THE CURSED INK OF ANGELO MARKADO

BLOOD & GOSPEL SAGA: The Cursed Ink Of Angelo Markado
Lolakwentosera
Philippine Copyright 2025

All rights reserved and any reproduction of and/or copying from this book whether through mechanical or digital means for commercial purposes is strictly prohibited. However part(s) of this book may be reproduced/copied without written permission for articles, reviews and/or further studies with special mention of the source.

ISBN: 978-621-8460-00-3

Book Cover Design & Layout by: Henri "KaliwetemARTe" Dalisay

Published by:
Lolakwentosera Book Publishing
lolakwentosera@gmail.com
lolakwentosera.com

THE CURSED INK OF ANGELO MARKADO

LOLAKWENTOSERA

Contents

Notes ii

1. The Year Of The Beast 1
2. The White Dusts 17
3. Azrael 33
4. Year One - Anno Bhiasti 49
5. The Mutation 65
6. Lumen 80
7. Haruki And Zovio 98
8. The Pranks 114
9. The Bloodless 127
10. Bersig - Love Match 143
11. Hiro Is Not A Hero 159
12. Nzo The Channak 175
13. The Truce 191
14. The Marriage Proposal 207
15. The Cursed Ink 220
16. Impossible Love 234
17. Sugar Rush 247
18. The Chase 265
19. The Vial 281

20 Hiro Her Hero	299
21 Her Second Life	314
22 The Water Vessel	330
23 The Blinding Light	339
24 Princess Sofia	355
25 Illuminaria	371
26 Doctor To The Barrio	386
27 The Cure	402
28 Child Birth	418
29 Another Child Birth	433
30 The Reunion	449
31 The Fab Five	462
32 Lumen Naria	477
33 Azhuangs Unite	492
34 The Arena	507
35 Cannonball	522
36 The Canaan Wedding	538
37 The Blessed Vessel	554
38 The Spear Of Fate	570
39 The Jabezzite Warriors	584

1

The Year Of The Beast

P RESENT DAY - **2025 AB** (Anno Bhiasti).

Immortality and youthful beauty—what others would consider a gift—was nothing but a punishment for Kein. An eternity of existence surrounded by feeble creatures—pathetic, weak humans and the bloodthirsty spawn of darkness known as the **sigbin**.

Inside his castle, a structure sculpted from a colossal iceberg in the heart of Antarctica, Kein, the immortal god, watched with muted curiosity as three of his most beautiful but bloodless sigbin ushered a trembling young man before him. At first glance, one might struggle to tell the difference between the two creatures. The sigbin could pass as human, their disguise nearly flawless—save for their philtrums, which were smooth and flat, a telltale mark of their true nature.

"Father..." one of the sigbin cooed, its voice a silky temptation. "We want to play, but...we can't calm him down." Humans taste better when they surrender to the feast—despite being the main course. His sigbin were begging him to feed the human his blood—a request he found utterly pathetic.

Kein, unimpressed, barely spared the human a glance. "That's because you're not the one he wants."

A male sigbin stepped forward, his touch languid and seductive as he caressed the young man. Fear turned to longing in the human's wide eyes, hope blooming despite the terror rattling his fragile frame. The scent of his blood—hot, thick, irresistible—filled the air, eliciting a primal hunger from everyone in the room. Even Kein, indifferent as he was, felt his lips part at the fragrance.

The male sigbin turned to him, expectant. "Father?"

Kein waved a dismissive hand. "Be my guest."

He wasn't in the mood to feed –he already had his favorite toy and pastime for now. Likewise, Caiphaiz, his most devoted servant, had been relentless in his insistence that he prepare for their journey to the City of Ruinae for the upcoming Festival of Avlam.

The sigbin beamed, its true nature surfacing—its skin darkened to a sickly green, scales rippling beneath its flesh. Before the human could scream, it lunged, a canal of sharp teeth piercing deep. Within seconds, the others descended upon him, their feast turning into a frenzy.

A tortured scream echoed through the garden of ice, reverberating off the frozen walls of Kein's domain. A smirk played on his lips. He had no interest in sharing the meal, but the sight of blood staining the pristine ice beneath him painted a cruel, beautiful contrast—one that suited his melancholic mood.

Before the human's final breath left his body, Kein felt it—a sudden vibration from the fruit he had held in his right hand since time immemorial. His eyes widened. "Abba," he whispered. He stood abruptly, his focus sharpening on the fruit.

Sensing his master's shift, Caiphaiz immediately ordered everyone out of the room.

Kein rushed outside, his feet carrying him into the heart of his genetically modified garden—a wonder of science and defiance against the laws of nature. In the midst of the Antarctic wasteland, a paradise thrived, frozen in time, created by Kein's will alone.

Once, he had the power to grow life effortlessly. Now, it was stolen from him. A curse. The land withered beneath his touch, the soil rejecting him, green turning to rot the moment he set foot upon it. But he had outwitted fate—science had become his ally.

Through technology and genetic manipulation, he bent the laws of nature to his will, creating an ecosystem that sustained him despite the divine punishment placed upon him.

At the center of his garden stood a tree unlike any other, its sole purpose to sustain the fruit he had carried for centuries. Kein knelt before it, reverently placing the fruit onto one of its branches. His heart thundered in his chest. How long had it been since he last saw Velial? He longed for his father's wisdom.

As he watched, the fruit shifted. Its once brown skin deepened—amber, then crimson, then the color of fresh, glistening blood. Kein reached for it, his fingers barely grazing its surface before something moved inside. A faint tremor at first, then more distinct—a writhing, living presence.

A hole tore open at the fruit's crown.

From within, a serpent's head emerged, green as poison, its forked tongue tasting the air. It wriggled free, its tiny body coiling around

Kein's hand, growing as it moved, sliding up his arm, across his shoulders. From a worm-like creature to an anaconda-sized beast, it slithered against his bare skin, tightening lovingly around his neck.

Kein exhaled, his lips parting. "Father, I missed you."

The serpent tasted his lips before whispering in his ear. "How long has it been?"

Caiphaiz, watching from the shadows, trembled.

"Too long, abba," Kein breathed. His fingers tightened around the fruit. "I tried to preserve it—I tried to keep you alive—but the fruit began to rot. I thought…"

Velial hissed, finishing for him. "You thought we failed?"

Kein nodded.

The fruit had begun to decay after the mutation of all his sigbin into bloodless hellions. In desperation, Kein had cloned trees to sustain it, keeping it fresh for centuries. But the final tree had withered. It would take years to create a new one.

Silence.

"Have you found the bleeding one?" Then, Velial's voice cut through the air like a blade.

"I have done what I can, Abba. I've gathered several leads and now await your arrival to set the plan in motion." Kein remembered the first time he heard about the bleeding sigbin decades ago.

<><><>

"*Adonai tricked us.*" *Velial hissed, its serpentine form coiling around Kein's body.*

"T-tricked?" Winding along his neck, he met the serpent's gaze, a flicker of dread in his perfect features.

"Yes! My transition should have been complete by now—yet I remain in this despicable form! Crawling. Writhing. Beneath your feet. Instead of walking beside you as I should!" The serpent's jealousy slithered through his words.

"How?" Kein's voice was strained. "The vaccine—SKi22 was—"

"One of your sigbin still bleeds." Velial cut him off, his tongue flickering against Kein's ear. "Adonai will use him to end you. He will be your death and the ruin of my plans."

Kein's expression darkened. "Impossible."

"But it's true. So find him." Velial's tongue slithered into Kein's ear canal, sending a jolt of searing pain through his skull. Blood trickled down Kein's face. "Turn the earth upside down if you must. Find him. End his immortality."

Kein trembled, his pain and rage intertwined. "Yes, abba. Right away!"

<><><>

For an entire century, he searched in vain—until, at last, he caught a break.

"I'm here now, child. Let's bring your plan to life, but first..." Velial coiled tighter, once again, crushing Kein's bones. The immortal one gasped—but he did not resist. "I missed you, my son... as I missed your mother, Evie." Its voice thick with venom, watching as blood seeped from Kein's nose, his eyes, his mouth.

With that, the serpent relinquished his grip, slithering downward, his body shrinking as he coiled toward Kein's navel—then, with a final twist, disappeared inside him. Kein convulsed—his pleasure and agony intertwined.

The sigbin outside howled, their bodies twisting, shifting, their grotesque transformation mirroring Kein's suffering.

And then—silence.

Bloodied and broken, Kein collapsed onto the frozen grass, clutching the fruit in his trembling fingers. A dark smile touched his lips. "Thank you, father... for your blessing." Then, as the blood drowned him, Kein lost consciousness.

The sigbin inside the castle could no longer contain their primal hunger. Their true, monstrous nature surfaced as they swarmed around Kein, drawn to the scent of his blood. Their tongues and fangs devoured the crimson nectar, lapping up every drop that spilled onto the icy floor.

Even Caiphaiz, usually composed, succumbed to the temptation. His lips traced Kein's torn flesh, cleaning the wounds with a reverence that bordered on worship.

Then, a sigbin approached, its voice a hushed whisper, "My lord, it's time."

Caiphaiz lifted Kein's almost lifeless body into his arms, his expression unreadable. Without hesitation, he carried him through the dim corridors of the castle, past the flickering torches that cast jagged shadows on the frozen walls.

Inside a secluded chamber, a young berhen lay sleeping, her breath soft, her form undisturbed—completely unaware of the nightmare about to unfold.

Caiphaiz gently placed Kein beside her, his pale body stark against the warmth of her living flesh. Then, with a final glance, he turned away, stepping out of the room and locking the door behind him.

Moments passed. Then, a scream ripped through the silence—piercing, raw, utterly consumed by terror. And the castle came alive with the sound of her fear.

<><><>

Not far from Kein's castle, in the quiet stillness of her room, Vahitna reached for a fresh blouse, unaware of the unseen force about to shatter her world. The moment it struck, her legs buckled beneath her. She collapsed to the floor, screaming, her body wracked with excruciating pain. The sound was unlike any human cry—a howl of sheer torment, primal and broken.

Her hands clawed at her dress, tearing fabric away as she revealed her swollen, pregnant belly. But this was not the pain of childbirth. Something inside her was thrashing violently, its movements unnatural, its fury uncontainable. Bones cracked. Flesh stretched. Organs ruptured. Yet, the child did not emerge.

Instead, it ripped at her from within, a prisoner in its own mother's womb—sharing in Kein's suffering, bound to his curse. And still, it remained. Unborn. Unleashed. Screaming.

<><><>

In Xego, chaos erupted as the sigbin suddenly collapsed to their knees, their bodies convulsing in unnatural spasms. Before the horrified eyes of the humans, their forms twisted and morphed, flesh warping as jagged green scales burst through their skin. Their eyes darkened, their jaws widened, and their bones snapped into grotesque new shapes.

A moment of paralyzed silence hung in the air.

Then—panic.

The realization struck like a lightning bolt. The sigbin were changing. Terrified of being devoured, the humans fled, screaming, their desperate footsteps thundering through the streets. Parents clutched their children, doors slammed shut, and the air filled with cries of fear and confusion.

<><><>

In the dense forest of the boundary dividing Cintru and Perlaz, a toddler was walking aimlessly –alone. Then an agonizing wail cut across the mountains. The toddler's – and the others – cries were unnatural—inhuman, laced with a suffering that no child should ever endure.

Then the toddler –Nzo, no longer looked like an innocent baby. His once soft, delicate skin was now covered in glistening serpent scales—deep green, jagged, and unnatural. His tiny fingers twitched, claws beginning to form, his round baby eyes darkening into something monstrous. Whatever Nzo had become... he was no longer just a child.

<><><>

In Zapad, every sigbin felt the raw, searing agony coursing through Kein's immortal body. As if tethered to their master's suffering, they fell to their knees, hands clasped in desperate prayer. Their forms began to twist and contort, muscles spasming beneath their skin as they shed the illusion of humanity.

Then, it began—a monstrous transformation.

Large, emerald scales erupted from their flesh, creeping across their limbs like a living curse. Their faces stretched and distorted, features warping into something reptilian, their jaws widening to accommodate fangs meant for devouring.

Shortly after, the sigbin gathered at the city square, recovering from the pain of their unified transformation. The lingering ache still pulsed through their bodies, a reminder of their connection to Kein and the power he held over them.

One of the sigbin, rubbing his sore limbs, muttered, "It's been a long time since something like this happened to us."

"Does it mean Kein has forgiven us?" another one asked hesitantly. "Will he finally return our blood after 300 years of this curse?"

Murmurs turned into a rising clamor as more joined in, their voices filled with hope, confusion, and desperation.

Then—

"Ouch!" A sharp yelp broke through the noise. One sigbin had cut the skin of another, watching closely for any sign of blood.

Nothing. The wound remained dry—lifeless flesh, cursed and hollow. The sigbin scoffed, putting his knife away. "Nope. That's not it." A hush fell over the crowd.

"It could be a new mutation," someone suggested, their voice uncertain.

"Or a new punishment." A collective groan of frustration and anger followed.

Exxon stood amidst the restless crowd, searching for one sigbin in particular. His sharp eyes landed on Goran, standing at a distance, quietly listening to the commotion. For someone small in stature, Goran commanded power effortlessly—a figure of quiet authority among the hellspawns.

Exxon approached, lowering his voice. "The delivery is here, boss."

Goran nodded once, then excused himself from the sigbin he had been speaking to. Without another word, he followed Exxon.

Hours later, they arrived at a warehouse, a vast space filled with hundreds of parked delivery trucks he inherited a hundred years ago from his father, Ehud –a notorious trafficker during his time.

Exxon led him to the center of the warehouse, where one of the trucks was waiting. With practiced ease, he unlatched the doors and swung them open.

The stench hit them first. Inside, hundreds of human corpses lay in a grotesque heap, the rotting scent of flesh thick in the air.

Goran stepped forward, examining the cargo. His gaze fell on a particular corpse of a woman, her body strikingly beautiful despite the death that claimed her.

He pulled her out, his fingers tracing the empty cavity where her heart had been ripped away. Then, slowly, he sank his teeth into her thigh.

He chewed—eyes fluttering shut, savoring the taste. It was nothing like fresh human meat and warm blood. But beggars couldn't be choosers. He sighed, pulling away and licking the remnants of a stale blood from his lips. "They will do," he murmured.

"Put them in the freezers. Sell them before they rot completely."

Exxon nodded, banging his fist on the truck's side. The engine roared to life, and the vehicle rumbled forward.

Goran exhaled. He missed the days when he could feast on the flesh of the living, the screams of humans echoing like music in his ears. But things had changed since his father Ehud no longer ran the business because he went missing. Good thing his new partner had a rare talent for crime—one that let him hunt human hearts without ever being noticed.

<><><>

In Perlaz, as Kein's suffering rippled through the world, every sigbin felt its impact. But none experienced it as intensely as Bufe, the ninety-eight-year-old sigbin, also known as a hukluvan—a rare and ancient breed of his kind.

Writhing in excruciating pain as he transformed, Bufe clutched his chest, his body convulsing. Though blind, his mind's eye was suddenly flooded with a vision –the berhen again. This time the bleeding sigbin was with her.

He remembered the last time he saw her vividly in his vision, decades ago…1925 AB to be exact.

<><><>

The berhen—a stunning, untouched beauty—bathing near a well. Her presence radiated purity, a contrast so stark against his cursed existence that it almost burned.

He could see her clearly, despite his blindness. Smell her. The hukluvan moaned, his frail hands trembling as he remembered another woman from long ago—his wife. The vision stirred something deep within him, something he thought had faded with time.

Near his bed, Vhinoe, his human great-great-grandson, was jolted awake by the noises. "Grandpa? What's wrong?" *Vhinoe rushed over, finding Bufe seated on the floor, his breathing ragged, his body unnaturally still—except for his mind, trapped in the vision.*

Bufe ignored him. He could still see her—the berhen. She stood with her back turned, the sun gleaming against her smooth, glistening skin. Dark waves of hair cascaded down her spine, her delicate figure outlined in golden light.

Then, she leaned forward—reaching into the well. Bufe's breath caught. This is different. He had daydreamed of her for centuries, but never had he seen what lay inside the well. Then he saw it. An ancient vessel, cracked and stained, emerging from the depths. Her hands cradled it gently, lifting it from the water as she began to bathe with it.

Bufe gasped—the vision snapped away. "Huh!" His body jerked, and he struggled to stand.

"Grandpa? What is it? A nightmare?" Vhinoe leaned closer, only to get shoved aside so forcefully that he stumbled and fell. Vhinoe groaned, rubbing his bruised back. "Ow! Seriously?"

Bufe grumbled as he groped his way back to the bed. "I don't sleep, doofus. How the heck can I have a nightmare?"

Vhinoe sighed and slid a few extra pillows under Bufe's head. "Fine, then what was it?"

Bufe's lips curled into a smirk as he whispered, "A beautiful vision."

"...Okay?" Vhinoe hesitated.

Bufe turned toward him, his expression sharp. "We have to find her."

Vhinoe arched a brow. "Grandpa, you're blind. You know that, right?"

SMACK!

"Ow!" Vhinoe doubled over, clutching his stomach where Bufe punched him.

Bufe raised his hands in mock prayer. "Adonai, forgive my grandson, for he is the dumbest of my descendants."

Vhinoe chuckled, rubbing the sore spot. "Okay, okay. Who exactly are we looking for?"

Bufe's smirk faded. His voice lowered, turning serious. "The berhen with her sacred vessel."

Vhinoe's laughter died in his throat. "W-what? A berhen? Why?" *His confusion deepened. Then, realization struck, and his face paled.* "G-grandpa... you're old. It's kinda weird that you're—"

THWACK!

The cane hit him on the head this time. "Not for me, you idiot!" *Bufe snapped.* "The berhen is the key to ending Kein's reign!"

Vhinoe's jaw dropped. "Oh."

Bufe sighed, his face softening. "When Kein falls, I can finally rest. I can finally die."

Vhinoe perked up. "Oh, well, that's—wait, I mean, uh—" *He quickly corrected himself, anticipating another hit.*

Bufe rolled his eyes. "You mean you can't wait for me to die."

"No, of course not! I love you! You're my favor—"

THWACK!

"Ow! What the heck!" *Vhinoe winced, dodging another incoming swing.*

"Stop joking and listen!" *Bufe snapped.*

Vhinoe sighed dramatically. "Fine." *He snatched the cane before his grandpa could strike again and tossed it far away.*

Bufe huffed, crossing his arms. "The berhen must meet with the one who still bleeds."

Vhinoe frowned. "Who?"

Bufe's expression darkened. "I've had visions of a sigbin. A special one. Angelo Markado—the Marked Angel."

Vhinoe tensed. He'd heard whispers of Angelo Markado before. But what did this sigbin have to do with Kein?

"We must bring the vessel to him."

Vhinoe exhaled, rubbing his temples. "So now we're looking for an old jar?"

Bufe growled. "No, you fool! Find the berhen, and you will find the vessel!"

Vhinoe nodded, finally serious. "Alright, I'll send my men to the market to—"

THWACK!

The flying kick sent him sprawling outside the cave. His guards outside snickered, trying—and failing—not to burst into laughter. Vhinoe groaned, dusting himself off. "Grandpa! I'm human, you know! I can die!"

Bufe scoffed. "Maybe I should just kill you and spare the world of your stupidity." He lifted his hands toward the heavens. "Adonai, please make Vhinoe's son smarter than him."

Vhinoe sighed in defeat. He wasn't the smartest, but darn it, he was strong.

Bufe settled back onto his bed, his tone grave. "The berhen, the vessel, and the one who bleeds must come together. Only then will Kein's reign end."

Vhinoe stood at a distance now, just in case. "Okay, but... how exactly does that end Kein?"

Bufe let out a deep, tired sigh. "I don't know... not yet." He closed his eyes, knowing sleep would never come. But perhaps, if he waited long enough, another vision would.

<><><>

A century later, he finally saw the bleeding sigbin and the berhen together—not as separate visions, but united at last. Alas!

<><><>

"Ahhh!" A deep, guttural scream erupted, scattering birds into a frenzied flight. Hendrix clutched the wall of his newly built treehouse, his body convulsing as searing pain flared across his skin.

It had been a long time since he had felt something this intense. It shook him to his core, sending waves of fire through his veins. He did not change form—except for one thing. Between his legs, his flesh had transformed. Green scales coated his length, sharp spikes protruding like the quills of an enraged porcupine.

Hendrix hissed, clenching his jaw. It wasn't the pain that bothered him. It was the fact that, despite the searing agony, he felt... ecstatic. "Darn it!" His fist slammed into the thickest tree trunk at the center of his house, almost splitting it in two, sending shattered pieces tumbling to the floor.

Unbeknownst to him, his body lit up—bright markings of different shapes and colors appearing all over his skin. They glowed briefly, then flickered, fading away just as the cries of the sigbin all over the fallen world died down. The inked marks vanished. The spikes on his body receded. And everything went back to normal.

Normal. Hendrix scoffed at the word. He wiped the blood off his knuckles. The tree he punched had cut his hand, but the wound was already healing. No scars. No trace. Just like always.

He leaned against the wall that now needed another repair. Every sigbin had been drained of blood. Yet, here he was. Still bleeding. Still regretting what happened a hundred years ago. His hand trembled slightly as he looked at his once wounded knuckle.
"I'm not normal like humans..." His voice was barely a whisper. "...and I'm not anomalous like sigbin." His eyes darkened. "What the heck am I, then?"

A beat of silence.

Then, a laugh—dark and bitter—escaped his lips. "A freak." The voice resembled that of an old friend he hadn't seen in such a long time.

2

The White Dusts

2019 AD (Anno Domini - The Year Of Our Lord)

It was torture for the serpent to stand in Adonai's presence. The One without beginning or end—the Alpha and the Omega—stood before His kneeling divine creations, His power saturating the air.

The serpent tasted it—Holiness. Absolute. Unshakable. And despite its resentment, it trembled in fear. It flicked its tongue, wishing it had knees to bend, like its brothers.

"Ah, you are finally here, brother." Azrael, the Giver of Death, acknowledged its arrival, lifting his foot to make way as the serpent slithered past.

It ignored him. The serpent's fury boiled inside. "I was the greatest of Adonai's creations! One mistake, and now I am this… this despicable, slithering beast—cursed to be at war with humans for all eternity!" Oh, how it longed to walk among its heavenly brothers again. Hopefully soon.

"Abba." The serpent honored Adonai in its own way, slinking up to the tree of the knowledge of good and evil—its favorite tree. The same tree that had caused its fall, yet it held only fond memories of the fruit it had once offered to Kein's mother.

Climbing the highest branch, it now towered above the other divine beings. But even as it exalted itself, Adonai's love still reached it. And that—that infuriated the serpent the most. *"How can You love me, Abba, yet continue to punish me?"* It had asked Adonai this before, when they were alone.

"I punished you for what you did, for what cannot be undone. But I still love you, for who and what you are—my creation," Adonai had always answered in His calm, majestic voice.

"Lies!" the serpent had hissed, but Adonai had remained silent, tolerating its insolence.

Now, the moment of decision has arrived.

"We are ready, Abba," Azrael announced, bowing low before Adonai, who stood one with His begotten Son, Yswh. Azrael dared not look upon the Divine Presence in front of him.

Very well. Do what you must, and I will take care of the rest, Adonai's Words echoed through the garden.

The serpent watched as Yswh exhaled a divine wind, sending it toward the tree of eternal life. Its fruits glowed, billions of them falling to the ground, transforming into pure, white dust. Another breath from Yswh sent the dust scattering toward the earth—His breath of life carried upon the wind.

"Go. Bring as many of My children back to this garden. The time has come for them to leave the earth and live with Me for eternity."

The army of divine creatures—hundreds of them—unfurled their gigantic wings and took flight, their mission clear: To harvest human souls. To bring them home. The serpent remained silent, its gaze dark.

"You are quiet, My child." Adonai's voice stopped it as it was about to leave.

"There is nothing to say, Abba."

They were alone now—the serpent and its Creator.

"You do not like My plan," Adonai observed.

"As always, You are too soft on them."

"Ah... jealousy. Your greatest weakness. Even from the beginning, when I first created humankind and you disapproved."

The serpent hissed. "And now You welcome them back into the garden You once exiled them from. What did they do to deserve eternal life with You?"

"Maybe because they are not as jealous," Adonai chuckled, teasing. The serpent coiled tighter around the branch. "The dust of eternal life will only reach those who choose to be with Me. Others will remain behind. And they will not be happy."

The serpent stiffened, its thoughts immediately turning to Kein. Adonai, omniscient and omnipotent, already knew what the serpent was thinking. "Not if I can help it," the serpent whispered.

"Ah... planning something again? Another test?" Adonai's voice carried no anger—only amusement.

The serpent knew its Father welcomed challenges. "Yes. A test. If these humans truly deserve Your love. I can do that, right, Abba?" Its forked tongue flickered, tasting the air.

Adonai smiled. "Of course. The gift of free will is yours, as much as it is theirs."

The serpent's eyes gleamed. "Very well. Goodbye, Abba." It slithered away.

"Goodbye, My child. I love you," And despite everything, Adonai meant every word.

The serpent thought otherwise. *Lies.*

<><><>

2076 AD – Over 50 years after the white dust from eternal life was poured down to earth, Sofia's eyes snapped open. She was still not used to not sleeping. Her body felt the same, yet different. She just didn't know how. At twenty-two, she was third in line to the Danish throne, but that no longer mattered.

She was a survivor of RPTR21—the virus that had plagued the world for decades. And she owed her life to Kein Serpens Industry (KSi) and their miracle vaccine.

It was her brother, Jens, who had fallen sick first. The infection spread rapidly through their household. She remembered bleeding from every orifice, moments from death, before receiving the KSi22 vaccine.

Then, darkness. When she woke up, she was in KSi's laboratory. That was years ago. And in all that time, she had never slept again. Dr. Peterson and his team monitored Sofia closely, keeping her under strict observation.

But for Sofia, the days dragged endlessly—a blur of sterile walls, repetitive tests, and unanswered questions. "When can I see my family?" she would ask. Countless times.

And each time, Dr. Peterson would smile, his voice as gentle as always. "Soon." That smile—it reminded her of her father, back when he was still alive. The thought sent a pang of sadness through her chest, and Dr. Peterson, as if sensing it, would reach out—his fingers ruffling her hair in a playful, comforting gesture.

Sometimes, his hand would brush against her cheek, the touch featherlight. And her heart would skip a beat. "Stop it, Sofia. He's just being kind." But kindness wasn't what made her breath hitch. It wasn't what sent a strange warmth pooling in her stomach. And it certainly wasn't what made her feel this hunger. A hunger for something more than food.

<><><>

Outside Sofia's room, Dr. Peterson stood with Kein and Caiphaiz, observing her through a one-way mirror.

Dr. Peterson felt honored and terrified to be in Kein's presence. The public rarely saw Kein Serpens. But to stand before him was to feel as though one stood before a god. Kein's impeccable black suit was tailored to perfection, hugging his lean, towering frame. But what truly unnerved Dr. Peterson were his eyes— Reddish violet. Cold. Ancient. Unholy.

Dr. Peterson cleared his throat, forcing himself to focus. "Her appetite keeps increasing. She doesn't sleep, and... her cells..."

Kein's gaze didn't move from Sofia, watching as she restlessly tossed in bed. "What about her cells?"

Dr. Peterson hesitated. "They're... not changing."

Kein's head tilted slightly. "Explain."

Dr. Peterson exhaled. "It's like she's... not aging."

Kein's lips curled slightly, but his gaze remained unreadable. "How about pain?"

"Oh yes, she feels pain," Dr. Peterson confirmed.

Kein's expression darkened.

Dr. Peterson shifted nervously. "It's time for my final round. Would you care to join me?"

Kein didn't answer. Caiphaiz stepped forward. "We'll watch from here."

Dr. Peterson nodded as he entered Sofia's room, relieved—unaware that, behind the glass, Kein's fingers traced the fruit in his pocket. Feeling its power and its promise. And most of all—its hunger.

<><><>

Sofia's eyes flickered open the moment she heard the doorknob turn.

Finally.

She had spent countless nights awake, restless, her body thrumming with an unfamiliar energy that she couldn't control.

"Good evening, Sofia." Dr. Peterson's voice carried its usual warmth, but there was hesitation in his eyes.

Sofia smirked. "Dr. Peterson." In a blink, she was right in front of him. Up close, the doctor seemed to have aged even more in Sofia's eyes. With his wrinkled skin and a thinning bundle of grayish hair, he looked more like a grandfather than a father now.

The doctor's breath hitched. "H-how did you—?" He hadn't even seen her move. His fingers twitched, instinctively pulling up his digital chart, recording the unexpected physical development.

Sofia, however, was barely listening. There it is again — that feeling of deep hunger that wasn't just for food. She had spent years in isolation, her body untouched, her mind drifting in a sea of endless wakefulness. And now, she knows why.

Her gaze flicked to Dr. Peterson's hands, remembering the countless nights he had been the last person to touch her before leaving the room. She had fantasized about him, obsessed over the sensation of his fingers on her skin—even if it was only clinical.

Enough waiting.

"Here, let me take a quick look at you," he said, leading her back to the bed. Sofia smirked.

"I'd rather take a look at you." Before he could react, she slipped off her hospital gown.

Dr. Peterson's entire body tensed. "Sofia—" Aware of the eyes watching him through the glass window, he knew he couldn't afford to lose his composure.

"What's wrong?" She stepped closer, her bare skin brushing against the fabric of his lab coat.

Dr. Peterson inhaled sharply. "Without Nurse Ida, we should skip—"

Sofia grabbed his hand, pressing it against her chest. "How's my heartbeat, doctor?"

Dr. Peterson swallowed hard. Her skin was warm. Too warm.

"Sofia, this isn't—"

"Shhh." Sofia tilted her head, watching his resolve crack as she slowly guided his hands against her skin.

Dr. Peterson's mind screamed at him to stop—but his body? His body was already lost. "Darn it..." His lips crashed against hers, hands roaming, gripping, exploring. The watchful eyes beyond the glass, forgotten.

Sofia gasped, arching into his touch, hungry for more.

The last remnants of his restraint shattered as he lifted her onto the bed, his mouth descending onto her in ways no medical textbook had ever prepared him for.

Ecstatic, Sofia's body was writhing under his touch, drowning in a sensation that was both pleasure and something else—something deeper. Something dark.

Dr. Peterson couldn't stop. Didn't want to stop. *I deserve this*, he thought, convincing himself that this was just another experiment, another test. He had devoted his life to his work to make up for losing his children to the virus. His ever faithful and loving wife is all he has... but then again...

This girl—this miracle—was offering herself to him. And he would take her. Hard. Fast. Over and over.

Sofia's eyes rolled back, her body arching as pleasure tore through her—wave after wave of something raw, electric, unholy.

And then— Everything changed.

As she came undone, her vision blurred—and for the first time, she saw it. The hunger inside her wasn't just lust. It was something else. Something primal. Something insatiable. And it wanted more.

She lowered her gaze to Dr. Peterson—his chest rising and falling, his hands still gripping her hips.

She smiled. "Thank you, doctor—"

A sudden, sharp pain tore through her skin. She froze, her body trembling, caught between agony and something far more intoxicating. Then, it happened. A sensation unlike any other—raw, primal, electric—ripped through her veins.

It wasn't just pain. It was liberation. She could feel it—her body morphing, shifting, becoming something more. Something otherworldly. Her smile faltered as a deep, guttural growl rumbled from her throat—low, dangerous, and completely inhuman.

Dr. Peterson opened his mouth to speak—but the words never came.

Sofia's vision sharpened. She could hear his heartbeat, could smell the blood pulsing just beneath his skin. And before she could stop herself—

She lunged.

Her teeth sank into his throat, the warm rush of blood filling her mouth, igniting a hunger that no pleasure had ever satisfied.

Dr. Peterson gasped, his hands clawing weakly at her, but she held him down, feeding like a starved animal. He tried to speak. To beg. To scream. But his voice was already gone. The hunger took over.

Sofia barely noticed when she tore into his chest, her fingers ripping through skin and muscle, digging deeper until—

There.

His heart. Still beating. Still warm. Still hers to devour. She took a bite. And moaned. It was better than any euphoric release. She rolled her eyes in ecstasy, savoring the taste, her body thrumming with newfound power. The moment was pure bliss. Until—

The door swung open. A scream.

Nurse Ida. Standing frozen in horror. Her eyes locked onto the blood-drenched scene before her.

Sofia, back in her old form and covered in red, with Dr. Peterson's lifeless body split in half beneath her.

For a long, chilling second, no one moved. Then—

Sofia licked the blood from her lips. She tilted her head, smiling wickedly. And with a voice that was no longer entirely human, she purred— "Oops."

<><><>

Behind the one-way mirror, Kein and Caiphaiz stood in silence. The doctor had been a pawn, a test subject—one of many. And he had failed.

"Should we intervene, my lord?" Caiphaiz asked, his voice eerily calm. Kein watched, completely still, his lips slightly parted, his gaze burning with something dark. Enjoyment.

"No," Kein murmured. His fingers traced the fruit in his pocket, feeling its warmth pulsing. "He was collateral damage."

A small, knowing smile played on Kein's lips. Sofia had passed her test. And her hunger was only beginning.

<><><>

2119 AD, a century since the white dusts spread.

The land, ruled by only two seasons—rainy and sunny—was once a virgin rainforest, untouched by corruption. Now, it was his private garden, carefully designed and nurtured with the help of the natives who had planted everything for him.

Kein sat on the soft earth, feeling the cool dirt against his skin—but he was careful not to touch anything. Because to kiss his skin was to wither and die. The garden, like everything he had ever loved, could never love him back.

It was the true curse of his immortality—not the eternal life itself, but the eternal longing. To love and hate forever while those around him withered into dust—

What a pity.

He sighed, finding solace in the single green fruit he always held in his hand—the last remnant of the man he used to be.

Before Adonai cursed him. Before he killed his brother. Before Aveel's blood stained the earth, poisoning it forever. Adonai, the Creator of the universe, had once placed his parents in a perfect garden—only to cast them out over one tiny mistake. Banished, they were forced to toil the earth, struggling to grow food from the sweat of their brow.

Kein hadn't minded. He loved the soil, loved the way it yielded to his hands, how he could coax life from the ground. But when he offered his finest crops to Adonai, he was rejected. Aveel, his brother, had spilled animal blood upon an altar—and Adonai had favored him instead.

Kein had gritted his teeth, his rage boiling.

"Blood? Adonai values blood more than the fruits of the earth?" Fine. If it was blood Adonai wanted—Then he would have it. And Kein had delivered, offering up his own brother's life.

"You are never to grow from the ground that you have littered with your brother's blood," Adonai's voice thundered. Of all his punishments, this was the most devastating. For a farmer, to be stripped of the earth's blessing was worse than death.

It was a cruel and eternal exile.

"Father." Kein opened his eyes, hearing the familiar hiss that yanked him from his reverie.

The serpent slithered toward him, irritation clear in its glowing golden eyes. Dirt clung to its long, spineless body, a reminder of its fall from grace. It loathed the filth—just as it loathed the One who had cast it down.

Kein once resented Velial, but over the centuries, he had come to see it as his true father. Adonai had rejected him, but Velial had told him the truth. His parents had been set up to fail—placed in a garden with temptation at its center, given a command they could not keep.

Adonai had been unjust. And Kein had paid the price.

"Why meet here? Take me to your cottage," the serpent hissed, its voice thick with displeasure.

"I'm sorry, Father." Kein brought the fruit to his lips, inhaling its scent. "This place gives me comfort."

The serpent flicked its tongue, its cold amusement seeping through its voice. "Because it reminds you of your crime."

Kein paused, studying the serpent's expression. "How did you know?"

A dark chuckle slithered from Velial's mouth. "Why do you think I always coil around a tree branch? It reminds me of when I first met your mother."

Kein exhaled sharply, kissing the fruit again. "Ah... when you seduced my mother. The only woman born from a man."

The serpent's tongue flickered, pleased. "Yes, I miss her. She saw me in my true form and liked me immediately. Without me, you would not exist."

Kein chuckled, shaking his head. "You make it sound like you made love to my mother."

The serpent hissed smugly. "Well, I taught your parents how. And for that, your mother's womb bore you."

It coiled around Kein's body, slithering over his shoulders, tightening against his neck. Kein made no move to stop it. "Painfully, I suppose." His voice was mocking.

"She was cursed to suffer in childbirth, after all." The serpent laughed, its forked tongue brushing against Kein's cheek.

"If I had it my way, I would have made love to your mother myself. She was beautiful in her nakedness. It was a pity she didn't even realize it—until I taught her how to think for herself." Velial spoke with smug pride.

Kein sighed, shaking off the thought of his mother's encounter with Velial in the garden.

"It's alright. We found a way to be one, after all." The serpent tightened its grip, the old ritual between them as ancient as their curse.

A long silence stretched between them, thick with understanding.

Then, finally— "You're melancholic, my son."

Kein exhaled.

"You aren't satisfied? Haven't you successfully slowed down Adonai's harvest?" The serpent's tongue flicked against Kein's lips, its kiss almost loving.

"We are successful. But there's... a side effect." Kein explained what had happened to Sofia and the other elites who had received the KSi22 vaccine decades ago.

The serpent listened intently, then smirked. "Ah. So they inherited your thirst for blood." Its forked tongue traced Kein's lips, drawing out a small shudder from the immortal god.

"But their taste for flesh? That... they got from you, Father."

The serpent laughed, coiling even tighter around Kein's body. "And this is why you halted the human trials."

Kein nodded. "I need to understand the full effects first."

For now, the frozen ones remained in Antarctica, safely contained. Until Kein could figure out how to control them. "But I still created other vaccines," he admitted.

The world was still dying. Without his intervention, humankind wouldn't survive.

The serpent scowled. "You are relying too much on science, my son. Our vaccine is perfect. The others won't stand against the dust from the Tree of Life."

Its voice hissed in Kein's ear, sharp and persuasive. "Adonai's plan will succeed if you hesitate."

Kein clenched his jaw. "Adonai is all-knowing. He must already know what we're planning."

"Yet He still gave humans free will." The serpent's voice turned silken. "Let's test Adonai's faith in humankind again." Its words slithered into Kein's mind like a whispered promise. "We won't force them. We'll offer it to them. If they choose us, we win—just like I won your parents away from Him."

Kein's breath hitched at the thought. He closed his eyes, aroused by the sheer power he could wield. His voice came out in a whisper. "Alright. We will move forward. The whole world will have the vaccine."

The serpent smirked, knowing it had won again.

"The side effect, though..." Kein was not really worried, only puzzled.

"We will deal with them later." Velial hissed.

Kein exhaled sharply, his fingers tightening around the fruit in his hand. "I just wish I could make them all like my son, Caiphaiz," he muttered, irritation lacing his voice.

The serpent coiled itself tighter around his shoulders, satisfaction slithering through its words.

"Ah, the old priest." It flicked its forked tongue. "Where is he, anyway?"

Kein smirked. "Around." He exhaled slowly. "Terrified of you."

Velial let out a soft, amused hiss. "Of course, he was taught—back when he was still human—that I am the devil himself." The serpent's voice was rich with pride. "The father of all evil."

Kein tilted his head, studying it. "Well, are you?"

Velial laughed softly, its tail tightening around Kein's arm like a lover's grip. "You call me your father. So tell me, Kein—" It pressed closer, its tongue flickering against Kein's jaw. "Are you evil, my son?"

Kein did not answer. The silence between them stretched—thick, suffocating, intimate. Finally, Kein sighed, his gaze distant. "If only I had more of this fruit." He turned it in his palm, watching the way the light danced on its perfect, immortal skin. "If I could feed it to all of them, they would be like Caiphaiz—immortal, but free from the hunger that your blood has cursed them with."

Velial let out a low, pleased hum, though its tone darkened. "You sound disgusted with me, son." It wrapped tighter around Kein's neck, a mocking embrace.

Kein let out a soft, breathless laugh. "Oh? Is there love between us, father?" His voice was quiet, edged with something unreadable. "Aren't we designed to hate?"

Velial leaned in, its mouth hovering near Kein's ear. "Then why pity the humans?" Its voice was a whisper, a temptation laced with venom. "Let them devour one another. Let the earth run red with their blood—just as you wanted."

Kein's jaw clenched. The serpent was pushing him, forcing him to make a final decision.

More silence.

Then, Kein turned his head slightly, his lips brushing the serpent's scaled face in something almost like a kiss. "Why did you ally with me on this?" His voice was low, thoughtful. "Why not let Adonai ruin me? Leave me to rot in this world while He harvests human souls for Himself?"

The serpent's coils loosened slightly, its voice turning almost gentle. "Because, Kein..." It sighed, mock sorrow in its tone. "If we trap enough souls here, Abba will mourn for them. He is known for His grace, after all." The serpent's eyes gleamed with malicious amusement. "We will use them to bargain. We will make Him remove both our curses—in exchange for the souls you make immortal."

Kein stilled. Then he laughed—a sharp, humorless sound. "Ah... And what makes you think I'd want to return to mortality?" His lips curled in amusement. "To be weak? To die from disease or be murdered like an animal?"

The serpent smirked, its whisper turning into a purr. "Because I know you, my son." It traced the tip of its tail along Kein's wrist, caressing it like an old lover. "You long to be a farmer again."

Kein froze.

3

Azrael

"You want to till the soil, to plant life with your own hands, to eat what you grow." The serpent's voice was like silk, smooth and dangerous. "You want to build forests that thrive under your touch. Not forests planted by others while you watch from a distance, mourning what you can never hold."

Kein's breathing quickened, his pulse hammering against his ribs.

The serpent's grin widened. "You were always proud of your harvests. That's why you offered them to Adonai, even knowing that He only favors the purest lamb, the bloodiest sacrifice."

It pressed its mouth against Kein's throat, inhaling the scent of his desire, his longing, his rage. Kein's fingers trembled around the fruit.

The serpent knew. Knew exactly what he wanted. Knew exactly what to say. "Imagine, Kein." The serpent's voice was barely a whisper now. "You, a farmer once more. And I—a divine creature again, free to walk between Heaven and Earth." Its voice shuddered with glee, with hunger, with victory. "It can happen, my son." It tightened around him, whispering in his ear.

"It will."

<><><>

2125 AD - Six years after the vaccine was made public.

It had been more than a century since the RPTR21 virus first emerged in 2019 AD, triggering a global pandemic that forever reshaped the world. And yet, even now, the chaos has not ended.

Despite the countless vaccines formulated by KSi, the virus continued to mutate, as if it had a mind of its own, its singular goal to infect as many humans as possible.

The world was in ruins.

Governments crumbled, economies collapsed, and people were dying—if not from the disease, then from starvation. Crime was at an all-time high. Countries surrendered their sovereignty, one by one, as their governments fell under the weight of the unrelenting pandemic. And now—the last remaining cities stood on the edge of the abyss.

Dr. Henry Mercado burst into the office, his breath ragged, his face dark with frustration. Across the desk, Dr. Wood barely flinched as he injected himself with the KSi22 vaccine—despite not being infected. Henry's eyes narrowed. "I need four."

Dr. Wood barely looked up, rolling down his sleeve, his fingers trembling slightly. "You know the protocol, Henry. You get one. That's it."

"That's not enough." Henry slammed his hands on the desk. He had just come from the hospital lobby, where the situation had spiraled into chaos.

The news had broken—India and China had officially lost the fight. They had stopped treating the virus altogether, waiting for the miraculous KSi22 vaccine rumored to cure even the most severe infections.

The announcement had sparked mass riots. Everywhere, people fought, screamed, and bled—desperate to survive, desperate for a chance at immunity. Inside the hospital, a strict lockdown had begun. Outside, the mob pounded on the doors, their voices a howling storm of fear and rage.

Henry had received one vial—just one. It meant that his wife and children—his entire family—would be left to die.

"Henry, please." Dr. Wood's voice was strained, his hand pressing against his temple, a dizziness overtaking him as the vaccine coursed through his veins. "More doses are arriving soon. We—the frontliners—have to receive it first. Then, our families."

Henry's jaw clenched. "The World Health Organization just announced the virus is now airborne." His voice was sharp, dangerous. "Do you think we have time to wait?"

Dr. Wood sucked in a breath, suddenly feeling nauseous—though he did not yet know why. "I'm sorry, Henry." He tried to reason with him, but the words barely left his mouth before Henry's fist slammed into the table. The metal frame rattled, stacks of files toppled to the ground, and for the first time, Dr. Wood jerked upright, alarm flashing in his eyes.

Henry stood there, breathing heavily, his fingers trembling with rage.

Then—

Without another word, he grabbed the syringe, his grip tight, and turned toward the door.

"Great..." Dr. Wood mumbled, his tongue suddenly feeling numb, his limbs weak.

Henry didn't answer. Instead, he slid the syringe into his pocket and left the room. The moment he stepped outside, the sound of fists pounding against the hospital doors grew louder. The crowd was getting restless. Desperate.

He knew it was only a matter of time before they were overrun. He didn't care. He had one vial. And he was going to his family.

Henry shoved past the chaos, ignoring the screams, ignoring the cries for help—ignoring the people who, just like him, wanted to live. Reaching the elevator, he punched the penthouse button, his heartbeat pounding in his ears. As the doors slid shut, muffling the sounds of the dying world outside, Henry closed his eyes.

And prayed he wasn't too late.

<><><>

"Henry!" Almira's voice trembled with relief and fear as she threw open the door.
They had met years ago, falling in love as nurses and doctors fighting a virus that had refused to die—a plague that had outlived generations.
Henry, a Southeast Asian doctor, and Almira, a local nurse, had chosen to dedicate their lives to Tel Aviv General—one of the last fortresses in a world that was falling apart.
For thirty years, they had served together. For thirty years, their family had been trapped within these hospital walls, never truly knowing the world outside the infection zones. Now, it was too late to leave.

Henry stepped inside, locking the door behind him. His eyes immediately went to Almira's face—to the thin, red line dripping from her nose.
His stomach dropped. "Almira... your nose."

Almira's eyes widened slightly before she wiped the blood away with the back of her hand. She exhaled shakily. "Oh..." Her voice was barely a whisper. Then, suddenly, she backed away. "Get out, Henry! I'm sick!"

Henry shook his head. "It doesn't matter." His voice was strained, hoarse. "I think I have it too. The virus has gone airborne."

Almira's shoulders sagged, a mix of exhaustion and acceptance settling into her bones.

Henry took a step forward. "How are the kids?"

Almira removed her useless protective gear, tossing it aside. "Hendrix is the worst." She swallowed hard. "He hasn't regained consciousness since this morning."

Before Henry could respond, a desperate cry rang out.

"Mom!"

Both parents spun around— And their hearts stopped.

Mae stood near Hendrix's bed, her hands stained with blood. Almira rushed forward, pulling her shaking daughter into her arms. Henry moved to Hendrix's bedside, his medical instincts kicking in. His son's skin was clammy, his breath shallow. Blood had pooled onto the sheets, seeping into the fabric like a stain that would never wash away.

Henry's hand trembled as he reached into his pocket— And pulled out the single vial. The only cure.

His throat tightened. "I only have one." His voice cracked, the weight of the moment crushing him.

Almira looked up. She knew what it meant. A slow, sad smile touched her lips.

And then—

"I'm ready to go." She kissed Mae's forehead, her touch gentle, final.

"No!" Mae's grip tightened, refusing to let go.

Henry wrapped his arms around them both, his voice low, steady. "I am too."

Almira and Henry smiled at each other—a silent understanding passing between them. They had spent a lifetime fighting together. They had built a family in a world that tried to erase hope. And now, they would leave it together.

"Mae, you have to survive." Almira pulled back slightly, her hands cupping her daughter's face. "You are the healthiest. You have to live."

"No." Mae shook her head fiercely. "You're the doctor, Dad! You can help more people than me!"

Henry smiled softly, pressing a hand over Almira's. "But I cannot live without your mother."

Almira's eyes glistened. "Nor can I, without your father." She wiped the blood from her nose, gripping Henry's hand like a lifeline.

Mae's voice broke. "You're willing to leave me behind?"

Almira brushed a tear from her daughter's cheek. "Because you have a future, sweetheart."

"And a purpose." Henry's voice was gentle, firm. "God's purpose for you. Trust Him, even when we're gone."

Mae's shoulders shook. "How about Hendrix?"

Henry's eyes darkened."I love your brother. But between a game developer and a nurse—" His voice wavered, but he pushed through. "I'd rather leave you behind. You can help more people. Hendrix would understand."

Mae's tears fell freely now, her body trembling. "I don't want to do this without you."

"Be strong, Mae." Henry kissed her forehead.

Almira did the same. For a brief moment, it felt like time had paused, giving them a second to memorize each other's faces— Before the world came crashing down.

–and then!

A loud bang at the front door made them all freeze. Screams erupted from the hall. Gunshots. Glass shattering.

"Give us the vaccine!"

"No!"

BLAG!

Henry spun around, locking the door to their room. He pushed a table against it, his pulse pounding, his mind racing. But it was useless.

A crash— And the door splintered open. Henry staggered back, the force knocking him to the floor.

Then—

Gunfire. People stormed in, faces twisted in desperation, weapons raised. Henry barely had time to think. With one last breath, he slid the syringe across the floor—straight to Almira. She caught it. Turned to Mae.

But the mob was faster. They ripped Mae away, shoving her to the ground. The vial hung between Almira's trembling fingers.

Mae's scream tore through the room. "Mom! NO!!!"

<><><>

That same night, Azrael followed the wisps of white dust, watching as they drifted like fireflies through the desolate streets. This place—once a quiet suburb—was now a graveyard of memories. Most of the houses stood empty, their walls crumbling, their doors hanging open like silent screams.

The street lights flickered—dying beacons in a dying world. The earth's moon was heavy, weighted by grief, loss, and the lingering cries of those still clinging to life.

Azrael, however, smiled. Not because he was cruel—but because he understood. Where there was suffering, there was love. And where there was love, there was a home for souls.

He spread his colossal wings and followed the dust into a house.

Inside, a family of three huddled together on a bed, their arms wrapped around one another. The little girl, no older than six, lay peacefully in her mother's arms, despite the blood that seeped from her skin.

The father held them both, his tears falling silently as he whispered, "I love you."

The mother kissed her daughter's forehead. "Rest now, my baby. I love you."

She then turned to her husband, brushing a tear from his cheek. "I love you."

He pressed his lips to hers, their love a quiet vow in the presence of death.

Azrael hovered above them, his presence unseen, his heart full of reverence for their final moments. The specks of white dust melted into their bodies, signaling that their time had come. With tender precision, Azrael descended. One by one, he kissed them, drawing their souls into spheres of light, glowing and warm. With a gentle touch, he placed them inside his satchel, already filled with the essence of countless souls.

"You will see each other again soon." He tapped his satchel lightly, as if comforting the souls inside. Then, with a beat of his wings, he soared back into the night. The further he flew, the more the air turned thick with decay. Smoke coiled through the sky. Flames devoured buildings.

The city was a living nightmare—a place where order had collapsed, leaving only madness behind. People screamed, fought, and killed—their souls still trapped in their bodies, destined for a darker fate.

Azrael landed lightly on a rooftop, observing as his brothers worked quickly below, gathering the harvest of the dead. A divine creature rushed toward him, wings slick with ash and blood.

"Azrael! Hurry!"

"What's happening?"

"Kein and the serpent's vaccine—" the angel's voice trembled. "It's locking their souls inside their bodies. We can't harvest them."

Azrael's breath hitched.

Then—

A voice. A silent, unseen command from Abba. Every angel froze, listening.

Then—

"Yes, Abba!"

And in a flash of light, they vanished—moving at the speed of divine will.

<><><>

Azrael reappeared inside a hospital, following the last wisps of white dust. But as he entered a room, his wings shuddered in horror. The dust—meant to bring eternal life—fell lifelessly to the floor, disintegrating upon contact with a human body injected with the vaccine. The patient, moments ago in a coma, convulsed violently, his mouth retching black gas into the air.

Azrael stepped closer. The man's body was still. He was alive—but dead. Azrael bent forward, his lips hovering over the man's mouth, prepared to take his soul. But the moment their lips touched—

Azrael jerked back, gagging. He covered his nose, his face contorted in disgust. "You are breathing, yet you are already dead." He turned away, his heart pounding.

The vaccine—it was defying the natural order. Trapping souls. Preventing the harvest. Azrael's wings tensed as he realized— The specks of eternal dust were fading from the air.

But the black gas—the rotting breath of the cursed—was spreading. He had to hurry.

Following the remaining trails of dust, Azrael flew toward the top floor. A mob had taken over, destroying everything in sight. Some of them were not meant for the harvest—they had already chosen a different fate.

But then—

A cry pierced through the chaos. "Mother! No!"
Azrael turned sharply. A girl was shoved against the wall.
"Mae!" A man, bleeding, weak, broken, tried to stand—
"Henry!"

Azrael acted instinctively. He swooped down, kissed Henry, and pulled his soul free—saving him before his suffering could continue. Then, before the man could violate Mae, he pressed his lips to hers, drawing her soul into his light.

But then—

"Hendrix... I love you. Please don't forget, Yswh loves you too." Almira's final words reverberated through the air. She plunged the syringe into Hendrix's arm.

Azrael's wings flared. "No!"

He darted forward, kissing Almira before she collapsed—ensuring her soul escaped before the vaccine took hold. Then he hovered over Hendrix, watching in horror as the vaccine ripped through his veins.

Azrael acted without thinking. He pressed his lips to Hendrix's— And breathed. A desperate, divine breath of life.

The young man's body convulsed. "AAAAAAAAAAH!" Hendrix screamed as blood burst from every pore.

Azrael saw his holy breath fighting the vaccine, pushing it away—but failing to expel it completely. Like oil and water, the two forces refused to mix. Instead, the vaccine retreated— Settling into one part of Hendrix's body.

His manhood.

Azrael's eyes widened. The vaccine had mutated, strengthening itself, leaving Hendrix's body in a war between divinity and corruption.

The young man stilled.

Azrael breathed deeply. He kissed Hendrix again— And this time, his soul did not leave. The vaccine held it captive. Azrael closed his eyes. "Abba, what should I do?" A whisper answered. He nodded. He exhaled one final time, watching as Hendrix's body lit up. Marks appeared across his skin—each one representing an element of creation. Then Azrael sighed, stepped back— And left him.

<><><>

Morning arrived. Azrael soared above the ruined city, his brothers suspended in the sky. Below them, the streets were lined with corpses. The white dust was gone. Only the black gas remained, moving as though it had a purpose.

A divine creature turned to Azrael. "Are we done?"

Azrael's gaze swept over the destruction. He clutched his satchel, now full of harvested souls. "For now."

"Should we follow the black gas?"

Azrael hesitated. Then shook his head. "Abba gave no such command."

And with that— They flew back to heaven, leaving behind the world that was no longer theirs.

<><><>

In Cintru, within the heart of his frozen domain, Kein's fruit began to pulse. It drank the black gas that swirled through the air, its once vibrant green skin darkening—fading into a sickly brown. Kein held it up, his fingers trembling slightly as he brought it to his nose.

The scent—rich, intoxicating, forbidden—made his mouth water. But he resisted. A deep, familiar hiss coiled around his ear.

"Be patient, my son." The serpent's voice slithered into his mind as it uncoiled from Kein's neck, its massive body slowly shrinking—smaller, tighter, thinner. It crawled down his arm, its form contracting further until it was no larger than a worm.

Then—

With a sharp bite, it burrowed into the fruit, disappearing beneath its surface. Kein watched, entranced, as the fruit shifted—its dull, brown skin darkening, twisting, transforming. A deep crimson hue bled through the surface, until the fruit gleamed—a perfect, blood-red gem in his palm.

Kein inhaled deeply— And laughed. A slow, rich, victorious sound. "We did it, Father." His grip tightened around the precious fruit as he pressed his lips to it, kissing it as one would a lover. "We did it!"

<><><>

The most powerful leaders of the world and its wealthiest elite gathered in Cintru, the glacial paradise of Kein Serpens Industries (KSi). The Antarctic—once a barren wasteland of ice—now stood as a thriving, modern haven, entirely under KSi's dominion. Within its impenetrable fortress, an event of monumental significance was taking place—the exclusive Survivors' Convention, where the fate of the world would be sealed.

Among the attendees was President Santiago 'Santi' Vicente III, leader of the second most populated country in Southeast Asia. He hadn't wanted to leave his homeland. He had hoped to oversee its rebuilding before passing on his reign. But how could he say no to the man who had healed the world—the mysterious benefactor behind the miraculous vaccine that had delivered humanity from the brink of extinction?

So, he boarded a private plane bound for the luxurious, castle-like headquarters of KSi, built atop a vast network of icebergs in the middle of the Antarctic Ocean. As the aircraft descended, Santi peered out the window—And what he saw left him breathless.

Cintru was alive. Against all odds, against all scientific logic, it had flourished—a gleaming metropolis of impossible beauty. It defied nature itself, rising from the coldest, most desolate region on Earth and turning it into a paradise. Towering crystalline structures stood amid vast green landscapes, their glass-like walls reflecting an eternal twilight.

Somehow, despite the subzero climate, lush forests, golden wheat fields, and blossoming orchards thrived across the city— A sight more dream than reality.

President Santi's breath hitched, his fingers pressing against the plane's window.

"Amazing, huh?" A smooth, velvety voice pulled him from his thoughts.

Turning, Santi found himself looking at their escort—Idris, a man who looked as though he had stepped off the cover of a fashion magazine.

"Where else in the world would you find a Rothschild's Orchid this size?" Idris gestured toward a massive, violet orchid standing several feet tall, its petals shimmering like silk spun from moonlight.

One of Santi's aides, a plant enthusiast, frowned. "Aren't those extremely sensitive to light?"

Idris chuckled, shaking his head. "Plants, flowers, and trees in Cintru don't require the elements of nature to grow." He winked. "We have ensured their survival by altering their genetic structure. Using advanced genome editing—the CRISPR-Cas9 method—we removed their weaknesses and granted them everlasting life." He flashed a charming smile, and the female staff nearly swooned.

Even Santi, at seventy-eight, found himself oddly fascinated—a rare male crush developing for the sheer brilliance of their guide. Still, the President's mind lingered elsewhere. His survival had been nothing short of a miracle. He had been dying of colon cancer, certain that his days were numbered— Then the virus had come, and with it, the vaccine that had changed everything.

Now, he felt stronger than ever, invigorated despite the sleepless nights. The doctors warned him of side effects, but he didn't care. And now, just as he had been preparing to step down, he had received a personal invitation from Kein Serpens himself. He couldn't refuse.

Not when he owed the man his life.

"Over there, Mr. President." One of his aides guided him to the table where ASEAN leaders were gathered. Pleasantries were exchanged—hugs, handshakes, and expressions of pure gratitude. For the first time in years, they could touch one another without fear.

"This place is unreal," murmured the Prime Minister of Singapore, his eyes sweeping over the magnificent architecture.

"I know, right?" Santi replied, still awestruck by the cathedral-like ceiling, impossibly high and adorned with golden etchings of celestial patterns.

The conference hall was sprawling, designed to be both modern and ancient at once— The glow of soft golden lights bathing the room in an ambiance of divine grandeur. Magnificent plants and floral displays framed the edges, filling the space with the scent of a perpetual spring.

They feasted like kings— For the first time in what felt like eternity, food was abundant, flowing without end. At one point, they had all been dying. Now, they were victors, indulging in life once more.

Then—
"Ladies and gentlemen..."

The hall fell silent as a holographic projection flickered above their tables. A figure materialized—Caiphaiz Prest. The audience stirred, murmuring.

"Is that him?" someone whispered. They had never seen Kein Serpens in person. Only his voice, his virtual messages, his philanthropic influence. His face remained a mystery.

"No, that's Mr. Caiphaiz Prest," the King of Brunei clarified. "Kein's second-in-command."

Caiphaiz's booming voice echoed through the hall. "Finally, we will heal together. Finally, the world unites!"

A montage of human suffering played across the screens—war, famine, disease, mass graves. The world before the vaccine had been a wasteland of horror. KSi had saved humanity, and now— It would lead them. As the presentation ended, emotions swelled. Laughter. Tears. Prayers.

And then—
A face appeared.

Kein Serpens.

4

Year One - Anno Bhiasti

For the first time, they saw him. And the applause was deafening. His youth. His beauty. His flawless, glowing skin. But above all—

His eyes.

Reddish violet. An inhuman shade. Yet, mesmerizing.

"Here he is, ladies and gentlemen!" Caiphaiz's voice trembled with reverence. "Leaders of the world, I am honored to present—Dr. Kein Serpens, Founder and Chairman of KSi!"

And then—

He stepped onto the stage. His virtual projection appeared on every table. Some fell to their knees, weeping, praying.

The worship began.

President Santi knelt, tears spilling down his face. It felt like a father had come to embrace his lost children—A savior, offering eternal peace.

Cries filled the hall.

"Thank you, Mr. Serpens…", "You are an angel from heaven…"

Kein smiled. Then he spoke. "People of the world, wipe your tears." His voice was divine—melodic, soothing, absolute.

They listened intently.

"With your permission, we will change our dating system." Kein's smile deepened. **"From Anno Domini to Anno Bhiasti."**

From the year of our Lord – Adonai to the year of the beast – Kein. A new beginning. A rebirth.

And with their blood as the seal— The contract was signed. Their souls are bound. And Kein laughed in victory.

Amidst the thunderous applause, the roaring cheers of adoration and devotion, Caiphaiz leaned in close—his lips brushing against Sofia's ear. His voice was smooth, deliberate, intoxicating. "It is time."

Sofia barely registered his words at first. Draped in a stunning emerald cocktail dress, she was a vision—elegant, alluring, lethal. The fabric clung to her flawless curves, shimmering under the golden lights, as though she were woven from the very essence of temptation itself.

"Yes, my lord." She turned swiftly, her heels clicking softly against the marble floor, slipping through the grand doors to prepare the others. Her emerald eyes—intensified by the dress—were locked onto the stage, where Kein stood, basking in his triumph.

The room worshipped him.

Kein raised a single hand, commanding silence with nothing more than a gesture. The crowd fell still, their eyes fixed on him, hanging onto his every word.

"The same contract will be sent to your countries," he announced, his voice smooth, hypnotic. "Your duty is to gather the signatures of all survivors in support of our agreement."

A pause.

Then—his smile widened, radiating an undeniable warmth. "You made history today, ladies and gentlemen!" With a flourish, he lifted a crystal goblet of deep red wine, the liquid within reflecting the golden glow of the chandeliers. "A toast!"

The crowd erupted into applause, lifting their own glasses—some with shaking hands, others with tears glistening in their eyes. KSi had no need to gather the DNA of the remaining humans.
They were mortal, their lives fragile and fleeting. Soon, their existence would be irrelevant.
"Now, the meeting is over, and it's time to celebrate! Take pride in what you've done!" Kein's voice rang through the vast chamber, brimming with excitement. And as if his words had been a silent cue, the lights shifted, the golden glow deepening into a warm, sultry hue. The air thickened with something intangible—something electric.

Then, the music began. A rhythmic pulse, soft at first, then growing, winding through the room like a sensual whisper. The great hall transformed, its center clearing to reveal a massive dance floor.
Soon, they arrived. A procession of beautiful men and women, young, vibrant, and flawless, strode in with effortless grace. Their bodies were draped in light, flowing fabrics, as if they had stepped out of a summer paradise—despite the frozen ocean surrounding them. They moved like living art, their presence both inviting and intoxicating.

And then, they danced. The energy in the room shifted, a feverish excitement taking hold. Laughter. Music. Bodies moving as one, lost in the intoxication of the moment.

The leaders, once so poised and controlled, found themselves letting go—drawn into the spellbinding atmosphere.

The entertainers mingled with them, weaving between the tables, pulling them into the lively, hypnotic rhythm.

Santi felt a soft hand slip into his. A blonde beauty, delicate yet undeniably powerful, smiled up at him, her expression both playful and inviting. "Dance with me, Mr. President?"

For a moment, he hesitated. He was old. His time for such things had long since passed. But her eyes held something familiar

—a youthful innocence that stirred a memory deep within him. His granddaughter. Cecilia.

She had died so young, stolen by the very plague that had nearly consumed the world. And now, here was this young girl, her age mirroring Cecilia's, smiling at him as if she had been placed in front of him for a reason.

He swallowed the lump forming in his throat. Then, with a faint smile, he took her hand. The music shifted, the beat slowing, the lights growing warmer still.

She wrapped her arms around his neck, pressing closer, her breath warm against his skin.

A fluttering sensation erupted in his chest, something unexpected—something that had been dormant for years. He stole a glance at the other leaders. They were all mesmerized, each one locked in an embrace with a partner just as beautiful.

The Prime Minister of India caught his gaze—his expression hesitant, his eyes questioning. "Is this... appropriate?" he murmured.

Santi hesitated, then shrugged. It felt good, though. "Well... when in Rome..."

The Thai prince chuckled, his arms wrapped around a young man. "Exactly."

Then—

A whisper against Santi's ear. "Mr. President... Please look at me."

He turned back, his gaze falling into those captivating blue eyes. The blonde's lips curled into a knowing smile. Her hands slid down his chest, her touch featherlight, yet charged with something potent. Santi's breath hitched.

She pressed closer, her soft curves molding against him. He felt his pulse quicken, his body responding in a way that startled him. A raging hunger stirred inside him—one that had been long forgotten. His body, once weak and failing, now felt alive.

"I chose you because I want you." Her lips brushed his ear, her voice a silken temptation. "Don't you want me, too?"

Santi swallowed hard, his hands instinctively gripping her tiny waist. "I... I want you... very much."

The blonde's smile deepened, her fingers tracing his lips, teasing. "Shhh..." Her touch was delicate, slow, yet deliberate. "No need to hurry..." Then, with a single motion, she slid the strap of her dress from her shoulder. The fabric pooled silently at her feet, leaving her standing bare, radiant, breathtaking.

Santi stared, mesmerized. She was a masterpiece, a vision straight out of a Renaissance painting— A living Monalisa, created for his pleasure. And he could no longer resist.

Amid the throbbing pulse of music, the intoxicated laughter, and the fevered cries of pleasure, Sofia and Hiro stepped onto the grand stage. Behind them, the sinful indulgence had begun—an unholy symphony of ecstasy and horror. But this—this was their true offering.

A gift for their god. Kein.

Sofia, draped in an emerald gown that shimmered like a serpent's scales, smiled seductively as she approached him.

Beside her, Hiro—a man carved from the very essence of beauty, with midnight-black eyes and a predator's grace—walked with silent reverence. Together, they presented their offering. The sacrificial lamb. The one who would begin the true celebration.
Kein stood at the center of the stage, exuding an unnatural glow, his raven-black hair falling like silk against his flawless porcelain skin.
Velial, now coiled around his fingers, shriveled—a mere worm awaiting its feast.
Kein turned to Caiphaiz, his most loyal servant, who stood at the edge of the stage, his eyes dark with unease. "Are you joining?" Kein mused.

Caiphaiz barely glanced at the writhing bodies in the crowd. "You have more than enough company, my lord." His tone was measured, his body tense. He wanted nothing to do with Velial, who now slithered down Kein's arm, burrowing deeper into the folds of his immortal flesh.
Kein chuckled, turning his attention back to his gift. She stood before him— Zonia. Barely twenty, with silky brown hair cascading over shoulders so delicate, so breakable. Her skin was pale, almost translucent under the flickering lights.
She clutched Hiro's arm, her breath shallow, her eyes wide with confusion. "H-Hiro?" Her voice was a trembling whisper, laced with naïve desperation. She had met him in Tokyo, at a victory gala celebrating the survivors of the plague. She had fallen madly, foolishly in love with this mysterious, chiseled stranger. She had agreed to a second date, never knowing it would take her across the world, aboard a

private plane, to a place that should not exist. To a man who was no man at all.

"Don't be afraid, my love." Hiro's gentle smile did not reach his eyes. "You are in the presence of our savior." With reverent grace, he pushed her forward.

Kein's crimson-violet gaze locked onto hers. Zonia shivered. She should have screamed. She should have run. Instead, she blushed. Her heart raced, her body betraying her— Drawn to him like a moth to a flame.

And then—

He kissed her. The world spun. The taste of his lips— Sweet. Unfathomably sweet. A forbidden nectar, more intoxicating than any drug. Her hands grasped at him, pulling him closer, craving more.

Kein chuckled, gently pushing her back. Zonia staggered, her head light, her pulse thundering. A haze of euphoria enveloped her. Hiro caught her, lifting her effortlessly and carrying her to the altar at the center of the stage.

The moment her body sank into the velvet softness, she gasped. The crowd's moans, cries, and laughter felt distant— Like she was floating, hovering between reality and delirium.

Hiro leaned over her, kissing her lips again, but— She wanted Kein's. Kein's tasted sweeter.

Kein felt Velial stir inside him—they are one. Slithering deeper, settling in his groin.

Sofia trailed her fingers up Zonia's bare leg. Zonia shuddered, fighting against the desire, the pleasure— But then—She saw Kein. His eyes held her captive. She felt her resolve crumble, her body surrender.

Hiro held her arms above her head, pressing soft kisses to her cheek, whispering words of devotion. Sofia's lips planted pressing delicate kisses on Zonia's feverish skin. Zonia's body arched, a whimper escaping her lips— Caught in the rapture of something she could not understand.

Then—

They bit her. A searing, white-hot agony. Zonia screamed, but— The wailing crowd drowned her out. Blood spilled onto the altar. Her vision blurred, her body burned— Yet euphoria intertwined with pain, twisting into something unspeakable.

Across the hall, Santi writhed in ecstasy. The blonde goddess, once an angel of temptation, now a snarling, scaly beast, was devouring his flesh. His own moans of pleasure and agony mixed with the sounds of crunching bone and tearing skin.

Somewhere, a woman screamed— Not in terror, but in rapturous delight. "Aaah... kill me! Kill me now!" A billionaire tycoon from Africa, her decadent body sprawled beneath the monster feeding upon her.

Santi heard her cries, saw the bloody glisten of her flesh, and— Understood. Understood that pleasure and pain were one and the same.

And then—

The blonde lifted her head, her red eyes blazing. Santi screamed. Her tongue split into two, and before he could recoil, it forced itself into his mouth— His soul burning away in the hellfire of ecstasy.

Back on stage, Kein sighed, brushing his fingers against Zonia's trembling body. Her blood pooled around her, staining the altar in sacred red. He was bathed in rapture— Just as he had been when his brother's blood soaked the earth beneath his feet.

Only now—

Now he had an army of eternal beasts to spill rivers of it for him. His beloved hellspawns would never die. They would never stop suffering. They would never stop thirsting. For the greatest pleasure came in repeating the torment endlessly—
Again.
And again.
And again.
"Enough." His voice cut through the madness, and Hiro and Sofia pulled away, licking the blood from their monstrous lips. They smiled at each other, clawed fingers intertwining, sharing a hungry, grotesque kiss.

Kein bit his lip, then turned back to Zonia. The girl was sobbing, convulsing in agony. He pressed his lips to hers, whispering,
"Shhh... taste me, my child." Then Kein took her purity -- violently.
Her cry melted into a moan— A moment of peace in the midst of carnage.

Then—

Her body twisted. Her eyes widened. Kein laughed, his voice pure sin. Zonia's chest exploded open, and from within, a serpent of shadows emerged, devouring her still-beating heart.
Kein's laughter filled the room, drowning the cries of the newly born monsters.

It was a celebration, indeed.

◇◇◇

15 Anno Bhiasti – (The Year Of The Beast)

Fifteen years had passed since Kein—the immortal—reset the calendar to exalt the beast, declare himself the god of the world, and unify all currency under a single digital system known as Koine.

Vahitna salivated, her eyes fixed on James' sleeping form. Her sharp senses scanned the world beyond their walls, attuned to the chaos lurking outside. For now, it was safe.

For now.

But she knew the truth—safety was an illusion. The sigbin — the hellspawns, as humans called them—had already discovered the full extent of their appetite.

Blood. Flesh. And worst of all— The pleasure of consuming their prey alive.

Yet Vahitna resisted. She hungered for James—his warmth, his scent, his very existence called to her—but her love for him fortified her against the beast inside. She could fight her urges, but she had no control over what waited beyond their home.

If the other sigbin ever found out James was still fully human... She couldn't let them have him. No matter the cost.

James stirred, shifting slightly. Vahitna steeled herself, her muscles tensing. She couldn't wake him. She had taken to sleeping apart from him. Not really sleeping, just sitting at a safe distance from their bed.

Now, she simply watched over him, guarding him from herself. She had forbidden herself to touch him. To get too close. If she inhaled too deeply... If she let her instincts take over... She might not be able to stop herself.

Some sigbin took time to realize what they had become. At first, they felt normal—until their first exposure to human flesh. A touch. A taste. A moment of weakness. The hunger awakened during intimacy.

At first, they didn't mean to harm their human lovers—until it became impossible to resist. Then came the bloody rituals— Sex, carnage, euphoria. A primal addiction, repeated endlessly, a spiral of indulgence from which there was no return.

When Kein declared himself god, resetting the world's calendar in his name, the sigbin fully embraced their new existence. They were eternal. Beautiful. Divine. And with their true power awakened, they no longer needed to hide their hunger. They could feast freely. And they did.

Rumors of war followed soon after.

<><><>

Vahitna had known something was wrong the moment she realized she couldn't give birth to Dinah. Nine months pregnant, she had been dying in a hospital bed, the RPTR21 virus devouring her from the inside out. She had been ready to go. To join Jordan, their 2-year old son, in whatever came next.

"I'll be with Jordan soon, honey," she had whispered, her voice frail, her fingers clutching James' hand. "See you on the other side, my love."

Jordan had died months before due to the same virus. She was at peace with her fate. James was not. "Please, baby—hold on. The vaccine is coming. Don't leave me!" He had begged, but her vision had already darkened, her body succumbing to the inevitable.

Then—

She woke up. James had smiled, tears streaming down his face, telling her— "Everything is fine." But it wasn't.

A month passed, and her pregnancy didn't progress. The fetus remained unchanged—alive, yet stuck in time. Other pregnant women suffered the same fate. Their babies were healthy, but frozen inside their wombs. James had blamed himself for allowing her to be inoculated.

She had forgiven him. But the truth was—none of them knew what was happening. KSi provided them with a medical facility, promising to find answers. When her C-section was scheduled, she had held on to hope.

Then—

She heard Dinah cry. James was there, sobbing, kissing her, whispering words of love. But the moment the umbilical cord was cut, the baby stopped crying. Dead. Her womb sealed shut. And she was pregnant again.

The cycle reset.

"I—I don't understand," James had sobbed, his voice breaking in the next room. "What's happening to my wife? To the others?"

Doctors gave senseless excuses, but Vahitna had stopped listening.

She had held Dinah's lifeless body, rocking her gently, kissing her tiny face. She hadn't wanted to let go. And when they tried to take her away— She had snapped.

"V-Vahitna!" James' horrified gasp shattered the air.

She looked down. Her hands were soaked in blood. Her mouth—Chewing. What remained of Dinah's tiny fingers. And then she screamed—A scream she never wanted to wake from.

Yet, fifteen years later, James still loved her. She didn't understand why. KSi gave them money, a home, security—but they would never be whole again.

"For as long as we have each other, everything will be alright." James still whispered those words, even now, as he traced the image of their unborn child on the ultrasound screen.

They had bought their own machine—a morbid attempt at hope. Dinah still moved inside her, but Vahitna felt nothing for her anymore. She had already eaten the real one.

<><><>

In the year of the beast (Anno Bhiasti), Kein's rule had divided the world. Most humans resisted—they refused to accept him as their Messiah. They refused to believe that the vaccine had been crafted from his blood, turning the sigbin into his children.

That the world was now his to command. But for many sigbin, Kein was a god. He had given them beauty, youth, immortality.

Yet there were exceptions—

Women like Vahitna, forever pregnant. Babies who never aged. The sick, the disabled, the elderly, all frozen in their conditions.

The vaccine had cured the virus, but it had never promised perfection. Hate crimes erupted. Humans feared the sigbin, and radical sigbin feasted on humans.

"Humans started this. We're just defending ourselves," a sigbin declared on the news.

"Self-defense?! We don't die! What the heck are they talking about?!" Vahitna screamed at the screen, enraged. She was not like them. She still cared about humans. Because she still cared about James.

"Let's not get involved in politics, my love" James always dismissed it, switching off the screen.

"They better stay away from you, or I will eat those monsters!" Vahitna uttered endless profanity as she was pacing back and forth in their kitchen, her nails digging into her own flesh.

James sighed, then pulled her into his arms. "I love you too."

She stiffened, her breath catching— His scent overwhelmed her senses. "D-Don't."

James pulled her closer. "I miss you."

She bit her lip. "I miss you too," she whispered. But she could already feel the change burning through her veins. She stepped back.

James looked hurt.

Vahitna clenched her fists. "I don't want you to see me like this." Vahitna turned away, controlling her transformation into a scaly green monster she had become.

A knock on the door interrupted the brewing argument. The homeowners' association meeting was about to begin. James wanted to kiss Vahitna, but she simply waved at him.

"The committee has decided—the new ordinance will be implemented immediately."

From where she hid after following her husband, meters away from the town hall, Vahitna couldn't see the speaker— But she knew his voice. The homeowners' association president.

They had gathered all human residents for an emergency meeting, though Vahitna—like the other sigbin—was not allowed to attend. It didn't matter. If she focused hard enough—and was at just the right distance—she could hear everything. Her kind always could.

"Wait a minute!" James. His voice rose in protest, firm, desperate. "Shouldn't we discuss this first? I don't want to be separated from my wife."

Vahitna's heart clenched.

"I'm sorry, James," another man spoke. His voice was heavy with grief. "I don't want to be away from my son either, but last night... he almost... he almost ate his mother. It came so close... I can't..."

Vahitna couldn't place the voice—but she understood his fear. She had seen it before. The moment of weakness. The hunger, winning.

"Well, my wife is different. She wouldn't even hurt a fly!"

Vahitna smiled at James' confidence. She loved him. She would never hurt him. But the others—the humans who feared what they didn't understand—didn't believe that.

"Still," a new voice cut in, sharp and indifferent, "humans will remain in the homes inside the village, while their sigbin family members will be relocated along the perimeter—to guard us against external attacks.

"It's that or leave."

Vahitna's blood boiled. Her fingernails dug into her palms, nearly breaking skin. She wanted to rip their throats out. To storm into that meeting and show them exactly why they should be afraid. How dare they try to separate her from James? She didn't care about the other humans. But James was hers. And she would not lose him.

"It's okay." James again. "We can manage." His voice was steady, calculated. "Maybe my wife doesn't have the same urges because..." he paused. "She's pregnant."

Vahitna grinned, pressing a hand against her still, silent belly. "That's my man."

◇◇◇

She was waiting in the kitchen when James returned.

"You heard." It wasn't a question. James knew she could hear everything. Still, his voice wavered. A small part of him refused to believe she could listen from that far.

Vahitna nodded, her worry etched into the lines of her forehead. Her voice broke. "I can't live without you."

James crossed the room, pulling her into his arms. "That won't happen." His whisper was gentle, determined. "We'll do whatever it takes."

Vahitna pulled back, studying his face. Her gaze lowered to his pulse—the soft, steady rhythm of life beneath his skin. James had lied to them. He had told them she felt no hunger. But she did. Every second of every day. She ached for his flesh—his blood, rich and sweet as honey. She could smell it. Taste it in the air. Her fingers curled into fists. She wouldn't fail. She wouldn't become like the others.

Her hand moved to the counter. She grabbed the butcher's knife—cold, heavy steel. She turned and pressed it into James' palm. "Whatever it takes." Her voice was calm, resolved.

5

The Mutation

James' throat tightened. He exhaled shakily, gripping the knife. He had always known it would come to this.

Vahitna laid down on the kitchen floor. She exposed her belly, her breath shallow.

James knelt above her, his hands trembling. Tears spilled silently from his eyes.

She stared at him, unblinking. "Do it."

James swallowed hard. Then—

He cut.

Vahitna stifled a scream, her fingers clawing into the tiles, her body seizing as pain ripped through her. "Ahhhhhhh!" Vahitna felt the knife tear through flesh and muscle, but— Her lips never formed his name. She refused to cry out.

Then—

A sharp, desperate wail echoed through the kitchen. James pulled their daughter free, cradling her against his chest. The baby screamed—a fragile, fleeting sound.

And then—

She fell silent. Her body limped. James' chest heaved, his arms tightening around her tiny form. His whole world collapsed— And yet, Vahitna only smiled. "Go," she whispered.

James hesitated, his fingers curling around Dinah's tiny, lifeless hand.

"Go. Now."

James stood. He took one last look at his wife. At the open wound that had already begun to heal. At the monstrous hunger glistening in her eyes. Then— He turned and left.

The moment the door clicked shut, Vahitna gazed down at the still body in her arms. A final, fleeting moment of silence. Then— Her teeth sank into the flesh. Blood filled her mouth, warm and familiar. She devoured it. And the hunger subsided.

For now.

This was how they survived. When they left the village, escaping the new law that would separate them, they had discovered a way. A way for Vahitna to satisfy her hunger—without turning on James. Her body never changed. Her womb never emptied. Every time, the baby died the moment it left her body. And every time, she fed.

But—

It wasn't always enough. There were nights when James' scent overwhelmed her. Nights when she watched him sleep, her mouth watering, her body shaking with restraint. Because James was alive. Because his blood was fresh. Because no matter how full she felt, James would always be more delicious than the dead.

<><><>

Vahitna sat motionless, watching her sleeping husband, her mind replaying the conversation they'd had before he drifted off.

"What if I drink your blood?" James asked, his voice quiet but unwavering. "Maybe I can be immortal too. The vaccine had Kein's blood in it—that's what caused your mutation. Maybe I can…" He leaned in to kiss her goodnight, but she stopped him, placing a hand on his chest.

"No! What if you die?" She searched his face, waiting for the usual laugh, the teasing grin—but James was serious.

"Just a drop," he stepped closer, eyes filled with determination.

"Nope, I can't risk it," she stepped back, avoiding his pleading gaze.

"Whatever it takes," he whispered.

Vahitna didn't response. Instead, she watched helplessly as James settled into bed, sighing.

"I'm dead either way." James' words shook her to her core.

War had been declared. Both races—sigbin and humans—had officially turned on each other. Streets would soon be drenched in blood, and the sigbin would feast. Humans, foolish as they were, still clung to their illusions of peace, believing their sigbin loved ones would protect them.

But love wouldn't win this war. Vahitna knew better. She knew humans would be casualties, nothing more. And James? He was human.

James stirred, rolling onto his side. Vahitna took a step closer. "What's wrong?" His groggy voice was thick with sleep, his eyes half-open. She stroked his hair, traced his cheekbone with her fingers. "Are you hungry again?"

She shook her head. The baby she had devoured last night would sustain her for three more days. "Let's do it. Whatever it takes." Before she could stop herself, she lifted her wrist, slicing it with a single, razor-sharp nail. The wound bled instantly, the deep red stark against her pale skin. She held it out.

James didn't hesitate. He gripped her wrist and pressed his lips to the wound, licking the dark nectar before her skin seamlessly healed. Silence stretched between them.

Vahitna waited. Her heart pounded. "Anything?" she whispered.

James sat still, thoughtful. Then— "Nothing." A deep exhale of disappointment. He flexed his fingers, testing himself. "I feel the same... except I'm not sleepy anymore." James licked his lips, as if savoring the taste. "Actually... I want more."

Vahitna's stomach twisted. Relief. And fear.

"Come here," James shifted, making space for her. "Lie with me."

"No." She turned away, forcing distance between them.

"Come on," he murmured, grabbing her hand. "If I have to die, I want it to be you."

Vahitna whirled to face him, eyes blazing. She was ready to scold him, ready to yell—

But his face was calm. Serious. Then, before she could react, James yanked her forward, sending her tumbling onto the bed. His lips crashed onto hers.

Vahitna's breath caught— Her body betrayed her. The kiss was electric, sending a wildfire through her veins. How long has it been? How long since they had touched? Since he had held her? Since she had felt human? Her body remembered. It responded.

"J-James..." She tried to pull away. Tried to resist.

But he only tightened his grip. His warmth, his heartbeat, the way he moved against her—it shattered her control. "Shhh..." His mouth devoured hers, and she gave in.

Vahitna moaned as James' hands roamed, exploring the curves of her still-bloated body.

"Ouch!" A sharp sting. Vahitna jerked away, tasting blood. James had bitten her lip—hard. She blinked, startled, as he licked the blood from her mouth. "James..."

His eyes burned with something wild. "I want more," he murmured.

And then— He bit her again.

Vahitna laughed—a sound she hadn't heard in years. The first real laughter since she became a sigbin. Something in James was changing. She could see it. She could feel it.

He kissed her again, and she didn't stop him. Didn't want to stop him. When she opened her blouse, she didn't need to speak. James latched onto her, feeding—just like a hungry child.

The sensation was intoxicating. Her body burned with pleasure, with a hunger different from before. He was draining her—but in the best possible way.

She let him. Until— James pushed her down. Vahitna gasped— Something was wrong. James was stronger. Stronger than he should be. His grip was tight, almost painful. His teeth sank deeper. She felt the change. Her own body reacted, her skin hardening, scales forming. She had transformed.

James should have recoiled. But instead, he only held her tighter, eyes burning with desire. He wasn't afraid. He was starving. The night became a blur of blood and pleasure—as Vahitna attacked her husband, feeding on him too. James, in return, made sweet-sweet bloodthirsty love to her.

Until the first light of dawn.

James was asleep. Vahitna lay beside him, her mind spinning. Something had changed. She could feel it. She touched James' skin— And froze. His wounds were gone. Healed. It had worked.

Vahitna let him sleep. She cleaned him, cleaned their bloodstained sheets, and cleaned the entire room. She waited. Waited for him to wake. She stood by the window, watching the full moon rise.

Then—

James' snoring stopped. Vahitna smiled.

Finally!

She rushed to their bedroom, excited to hold him again— Only to be met with teeth and claws. A wild beast—a creature that once was James— Tore into her belly. And ripped their child out.

<><><>

999 Anno Bhiasti. For over nine centuries of Kein's rule as the god of the new world, humans fought a losing war against the sigbin—immortal hellspawns that refused to die. As a result, their numbers dwindled, forcing them into hiding at the very edges of the world.

Their last hope had once been the azhuang, created as a safeguard against the sigbin. But the plan backfired. The azhuang turned out to be useless by day, spending all their time asleep, and deadly at night, when they awoke hungry—for human blood. With this unintended betrayal, humanity found itself at war with two monstrous races, a battle they could never hope to win.

Amid the chaos, a group of foresighted survivors established Perlaz, a hidden stronghold in Southeast Asia. Sympathetic sigbin helped erect towering barricades and labyrinthine roadblocks to prevent their more predatory brethren from breaching the territory. At the heart of the settlement, a thriving human colony took root, struggling to preserve what was left of their kind.

Leading Perlaz's defenses was Bufe, a blind, 98-year-old sigbin known as a hukluvan—one of the so-called "useless immortals," despised by radical sigbin for being either sick, disabled, or unwilling to partake in the senseless slaughter.

Once a decorated military doctor in the ChinDia War of the late 21st century (Anno Domini), Bufe had fought both pandemics and battlefield horrors as a human. Now, as a sigbin, he stood at the helm of brigada, a military force of humans and peaceful sigbin, sworn to protect Perlaz's inner sanctum.

His channaks—sigbin children who rejected war—patrolled the outer barricades, ensuring the safety of Perlaz's expanding colony.

Now, under the watchful eyes of thousands of brigada soldiers and sigbin warriors, Kein stepped off his plane just outside the marked borders of Perlaz.

Beside Bufe, Reeva, a twelve-year-old channak warrior, clenched her fists. Although frozen in time due to the vaccine she received just before her first menstruation, her sharp mind and battle prowess made her one of Perlaz's most formidable young leaders.

"I may be blind, but I can feel your unease," Bufe murmured, sensing Reeva's tension.

Reeva swallowed her anger. "What does he want?"

"We're about to find out," Bufe replied, gripping his cane.

Despite nearly a thousand years passing, his resentment toward Kein burned as fiercely as ever. Not for turning him into a sigbin—he had long accepted that—but for being the source of everything: the curse, the suffering, the war that had pushed humanity to the brink of extinction.

The ground beneath them trembled slightly.

"What is that sound?" Bufe asked.

"The plants," Reeva whispered in horror. "They're dying."

From the moment Kein had stepped foot on Perlaz's soil, the surrounding vegetation withered and turned to dust—a reminder of his ancient curse.

"He's with that strange man again," Reeva continued, trying to keep her voice steady. "And a handful of sigbin."

"Ah... Caiphaiz," Bufe spat. "The high priest. Kein's second-in-command."

Reeva smirked. "Well, in this part of the world, you're in charge. I'm your second-in-command."

Bufe let out a dry chuckle, then turned his attention back to their unwanted visitors.

Kein stopped, sensing the hostility from miles away.

"That's far enough, cursed one," Bufe said, his voice steady but firm.

Kein halted.

The chosen meeting place—a rocky valley far from Perlaz's inner borders—was open and vast, surrounded by towering mountains where hidden channak warriors lay in wait. Every sigbin and human soldier present was ready for battle, their weapons locked on Kein's entourage.

"What do you want, cursed one?" Bufe repeated. He would never acknowledge Kein as a god.

Kein's sigbin growled at the insult, and the air grew heavier with tension. Channak warriors shifted into position, awaiting the order to attack. But Kein raised a hand, silencing his own men.

"I come in peace, my child," he said smoothly.

"If you do, you should have stayed away," Bufe shot back. "If you truly cared, you'd be destroying your own monsters—the hellspawns slaughtering humans! Yswh's creations! The true children of Adonai!"

Kein exhaled, gripping the fruit in his right hand. "You are my creations too," he said, his voice unnervingly calm. "You are my blood. My children."

"No!" The hukluvans and channaks shouted in unison.

Kein let their fury pass before speaking again. "Very well," he said. "I understand your anger. I came personally to tell you this war ends today."

Silence.

Bufe's grip on his cane tightened, waiting for Kein's deception.

Kein took his time, letting the words settle before continuing. "I propose a new order," he said. "The world will be divided into three continents. The North will be for hostile sigbin, closest to me in Cintru, where I will contain them, the MidLands will be a neutral zone for humans and peaceful sigbin who choose coexistence, and the South – Your territory, Perlaz, which I will expand and reinforce."

Reeva exchanged glances with Bufe. They remained silent as Kein elaborated.

"I will send supplies, weapons, and technology to secure your borders," Kein promised. "I will personally oversee the relocation of human refugees here, ensuring their safety. I will restrict global transportation, preventing unwanted crossings between territories."

Reeva folded her arms. "And the azhuang?" She had never encountered them personally, but the stories from refugees were enough—soulless, bloodthirsty creatures that preyed on humans just as much as sigbin did.

Kein's expression darkened. "I will wipe them out," he declared.

The murmurs among Perlaz's sigbin grew louder. The azhuang were not true immortals—they could be killed. If Kein was willing to exterminate them, was he really on their side?

Bufe raised a hand, silencing the discussions. "Why?" he asked, suspicion lacing his voice. "Why would you do this?"

Kein held his gaze. "Because I value human life," he said.

Bufe almost laughed at the blatant lie.

Reeva, however, made the final call. "Make it happen," she said, her voice sharp. "Then we'll believe you."

Kein nodded and left without another word.

<><><>

"What's on your mind, my lord?" Caiphaiz asked, watching Kein in the dimly lit cabin of their bullet jet. The air between them was thick with unspoken thoughts as they sped toward Cintru, leaving Perlaz and its unwelcome hostility behind.

Caiphaiz's jaw clenched as he recalled their meeting with Bufe. That despicable hukluvan had the audacity to insult Kein to his face—to call him cursed. The high priest seethed at the memory, barely able to contain his rage.

"You should have silenced him," Caiphaiz muttered under his breath. "He's nothing but an old piece of immortal garbage. Useless, weak, and blind."

Kein, however, remained lost in thought, unmoved by his second-in-command's anger. His eyes were fixed on the darkness outside, fingers idly stroking the fruit inside his coat pocket. Sofia and the others...?" Kein finally spoke, deflecting Caiphaiz's frustrations.

Caiphaiz inhaled sharply. He knew this question was coming.

The first-generation sigbin—the very first immortals birthed from the fusion of Kein's blood and Velial's venom—had begun to mutate. It started slowly: a pallor they couldn't shake, a lethargy that seeped into their bones. Then, one by one, their veins dried up—their bodies no longer capable of producing blood.

They were becoming something else. And for the first time in over a thousand years,

Kein had known fear. "Find out what's causing this mutation!" Kein had raged when he first heard of it. "They cannot be without blood! They must have blood in their veins!"

Scientists from K.S. Industries worked tirelessly, dissecting, experimenting, and testing solutions. But no cure was found. Now, Sofia and the others were back in containment—lab rats once again, their bodies studied like failed experiments.

Caiphaiz sighed. "There is still no progress, my lord."

Kein's grip tightened on the fruit, remembering...

<><><>

"I miss you, my lord," Sofia whispered, her voice trembling.

When Kein had last visited her in the lab, she had reached for him, her hands frail, her body shrouded in a sterile hospital gown. The scent of death clung to her—cold, empty, unnatural.

Once, she had been among his most cherished sigbin—a beauty who had ruled over men with a mere glance. Now, she was a walking corpse.

Kein did not respond at first. He simply stared at her, taking in her hollowed-out features, the lifeless gray tint of her skin. She was no longer worthy. "I miss you too, my child," he finally said, masking his revulsion behind a gentle tone. "Be patient. We will find a cure, I promise."

When she leaned in to kiss him, he barely touched his tongue to her lips before pulling away—disgusted.

Then he turned and walked out.

<><><>

In his growing desperation, Kein sought his father's counsel. Sacrificing another tree from his garden, he awakened Serpens from his slumber.

The massive serpent coiled sluggishly around the dying branches, flicking its tongue in irritation.

"I live for blood, Father," Kein confessed, his voice unsteady—an emotion he was not used to feeling. "I cannot survive without it. Can you find answers for this anomaly?"

Velial hissed thoughtfully, his massive golden eyes flickering. "I will, my child," the serpent assured him, though even he sounded uncertain. "But I am still waiting for Adonai to summon me. He has been silent since we took over His beloved world."

That, more than anything, troubled Serpens. He had expected resistance. He had expected divine wrath. Yet Adonai had done nothing. Why? Why had He abandoned His own creation?

<><><>

Kein paced the length of his garden, feeling something foreign creep into his heart—something vile and human.

Fear.

He clenched his fists. No. He was Kein Serpens. The god of this world. If he could not drink from the blood of his sigbin, he would ensure another source remained flowing. "The humans," Kein whispered to himself, a new plan forming in his mind. "I must secure them and stop this bloody war. Without the blood of my sigbin, theirs must remain flowing."

This—this was why he had spared Perlaz. It had nothing to do with kindness. Nothing to do with justice. He needed a thriving human population—not just for balance, not just for order. For blood. For his survival. For his pleasure.

This was why he had endured Bufe's insults and humiliations. Because in the end, it didn't matter. Bufe could call him cursed. He could spit and curse Kein's name to the heavens. But so long as his blood ran red, Kein would let him live.

For now.

<><><>

Months passed. Bufe and his warriors stood vigil at the border, awaiting Kein's move, never letting their guard down.

Then, the first skyraptor appeared.

One by one, helicopters delivered human refugees, along with weapons, technology, and supplies—everything Kein had promised.
"He was telling the truth," Reeva admitted as they worked to resettle the survivors.

<><><>

After visiting Perlaz and forging a deal with Bufe, from Cintru, Kein addressed the world through an augmented reality feed. His voice echoed across continents as his divine decree rippled through every screen, every city, and every heart. "The war ends today."

The new world order had arrived. Kein laid out his vision: the world would be divided into three territories, each serving a distinct purpose. But the world did not welcome his declaration.

Across cities and strongholds, radical sigbin erupted in protest. Their monstrous roars filled the streets, defying their creator. Humans, too, trembled at the weight of this announcement, their fragile hope hanging by a thread.

<><><>

In the chaos of the rioting crowd, Vahitna and James stood side by side—predators among sheep—watching the world burn in resistance. But when Kein ordered the annihilation of all azhuang, the protests turned into an all-out frenzy.

For nine centuries, Vahitna and James had lived in isolation, lurking in the shadows south of the Mediterranean Sea.

James, a nightborne predator, was sensitive to sunlight but remained young and lethal. Together, they had built a legacy of fear—hunting human villages, targeting pregnant women, and devouring life before it could even begin.

James feasted on the mothers' hearts. Vahitna devoured the unborn. But now, Kein threatened to strip everything away from them. No one. Not Kein. Not anyone.

She would not allow them to take her husband away—dead or alive.

<><><>

Kein's voice resonated through the world, commanding all who bore his accursed blood to listen.

"This is an urgent call to all my sigbin children." His glowing, violet-red eyes bore into the camera as he sat atop his throne in Cintru, exuding absolute control. "Stop hunting humans and follow the new laws I have set forth. All sigbin who cannot live in harmony with humans must proceed to the northern lands. Settle in Zapad... or reside here in Cintru, where I will deal with you personally."

A collective shudder rippled through the sigbin who knew of Kein's punishments in Cintru. Kein was merciless. His torments were eternal. "Sigbin with human families must make a choice." His next words sent a shockwave through the sigbin ranks. "Separate from your human companions and send them to Perlaz, where they will be left in peace to grow and repopulate... or move to Xego, the neutral ground. There, humans and sigbin may coexist—provided that you uphold peace and order. No more war!"

The world held its breath. But the sigbin refused. Cries of outrage erupted. Families clung to their human loved ones, rejecting the divide Kein demanded. They would not give up their humans.

"Obey me," Kein thundered, his voice shaking the very air itself. "For I have cursed you!"

The sigbin froze.

"You know my power. I am your God. I am your creator. End this war... or suffer the consequences." Then, without hesitation, Kein turned to the sigbin kneeling beside him.

In a swift, merciless motion, he decapitated the sigbin in front of the world. The head rolled onto the floor—bloodless.

6

Lumen

The riots fell into silence.

Kein lifted the undead's head, staring into the camera, his serpentine smile curling at the edges of his lips. "This will happen to you."

A shudder spread across the sigbin.

"You will dry up. You will wither. You will suffer a bloodless existence." Kein let the silence sink in. Then, his voice softened, dripping with deceit. "Obey me. Change your ways. And maybe... just maybe... I will change my mind."

The sigbin knew hunger. They knew fear. And they knew Kein was not lying. The mutation—the slow, agonizing loss of blood—was happening. And if Kein had the power to curse them, then surely... He had the power to restore them. With that, the sigbin across the world bowed in submission.

<><><>

In the shadows, Velial coiled in satisfaction. "Tell your children the mutation is their punishment for disobedience," the serpent had whispered to Kein before the broadcast. "Make them fear you. Make them believe your curse is real. Do not appear weak. Do not appear uncertain. Make them worship you in fear, and they will bow to you."

Kein had followed every word. And the world had crumbled beneath his feet.

<><><>

Far away, in the stronghold of Perlaz, Bufe trembled in agony as Kein was addressing the nation. Sitting in his chamber, the blind, ancient sigbin groaned, his body writhing as he felt Kein's false curse rippling through their kind.

"Grandpa!" Melvin, his grandson and a brigada general, rushed into the chamber. The young warrior knelt beside him, watching as Bufe's face contorted in pain. "Grandpa, what's happening? What do you see?"

Bufe's gasping breath filled the air. Then, in a sudden moment of clarity, his trembling hands reached for Melvin's knife.

Before Melvin could stop him, Bufe slit his own arm open. "Grandpa!" Melvin lunged forward, but the wound sealed itself instantly.

Bufe stared at his own flesh, not seeing anything but feeling everything. His heart sank. Melvin's breath hitched as he took the knife back after telling Bufe that he was not bleeding

Silence.

"What did you see?" Melvin asked, knowing his grandpa saw a vision.

Bufe's lips trembled. "A bleeding sigbin with blinding marks all over his body." He whispered, dread creeping into his voice.

<><><>

In 1925 Anno Bhiasti, a hundred years before the present day, every sigbin had become bloodless—except for one.

Tasty virgin heart available inside - this was the infamous tagline of Isla De Parthena, a high-class brothel chain with branches scattered across Zapad and Xego. But its allure wasn't just about lust—it was about bloodless pain.

The club's prized attractions were the **athenas**—virgin sigbin hellspawns, whose bodies defied biology. Despite engaging with their clients, they remained physically intact, their bodies resetting after every act. But beyond their eternal purity, it was their distinct scent that drew in the wealthiest and most powerful sigbin. The heart of an athena was a delicacy, a euphoric fix that no drug could match.

Over the centuries, Parthena's athenas had evolved from pleasure providers to something far more sinister. Now, customers came not just to indulge—but to torment. The sigbin didn't just want virgin flesh; they wanted to see athenas being sacrificed repeatedly.

Hiro, the young man present during the first Festival Of Avlam at Cintru, pushed open the doors of the brothel's bar lounge and was greeted by dim golden lights and the thick scent of spiced liquor and sweat. But beneath it, faint yet unmistakable, was something else—something sweet, something hauntingly familiar.

His heart pounded. He knew that scent. Even the memory of it made his stomach knot and his mouth water.
"Hi, Uncle Hiro!" A bright voice cut through the noise.

Lumen.

She waved at him enthusiastically from behind the kitchen's glass partition, oblivious to the effect she had on him.

Hiro forced a strained smile, his body already betraying him, heat pooling at his core. He gritted his teeth. Dang it! Not again. Every time he saw Lumen, the hunger intensified. It was wrong. He knew it. He should have stopped coming to this brothel. He should have left Xego altogether. But he couldn't. He was addicted—not just to her scent, but to the sheer innocence in her eyes.

And she had no idea how much danger she was in. Right now, the air-tight barrier surrounding her in the kitchen kept her safe. But for how long?

"Where's your grandpa?" Hiro asked, signaling the bartender, Ben, for his usual drink.

Lumen smiled. "He's downstairs in the dungeon with Uncle Hendrix and Papa."

Hiro clenched his fist. She barely showed any skin in that shapeless dress, and yet, everything about her was maddeningly intoxicating. He threw back his drink in one go and waved goodbye before heading down the basement stairs.

The basement was damp and grimy, resembling a dungeon more than a meeting space. Partitions divided the area into storage rooms, but the real business happened at the farthest section, where Hendrix and the others were gathered.

Lumen's father, Hugo, greeted Hiro with a weary nod. Beside him sat Baby Nzo, perched on his high chair in green overalls, his small frame belying the sharp intelligence in his piercing black eyes. Though only two years old (in human years), the channak child led the underground movement like a seasoned war strategist.

Hendrix, however, barely acknowledged Hiro. Once his closest ally, now his reluctant partner, the tension between them was palpable. But for Lumen's sake, they put aside their differences.

"I have great news," Hiro announced, lowering himself into a crate. "I found a way to get Lumen safely to Perlaz."

Hugo exhaled sharply, his hands trembling as he ran them through his graying hair. "Finally…" he murmured, voice cracking. The burden of protecting his daughter had aged him beyond his years.

Across the table, Nzo sucked his thumb, kicking his legs. "Missing berhen, more, yes, more, again," the toddler muttered, his baby voice eerily serious.

Hiro stiffened. So that was why the room felt like a funeral.

The recent news of a missing high school girl had spread across Xego, but only Nzo and the others saw the pattern—berhen were disappearing. Yet, the city's authorities refused to entertain the possibility of a targeted conspiracy.

"I heard," Hiro muttered, lowering his gaze. That girl was already dead. He knew it. They all did.

"Can you really get Lumen out? The airports are still…" Hendrix interjected, his protective instincts making him distrustful.

"Who says we're using public transportation?" Hiro shot back smugly.

Hugo looked between the two men, his eyes brimming with gratitude. "I can't thank you both enough."

Nzo, however, wasn't satisfied. "Lumen first, okie-okie?!" the toddler insisted, slamming his tiny fist onto the table.

Hiro and Hendrix stiffened. A heartbeat later, the air shifted. Their bodies tensed, their breathing shallowed. Something sweet and overpowering filled the room.

Darn it!

Hiro knew that scent. Hendrix did too.
And judging by the way Nzo screamed, they weren't the only ones.
"No! ILLUMINATA, Out!"
Hugo barely had time to react before grabbing his daughter and shoving her into the nearest sealed chamber, locking the air-tight door behind her.
From inside, Lumen's eyes widened in confusion. "Papa—?"
"STAY IN THERE!"

Hendrix clenched his jaw, fighting the transformation clawing its way to the surface. His pupils dilated, his breath ragged.
Hiro trembled, his scales beginning to form from his ears down to his neck. Her scent was too strong today.
"You out? Okie-okie?!" Nzo's tiny voice cut through the tension, his sharp baby teeth gnashing.
Hiro didn't answer. He bolted, holding his breath.

<><><>

The back alley behind the brothel was cold and reeked of urine and vomit. But to Hiro, it was fresh air. He leaned against the wall, trembling, his claws digging into his palms.
He yanked his pendant from around his neck, opening the small vial inside. With shaking fingers, he dabbed a single drop of red liquid onto his tongue.

Blood.

Instantly, his body calmed, the feverish hunger subsiding. He exhaled. That was too close. If no one had been there, he would've taken Lumen in an instant. He cursed under his breath, but deep down, he knew—it wasn't just hunger.

It was her.

<><><>

Back inside, Hendrix had just finished tossing a group of injured sigbin onto the street after a brutal bar fight. Like them, the clients had caught Lumen's scent at the bar, but they were adamant about searching every room for a special Athena—willing to pay any price to find her.

This was the reason why Lumen slipped into the basement to hide, interrupting the ongoing meeting to warn them about what was happening upstairs. The sudden intrusion caught everyone off guard, forcing Hiro to retreat into the alley.

Tani, one of the discarded sigbin who got a beating from Hendrix, crouched by the gutter waiting for his broken jaws to heal. "You smelled it, right?" he murmured.

His friend, Oskie, groaned as he reattached his severed arm, his eyes narrowing. "Yeah. What was that?"

"I've been to every Parthena in Xego," their third companion, Cody, added, snapping his dislocated jaw into place. "That one is different."

Tani smirked. "They're hiding a berhen in that brothel." Oskie licked his lips, excitement flashing in his eyes. But Tani stopped him. "Not for you, idiot. We'll sell her."

"To who?" Cody asked. Tani dialed the neural implant on his wrist, smirking. "The Governor's son."

◇◇◇

"Ben, hit me!" Hiro slumped into the seat next to Hendrix who was rolling his shoulders after the bar fight had finally died down. Business resumed as usual—dim lights flickered, the scent of sweat and alcohol thick in the air, and the slow, hypnotic thrum of seductive music filled the room.

On stage, Cindy and Zonia —the same woman Hiro had once offered to Kein at the altar during the first Festival of Avlam— twisted gracefully around their poles, their skin glistening under neon lights, clad in nothing but high-heeled boots.

Ben, unfazed as ever, slid Hiro's usual drink across the bar. Hendrix, opting for something simpler, took a deep swig straight from his beer bottle, his gaze distant as he waited for Nzo to return from his usual rounds.

The kid was out roving the area, scanning for more unwelcome sigbin lurking too close for comfort.

Hiro smirked and downed his whiskey in one gulp. "So, there's still some fight left in you, huh?" he quipped, his voice laced with sarcasm.

Hendrix barely reacted. Instead, he tilted his bottle back, draining the last of his beer before slamming it onto the counter. "Let's talk." Without another word, he pushed off his stool and strode toward the exit, not even sparing Hiro a glance.

Hiro huffed, a smirk tugging at his lips as he gestured to Ben for another round. "I prefer to fight, though."

Hendrix hesitated at the door for a beat before sighing. "Alright." He stepped outside.

Hiro grinned. *That's more like it.*

Just as Hiro rose to follow, Nzo strolled in, his sharp eyes flickering between the two. "'Bout time." The kid smirked knowingly as he watched Hiro trail after Hendrix, remembering how the toodler met the bleeding sigbin.

<><><>

In **1521 AB**, when most sigbin still bled, Hendrix stepped out of his hotel early, eager to explore the renowned City of Ruinae. The business district was alive with holographic billboards and augmented reality ads flashing across towering skyscrapers.

He smirked as he spotted his gaming name -- Haruki, displayed on nearly every screen. His creations had taken over the city, proof that he had carved out a legacy in this new world.

Settling in Xego had been a long time coming. For over a millennium and a half, Hendrix had wandered, unsure of where he belonged. Waking up as a sigbin after his near-death experience in a Tel Aviv hospital (that no longer exists nowadays) had been a lonely and disorienting transition. His family was gone, his human ties severed. But his mind, sharp as ever, found purpose in the one thing that had always anchored him—gaming.

Decades passed before he fully embraced his new life. The gaming industry thrived as the global economy flourished under Kein's reign. Hendrix leveraged his pre-existing skills to build his empire. As Haruki, he didn't just play games—he designed them, creating expansive open-world RPGs where players could code their own stories. The unpredictability of each simulation made his games addictive, drawing in millions across all three territories.

His nomadic lifestyle fed his creativity. He dived into the ocean's abyss, trekked through the most treacherous jungles, and raced across scorching deserts, all to gather inspiration for his ever-evolving digital realms. But when Kein divided the world into Zapad, Xego, and Perlaz, his travels became restricted. While Zapad, a haven for the most violent sigbin, had fueled his thirst for blood sports and combat simulations, Xego offered something new—a balanced, structured civilization where humans and sigbin coexisted.

He was looking forward to a new adventure that had just begun.

–then

"GET OUT OF HERE AND NEVER COME BACK, YOU PERVERT!"

BLAG!

Hendrix barely had time to react before something—or someone—collided with him, sending him sprawling onto the pavement. He groaned, blinking in confusion, as an awful stench assaulted his nostrils.

What the hell just hit me? He sat up and found himself face-to-face with a tiny toddler, wearing nothing but a filthy, sagging diaper. The child's chubby half-exposed butt had landed right on his face.

Hendrix flinched, shaking his head in disbelief. The kid reeked of spoiled milk and alcohol. "Are you alright, kid?" Hendrix asked, instinctively reaching out.

The child hiccupped, staring at him with bloodshot eyes. "H-hick! Me..Nzo want Mimis. Lots-lots Mimis!" The toddler slurred, waving his stubby arms toward a lingerie store with a smashed-out front window. "In there, hick! Okie-okie?!"

Hendrix raised a brow, struggling to process what he was seeing.

The child was drunk. It was rare to encounter channaks—the infant sigbin abandoned by their parents. Most of them never made it outside Perlaz, where the hukluvans protected them. This one, however, was here in Xego, alone, reeking of alcohol, and mumbling about "Mimis".

Despite the absurdity of the situation, Hendrix found himself instantly liking the kid. He lifted the child into his arms. "Mimis? Who's Mimis?"

The toddler hiccupped again, blinking blearily before grabbing Hendrix's collar. "Yes! Mimis! Hick! Like this!"

And then—CHOMP!

The little hellspawn sank his tiny fangs into Hendrix's nipple and pinched the other one.

Hendrix let out a very undignified yelp. "WHAT THE F—!?"

<><><>

Hendrix found the diner that the sigbin had directed him to. He hadn't expected much—maybe a quiet place to drop off the foul-smelling, drunken toddler he had somehow become responsible for. But as soon as he stepped through the doors, his expectations were shattered.

When the channak, whom he initially thought was cute, attacked him, he was caught completely off guard. Small but unnaturally strong, the baby bloodhound latched onto his chest like a wild animal, scratching, pinching, and—most disturbingly—trying to suck his nipples.

Hendrix struggled to pry the baby off him, but Nzo was fast, relentless, and unreasonably agile for something in a diaper. They tumbled into the street, causing a commotion, yet passersby merely laughed. Others placed bets on the outcome of the bizarre brawl.

Hendrix had assumed Xego was a civilized continent—clearly, he was mistaken.

It took nearly tearing the kid apart to finally subdue him. The laughter of the spectators died down when Hendrix, now exhausted and visibly disheveled, managed to restrain the struggling, foul-mouthed toddler using his jacket.

"Just take him across the street," a sigbin chuckled. "Three blocks down, you'll find a yellow-and-blue diner. His family will take care of him."

"Thanks for the koine," another sigbin, who had apparently bet against Nzo, grinned at Hendrix.

"He usually fights better when he's drunk," another gambler muttered, disappointed after losing a hefty hundred koine points.

"Only if his drink has breast milk in it," the winner added with a smirk.

"Disgusting," a third bystander grimaced.

What kind of place is this?! Hendrix thought. He contemplated just leaving the baby there, but despite everything, he couldn't bring himself to abandon the little menace.

Dragging the still-struggling toddler, he followed the directions to the diner.

<><><>

The moment Hendrix stepped inside, a delicious aroma hit his nose. His stomach grumbled, reminding him that he hadn't eaten since the night before.

"Grandpa!" A beautiful woman in her thirties rushed toward them.

Hendrix froze for a moment, still unaccustomed to their presence. Back in Zapad or the wilderness, their kind never distracted him. But this was Xego—a place where he could no longer ignore them.

The woman gently took the child from his arms. "Thank you. Where did you find him?" A man, also human, stepped forward.

Hendrix explained the chaotic scene that had unfolded in the streets.

"I'm sorry about that," the woman sighed. "Come in—let me serve you something to eat before you go."

The couple introduced themselves as Cathy and Jonathan, and their warmth caught Hendrix off guard. He had met humans before, but they had either feared him or treated him with open hostility.

The contrast intrigued him. Before he knew it, they had ushered him into the kitchen, away from the prying eyes of the other diners.

<><><>

Hendrix watched as Cathy bathed the drunken toddler in the kitchen sink. Nzo was babbling nonsense, alternating between giggling like an innocent child and cursing like a seasoned sailor.

"Grandpa, how old is this little crap?" Jonathan muttered, throwing Nzo's soiled diaper into the trash with a look of absolute disgust.

Cathy, now drying the toddler on the dining table, laughed. Jonathan rolled his eyes, then handed Hendrix a steaming cup of coffee.

Hendrix chuckled when Jonathan pinched the channak's bare butt cheek. Nzo, still in a drunken haze, frowned in annoyance—then, out of nowhere, threw a fork directly at Hendrix's forehead.

Bullseye.

"Grandpa!" Cathy and Jonathan gasped. Cathy smacked the kid's tiny hand, but Nzo merely blow spit bubbles, watching Hendrix with wide, unblinking eyes.

The humans turned to Hendrix, apologetic and wary. Other sigbin might have thrown the child into the streets or retaliated with force. But instead of getting angry, Hendrix burst into laughter.

The absurdity of it all—the baby, the fork in his forehead, the sheer insanity of the moment—was just too much. He pulled the utensil from his skull, blood trickling down his face, and continued laughing.

Nzo joined in, giggling like an innocent child, which only made Cathy and Jonathan laugh along in relief. The kitchen filled with warmth and mirth, an unexpected contrast to the madness outside.

The laughter was cut short by the sudden slam of the kitchen door.
"Where is that little bastard?!" A heavy-set woman stormed in, her presence commanding.
Another human, Hendrix noted, intrigued.
"He's here, Trix—drunk as usual," Jonathan sighed.
"He keeps saying you broke his heart for moving away," Cathy added, tying Nzo's tiny bathrobe.
"Darn him!" Trix growled, marching toward the table.

Hendrix smirked into his coffee, amused by the human drama unfolding before him.
"Never mind them—eat," Cathy insisted, placing a plate of food in front of him and handing him a fresh fork—this time, for eating, not impalement.

Meanwhile, Trix grabbed Nzo by his fresh diaper and, without hesitation, slapped him across the face. Hard. Left. Right.
Blood dribbled from the baby's nose and lips.
Hendrix instinctively tensed, about to intervene, but Jonathan discreetly signaled him to stay out of it. He had no choice but to just take another sip of his coffee, eyes flicking between the scene and his plate.
"Mimis!" Bleeding but suddenly sober, Nzo stared at Trix. Then, without warning, the toddler leapt onto her, grabbed her blouse, and—tore it open. "MIMIS!" Nzo latched onto her breast, sucking hungrily.

Hendrix froze, fork midair.

Trix, utterly unfazed, cradled the baby against her chest, sitting down as though nothing had happened. The kitchen remained eerily calm.

Even Jonathan continued drinking his coffee, completely unfazed.

Meanwhile, Hendrix struggled to process what the heck he was witnessing. It was bizarre. Disturbing. And yet...he couldn't look away. Milk flowed freely from Trix's other breast as the toddler squeezed it with his tiny hands.

Hendrix's grip on his fork tightened. He had fought in blood battles, brutal tournaments, and witnessed atrocities in the darkest corners of the world.

But this... This was something else.

Slowly, Nzo turned his head, his tiny mouth still latched onto Trix's breast. His glowing eyes locked onto Hendrix. Then, without breaking eye contact—

The channak spit milk directly into Hendrix's open mouth.

<><><>

1925 AB -- Smiling at the memory, Nzo watched as Hiro and Hendrix leave the bar, already knowing where they were headed.

From Nzo's bar at parthena, Hendrix and Hiro found themselves again inside the arena. The arena was empty, its underground walls lined with the scars of past battles, the air thick with the scent of blood, sweat, and old grudges.

It had been decades since the last time Hendrix and Hiro clashed like this—not as enemies, not as mere allies, but as brothers forged in blood and war.

For all their disagreements, all the tension brewing between them, this was their language. Here, fists spoke louder than words. Hiro flexed his fingers, the memory of Hendrix's taste still fresh in his mind. Hendrix cracked his knuckles, remembering the feel of Hiro's fangs sinking into his flesh.

How long has it been? A couple of decades, maybe more. Yet, in this moment, as their eyes met under the dim, flickering lights, they both knew—some things never change.

"I don't think this is the right time to fight, Zov." Hendrix is still appealing at the last minute. His voice was calm, but the weight behind his words was heavy. Across the arena, his estranged friend stood rigid.

Hiro flinched at the sound of that name—his old name. It had been a long time since anyone had called him that. A warmth stirred inside him, but he crushed the feeling before it could settle. No. Memories like that were best left forgotten.

Yet Hendrix felt it too. Standing at the center of the arena again after more than a century of avoidance, nostalgia clawed at him. And with Hiro—Zov—before him, the sentiment grew stronger. He had to admit it—he missed his spirit-brother. No matter how much time had passed, no matter how much had changed, his bond with Hiro remained. They didn't share blood, but they were family.

"Enough whining," Hiro muttered, yanking off his shirt. He took a fighting stance, his expression unreadable.

Hendrix exhaled sharply, shaking his head. A growl of protest rumbled in his chest, but he said nothing more. He simply braced himself.

Hiro struck first. As always. A rapid three-hit combo came at Hendrix's right ear—a feint, a distraction. Hendrix countered smoothly, blocking the left jab and dodging the right hook. Then—a flash of silver. A hidden blade sprang from Hiro's skin, slicing through the air toward Hendrix's neck. So typical. Hendrix had expected nothing less.

When the sigbin lost their blood, Hendrix designed an avatar with an advantage—one that could hide weapons within its body. With regeneration at their disposal, sigbin hellspawns adapted quickly. What began as a mere game mechanic soon became a real-life trend. Despite the pain of embedding weapons under their flesh, many adopted the technique.

Hendrix never imagined Hiro would follow the fad. But he had already noticed the telltale discoloration on Hiro's skin on their way to the arena—subtle, but clear to his sharp eyes. There are at least a dozen weapons inside him.

As Hiro lunged again, Hendrix seized his arm, twisting it violently. Flesh tore. Metal clattered. The embedded knife ripped free, taking a chunk of Hiro's left arm with it.

"Arrrgh!" Hiro gritted his teeth against the pain.

He wasn't backing down. It's foolish to hope, Hendrix thought to himself. *Fine, then.* Hendrix flung the knife aside and shoved Hiro away, sending him skidding several meters across the arena floor. One down. Less than a dozen to go. If Hiro wanted a fight, he would get one. But Hendrix's goal wasn't to win—it was to disarm him, to protect him.

Hendrix remained on the defensive, but the moment Hiro charged again, he shifted tactics. He moved faster, became unpredictable.

Hiro, who always led the attack, wasn't used to being on the back foot. That hesitation—that brief moment of uncertainty—was all Hendrix needed. With a devastating kick, he sent Hiro flying. The impact threw him onto his back, but Hiro barely hesitated before flipping onto his feet again.

Now, the real fight was beginning.

That rush—that feeling—Hiro had nearly forgotten it. The euphoria, the thrill. The reason he once loved Hendrix like a brother. Don't get caught up, fool. Hiro gritted his teeth. He's not your friend anymore.

The battle wasn't over. Between the echoes of love and the sting of resentment, Hiro steeled himself for a more aggressive assault. Another hidden weapon glowed beneath his skin, ready to emerge. But before he could make a move—Hendrix was already there.

A blur. A rush of wind. And then—searing pain. Hendrix ripped Hiro's right arm clean off.

"AHHHH!" Hiro dropped to his knees, screaming as bloodless pain tore through his body. Despite the torture at Hendrix's hands, he couldn't shake the memory of the pleasure he once felt meeting his best friend—the brother he now despised.

7

Haruki And Zovio

In **1521 AB**, after his brief encounter with the channak Nzo, Hendrix was ready to settle down in Xego for work

"Haruki! Finally! In flesh and blood." Hiro's voice was filled with excitement as he greeted Hendrix with a firm handshake, his grip exuding the thrill of finally meeting his legendary gaming partner in person.

"Zovio, the man himself!" Hendrix matched his enthusiasm, gripping Hiro's hand tightly before tapping his shoulder in a brief but solid man's hug.

With that, they stepped into the VIP lounge of Hajji Towers—the tallest, most modern cylindrical skyscraper in the City of Ruinae. The sheer scale of it was a testament to Hajji Inc.'s dominance, a conglomerate that had built its name on technology, entertainment, and power.

Tonight, however, wasn't just about business. It was about forging something greater.

Hendrix and Hiro wasted no time introducing their teams—gamers, coders, and technical specialists—the brightest minds assembled to develop and produce world-class RPGs for the ever-growing market.

"This, my friend, is your gaming cave." Hiro led Hendrix through a futuristic colonnade connecting Hajji Towers to the Hajji Olympus Interactive Headquarters—a cutting-edge facility dedicated to game development, AI integration, and immersive virtual reality technology. It was a gamer's paradise, built with one purpose in mind: to house the creative genius of Haruki.

Hendrix let out a low whistle, his eyes darting across the state-of-the-art equipment, the holographic servers, and the AI-driven design labs. His team stood frozen, in absolute awe of the tech marvel surrounding them. "Sweet!" Hendrix muttered, running his fingers over a sleek gaming console. "I thought I'd be working from home."

"You can't work from home, Haru." Hiro folded his arms, smirking. "Fart it! I built all of this for you!"

Hendrix turned, meeting his old friend's gaze. He saw the sincerity behind the words.

"Darn, Zov... this is—wow," Hendrix admitted, genuinely impressed.

"So?" Hiro's voice was expectant, a knowing smirk creeping onto his face.

Hendrix let out a breath, shaking his head with a grin. "Of course, I'll work here. Hell, I'll probably crash here more often than I should."

"Great." Hiro's eyes gleamed. "Remember, all of this is yours, but every brilliant game your mind produces? That's mine."

Hendrix laughed, shaking his head. Same old Zovio—always the businessman.

◇◇◇

Hendrix and Hiro had known each other for over a century, yet this was the first time they met in person.

As Haruki (Hendrix) and Zovio, they had dominated the online gaming world, their avatars becoming icons in the RPG community. But while Zovio was a well-known competitor, Haruki was something else—a legend.

Hiro played for fun. Hendrix played like his life depended on it. And that difference was why Haruki became a phenomenon—a name whispered with awe and respect in gaming circles. His games, his strategies, his world-building—it was unrivaled. And yet, no one knew his face.

Hendrix had spent centuries crafting his 'alter' in the new world, keeping his true identity hidden. Only a select few knew that behind the legendary avatar of Haruki stood a sigbin whose genius for game development had made him a global force.

Hiro saw the potential in Haruki's work long before anyone else did. "Your products are great, Haru, but your business model sucks!" Hiro would often tell him during their gaming sessions. "Let me handle the business, you focus on creativity. That's what you do best."

At first, Hendrix refused. He had no interest in wealth, power, or business. But Hiro was relentless. Eventually, after much persuasion—and billions of koine on the table—Hendrix gave in. And just like that, Haruki became a subsidiary of Hajji Inc.

Now, all Hendrix had to do was what he did best—create.

<><><>

"How's Xego so far?" Hiro asked, tinkering with one of the interactive walls in Hendrix's gaming lab.

"Not bad. Brighter, cleaner than Zapad." Hendrix shrugged, focused on encrypting his accounts on the server mainframe.

"Cleaner? Hah!" Hiro scoffed. "Zapad is a dark hellhole compared to Xego."

He wasn't wrong.

Zapad was a chaotic wasteland—a breeding ground for radical, violent sigbin. There was no order, no structure. Just blood, lust, and lawlessness. If you weren't tough, you would be subjected to eternal life of being a bottom feeder. That was the rule of Zapad.

Hendrix had lived there for decades, and it had shaped his understanding of violence. But Xego was different.

"Have you met anyone interesting? sigbin here are generally... nicer." Hiro smirked, planning to bring Hendrix in one of his parthenas to have a taste of his fresh athenas.

Hendrix chuckled, shaking his head as memories of Nzo flashed in his mind. "Yeah," he admitted, "The kid's a darn menace."

"Oh yeah, Nzo." Hiro grinned. "He's famous in this part of town." Hiro laughed harder when Hendrix recounted his first encounter with the wild channak.

"So." After sharing laughter and small talk, Hiro finally turned to face Hendrix, curiosity gleaming in his eyes. "Ready to tell me the secret? Why do gamers go crazy for your RPGs?"

Hendrix smirked, leaning back in his gaming chair.

Hiro studied him for a moment. Up close, Hendrix was different. Most sigbin had smooth, almost flawless skin, but Hendrix's philtrum wasn't as flat—almost... human. It was subtle, but Hiro noticed. There was something unusual about him.

But before Hiro could dwell on the thought, Hendrix's expression shifted. "What about my request?"

Hiro's grin returned. "I thought you'd never ask." With a tap on the wall's interface, a hidden section of Hendrix's gaming cave slid open—revealing something far grander than any tech lab.

A massive indoor arena sprawled before them—floodlit, fully equipped, and battle-ready.

Hendrix's breath hitched. It was identical—if not better—than the deadly gladiator fields of Zapad, where sigbin fought to the death. This was his true request. Hendrix had no use for luxury. He didn't care for the money or the power.

But an arena? A place where he could fight, test his skills, and perfect the brutality of his RPG simulations? That was the real prize. Hendrix shook his head in amazement. "Now you're talking," he muttered, shedding his jacket.

Hiro grinned. The game had just begun. "Got a new game brewing in that mind of yours? Do spill!"

Hendrix smirked. "How about a warrior Channak?"

Hiro burst into laughter, instantly recognizing the inspiration behind the idea. "Good luck with that! Knowing that crazy drunk… tough luck, bro. Tough luck." He chuckled, shaking his head.

*** <><><> ***

Hiro knew exactly who Nzo was: the infamous toddler sigbin of Xego. Nzo's family had been allowed to settle in Xego after the war, when the world was divided into three factions. His arrival marked a turning point, symbolizing the possibility of peaceful coexistence between humans and sigbin.

As a result, Nzo became the poster child for the harmonious future they envisioned, and his story played a pivotal role in building Xego's reputation.

Over the years, Hiro had crossed paths with Nzo on numerous occasions, usually at his father's grand parties or ceremonies where Nzo's presence was required. As Xego grew more established as a haven for both races, Nzo slowly faded from the spotlight, but still remained a prominent figure—a famous, occasionally drunken channak whose antics entertained locals and visitors alike. His occasional disruptions in the City of Ruinae kept him relevant, and both sigbin and tourists found him amusing enough to tolerate.

One day, determined to get closer to Nzo and persuade him to fight in the arena, Hendrix dragged Hiro into Nzo's coffee shop, a quaint diner where both humans and sigbin mingled. Hiro found the place dull, until he saw Cathy, Nzo's granddaughter.

Despite Cathy being married with children, Hiro couldn't shake the strange pull he felt toward her. At first, he resisted her warmth, her friendly smile, and her effortless charm, but eventually, he became a regular visitor, even on days when Hendrix wasn't with him.

"Hi Mr. Hajji, your usual?" Cathy would greet him with a smile, her toddler in tow. Hiro, though usually unfazed by humans, couldn't help but feel drawn to her. She was in her late thirties, confident, and comfortable in her own skin, unlike the other humans Hiro had encountered, who often showed weariness in the presence of sigbin.

"Yes, please," Hiro would reply, already counting the moments until Cathy's husband and even Nzo would leave, so he could steal a few more moments of her attention. He'd watch her, consumed with an intense longing to be near her, to touch her. *Stop it!* he'd scold himself. *She's just a human. She's not even a berhen.*

In his long life, Hiro had encountered and bedded beautiful women, both human and sigbin, yet Cathy was the only one who seemed to shine in his eyes. She was fearless around him, unlike others who instinctively shrank away. Her confidence and unguarded nature captivated him.

"How's your day, Mr. Hajji?" she'd ask as she served him his coffee.

"Mr. Hajji is my father. Just call me Hiro," he'd correct her, feeling a strange compulsion to share more than just pleasantries. Sometimes their conversations were as trivial as the weather, but other times, Hiro found himself spilling truths he hadn't meant to.

"Really? Your father must have loved your mother very much!" Cathy once said, wiping away a tear. Hiro didn't enjoy talking about his mother, but Cathy had a way of drawing it out of him.

"He did," Hiro replied, his voice unsteady. His mother had survived the pandemic as a human, and his father had fought in the wars to protect her. Hiro's father never once lusted after his mother's blood.

When Hiro, driven by curiosity, attacked her in a moment of madness, his father had decapitated him without hesitation. Throughout her life, his father had stayed loyally by his mother's side.

"That's why your father formed Xego, isn't it? I understand now," Cathy said, her words wrapped in admiration. "Your father is a hero, and you must be too."

"I'm not," Hiro replied quietly, genuinely believing it.

"Well, you are in my book," Cathy insisted, her smile warm and comforting. "Any sigbin strong enough to respect humans like us is a hero in my eyes."

Hiro's heart melted at her words, and just as he thought he might say something more, Hendrix arrived, breaking the moment.

"Oi! You're here early!" Hendrix greeted, and Hiro felt a pang of jealousy when Cathy smiled at him the same way she did with him. But Hiro understood that Cathy's warmth was just who she was—welcoming and genuine to everyone, whether sigbin or human.

"Yup, done with the meeting," Hiro replied, grateful that Hendrix had come just in time to prevent him from doing something foolish.

Though Nzo occasionally joined them, Hiro always felt awkward around the baby, who seemed to have a strange distance from him. Nzo, despite being close to Hendrix, seemed colder toward Hiro, as if sensing something in him that Hiro couldn't quite understand.

Can Nzo see through me? Hiro often wondered. Does he know what I feel for Cathy? Hiro kept his distance, careful not to let the child pick up on his inner turmoil.

One day, Cathy invited him to a small gathering of friends and family. Hiro, used to spending his sleepless nights in the arena or indulging in destructive behaviors, found himself intrigued by her invitation. He accepted, curious about what it might mean to be part of something normal, something human.

The event turned out to be a mini-concert and, strangely, a religious gathering. Kein was the only god worshipped by all races, and Hiro knew he wasn't welcome there. Humans and sigbin alike seemed tense upon his arrival.

"Hey, you!" Hendrix looked surprised when Hiro entered, and Nzo's defensive posture only added to the unease in the air. Hendrix, though, was there for the company of humans and paid little attention to the undercurrent of tension.

"Grandpa, don't worry. Mr. Hajji is a friend, right, Hiro?" Cathy's reassuring voice broke through the awkwardness, and Hiro, despite his discomfort, agreed. "Y-yes, you can trust me."

Cathy, now dressed in a simple but beautiful outfit, looked stunning to Hiro. Her presence seemed to change everything, and for the first time, Hiro felt an unfamiliar ache in his chest.

Later, as the music filled the air, Hiro couldn't help but feel moved by the performance. Cathy, singing with the band, poured her heart into a song about love, hope, and passion—emotions Hiro had buried deep inside. Tears welled in his eyes as he listened, the weight of his past pressing down on him.

Unable to bear it any longer, Hiro excused himself and stepped out of the room. Nzo, ever observant, guided him to a private space where he could collect himself. Hiro was surprised by the compassion Nzo showed, though he couldn't shake the feeling that the channak knew more than he let on.

That night, Hiro's emotional pain consumed him. Alone in the prayer cell, he shed his human form, his monstrous appearance taking over as he wrestled with his own inner hellspawns. Confused and torn, Hiro wept silently, knowing that his desire for Cathy wasn't just lust—it was something deeper, something that was slowly breaking him apart.

After that night, Hiro distanced himself from Sofia and found solace in the arena, with Hendrix and, in a strange way, Cathy. His life had changed in ways he didn't fully understand, but one thing was clear: his heart had been touched, and there was no turning back.

<><><>

Meanwhile, at the border of Zapad and Xego, Ehud's stomach rumbled—not from mere hunger, but from a deep, visceral craving. Nothing compared to the ecstasy of consuming a fresh human heart, still warm and pulsating, ripped straight from a living body.

From his vantage point, he spotted a convoy of vehicles discreetly approaching. His lips curled into a sinister smirk. The border patrol, bribed beyond refusal, had long turned a blind eye. "How many?" Ehud asked, his tone as sharp as a blade.

"A hundred and counting. Enough to keep you fed for a week," Achmed, his towering 6'7 associate, responded coolly.

Though massive in stature, Achmed lacked the aura of menace that surrounded Ehud's smaller frame. A former human trafficker before becoming sigbin, Ehud had mastered every dark and twisted craft necessary for survival.

As the cargo was unloaded, Ehud watched intently. According to the new laws, all human corpses were to be cremated, ensuring that sigbin wouldn't desecrate graves for food.

But the truth?

While mourners took home sealed urns filled with synthetic ashes, the real bodies were delivered to black-market meat traders in Zapad. Ehud approached one of the crates, pried it open, and sank his teeth into a cold, frozen corpse. His face twisted in disgust.

"Ugh!" He spat out the rancid flesh, barely able to swallow.

"That one had a long wake," Achmed chuckled, patting Ehud's shoulder in mock sympathy. Ehud growled, frustrated. "Humans! If only I could get my hands on one of them while they're still alive."

Achmed smirked knowingly. "Hah! You wish," he muttered, a glint of amusement in his eyes.

As the last trucks departed, leaving behind only Achmed, Ehud, and a handful of trusted men, Achmed finally spoke again. "Lord Kein is grateful for your cooperation," he said smoothly. "He wants Zapad stable until the humans repopulate. Then, you'll be rewarded generously."

Ehud snorted. He had heard that lie before. Promises of great rewards from Kein meant nothing to him. At the end of the day, he relied only on himself. "Yeah, sure," he muttered, unimpressed.

Then, his eyes darkened with hunger. "Now, show me." Achmed nodded and signaled for a smaller truck to move forward. Ehud stepped toward it, his heart pounding in anticipation. With a swift motion, he unlatched the doors and pulled them open.

Inside, among dozens of fresh, naked female corpses—each one missing its heart—lay a man, bound and struggling.

"Help! Help!" the captive gasped, his gag loose, his desperation palpable.

Ehud's grin widened. He pulled out his device, and with a few taps, airdropped koine points into Achmed's account. Officially, Ehud was merely following Kein's orders—ensuring that all human remains were delivered as per the new laws.

Unofficially?

The sigbin of Zapad were restless. Sick of rotting flesh. Tired of Kein's so-called curse. So, Ehud adapted. Every so often, a "stray" human found their way into his grasp. "What Kein doesn't know won't hurt him," he reasoned.

They weren't waging war on humans. But...who said they couldn't enjoy the occasional indulgence?

"Enjoy," Achmed said, confirming the transaction.

Ehud barely heard him. He was already inside the truck, looming over his prey, his claws poised. A heartbeat away from his next meal.

<><><>

1621 AB, a century after moving to Xego, arena became Hendrix source of inspiration --his life.

"Darn it! Your blood stings, bro!" Hiro grimaced, wiping Hendrix's blood off his face.

Both stood half-naked and bleeding inside the arena, locked in a brutal simulation of the latest game Hendrix designed—set for release on their 100th anniversary.

A century had passed, and just as Hiro predicted, Haruki's gaming brand had exploded a hundredfold. Back-to-back blockbuster releases kept the market in a frenzy, turning Hajji Inc. into the world's leading gaming empire—all thanks to Haruki's creativity.

"Sandy, reset!" Hendrix snapped, tired of Hiro's whining.

In an instant, high-pressure water jets blasted them clean, washing away the blood as the arena's setting morphed from a tiled pit into a sprawling grassy football field.

"I swear, I'm not cleaning up after you boys again," Sandy muttered, rolling her eyes as she adjusted the lighting—keeping it dark and foggy.

"Great work, Sands," Hendrix called out toward the booth. Though stationed at the farthest end of the arena, he knew she could see him clearly. Sandy blushed. She'd been crushing on Hendrix ever since she joined his team decades ago.

Craig patted Sandy's back approvingly. Beside him, Lane adjusted the camera, ensuring they recorded every detail of the fight for Hendrix's new game.

"Come on, no more excuses. Fight! Most of the blood is yours anyway," Hendrix tossed away his towel and assumed his stance.

"You may not bleed easily, but your blood stings like hell," Hiro muttered, standing opposite Hendrix, still dripping wet.

"Yours stinks, though," Hendrix countered, watching Hiro's movements carefully.

"Oh, come on! We all agree his blood is disgusting," Hiro scoffed, glancing at the booth where Lane and Craig raised their thumbs in agreement. They had fought Hendrix enough times to know—his blood is hurt to touch.

"That's because my blood is clean," Hendrix smirked, shifting to the left.

"Is that so? Pretty ironic for an immortal to be such a health freak. Scared of dying, Ruki?" Hiro teased, circling to Hendrix's right, looking for an opening.

"So, you're calling me a freak?" Hendrix chuckled.

"I'm saying quit being a good boy," Hiro grinned, still studying Hendrix's stance.

"Makes me a better fighter, though. Try it sometime—clean your blood of all the crap." Hendrix inched closer, provoking Hiro.

"Me? Give up alcohol and drugs? In your dreams, bro." Hiro laughed.

Drugs and alcohol were sigbin's way of life. Overdosing wasn't just common—it was their version of a nap. Hiro and the others were always high during fights, their tolerance for pain and heightened thirst for violence transforming these battles into euphoric bloodbaths.

For Hiro, nothing compared to the high of the arena—even the wildest nights at Isla De Parthena or feasting on a virgin's heart paled in comparison. Yet no matter how intoxicated his opponents were, Hendrix was always faster, stronger, and smarter. Outside the arena, he was a gaming prodigy. Inside, he was a beast. His usual gentleness vanished, replaced by razor-sharp focus and brutal efficiency.

"Enough with the girl talk—fight already!" Joreel yelled from the booth. The seven-year-old channak had once lived in Perlaz but took a different path, becoming one of Hendrix's top coders. Though he occasionally stepped into the arena, his real place was at the booth—capturing simulations and coding them into Hajji Inc.'s augmented reality games.

Hiro was the first to strike—double jabs followed by a sneaky left hook aimed at Hendrix's kidney.

Hendrix let Hiro land the hit, already anticipating his next move. The moment Hiro reached for the samurai tucked into his waistband,

Hendrix exploited the opening, executing swift triangular footwork to snatch the weapon instead.

Hendrix wasn't fond of weapons. What's the point? They barely affected immortals, serving only to make sigbin bleed.

For Hiro, however, weapons were everything. They weren't just tools—they were branding. Weapons defined gaming avatars, building their legend in the RPG world. Hajji Inc. raked in billions by incorporating innovative weaponry into their games.

Hendrix tolerated the obsession, indulging gamers who romanticized old-school combat. The bloodier the fights, the more players became addicted. Every time Hendrix launched a gruesome new game, Hiro anticipated skyrocketing sales—and he was never wrong.

With a single calculated strike, Hendrix slashed Hiro's back. Blood erupted like a crimson rain, splattering across the arena. Hendrix smirked. Perfect. Sandy would have captured the shot beautifully, and Joreel would have a field day coding it.

As expected, the customers craved more blood. Hendrix would give it to them. He stepped back, dodging Hiro's blood, but some splattered onto his arm. He clenched his jaw. It wasn't the sight of blood that bothered him—it was the smell. The stench was repulsive. Rotten, vile, unnatural.

Hendrix also noticed that through time, Hiro's blood, just like the others, is getting thicker and darker. However, he didn't comment much about it knowing how sensitive sigbin are, sensing that the changes have something to do with Kein's curse. Hendrix, as always, doesn't care because politics has nothing to do with his game.

When he saw that more blood was about to gush out of Hiro's wound, Hendrix elevated high in the air and landed on his feet, meters away, facing Hiro.

"Woah!!!"

"What the heck?!"

Sandy and Craig exchanged stunned looks before scrambling to check the footage. Had they captured that insane moment on screen?

"H-how did he do that?" Lane stared at the monitor in disbelief. He had caught it on playback but missed seeing it live.

Joreel barely glanced up from his coding. "He always does that—surprises us with new moves," he muttered, unfazed. He had seen Hendrix pull off countless jaw-dropping stunts before.

Even Hiro was momentarily stunned when Hendrix had glided behind him with unnatural ease. But Hendrix himself was oblivious—he wasn't trying to impress anyone. He was just instinctively avoiding Hiro's blood.

The smell.

That putrid, stinging odor that no one else seemed to notice. Hendrix had asked the others about it before, but they only looked at him strangely, insisting that if anything, it was his blood that reeked.

"It doesn't just stink, man. It's hot and itchy too," Craig had once complained.

Hendrix had only shrugged it off. As far as he was concerned, they were just making excuses for getting their asses handed to them in the arena.

"I tasted your blood once," Lane had admitted with a grimace. "I vomited all my insides, man. That's how bad it is."

Hendrix had no idea why they kept drinking each other's blood during simulations. The whole thing disgusted him. Watching fighters bite into each other, licking the blood off their opponent's skin, made his stomach turn.

Yet, gamers loved it. They found the brutality intoxicating—some even arousing. Hendrix indulged their obsession by coding it into his games, making it as graphic as they wanted. But for him to try it? Even the thought of drinking blood sent a sharp, stabbing pain through his chest—like a knife twisting into his heart.

"Bloody hellhounds! How did you...?!" Hiro's voice was laced with shock and pain as he struggled to process what had just happened. Before he could react, Hendrix moved again—this time, soaring effortlessly before crashing down onto Hiro's back with bone-crushing force.

8

The Pranks

A sickening crack echoed through the arena as Hiro collapsed, his spine momentarily shattered. Agony seared through him, intensifying as he forcefully reset the broken bone in place.

"More?" Hendrix loomed over him, unfazed.

"Nah." Hiro spat onto the ground, wincing. If he had been fighting Lane or Craig, he could have gone all night—drinking their blood always gave him a boost.

But Hendrix's blood? He'd tasted it once by accident, and it had made him weak. Something was off about it. Even the others had noticed. But Hendrix's explanation about "healthy living" was complete bullcrap!

"It's okay, guys. We got great footage. Good work, boys!" Sandy called out, wrapping up the night. As they packed up, Hiro and Hendrix reviewed the fight footage.

Despite taking most of the hits, Hiro had to admit—he looked badass on screen. Hendrix always had a way of making his opponents look good, bringing out their best moves, staging the perfect shots.

Then, they all saw it. Hendrix. Flying.

"Holy crap!" Hiro muttered, staring at the screen. Even Hendrix looked surprised. "See that? How the heck did you—?" Hiro turned to him, dumbfounded.

Hendrix just shrugged. "Told you—healthy living." He grabbed his gear, already heading for the exit.

"Where the fart are you going? I thought we were coding this!" Joreel called after him.

"Need to run first. I'll be back later." Hendrix's adrenaline was through the roof. He needed to burn it off. *Running always clears my head.* Besides, he had to admit—clean living did have its perks. *How else could he fly?*

"What about you, boss?" Sandy asked Hiro.

"Athena, I need to feed me some good old red." *And a virgin's heart*, Hiro thought.

Later, when Joreel, the channak, was alone reviewing the footage, something caught his eye. It happened so fast that he had to rewind and play it back multiple times. During the moment Hendrix slashed Hiro, a few drops of blood splattered onto his arm.

That's when Joreel saw it—something emerging from Hendrix's skin. At first, he thought it was just a trick of the light, but as he slowed the footage, the details became clearer. Drawings—no, symbols. Vivid, intricate tattoos that flared to life, burning like they were engulfed in flames. But just as quickly as they appeared, they vanished.

By the next frame, Hendrix was simply soaring through the air, as if nothing had happened.

◇◇◇

If not in the arena, Hendrix and Hiro's friendship was forged—and strengthened—through their over-the-top pranks on each other.

"Ahhh!" Hendrix's scream echoed through the room as two snarling wolves lunged at him, their fangs barely missing his throat but successfully tearing through his shoulder blade. His blood splattered across the brand-new carpet—the one he had just installed.

With a furious growl, Hendrix knocked the wolves unconscious before they could finish their attack. His chest heaved as he examined them, making sure he hadn't hurt them too badly. His body was already healing, but there was no saving the furniture and appliances wrecked during the chaos.

Laughter erupted from across the room.

Hiro.

The bastard was laughing his ass off, thoroughly enjoying the destruction.

"Heck, Zov! Where did you even get these? Aren't they extinct?" Hendrix huffed, still eyeing the wolves sprawled on the floor.

"Happy birthday, Ruki," Hiro grinned, flicking on the lights, still breathless from laughter.

Hendrix had barely stepped into his apartment for some much-needed rest after days of coding his latest RPG, and this was the welcome he got?

"Go to hell!" Hendrix grumbled, yanking off his blood-soaked shirt to inspect his freshly healed shoulder.

Hiro clapped him on the back, smirking. "Looking forward to your counter-prank."

"Oh, you better be," Hendrix muttered, already scheming as he surveyed the disaster that was once his perfectly arranged living room.

As if the bloody fights in the arena weren't enough, Haruki (Hendrix) and Zovio (Hiro) had to bring their battles outside of it too. Sandy, the only female sigbin member of Hendrix's team, simply couldn't understand them.

"How can you guys even be friends?" she asked, exasperated, after witnessing yet another of their ridiculous pranks—this time involving Hendrix and Hiro completely wrecking her state-of-the-art arena design.

Craig, barely paying attention, continued munching on his lunch. "Men are takers, Sands. Women are givers." Hendrix and Hiro, still fresh from their latest act of destruction, casually joined them at the table.

"I'll pay for the damage, Sands. Promise." Hiro grinned, clearly having the time of his life.

"I still don't get it!" Sandy huffed, pushing her plate aside, her appetite ruined.

Lane smirked, adopting a dramatic, effeminate tone. "Women are always like, 'Oh, you're so pretty tonight!' and 'No, please, your shoes are way more beautiful!'" He batted his eyelashes for effect.

The men roared with laughter.

"What's wrong with that?" Sandy shot back, still fuming over her ruined set.

"Men," Craig said between bites, "the more we like each other, the more we mess each other up. Right, bro?" Without warning, he punched Lane in the arm, smashing muscle and bone. Not to be outdone, Lane twisted Craig's arm until it cracked. Both men winced in pain—while laughing hysterically.

Sandy groaned and turned to Joreel, hoping for some sanity. He just shrugged. Boys will be boys. Ugh. Sandy sighed, rolling her eyes as she stomped back to her station. Someone had to clean up after these doofuses.

Several days later, Hiro stormed into Hendrix's office, his fury palpable. Without warning, he pounced on Hendrix, slamming him into the desk. Hendrix had just hacked into Hiro's financial reports and made it look like he was embezzling from the company.

"Darn it, Hendrix! My father presented this during the board meeting!" Hiro roared, his fist connecting with Hendrix's face, breaking his nose in two places.

Hendrix just laughed, blood trickling from his split lip. He spat out a broken tooth and flashed a grin. "You're really mad, huh?"

"What!?" Hiro paused, momentarily startled. His fist hovered over Hendrix's face, unsure whether to hit him again or to process why Hendrix was so happy despite the bloodied mess.

Joreel chuckled from the corner. "You called him by his name, boss."

Sandy, standing nearby, looked ready to snap. She could handle the violent, simulated fights all day long, but random attacks without a clear punchline were driving her to the edge. Was this a prank? A real fight? Even she couldn't tell anymore.

Meanwhile, the rest of Hendrix's team was watching the scene unfold, eagerly placing bets on who would come out on top. By now, they were used to Hendrix and Hiro's pranks—they never knew where the line between a joke and a fight really was. But, oddly enough, no matter how messed up the prank got, it only seemed to strengthen their bond.

Hendrix, still laughing through the blood, rolled around on the floor.

Sandy slammed her fist down on her desk, a frown deepening on her face. "This is ridiculous."

Hiro straightened up, still eyeing Hendrix warily. But then, seeing the chaos and feeling the tension break, he let out a laugh and pulled Hendrix to his feet.

Everyone in the room, even Sandy, couldn't help but join in the laughter, despite themselves.

"I will get you for this, Ruki!" Hiro yelled as he stormed toward the door, slamming it behind him.

"Bring it on, bro!" Hendrix called after him, laughing so hard that he had to pause and wince. He felt his nose shift back into place, though it hurt like hell. They had a running bet. Anyone who screamed their real name out of anger during a prank would lose the game.

Hiro just lost.

Hendrix coughed from laughing too hard, his victory in clear view.

Months later, Hendrix stormed into Hiro's office, seething with anger after discovering that his latest code was deleted from the central server. "I'm going to tear you apart, you'll regret—" His words died in his throat when he saw Hiro's father sitting calmly at the conference table, engaging in a discussion with Hiro.

"Father, remember the famous Haruki?" Hiro stifled a laugh as he casually introduced Hendrix to Mr. Hajji, who Hendrix had met only during formal company meetings.

Hendrix, flustered, immediately apologized to Mr. Hajji for his outburst.

"I always support my son in everything he does," Mr. Hajji said with a warm smile, patting Hendrix's shoulder as he stood up to leave. "If you're sleeping together, I'm happy for both of you."

Hendrix stood frozen, shock and embarrassment flooding his face. Hiro, unable to contain himself, roared with laughter, his amusement echoing throughout the office as employees outside giggled, unaware of the situation's context.

"Ruki, your face... hahahaha! You should've seen your face, darling!" Hiro laughed, unable to hold it in.

"Darn you!" Hendrix growled as he stormed out of Hiro's office, still red with fury.

"I love you, my doll..." Hiro called after him, his lips puckering in mock affection as he chased Hendrix down the hallway.

The employees watched with a mix of confusion and amusement as the two bosses ran around like children, utterly unbothered by the chaos they were causing.

<><><>

Whenever the pranks became too intense, Hendrix would throw Hiro into the arena to settle things, with their antics concluding in a satisfying, bloody fight. Their longest brawl lasted for three days and two nights, and it only ended when Sandy, in a fit of rage, showered them with bullets from a high-caliber machine gun. That's when they finally broke off their unofficial combat simulation that had been destroying her arena.

"GET OUT of my set, you bloody asswipes!" Sandy screamed, livid with frustration. Craig and Lane had to drag the two bleeding hellspawns out of her sight, each holding one by the arm.

To make up for the destruction of her arena, Sandy decided to make the most of the situation. She set it up so Hendrix and Hiro could record their own fights even when they were alone. She'd given up on trying to keep them out of her arena; there was no stopping them anyway. At least now she could benefit from the chaos by making her recording process easier. To her surprise, she discovered that their unrehearsed, near-death fights were more organic and raw than anything they'd simulated.

"The best footage we get is from their real fights," Lane and Craig would joke, reflecting on the recorded footage the day after.

<><><>

Later, as they lay on the arena field recovering from their grueling battle, Hiro, in a rare serious moment, turned to Hendrix.

"Seriously though, I don't blame my father for thinking you're into me. I haven't seen you with anyone. Don't you get lonely? Don't you want me, my love?"

Hendrix punched Hiro square in the mouth before the latter could even make a move to kiss him. "Dream on!" Hendrix snapped. Of course, he got lonely, but the thought of intimacy terrified him. He couldn't bring himself to even consider it, particularly when his physical insecurities made him feel repulsed by himself. His body doesn't transform into scally green monsters like other sigbin, but he has a terrible secret down there. How could anyone, let alone a woman, want to sleep with him when he couldn't stand his own inner monster?

"Dream on?! You haven't seen me in bed, my friend. My lovers adore me," Hiro shot back, kneeling on the grass and pumping an imaginary partner. Hendrix rolled his eyes—he was well aware that sigbin were polysexual and didn't care about sex or gender.

"I'm sorry, but unless you have genuine female parts, you'll never have my body," Hendrix retorted coldly. With that, he kicked Hiro away from him, signaling the start of another vicious round of their brawl. It was Hendrix's way of telling Hiro, in no uncertain terms, that he was straight.

He couldn't ignore the fact that, deep down, he craved the kind of relationship his parents had—one built on love, acceptance, and intimacy beyond just physical pleasure. His insecurities made him desire someone who would embrace all of him, flaws and all, and stay with him beyond the bedroom.

But the idea of finding the right woman who fit that ideal seemed exhausting to Hendrix, so for now, he focused all his energy on the game. He had neither the time nor the desire to pursue casual encounters.

In the days that followed, Hiro was left fuming as he stared at a deep fake video of himself as a woman, surrounded by three avatars—each one a famous RPG character created by Hendrix. The video was saved to the office server, and as soon as the employees logged into their units that Monday morning, it was the first thing they saw.

"Ruki!!!!" Hiro screamed in pure rage, his fists clenched in fury as he realized the prank Hendrix had pulled.

<><><>

Amidst the bloody brawls and relentless pranks, a deeper bond began to form between Hendrix and Hiro, a bond that neither could deny. Hendrix had come to value the trust and creative freedom Hiro constantly offered him. He knew Hiro always fought for him, even when his plans seemed reckless.

"You treat him like he's one of us," a board member would comment.

"He's just an employee, Hiro," another would add.

"What's with the special treatment?" they'd question.

But Hiro never budged. *He's not just an employee. He's my family,* Hiro thought, a fierce protective instinct rising within him.

For Hendrix, it was different. He had made Hiro belong, not just to the empire, but to something real, something grounded. Hiro, who had once been a strange and untouchable figure within the empire he helped build—his father's legacy, a looming presence in Xego—finally found his place. Hendrix helped him step down from the pedestal of status and see the world around him through different eyes. Under Hendrix's influence, Hiro became not just a figurehead, but a man who felt truly seen.

And Hiro, for the first time, loved who he had become. In the beginning, he thought his feelings for Hendrix were that of a typical bromance laced with a bit of a sexual tension — he can swing both ways afterall. He would have crossed that line but he never once felt the same tension from Hendrix, confirming that his friend was one of those old fashioned kind. And so, Hiro never pursued it.

Despite spending much of his life in Xego, Hiro had never bothered with humans, finding them weak and unnecessary. Yet, Hendrix changed that, showing him a world of emotions he hadn't known he was capable of feeling. Through Hendrix, Hiro discovered a new depth of connection, one that went beyond anything he had ever imagined.

Yet through Hendrix, he also endured unbearable pain—no battle within the arena could ever compare.

<><><>

1925 Anno Bhiasti -- Fast forward three centuries, and back in the arena where their friendship was forged, Hiro watched helplessly as Hendrix broke his arm and tore yet another weapon from his knuckles.

Even before Hiro could begin to heal, Hendrix launched a savage attack, forcing Hiro into the air in a blur of unexpected moves. Hendrix wrenched another weapon from his thigh and hurled it out of reach, leaving Hiro disoriented and vulnerable.

Then, as if from nowhere, a violent sandstorm engulfed them, blinding Hiro. Before he could react, Hendrix sliced open Hiro's back and removed another implanted weapon, a high-caliber gun, with surgical precision.

One by one, Hiro's weapons were stripped from his body, his flesh torn and his bones shattered from the waist up. But it was his fury that kept him from succumbing to defeat. This fight was far from over; Hiro had more to give, and he was determined to emerge victorious.

Hendrix's final strike sent a wave of agony through Hiro's body. He wailed in torment, the butcher knife that Hendrix pulled from inside his torso now slashing his leg open to extract another hidden weapon. The pain was unbearable—it felt as though Hendrix was setting his leg on fire. Hiro fought to keep his screams in check, biting down hard on his tongue to stifle the sound, but the searing burn within him was excruciating.

Then, finally, Hendrix stepped back, his eyes scanning Hiro's battered body, still searching for any hidden weapons. The pain didn't stop—it only grew more intense—but Hiro's will to win remained unshaken. Despite the damage, he had yet to give up. He would not be defeated so easily.

The arena, as always, recorded the brutal fight. The footage revealed Hendrix hovering in the air, his movements graceful and controlled as if he had wings. His command over the ground was evident, with the earth shifting beneath his feet as though responding to his every step.

Most shocking of all, his hand appeared to be engulfed in flames as he reached into Hiro's leg, burning it from the inside. Hendrix, aware of the cameras capturing every moment, glanced around, he would need to erase all traces of this encounter once it was over.

Because --

There was something he didn't want recorded—not just the fight, but an unspoken secret Hiro and the others must not know about him. The question burned in Hendrix's mind: when would Hiro stop obsessing over these battles? Once, their duels had been exhilarating, an addiction of sorts, when both were dripping with blood. But now, Hiro was little more than a collection of bruised flesh and broken bones. The thrill had drained from their clashes, leaving only emptiness.

Hendrix's thoughts were momentarily distracted by the cameras, a rare lapse in focus as his mind briefly shifted—calculating the angles that would obscure most of their fight from view. That was when Hiro, in a final act of defiance, unleashed a hidden dart—one that flew from the most unexpected place. As he struggled to rise, Hiro smiled despite the pain, a deep breath filling his lungs as he forced his stomach to contract. The weapon, lodged deep within him, shot forward with deadly precision.

"No!" Hendrix shouted, narrowly dodging the dart, but it still grazed his cheek, the sharp point piercing through his flesh. He recoiled, blood dripping from the wound as he staggered backward, desperately hiding his bleeding face. This was what he feared most. The one thing he could never let Hiro discover—that even in a world where sigbin were meant to be bloodless, he still bled.

Hendrix could feel the warmth of his own blood dripping onto the ground, and the panic set in. He knew Hiro was behind him, ready for the next strike. The fight wasn't over, and Hiro had just proven that he was still a force to be reckoned with, no matter how broken he appeared.

Hendrix waited for his wound to close, desperately covering the bloodstains on the ground with dirt. He smeared more dirt across his face to conceal any remnants of the wound, ensuring no trace of blood would be visible when Hiro attacked.

As expected, Hiro charged from behind. He poised himself for a powerful kick, the sharp samurai blade embedded in his heel ready to slice through Hendrix's neck, certain to decapitate him.

But Hendrix was prepared. A sudden sandstorm, erupted in his direction, swirling around Hiro like a tornado. The gusts of wind threw him into chaos, spinning him through the air as his weapons were ripped from his body—both his visible and hidden blades were torn away by the relentless force.

Amid the storm, Hiro's senses dulled. He couldn't see Hendrix's left arm shoot through the whirlwind to grab him, nor could he anticipate the horrifying act that followed.

With unyielding force, Hendrix's hand delved into Hiro's most intimate space, before firing the gun he had hidden there. Hiro felt the searing pain as bullets shredded his insides, the force of each shot splintering his torso and spilling his organs out.

Hendrix unloaded the weapon, firing relentlessly until the last shot rang out, before pulling the gun free. The feeling of his own weapon tearing through his body was humiliating, but what followed—Hendrix's arm digging deep into him—was worse.

Hiro screamed in agony, his internal organs spinning in the vortex of dirt around him, but the pain overshadowed everything else. He felt his body writhing in torment, helpless and broken, knowing it would be a long time before he could heal—if ever.

But Hendrix wasn't finished. He appeared in the maelstrom, moving with an eerie precision, as if he were part of the tornado itself. Balanced by the wind, Hendrix's blades sliced through Hiro's flesh with ruthless efficiency, each strike disarming him further, severing the embedded weapons one by one.

Hiro screamed again, but this time the pain wasn't just physical. Amid the agony, a hollow longing grew inside him for Haruki—his brother, who had left him in the past. In this moment of anguish, Hiro realized how much he needed Haruki, wishing he had never abandoned him, wishing everything was all a prank, much like before...

9

The Bloodless

In 1700 AB, the sigbin world was blissfully unaware that this marked the beginning of their downfall.

"Zov... my brother, listen to—" Before Hendrix could finish his sentence, Hiro was already at his throat. The walls of Hendrix's office trembled as the two best friends clashed once more, their raw power shaking the very foundation of the room.

"You have no idea what I have planned for you!" Hiro spat, his fury burning hotter than ever. Hendrix would never have the last laugh at his expense—never!

"I know, brother. That's why I want a truce." Hendrix's voice was calm, even humble, as he refused to fight back, despite knowing he could easily overpower Hiro. He had gone too far this time, and he knew it. The deep fake video—the prank that transformed Hiro into an exaggerated, humiliating version of himself for the world to see—was a mistake. And now, Hiro had devised the perfect revenge: one that would expose Hendrix's real identity, merging his carefully cultivated alter ego, Haruki, with his true self.

Hendrix couldn't allow that.

He had only one option. He uttered their sacred safe words—"*my brother*"—signaling a temporary ceasefire. Their unspoken rule was clear: a prank war hiatus lasting at least a decade, unless some extraordinary event triggered the mischief cycle once more.

"Well, I don't want a truce!" Hiro snapped, but despite his anger, he released Hendrix. A deal was a deal. Their safe words were sacred, no matter how much Hiro seethed. "Alright! I'll save it for next time," Hiro promised, flashing a wicked grin.

"Thanks," Hendrix muttered, though unease crept into his chest. Hiro had let it go far too quickly, and that was never a good sign.

"On one condition," Hiro added, his smile turning devilish.

Here we go, Hendrix thought warily.

That night, Hendrix found himself in one of Isla de Parthena's infamous bars, just outside the City of Ruinae—one of Hiro's own establishments where they will hide Lumen and Nzo's family over 200 years later.

"Enough with this clean-living bullcrap. Come on!" Hiro dragged him inside, fully intent on corrupting his straight-laced best friend. He had originally planned to set Hendrix up with three Athenas while he watched, but Hendrix haggled the number down to one—along with three bottles of beer.

Hiro agreed, relenting for now. It was, after all, the first time they would drink together. Too bad Hendrix refused to take anything stronger. "A virgin who's never tasted alcohol in his life—crap! You're practically a saint, Ruki... not a hellspawn!" Hiro teased, shoving him inside the bar.

Hendrix simply endured the insult, willing to humor Hiro just to get it over with.

As expected, Hiro tricked him into drinking past his limit. Now, sprawled across a luxurious hotel suite, Hendrix realized—too late—that his drinks had been spiked with something far more potent.

"It's just whiskey, Ruki. Man up, virgin boy!" Hiro roared with laughter, his amusement at Hendrix's state filling the room.

The world spun. Hendrix felt as though he was floating, the walls bending and twisting around him. His mind struggled to hold onto a single coherent thought. Hiro had told him to wait. Wait for the athena - virgin sigbi – who would 'solve his purity problem.'

An Athena stealing my virtue, huh? Hendrix chuckled to himself, feeling utterly ridiculous.

A vague memory surfaced—the crude talk among his sigbin peers, Hiro especially, about their wildest conquests. He had never paid much attention before, uninterested in their endless brags and depraved tales. But now, in his intoxicated haze, those stories lurked at the edge of his mind.

The talk of blood-drinking. Heart-eating. None of it had ever resonated with him. He had always held onto the beliefs his parents instilled in him—the sanctity of love, the significance of marriage. And yet, here he was, his body betraying him, his mind clouded.

Hendrix exhaled heavily. Drinking with Hiro had helped dull his anxieties. But now, something else was clawing at the edges of his thoughts. A deep unease. Something wasn't right.

Hendrix knew that when provoked—or in a violent mood—sigbin transformed into monstrous, green-scaled creatures. He had fought plenty of them in the arena. Others claimed that the same transformation occurred during intimate encounters with Athenas.

Yet, Hendrix could never recall changing form himself, no matter how intense his emotions got in the arena.

"I'm impressed by your calmness, Ruki," Hiro had once remarked.

Hendrix had only chuckled at the time. Oh, I change form, alright... just not in the way you all expect. His transformation—his secret—had always been his greatest vulnerability, one he guarded fiercely. It was the reason he kept his distance from intimacy.

He remembered the night Sandy had tried to seduce him. He could have said yes—she was brilliant, the mastermind behind the arena's deadly design, and undeniably beautiful with her striking red hair. But the thought of being exposed, of revealing himself in such a way, was unthinkable. He had declined her advances as politely as he could. At first, she was offended. But in the end, they became closer as friends.

"Sandy thought you were into me," Hiro had once told him over coffee at Nzo's.

"When did she say that?" Hendrix had asked, only half-interested, distractedly scanning the code Joreel had sent him.

"In bed," Hiro had smirked. "Since you rejected her."

Hendrix had simply nodded. "Ah."

He knew Hiro had expected jealousy, but there was none.

"So?" Hiro had pressed.

"So what?" Hendrix had sipped his coffee without looking up.

"Are you?" Hiro's voice had turned playful. "Into me?"

Hendrix had paused, amused by the question. Deep down, Hiro already knew the answer. And Hendrix knew that, given the right circumstances, Hiro wouldn't mind if things took a more... unconventional turn between them.

"Depends," Hendrix had finally said, a smirk tugging at his lips. "Do you have a female part I can enjoy?"

Hiro had thrown his head back in laughter. "Have you ever even seen one, virgin boy?"

Hendrix had shut him up the only way he knew how—by dragging him into the arena and kicking his ass.

Now, lying on the hotel bed, intoxicated beyond reason, Hendrix let the weight of his thoughts dissolve into the haze. Can I do this? His mind fought against itself. Stop overthinking. Just get it over with.

He didn't even know what he had been drugged with, but the sensation of floating, of sinking into the abyss of oblivion, was intoxicating in its own right. He welcomed it. For once, he wanted to let go. To just be.

Maybe he was too far gone to perform, anyway. He exhaled, heavy-lidded eyes slipping shut. Sleep –wishing he could. That's what he needed.

He didn't notice when the blonde Athena slipped into bed beside him. "Oh... hello... h-how did you...?" Though startled, Hendrix didn't resist as the athena began removing his clothes. He was too captivated by the depth of her emerald-green eyes, too lost in their hypnotic pull to put up a fight.

He shook his head, trying to snap himself out of it. What the heck is happening? The last of his garments slipped away. "W-Wait!" His voice wavered as he caught her wrist. Something inside him was stirring—something unfamiliar, primal.

Beth was good. Too good. And despite the alarm bells ringing in his mind, his body responded in ways he couldn't control. "C-can we just talk for a bit?" He asked, desperate for a reprieve. For some air.

Beth only smiled, pressing soft kisses along his jaw. "Mmm... about what?"

"L-like... your name," he stammered, dazed by her warmth.

"Call me Beth," she murmured against his lips, her breath tinged with something sweet and intoxicating. She was high too. Of course she was.

"Okay, Beth... Ahh... let's... wait... ohh—" Hendrix tensed, torn between hesitation and the new, dizzying sensations Beth was introducing him to. His body betrayed him, his resolve slipping fast.

"Talk all you want, sweetie. My mouth is busy," she whispered into his ear, her voice dripping with honeyed amusement.

A shiver ran through him, his skin erupting in goosebumps. But his body hair wasn't the only thing standing now.

Crap.

Hendrix struggled weakly, but Beth was quicker, pinning him down with practiced ease.

"Please, just let go..." she coaxed, her gaze locking onto his. "Let me make you happy, okay?"

Hendrix swallowed hard. There was something in her eyes—something pleading, almost desperate.

"This isn't your famous arena, love. No one has to bleed here, right?" she added, tilting her head with a knowing smirk. She knew who he was. Of course she did. He is Hiro's best friend, so he deserves nothing but the best.

"A-alright... but I don't... I mean, about drinking blood..." Hendrix tried, his voice barely above a whisper.

Beth laughed softly, running a teasing finger down his chest. "I know, sweetie. Hiro told me all about your kinks... I'll play along."

There was something off about her laugh. A forced lightness.

"Don't worry about anything," she assured him, but there was a weight behind her words. "It'll be the death of me, but a little torture can still be fun." She smiled, but it didn't quite reach her eyes.

Beth needed blood. It was the only way to numb the pain of what was coming. But tonight, she had to make do with drugs instead. It wouldn't be enough—it would still hurt like hell—but for Hiro, she'd endure it.

"D-don't worry. I won't... eat your heart," Hendrix promised, surrendering to her kiss. The words tasted strange on his tongue.

Beth let out a soft chuckle. "Oh, sweetie... I've heard that promise before." She traced a gentle finger along his jaw, her smile wistful. "Pity," she whispered. "That's the best part of the ceremony."

She knew the truth. Sigbin always ate the virgin's heart. It was in their nature. Hendrix was no different. And Hiro had promised her the sun and the moon to make his best friend happy. Beth would give him everything—her body, her blood, and if fate was cruel enough... maybe even her heart.

Beth kissed Hendrix again, pleasantly surprised. He didn't know how to kiss at first, but he was a quick learner—so quick it amazed her. Despite his powerful, muscular build, he touched her with a gentleness that sent shivers down her spine.

She had braced herself for something rough, violent even. She had heard of Hendrix's reputation in the arena—the brutal, unstoppable force that left his opponents broken. She had mentally prepared for the torturous death she might suffer in his hands. But this?

This was not the monster she expected.

His hands traced her skin with care, his lips moving with an almost reverent softness. It was as if she were something fragile, something precious. For a moment, she was no longer Beth the athena, no longer a sigbin seductress—just a woman, cherished and adored.

It stirred something in her. A memory. Once, before she became what she was, she had longed to be loved by a true gentleman. Now, in Hendrix's arms, she played the role of the delicate damsel she had once dreamed of being—and she enjoyed every second of it.

Hendrix, encouraged by her responses, grew bolder. He kissed her deeper, touched her with increasing confidence, his body learning hers with every motion. Beth let him take the lead, prolonging their foreplay, savoring the intoxicating mix of tenderness and hunger.

But soon, she couldn't wait any longer. She pulled away from his lips, her hands gliding over his body, desperate to explore every inch of him.

"Ohhh..." Hendrix moaned, his head tilting back in bliss.

Beth expected him to transform at any moment—surely, the pleasure would awaken whatever beast lay dormant within him. But nothing happened.

Until she was face-to-face with it.

A monstrous, thorn-covered form now loomed over her, green and menacing. Hendrix's true self, fully revealed. Beth's breath hitched. Her pulse pounded. *This... this is what he was hiding...* But when she looked up, Hendrix wasn't even aware of her reaction. His head was thrown back, his chest rising and falling rapidly, completely lost in the moment. She hesitated. Then, she carried on.

Slowly, Hendrix relaxed beneath her touch. Beth had seen everything—yet she said nothing. Whether out of politeness or familiarity, Hendrix couldn't tell. Maybe she had already encountered others like him. Maybe... he wasn't a freak after all.

"Teach me..." he murmured between kisses, mimicking her movements, eager to learn.

"Hmmm?" Beth asked, her initial shock fading, replaced by something unexpected. Enjoyment.

"I want to make you happy." He rolled over, pinning her beneath him this time.

Beth stilled. It wasn't fear that held her breath—it was something deeper. Something dangerous. No one had ever said those words to her – make her happy. She gazed into his eyes, touched by the sincerity in them. With a slow, inviting smile, she surrendered.

And Hendrix, with her guidance, pleasured her in ways she had never known. No one had ever taken such care, such patience, to ensure her pleasure. By the time he was done, she was utterly spent—heavenly, blissfully lost in him.

She could do this forever. If not for the taste of his blood. The moment she attempted to drink from him, bile rose in her throat. His blood was wrong. Burnt, stinking, like fire and rot. She barely managed to swallow down her revulsion, but her body betrayed her. Beth gagged, nearly vomiting into her mouth.

Hendrix, ever the gentleman, looked at her with concern. "Sorry about that..." he said softly. He was aware of how his blood tasted to others.

Beth exhaled shakily. She couldn't take it anymore. Whatever tenderness she had indulged in was now eclipsed by something more primal. She grabbed him, eyes blazing with urgency. "Stop holding back," she demanded. "Take me. All of me. With everything you've got."

Hendrix didn't need to be told twice. High on something, delirious with lust, he followed her lead—took her in his arms and gave her everything, without restraint.

She didn't break. She wanted more. And he gave it to her. By the time it was over, he was drained. Exhausted. But satisfied beyond words. Lying on his back, staring at the ceiling, Hendrix let out a breathless laugh.

If this was Hiro's prank, I'd gladly do it over and over again. Still lost in the haze, he turned to Beth, capturing her lips once more—only to freeze. Something was wrong. He pulled back.

Beth didn't move. Her body lay limp beneath him, eyes staring blankly at nothing. Her chest... open. Hollow. The bed beneath them, drenched in blood.

Hendrix bolted upright, horror washing over him in a crashing wave.

No.

No, no, no!

He scrambled off the bed, hands shaking as he reached for his clothes. *How? How the hell did I eat her heart?* His breath came in short, panicked gasps as he zipped his pants, mind spiraling into a nightmare he couldn't wake up from.

Then—

Beth moved. With inhuman speed, she sat up, eyes snapping open.

Before Hendrix could react, she lunged, grabbing him and dragging him back down onto the blood-soaked bed.

A wicked grin spread across her lips. "Again," she whispered, giddy with delight.

<><><>

"That's my boy!" Hiro smirked, throwing a playful punch at Hendrix's shoulder. "Beth couldn't stop bragging about you, bro. Called you her greatest ever. Darn, man, that hurts!"

Hendrix chuckled, rubbing his arm where Hiro had hit him. He had spent the entire weekend with Beth, indulging in his newfound vice—her. A lingering guilt gnawed at him for the way he kept pushing her limits, but he couldn't stop himself. He was hooked. And thanks to Hiro, he now had a taste for alcohol, too.

Sorry, Mom, he thought, not really meaning it.

The years that followed were nothing short of spectacular. Hendrix thrived—successful, wealthy, a respected sigbin. He had friends on both sides—humans and hellspawns alike. Nights were spent drinking with Hiro, reveling in the same thrill outside the arena that they shared within it. In his downtime, he enjoyed the warmth of Nzo's family and the sleepless nights with Beth.

"Don't sleep with anyone else but me, you hear? I'll cut you off if you do." Beth's voice was firm, her monstrous form briefly flashing as she glared at his grotesque form.

Hendrix laughed—until he realized she wasn't joking. "O-of course! I won't sleep with anyone else. Promise!"

Beth studied him, then softened back into her ethereal beauty. "You're mine."

Hendrix spent the rest of the night making it up to her. Life was good. Perfect, even.

Then—
BOOM.

<><><>

In a single day, in 1725 AB, everything changed. The celebration in The City of Ruinae, Xego, marked seven hundred years of peace under the Treaty of Avlam. The thousand-year war had ended, yet this was also the day that all sigbin stopped bleeding. The last drop of their eternal blood, drained, and Kein couldn't stop it from happening.

He stood in the penthouse of Hajji Towers, overlooking the city. Below, humans and sigbin coexisted under his rule.

"It is time, my son." Velial's voice slithered in his ear.

Kein turned, facing the serpent that had guided him for centuries. The last drop of blood had dried from the sigbin race. The final mutation was complete. Velial uncoiled. Kein braced himself. And in the most agonizing moment of his immortal life, Velial entered Kein's body.

The serpent devoured him from the inside out, splitting him apart bone by bone, nerve by nerve—ripping out his still-beating heart. And across the world, every sigbin felt his pain. They howled in agony, their bodies twisting into monstrous forms.

The world wept. The sigbin repented.
"Forgive us, my lord!"
"We will wait for your forgiveness!"
"Give us our blood back!"

Meanwhile, in his house... a lone sigbin sat in his room, coding an RPG game, oblivious to the world-changing event.

Hendrix.

Even as Kein and Velial became one, Hendrix sat in his darkened study, unmoved, untouched.

Until—

"Ahhh!" A burning sensation erupted across his skin as the monster between his legs changed form. He ran outside, stood shirtless as the snow fell on his half-naked body, calming the fire raging within. Unaware that across his skin, glowing inked marks had begun to take shape—

Marks that would define his true purpose.

The news exploded with reports of the phenomenon. Sigbin, once untouchable predators, now begged Kein for a cure, swearing to protect human lives in exchange. But Kein did not answer.

<><><>

As the years passed, resentment festered. Riots erupted in every major city. New laws were enforced—strict protections for humans who had never smelled so tempting to starving sigbin. Hellspawns no longer just craved flesh; they envied humans for the one thing they no longer had—blood in their veins.

Hendrix watched his friends spiral into despair. Even Beth stopped coming to him, ashamed of her own emptiness. "You know I don't have a blood fetish, right?" he reassured her, desperate to hold on to what they had.

Beth trembled in his arms, tears wetting his shirt. "D-do you love me, Hendrix?"

The question hit him like a blade to the gut. He opened his mouth, but no words came.

Beth's tearful eyes searched his face. Then, without another word, she pulled away and walked out.

Hendrix never saw her again. Looking back, Hendrix wondered if he should have just said yes—even if he wasn't sure what he truly felt.

<><><>

Hiro moaned as Sofia's tongue moved against him, fierce and relentless. "Are you back for good?" she asked between heated kisses.

"Yes!!!" Hiro screamed in pure ecstasy, reaching the peak of satisfaction.

The curse Kein had foretold centuries ago finally arrived, shattering the sigbin population. The hellspawns, once feared for their violence, were left cursed and bloodless, victims of a punishment long in the making.

Though most of the world mourned the monstrous transformations of the sigbin, the continent of Perlaz—home to Bufe, the brigada, and the channaks—remained indifferent.

Hiro, trying to escape the turmoil, lived as normally as possible. He felt unchanged, though there was an unsettling dryness to his being. Still, his appetite was the same, his strength undiminished, his bodily functions unaffected.

Curious, he cut into his own arm, expecting pain, but instead felt as though a butcher were slicing frozen meat. The lack of blood, and the way his wound healed without leaving a trace, shook him to the core.

Years passed, and the world descended into chaos. sigbin in their prime—young, strong, and once full of violence—fell into depression. Riots erupted across cities, and rumors of another world war spread. The citizens of Xego, fearing for their future, fled to Perlaz.

In response, Hiro's father, Mr. Hajji, implemented strict laws from Cintru. Any sigbin found harming humans was deported for punishment. Human burials were banned, cremation became mandatory, and female humans who reached puberty were relocated to Perlaz.

Sigbin and humans were forced to coexist under harsh new laws, creating a fragile peace. But beneath the surface, Hiro and his kind were spiraling into despair. Unable to cope, Hiro packed his bags and left Xego without a word –to meet an old friend.

Sofia.

She stood at the doorway of her chateau in Cintru, arms crossed. "So, you came crawling back," she said, expecting to berate him. But when she saw his face, something shifted inside her.

She remembered the pain of becoming bloodless centuries ago, with no one to turn to. As one of the first sigbin to be healed during the initial vaccine testing, Sofia had lost her blood before most others. Kein, once so affectionate, grew distant, no longer needing her as he once had.

Sofia met Hiro a year before the feast—the first year of Anno Bhiasti. He was young, innocent, pure in the ways of the sigbin, and she taught him much. When she became bloodless, it was Hiro who saved her, offering his blood and showing her a way to keep living.

They had shared joy and passion until Hiro grew distracted by his own online empire. He left their home in Cintru, barely a goodbye –and for centuries, they drifted apart.

Sofia was proud. She wasn't the type to beg, especially not to a man like Hiro. She was a royalty. She was sure Hiro would come back to her eventually. And when he did, she promised herself she would send him away for good, returning the favor he had once given her.

But the day of reckoning arrived, and instead of anger, Sofia found herself embracing the crying Hiro. She tore his clothes off and showed him how to live again, even without blood. The tongue lashing she had planned was replaced by a passionate reunion. In that brief moment, Hiro finally felt like he was home again.

<><>

Back at the arena, Hiro was a long way from home—stripped of every weapon he had meticulously embedded across his body in preparation for this long-awaited duel with Hendrix. He now understood this wasn't a prank. Invoking the magic word was useless, and his pride wouldn't allow him to beg for mercy.

But Hendrix wasn't looking for Hiro to beg. It was the other way around.

He had come to beg—that was the real reason he finally agreed to meet at the arena after decades of absence. He understood now: living without blood had taken its toll on the sigbin. And his own life, as the bleeding one, had been just as miserable.

10

Bersig - Love Match

As the decades passed, Beth was gone—and so was Hiro. He had vanished without a word of farewell, muttering something about Sofia, a name Hendrix had never heard before.

"He could be with his father in Cintru, begging Kein for a cure," Craig once suggested.

"I hope he comes back successful," Lane added.

Hendrix had never set foot in Cintru. He had no reason to go there. Yet, every time he missed Hiro, the temptation gnawed at him. It didn't help that the arena had been empty for years. Who wants to fight when there's no blood to spill?

When being around the down-spirited sigbin became unbearable, Hendrix turned to Nzo and his family. Jojo, Cathy's great-great-grandson, now managed Nzo's diner, and over the years, Hendrix had witnessed generations of Cathy and Jonathan's family grow, age, and pass on. But it was their deaths—Cathy's and Jonathan's—that he mourned the most. Even Hiro had struggled when Cathy passed centuries ago.

"No blood, no care-care, Nzo okie-okie!?" Nzo had shrugged when Hendrix asked how the channak felt about the curse. They were at the diner, the place Hendrix frequented after work or when he needed to clear his head.

"Don't you feel dry? Different?" Hendrix asked. For him, nothing had changed—but he hadn't dared wound himself to test what others described as cutting through frozen meat and feeling awful afterward.

"No-no," Nzo said simply.

Hendrix figured that since Nzo never drank blood or indulged in carnal desires, maybe it wasn't essential to him. If anything, if it were breast milk that had dried up, Nzo would probably declare another world war. The thought made Hendrix chuckle.

"I feel uncomfortable around other sigbin... Sometimes it's like they're looking at me and—" Girlie, Jojo's wife from Perlaz, shuddered, unable to finish her sentence. She was pregnant—with twins.

"Hide-hide, okie-okie?!" Nzo warned, his pacifier forgotten as he fixed Jojo with a serious stare.

"We are careful, Grandpa," Jojo reassured him, wrapping an arm around his wife. He told her to stay in the kitchen when sigbin customers were around and to serve only humans. They both agreed. But they also agreed that they always felt safe around Hendrix.

"They're jealous of your blood," Hendrix warned. "Just don't go out much."

"Yes, Uncle Hendrix." Jojo kissed his wife's forehead before sending her off to the kitchen.

With the arena empty and his team unmotivated for bloodless simulated fights, Hendrix threw himself into work and online gaming, shutting out the world. Meanwhile, the city streets became a new kind of battlefield—sigbin, driven mad by hunger and frustration, turned on each other. Riots erupted, leaving buildings in ruins and city landscapes scarred.

More decades passed. Still, Beth and Hiro were absent from Hendrix's life.

But he witnessed the birth of Nzo's grandsons, watched them grow from infants to old men, saw them take wives and raise children, living out their brief but fulfilling lives. Sometimes, Hendrix envied them. Immortality isn't always fun and games.

A century later, things began to settle. The riots slowed, destruction became occasional, and bloodless sigbin slowly adapted to their new reality. Then, finally, a spark of change.

"The team's ready to open the arena again," Sandy announced one day, excitement in her voice.

"We can still capture the simulation," Joreel added. "I'll incorporate the blood in the code."

"I'll code in the weapons under their skin," Hendrix added.

"I'm volunteering to have the deadliest weapons inside me for simulation at the arena," Craig raised his hand. It would hurt big time, but he's all for it.

The others agreed, excited.

With the arena reopening, Hendrix felt a flicker of hope. Maybe Hiro would come back.

"Are you fighting, boss?" Lane asked.

"You bet," Hendrix said, a grin creeping onto his face. Suddenly, he missed Hiro more than ever. The arena wasn't the same without him.

"Okay. Tomorrow then." Craig cracked his knuckles, eager for battle. And just like that, Hendrix was back where he belonged.

That night, after his long run, Hendrix froze in surprise—and then pure exhilaration—when he saw Beth waiting for him in his driveway.

"Long time," he said, drinking in the sight of her.

Beth's beauty hadn't faded. If anything, she looked even more striking under the moonlight. Without a word, she pulled him into a tight embrace.

"I know. I missed you," she whispered before kissing him deeply.

Desire shot through Hendrix like wildfire. "Where have you been?" he moaned against her lips, barely managing to control himself. It felt right to at least ask before he lost himself in her.

Beth had spent years wandering through Zapad, trying to reconcile with the bloodless version of herself. Tired of running and going nowhere, she had finally made a decision—to come back. To be with Hendrix. To confess that she loved him.

She knew he didn't feel the same way. But she didn't care. "Are you sure you don't mind?" she murmured as they collapsed into bed together. Beth knew Hendrix didn't care about blood, but that wasn't her real insecurity.

"Yes," Hendrix muttered between kisses, his hands roaming her body. She wasn't as soft and warm as before, but she was still intoxicating.

"Hmmm, you smell good... different, but good," Beth whispered in his ear as she moved against him, sending shivers down his spine.

Then, she stilled, her gaze locking onto his. "You don't care about my blood... but your monster does," she mused, eyeing his partially transformed form.

"Let it starve," Hendrix growled, about to reclaim control—until he realized something was wrong. Beth felt dry. Too dry. Like an empty husk.

Then —pain.

"Ah!" Hendrix tasted blood as Beth's teeth sank into his lips. His breath hitched. What the hell?

Beth's eyes widened in shock as she pulled back, staring at the crimson streak on his mouth. "I... Impossible," she stammered. The scent of his blood filled the air. Something shifted in her.

Before Hendrix could react, Beth's form twisted—her monster took over. She lunged. Her claws gripped his face, her mouth latching onto his bleeding wound. She sucked desperately, frantically—her body trembling, her hunger unhinged.

Hendrix struggled to push her off, but she was too strong, too wild—until, just as suddenly as it started, Beth went limp. She collapsed in his arms, motionless.

"B-Beth?" His voice cracked as he shook her.

Nothing.

Panic surged through him. I killed her. Crap! I killed her.

<><><>

While Hendrix had demons of his own to face, somewhere in Zapad, Sofia and Hiro lay in bed, still high on drugs, both of them pretending to be satisfied.

"Do you miss it?" Sofia asked, her head resting on Hiro's chest.

"Terribly," Hiro sighed, his voice thick with longing.

"Me too," she replied, flinching slightly when Hiro squeezed her tighter.

They were talking about the old days, when they could feed off each other's blood, their bond once stronger than anything else.

"I like this too... occasionally," Sofia chuckled, though her words didn't carry much meaning.

"The human kind?" Hiro asked, kissing her forehead, trying to play the gentleman, like something out of an old story.

"The boring kind," Sofia said, and they both laughed, the shared humor light but empty.

"Are we set?" Sofia asked, her gaze fixed on Hiro as he dressed.

"Yes, I already told Ehud where to meet me," Hiro answered, a hint of excitement in his voice as their plans took shape.

"I'm really glad you're back on board. I missed you," Sofia said, walking toward the receiving area, watching him prepare for their next move.

Hiro didn't answer. She had been saying the same thing over and over ever since he returned, crying on her shoulder for having lost all his blood. He never shared the real reason he had stayed away for so long. He told her it was the work he had done in Xego that had forced him to leave. "I don't fit in Xego anymore," he had said when he came back to her, now a bloodless sigbin. Sofia didn't press further.

"Are you off to see Caiphaiz?" Sofia asked, kissing Hiro one last time before letting him go.

"Yes, I need a better hit. To be honest, you suck!" Hiro said, his hand brushing against Sofia's hard body in jest.

"And you're full of crap!" Sofia shot back, punching him in the gut before pushing him out the door.

"Hi, Dimas," Hiro greeted smugly as he passed Sofia's current companion. He liked to mess with Dimas, teasing him.

"Bye, Hiro," Dimas replied coldly, eyes narrowed.

Dimas entered, and Sofia, now sprawled on the sofa bed, greeted him with a playful grin.

"Jealous, my love?" she asked, tracing the scar that ran from Dimas' right eyebrow all the way to the back of his skull. To Sofia, it only made him more breathtaking.

Dimas shook his head, lying.

"Come here," Sofia beckoned from the side of the sofa, clearing space for him to sit beside her. She dabbed some blood from the vial hanging on her necklace and smeared it on her lips.

Dimas smiled and kissed her, savoring the taste. "I love you," he said, his eyes glowing with adoration.

"I love you more," Sofia whispered, before biting into Dimas' neck and drinking deeply. He moaned in pleasure, determined to be a better lover to her than Hiro had ever been.

<><><>

Days later, Hiro joined Caiphaiz in the shower, where blood flowed freely.

"Slow down, boy," Caiphaiz cautioned, pulling his bleeding arm away from Hiro's eager mouth. Hiro's eyes were wide, dilated, consumed by the intoxication of Caiphaiz's blood.

The euphoria coursing through him was overwhelming—so powerful that it could last for days. In this state, Hiro was vulnerable, and Caiphaiz could do as he pleased with him.

When Caiphaiz finally pulled away, he rewarded Hiro with several vials of his blood, ensuring Hiro wouldn't suffer the painful withdrawals.

"Thank you, my Lord," Hiro murmured, his voice thick with gratitude as he cuddled up to Caiphaiz, one vial now dangling from a chain around his neck like a prized possession.

"Use it sparingly," Caiphaiz said, his tone both playful and warning. "Enjoy."

He watched Hiro leave, his mind lingering on the boy. Of all the sigbin Kein had created, only a few had captured his attention, and

Hiro, from the moment he arrived in Cintru with his father, was one of them.

Caiphaiz was different from the others that's why he still bled. Created by Kein through a unique method. He shared the immortality and vulnerability of the sigbin, but lacked their strength, their insatiable thirst for blood, and their carnal nature.

Hiro, however, had invoked a desire in Caiphaiz that he couldn't quite explain.

Though Hiro had been naive when they first met, Caiphaiz had taken him under his wing, guiding him through Sofia's influence and preparing him for the feast. Despite Hiro's emotional volatility, he had always been Caiphaiz's favorite sigbin, and the priest would do anything to keep him happy.

<><><>

From Cintru, Hiro made his way to Zapad to meet Ehud at the border. As they approached the checkpoint of Xego, they simply presented Hiro's ID, embedded in his palm.

The border patrol instantly recognized him as the governor's son and, eager to grant him passage, waved them through without hesitation.

"Are you all set?" Hiro asked, glancing over at Ehud, who was driving the truck. With Hiro on board, Ehud's role had shifted. No longer waiting for fresh meat supplies to arrive at the border, Ehud now had the privilege of personally selecting the shipments. This new arrangement thrilled the smuggler.

"Yes, everything's in order, thanks to you," Ehud replied, pulling over to the side of the highway inside Xego's territory. It was here that Hiro would part ways with him. "This is where I leave you," Ehud said, his voice tinged with excitement for the task ahead.

"Call me when you're back," Hiro warned, his tone serious. "Be careful near the Perlaz border."

"Don't worry, boss. We know a thing or two about making channaks dance to our tune," Ehud chuckled, amused by his own private joke.

Hiro had no interest in the intricacies of smuggling—he only cared about getting what was his.

<><><>

Days later, Hiro stood on the balcony of his mansion, watching as Ehud's trucks pulled up to the driveway.

"This will be your new home," Ehud announced, leading a young woman inside. "You're fortunate BerSig matched you with someone so wealthy and powerful in Xego," he added, watching as the young berhen took in the lavish surroundings, her eyes wide with awe.

"Presenting your husband-to-be, Mr. Hiro Hajji, CEO of Hajji Inc.," Hiro heard Aldred, his butler, announce as he descended the stairs to greet their guests.

"Hello, Abby," Hiro said, flashing a warm smile. The berhen, overwhelmed by the grandeur of the mansion, couldn't help but blush at the sight of him. Her scent, sweet and intoxicating, already seemed to fill the air.

"H-hi, Mr. Hajji," she stammered, clearly taken aback by Hiro's handsome appearance. They had only exchanged brief conversations before this moment, and she was still getting to know him.

At just 21, Abby was strikingly beautiful, her small, heart-shaped face radiating innocence. Hiro had personally selected her from a pool of candidates, swiping right as soon as he saw her profile. In Perlaz, pure maidens were eager to escape the rules of Vincot – a place where maidens await their suitors – and find alternate routes to marriage.

"Please, call me Hiro, sweetheart." Hiro gently took her hand, pressing a soft kiss to her palm. She blushed, biting her lip in excitement. Hiro smiled, though his thoughts were elsewhere. I'm freaking hungry, he thought, his desire gnawing at him.

"Ehud, are you set with Sofia?" Hiro asked, not even looking at him.

"Yes, I've got something special for her too," Ehud replied, a mischievous grin spreading across his face. He wanted to show Hiro the contents of his trucks, but he knew Hiro would be busy with his new fiancée.

"Great! You may go. I'll take care of beautiful Abby here." Hiro winked at the berhen, who bowed her head, clearly delighted.

"Alright, enjoy!" Ehud said, his grin widening as he left, clearly pleased with the day's events

<><><>

In the passenger seat of Ehud's truck, another berhen waited patiently. Surrounded by a feast of temptation, Ehud reveled in every minute of his work.

"Don't worry, sweetie," Ehud said, casting a glance at her. "Your husband-to-be is wealthier and more powerful than Abby's fiancé. You're in good hands."

The human berhen smiled shyly, adjusting her appearance in the rearview mirror. She wanted to look perfect for the man who had chosen to marry her — one of the wealthiest in Xego, or so she had been told. She reassured herself that her parents would understand her decision once she contacted them after settling in Xego.

The initial shock would pass, and she would prove to them that she had made the right choice in seeking love here, away from her old life.

Ehud grinned as he signaled his men to follow. Several trucks pulled away from Hiro's mansion, each loaded with humans — some kidnapped, some killed in the hunt, and others who traveled willingly.

After watching Ehud leave, Hiro turned his attention back to his guest.

"Aldred, my bride must be tired and hungry. Please attend to all her needs while I return to work," Hiro said, planting a soft kiss on Abigail's forehead.

"Yes, my lord," Aldred responded with a bow. Hiro's gaze lingered on Abigail for a moment, brushing his fingers over her lips, savoring the softness of her skin. *Soon, my love. Soon*, he thought, the monster inside him stirring with anticipation.

"A-are you leaving already?" Abigail's voice trembled, a hint of disappointment coloring her words. She had hoped for more time to get to know the man she was about to marry.

"Yes, sweetheart," Hiro replied, his tone apologetic yet firm. "I'll give you all the time you need to prepare for our wedding. I'll marry you as soon as possible." He placed his wrist on Abigail's handbag, transferring koine credits into her digital wallet with a few swift movements."

Aldred, take Abigail to Ruinae tomorrow for a shopping spree," Hiro instructed, his voice carrying authority. Aldred bowed once more.

"Promise me you'll enjoy yourself," Hiro said, pulling Abigail into a brief but tender hug.

"Alright, m-my love," Abigail stammered, her excitement building at the prospect of buying whatever she desired. Life in Perlaz had been harsh, and the thought of a life filled with luxury seemed almost too good to be true.

With that, Aldred guided Abigail upstairs, her heart fluttering with anticipation for the life ahead.

<><><>

After meeting with his fiancée, Hiro descended into the basement—now transformed into an opulent honeymoon suite. The decor was both extravagant and exquisite, a wedding gift for his lovely wife, Mei Zhen, who awaited him in all her radiant beauty. They had married just yesterday, and he had told her to rest, preparing herself for the honeymoon.

Mei Zhen, much like Abigail, was an oriental beauty—petite, with smooth, pearly-white skin, a delicate nose, and smiling, almond-shaped eyes. Hiro had a particular taste, in both women and food. He could indulge in anything, but brunettes remained his favorite.

"Finally!" Mei Zhen threw her arms around him, her enthusiasm boundless. She wore a silky, provocative piece of lingerie that clung perfectly to her frame, accentuating every curve.

"Careful, my love," Hiro murmured, a smirk playing on his lips. "Don't tempt me. I'm still a sigbin—a monster who married a human out of rebellion… and love."

They hadn't lied about the berhen they recruited from Perlaz, which was why their dating app was called bersig—the forbidden romance of berhen and sigbi. The app lured humans into matching with wealthy, desirable sigbin husbands, promising love despite the lurking danger.

There was something peculiar about human women who believed their love could transform bloodthirsty predators into angels. Hiro found it amusing. Tsk. Clueless creatures… but lucky me.

"Sorry," Mei Zhen giggled, looking up at him with complete trust. "I just know you'd never hurt me." She was young, innocent, hopelessly devoted.

Hiro lifted her chin gently, forcing himself to meet her gaze. "I don't deserve you," he said softly. "Risking your life just to be with me..."

Mei Zhen's eyes glowed with unwavering determination. "It's love. The moment I saw your profile picture, I knew. Human or sigbin, it doesn't matter to me." She pressed herself against his chest, listening to his heartbeat—fast and eager.

Hiro inhaled deeply, savoring her scent. "Aren't you afraid that we won't work out?"

"Oh, but we will!" Mei Zhen beamed. "I've heard success stories from other berhen who joined BerSig. They're so happy with their sigbin husbands, and I intend to be just as happy with you."

Hiro laughed, unable to suppress his delight. He pulled her close, embracing her warmly. "I love you," he whispered, his tone shifting, growing quieter.

Mei Zhen felt the change instantly. She pulled back slightly, searching his face. "What's wrong?"

Hiro held her gaze, his fingers tracing the curve of her jaw. "If I hurt you tonight... tell me."

Her smile turned mischievous. "I'll only tell you how much pleasure you're giving me. How about that?" She had spent countless hours watching videos, preparing for this very night. She intended to make her husband's first night unforgettable.

Hiro, however, didn't smile. His grip on her waist tightened slightly. "I'm serious. Tell me to stop."

Something about his voice sent a shiver down Mei Zhen's spine—but instead of fear, she felt exhilaration. He loves me. He really loves me! "Never!" she vowed, holding him tightly.

Their wedding had been simple and intimate, yet the absence of her family in Perlaz still stung. They had refused to support her decision, forcing her to sneak across the border just to follow her dream.

Hiro exhaled slowly, his fingers brushing through her hair. "Fair enough." Then he gently pushed Mei Zhen away, gazing at her with adoration before slowly peeling off her delicate lingerie. His hands trembled—not with nervousness, but with sheer excitement.

She had no idea how much happiness she had given him, how much he had enjoyed playing house with her. Promising her a life as his wife, showering her with everything money could buy.

Yes, Mei Zhen had even posted glowing testimonies online for her family in Perlaz, proving how well she was doing. She had recorded countless videos, documenting her seemingly perfect life in Xego, her digital presence immortalized.

Every movement, every smile, every word—her voiceprint, faceprint, even her body scan—was meticulously mapped through an RPG-like format, accessible to her loved ones in Perlaz for years to come. Even long after Mei Zhen was dead.

Hiro and Sofia had perfected this berhen-smuggling scheme in **1300 AB**—a twisted gift from Hiro to Sofia, his bloodless sigbin partner, who had once wallowed in misery. Hiro handled the system's setup while Sofia took charge of the ground operations—recruiting qualified sigbin hellspawns from Zapad to smuggle humans from Xego and Perlaz.

They took the heart of the berhen, while Ehud, if lucky, got all the fresh meat he needed to supply his clientele in Zapad.

Hiro had once thought himself a fool for leaving Sofia after two centuries to settle in Xego as Hendrix's partner. But now, he was back—his absence nothing more than a brief intermission in their ever-thriving berhen smuggling business.

Their work was flawless. No longer just an underground market for fresh meat, they had expanded, supplying berhen-on-demand to the wealthiest sigbin across Zapad.

Ehud oversaw the operations, while Sofia controlled the most influential and powerful sigbin in Cintru. Hiro, ever the strategist, managed the affairs of Xego, ensuring their recruitment system operated seamlessly—luring, rather than abducting, berhen to avoid drawing unwanted attention.

Their scheme was perfect.

Flawless.

Just like Hiro's wife.

With an effortless motion, he lifted Mei Zhen into his arms and carried her to the heart-shaped bed, a cruel imitation of romance. He had given her a fairy-tale life—except instead of being married to a prince, she had wedded a hellspawn. And now, she would finally learn what that truly meant.

Hiro kissed Mei Zhen passionately, his lips hungry, his grip careful. One wrong move, and he could break her like a fragile twig.

Mei Zhen moaned softly, oblivious, as his lips traveled from her mouth to her neck. "Hiro..." Mei Zhen's voice trembled, and Hiro felt the anticipation clawing at his insides.

His excitement swelled, but he was determined to prolong the torment. He wanted to savor the moment, to ensure his bride's night was unforgettable before—well, Hiro smiled darkly to himself. The moment would come soon enough.

Mei Zhen convulsed beneath him, her body writhing in pleasure as Hiro explored every inch of her. His control was slipping, but he fought to hold it together.

"Hiro... my love... please, take me now," Mei Zhen pleaded, her voice strained, gasping for air.

11

Hiro Is Not A Hero

As much as Hiro craved his human berhen bride, he held back. No, she was not yet his to claim completely. She must remain untouched—her purity intact. Only then would he savor the full pleasure of consuming her heart.

When Mei Zhen screamed, the release shuddering through her body, Hiro's hunger roared. His throat burned with the need for more, but he forced himself to hold back. The beast within stirred, but Hiro would wait. His patience, though frayed, remained.

Not yet. Hiro whispered the words to himself as if they were the only thing anchoring him to sanity. He repeated the ritual—seducing, teasing, withholding—until he could bear it no longer.

"Huh! Aaaaaaa! Awwww!" Mei Zhen's cries were filled with agony and ecstasy as Hiro's claws tore into her chest.

Blood splattered across her face, staining her once-beautiful skin. She struggled against him, but Hiro's grip was iron, her limbs pinned beneath his monstrous form.

"No!" Her scream echoed in the basement, muffled, but upstairs, Abigail soaked in her bath, blissfully unaware of the horrors unfolding below.

Mei Zhen's wailing was a symphony to Hiro's ears. She begged him to stop. She pleaded, but Hiro had never promised her mercy. Her voice only made him hunger more.

Finally, when Hiro sank his fangs into her still-beating heart, he was no longer a man. He was a grotesque, green-scaled monster. With a low moan of satisfaction, he bathed in Mei Zhen's blood, reveling in the warmth as it soaked his body.

Her beauty had faded. No longer the vibrant woman she had been, Mei Zhen lay in a lifeless heap on the bed, eyes wide open, her mouth hanging agape. Life had drained from her eyes, leaving only the hollow stare of a corpse bride. Her fairy tale had turned into a nightmare.

When Hiro had consumed all she had to offer, he took the last of her—her purity—just as he had planned.

Aldred was already in the room when Hiro emerged from the shower, his body cleansed of Mei Zhen's blood, his hunger satisfied, his stomach full. "My lord," Aldred greeted him with a bow, offering a clean towel.

"She's all yours," Hiro said coldly, stepping past him. "Enjoy."

Aldred beamed, his fangs glinting as he shifted into his own monstrous form, already eager to feast on the remains.

As Hiro ascended the stairs, he found his mind drifting. He needed a new bride. Abigail was next, but Hiro had to be patient. He would make sure Abigail fell madly, obsessively in love with him before their wedding. He couldn't afford any mistakes. He had to start the courtship early.

Passing by a large mirror in the hallway, Hiro paused. He gazed at his reflection—a handsome man with eyes that always seemed to smile, friendly and charming. His looks disarmed, but there was something beneath the surface that others found unsettling. A coldness. A mystery that made even the bravest sigbin hesitate in his presence.

But Hiro knew the truth. Beneath the charming exterior was a man in pain—a man who longed for the innocence he had lost. His monstrous form was a curse, but deeper still was the yearning to be more than the monster he had become.

The guilt weighed heavily on him. The sadness, the unspoken regret—it all clawed at his heart, a silent reminder of the heinous crimes he had committed.

As Hiro stared at his reflection, his face shifted. The smooth features, the handsome eyes, melted away, replaced by the grotesque visage of the creature he had become. For a moment, he remembered Hendrix—before the betrayal, before everything changed.

He thought of Cathy, too, the love of his life, whose sad smile haunted him still. She had been his light, and her death had shattered him. "I didn't kill them, Cathy. He did!" Hiro's voice cracked, the words laced with madness, as he shouted at his reflection.

As if Hendrix himself stood before him, Hiro screamed, "It's all your fault!" He struck the mirror with all his strength, the glass shattering with a deafening crash. The sound echoed through the house, causing Abigail to jump, her bubble bath interrupted by the violent noise.

Hiro's fist throbbed, the adrenaline surging in his veins. He stood there, breathing heavily, his reflection now nothing but shards of broken glass. His heart, too, was shattered—irreparably so.

<><><>

1925 Anno Bhiasti -- Back in the arena, where words could never capture the full depth of his hatred for Hendrix, Hiro wanted to scream…**It's your fault!** But his throat was too raw, his breath too shallow. He could barely form words.

Flat on his back, in a twisted mass of agony, his body impaled by more than a dozen spears that pinned him to the ground. The tornado that had once ravaged the battlefield had long since dissipated, but Hendrix had tossed Hiro into a pit, his body crashing like a ragdoll into a bed of sharp, metallic spears.

Hiro's skin screamed in agony as the barbed tips tore into his frozen flesh, each puncture sending waves of blinding pain coursing through his veins.

Hendrix might not have been in the arena for long, but Sandy had kept him well-informed of its deadly design. The traps, the snares, the obstacle courses—it was all a twisted maze Hiro hadn't anticipated. He hadn't set foot in Xego for years, and now he realized that Hendrix had seen this fight coming from the very beginning. From the moment he had stepped into the arena, Hiro had been set up, the noose slowly tightening around him.

Hiro knew it would take days—maybe weeks—to free himself from this trap. Every movement would be agony. He clenched his jaw, trying to steady his breath through the shock. But beneath the pain, there was something far worse creeping in: exhaustion. Defeat.

A searing, gnawing anger that burned hotter than any of his wounds. He waited, eyes fixed on the darkness above, hoping for Hendrix to appear, to stand over him with that smug, victorious grin. Hiro knew it was coming—the moment when his enemy would gloat, taunting him for his defeat.

But when Hendrix finally descended into view, it wasn't with words of triumph. Instead, he was holding a massive steel wall—heavy, jagged, and unforgiving. With a roar, Hendrix threw it into the pit with a crash, and Hiro felt the ground shift beneath him as the metal sheet slammed down on top of him.

Trapped between the cold earth and the crushing weight of the steel, Hiro's body was further impaled by the spears still embedded in his flesh. The spikes dug deeper into his frozen form, locking him in place.

Despair sank into Hiro's chest like a lead weight. There was no escape—not without help. Hendrix would bury him alive, if not in this pit, then with a load of dirt. Hiro knew that, without assistance, he would remain here—broken, trapped—until the earth swallowed him whole. Weeks. Months, perhaps, before anyone would find him. And by then, his body would be nothing more than a husk, rotting in the dark.

A sharp, ragged scream tore from Hiro's throat as Hendrix leaped onto him. The ground trembled beneath them, and the metal wall pressed down harder, forcing Hiro into the jagged spikes beneath him. The pain shot through him like wildfire.

Hendrix cursed. "Darn it" The words were a growl of frustration. He had miscalculated, and one of the sharp spikes had caught him, tearing into his skin as he leaped into the pit. Blood seeped from the wound, staining the air with its bitter metallic scent.

Accidents like this ignited Hendrix's fury, a fury that was hard to control. It was the very reason he stopped fighting—especially with his best friend, Hiro.

His hand trembled as he inspected the wound, checking carefully to see if his blood had seeped through the jagged metal to Hiro's exposed skin.

Hendrix was determined—no matter what—to protect his brother. But Hiro had no idea just how deep the danger ran. By challenging him, by asking to fight, Hiro was walking blindly into a storm. A storm that would only consume them both.

To face a sigbin like Hendrix, especially one bleeding out with rage, was more than reckless—it was a death sentence.

"Darn you! Get off me, you son of *&^!" Hiro screamed, feeling Hendrix's weight bearing down on him. Each step from his enemy pressed the heavy metal sheet harder against his chest, crushing his lungs and making it nearly impossible to draw a breath. The metal was pinning him in place, a cruel iron cocoon that held him immobile, but it also shielded him from Hendrix's bleeding wound—now sealed and healing.

Hendrix wiped the blood away with a careful, almost deliberate motion, making sure not a trace of it remained visible. His hands moved swiftly, obscuring the evidence, as if trying to erase any sign of the wound that might betray his vulnerability. He was determined that Hiro would see nothing—nothing that could reveal the cracks in his facade.

"Shut up, Zov!" Hendrix snarled, his voice dripping with anger and frustration. "Shut up and listen to me... just this once... please, *my brother...*" Hendrix's tone shifted, heavy with an emotion Hiro hadn't expected. The words were thick with sorrow and a desperate plea, as if something deep inside him cracked.

Hendrix teetered on the edge of emotional collapse. As always, he had triumphed over his brother, Hiro, in the arena—but winning his trust was the real battle.

Too many secrets weighed him down. Deadly secrets that only Nzo and his family knew, whether he wanted to or not.

<><><>

A couple of years ago, in 1923 AB, Hendrix was drowning in despair.

"Hendrix! DRIIIIIX!" Tiny fingers jabbed into Hendrix's nostrils, yanking his head up.

"Hatchew! Quit it, kid!" he grumbled, swatting Nzo's hand away. He was drunk. Again.

With the entire sigbin population struggling to cope with their bloodless existence, they sought solace in extremes—sex, drugs, violence. Hendrix? He drowned himself in alcohol. Three bottles had turned into three barrels. Over the decades, his tolerance had climbed so high he now mixed his beer with hard liquor just to feel something.

"Lousy, stupid drunk!" Nzo scowled before leaping onto Hendrix's lap and twisting his nipples through his shirt.

"STOP! STOP IT!" Hendrix yelled, jerking back. He didn't want to sober up. When he was intoxicated, he could forget.

"No sleeping! Don't! Okie-okie!?" Nzo shrieked in his ear as Hendrix's head drooped again.

"Hah! How I wish!" Hendrix tried taking another swig from his bottle, but Nzo knocked it away. Beer sloshed over his shirt.

"Yeah, sleep can't, okie-okie?!" Nzo giggled, stuffing his own feeding bottle—filled with milk and cognac—into his mouth.

Crap. I wish I could sleep, Hendrix thought, disoriented.

"HENDRIIIIX!" Nzo shook him violently.

"What?! Whaaat? Where're we?" Hendrix slurred, blinking. They were still in Isla De Parthena's bar. When he was drunk, the world blurred just enough to make his endless life feel less unbearable.

"Come me diner. Come, Drix...huh?" Nzo had been pestering him for years to visit his family's coffee shop.

"I can't," Hendrix muttered, his eyes half-closed.

"Why?!?" Nzo slapped him.

"'Cause I'm always with you here," Hendrix flicked the toddler's forehead.

"Oh! Right. Okie-okie!" Nzo cackled, momentarily forgetting his anger—until Hendrix shoved him off. "Hey! No! Don't going?" Nzo pouted as he landed on the bar table like a discarded toy.

"I'm gonna pee. Wanna watch?" Hendrix shoved Nzo's tiny arms away when the kid tried clinging to him, throwing a baby tantrum.

"Eww! No Nzo watch little hotdog! Okie-okie?!" Nzo scrunched his face in disgust. With only a few customers left, they practically had the bar to themselves.

"Hah! My monster is not—" Hendrix mumbled something unintelligible as he stumbled toward the back door.

The cold air hit Hendrix as he leaned against the wall, unzipping his pants. He decided he'd go to work after this and leave Nzo behind.

Then—two brawling sigbin stumbled into the alley. Hendrix ignored them, closing his eyes while relieving himself. He was too tired, too drunk, too—

THUD!

"Urgh!" Something hard struck the back of his head. "Dude, Me no fight. Just git," he slurred, imitating Nzo's speech at the sigbin who had thrown a trash can at him.

The giant sneered. "Do I look like I care? The other guy ran, and you're here, so... let's do this."

A fist swung at Hendrix's face. He ducked—barely—zipping up just in time. Some sigbin still hadn't accepted their bloodless fate. They turned to non stop violence, lashing out in blind fury.

"I said, piss off!" Hendrix tried pushing past, but the monster blocked him, unmovable.

A punch landed in his gut. Hendrix doubled over. Pain exploded through his stomach. Then—he laughed. A raw, unhinged laugh.

The arena. He remembered the arena. The thrill of the fight. The euphoria. He missed it. Darn did he miss it. *I miss Zov.* He hadn't seen Hiro in like forever. His laughter only fueled the rage of the drunken giant sigbin. When Hendrix looked up, his opponent had already shifted into his monstrous form. The fight was on.

Hendrix fought defensively, slipping into the familiar rhythm of combat. But without blood, it felt hollow. He broke bones, dodged attacks, but there was no satisfaction.

Then—CRACK!

The sigbin head-butted him. A jagged knife embedded in its forehead tore into Hendrix's skin. Too drunk to react in time, Hendrix staggered back, feeling warmth trickle down his face.

Then—realization.
Blood.

His own blood. His body began to heal, but the scent was already in the air. The hellspawn froze, nostrils flaring. Hendrix wiped his face, smearing red across his skin. No, no, no... Despite the initial shock, the sigbin's eyes lit up.

Hunger. Pure, desperate hunger.

"No! Don't! Stay away from me!" Hendrix stepped back, frantically searching for an escape. The alley was a dead end. The sigbin trembled, staring at the blade coated in Hendrix's blood.

"W-what are you?" The monster pulled the knife from its skull, lifting it to its mouth.

"NO!" Hendrix lunged—

Too late. The sigbin's tongue flicked over the blade. Instantly, its body seized. Then—it collapsed. A lifeless heap on the alley floor. Hendrix panted. His hands trembled. Then he noticed—

Nzo.

The toddler stood behind the fallen sigbin, mouth open in shock. Hendrix slumped against the wall, clutching his head. "Crap."

He dared not touch Nzo. The kid was as important to him as Hiro.

<><><>

Hendrix remembered—it all started with Beth.

"Beth?! Beth?!" Hendrix shook the unconscious sigbin, but she remained unresponsive. Horror gripped him—not just at what had happened to Beth, but at the realization that his own blood still flowed. After all these years, he had never checked. Without the arena, he had never been wounded—not while running, not while working on his games.

Beth wasn't dead, not in the way he used to kill her. Sleeping? No. How?! We don't sleep. Then, he heard it—a snore. Beth was breathing, her chest rising and falling in a peaceful rhythm. A new kind of fear settled in. Sigbin had been awake for nearly two thousand years.

Relieved, yet unnerved, Hendrix couldn't shake the feeling that his blood had something to do with her condition. *What is going on?* With no one to turn to, he threw himself into researching whatever he could online:

Bloodless sigbin Why hellspawns don't sleep Side effects of KSi22 vaccine

Nothing. His searches yielded nothing useful, only deepening his frustration and helplessness.

What did I do to be spared from Kein's curse? Wait... am I really spared? Should I go to Cintru and ask Kein? "Ahhh!" Hendrix pulled at his hair in frustration. But something in his gut told him—he could trust no one.

Now, he had more than just what was between his legs to be ashamed of. No one could discover that he was still bleeding. Not until he found a way to wake Beth.

Days turned into months. Months into years. Still, Hendrix hoped that one day, Beth would open the door when he came home. Every day, he visited her in the basement, which he had transformed into a cozy bedroom. She lay peacefully on a soft bed, like a princess from the ancient fairy tales.

Can a true love's kiss wake you?

The thought was pathetic. Desperate. But he was out of options. So, every night, he pressed a gentle kiss to her lips—only to leave disappointed.

Beth's disappearance couldn't go unnoticed forever. Her friends might start looking for her. Hendrix couldn't afford that risk.

From then on, he avoided the arena, where even a simulated fight could expose him. His team didn't take his absence well.

"Boss, I designed a new arena," Sandy coaxed, showcasing intricate lairs, lethal traps, and brutal obstacle courses. But Hendrix had to refuse. Again and again.

Then, after decades of absence, Hiro returned. Hendrix was ecstatic. They traveled to Isla De Parthena to celebrate, but instead of brawling in the arena, they spent their time lost in online games.

"Let's do it! I tried the arena with Craig and Lane the other day—it's cool. Not as amazing as before, but still..." Hiro tried to convince him.

"I'm done with the arena," Hendrix said flatly.

The words cut deeper than he intended. It wasn't the fights that Hiro mourned—it was Hendrix's refusal.

Hiro tried again. "Come on, my brother." He used their safe words, but Hendrix still shook his head. Among everyone, Hiro was the last person he wanted to harm with his blood.

"It doesn't work that way, Zov. This isn't a prank. I'm just bored of the arena... maybe a little depressed too, after losing—ehrm, losing our blood."

A lie. A desperate, obvious lie. But better that than the truth.

Hiro took it personally. He had returned to Xego, trying to accept his bloodless existence. The hunger still gnawed at him, the guilt of devouring human hearts never truly fading. He had wanted to be better—to be the hero Cathy once believed him to be. Hendrix was supposed to help him through it.

Instead, Hendrix's refusal shattered their bond. They avoided each other until they became completely estranged.

Maybe it's for the best. I just want you safe, my brother, Hendrix told himself that, but it didn't make the ache in his chest any easier to bear.

He heard from the others that Hiro still visited Xego but refused to see him. The decades dragged on. Hendrix learned to compartmentalize his pain, burying it under the weight of too many secrets.

A lover, cold and sleeping in his basement. A body, still bleeding, without explanation. A best friend, lost to him. And now, Nzo knew the truth. A toddler—too young to understand, but too dangerous to ignore. Hendrix would protect him and Hiro. No matter the cost.

<><><>

Back in the arena, Hiro's fury reached a tipping point. "Get off me! Darn you! I'm gonna—" Hiro thrashed violently, every muscle in his body straining against the hold restraining him. He refused to be trapped like this. Not here. Not now.

"I need you, brother... Zov... *my brother*, please listen to me." Hendrix's voice cut through Hiro's rage—raw, desperate. "I'll tell you a secret."

For a moment, Hiro froze. The safe words. Hendrix had spoken their safe words – my brother. His breath hitched as the haze of fury clouding his mind began to clear. *Why? Why was Hendrix saying this? Why now?*

Hiro's body remained tense, his instincts screaming at him to resist, to fight—but then, something warm and wet splashed against his face.

Drip. Drip. Drip.

His pulse pounded in his ears as he looked up. Hendrix was crying, hoping...hoping that Hiro would understand him, just as Nzo did.

<><><>

A year ago.

"Darn it, kid. There's no more room down here," Hendrix grumbled, staring at the growing pile of snoring sigbin in his basement.

"Okie, meh bassment okie-okie?! Uuuh!" Nzo strained, trying to drag the unconscious sigbin they'd ambushed near Nzo's diner. But the hellspawn was far too heavy for the little channak to carry.

"About time. Your basement is bigger than mine. Hendrix folded his arms, watching in amusement as Nzo nearly toppled over from the effort. "Are you sure this one knew about Lumen?"

"See? Gang, okie-okie!?" Nzo triumphantly held up a burnt nanochip he had cut from the sigbin's armpit.

Hendrix exhaled sharply. They had already captured too many of Lumen's enemies—sooner or later, someone important and powerful was bound to come looking. "We need help, kid. We can't keep doing this..." With a grunt, Hendrix lifted the unconscious sigbin and tossed him onto the heap like a sack of garbage.

"Okie, okie!?" Nzo huffed, finally reaching the bottom of the stairs. His little chest heaved with exhaustion, but he was grinning. At least Hendrix had helped this time.

Effit! Me help-help too! Nzo thought, determined. The memory of discovering Hendrix's secret in that alley was still fresh in his mind.

<><><>

"Oh-oh, nap-nap. Huh! Magic? Okie-okie?!" Recovering from his initial shock, the toddler inspected the sigbin lying motionless on the ground. Nzo had followed Hendrix into the alley minutes earlier, knowing the drunk sigbin would sneak off again after taking a leak.

The channak had seen everything—the moment the massive sigbin attacked Hendrix and how the fight ended in his friend's favor.

Hendrix pulled himself together, standing up slowly. He watched the channak warily, unsure of what to do next.

"Don't! The blood…" Hendrix warned, his voice sharp as he saw Nzo reaching for the knife still clutched in the sigbin's hand.

"Wiii, noice. Very noice! Okie-okie!?" Nzo chirped, inspecting the scene with interest. He had noticed something different about Hendrix ever since they started frequenting the parthena bars.

His grandchildren often asked why Hendrix no longer visited the diner, but Nzo couldn't tell them the truth—that his old friend preferred drowning himself in booze rather than spending time with humans. Nzo had seen other sigbin lose control before, but it puzzled him that Hendrix's depression had only set in decades after they had all stopped bleeding.

"Kid, I…" Hendrix started, but his voice trailed off.

"Me, Nzo know, okie, okie!" Nzo nodded, his eyes scanning every inch of the unconscious sigbin, who now looked almost human.

"What are you thinking?" Hendrix asked, nudging the blood-stained knife into the sewer with his foot.

"Peek-a-boo, trash-trash! Okie-okie?!" Nzo grinned innocently.

Hendrix blinked. "Y-you're not gonna tell on me? W-why?"

Nzo shrugged. "Coz-coz…" He tried to reach for Hendrix's healed wound.

"D-don't!" Hendrix recoiled, but before he could react, Nzo tossed a dirty bib in his face.

"Wipe-wipe, stupid! Blood, okie-okie?!" The channak huffed, suddenly slipping back into his baby boss persona.

Hendrix sighed, defeated, and wiped his face. He had no choice—he had to take Nzo back to his basement and figure out what to do with the unconscious sigbin.

When they arrived, Nzo wandered around, his eyes landing on something unexpected. "Oh, Beth."

There she was, lying peacefully on her bed—clean, beautifully dressed, looking almost as if she had simply dozed off rather than been trapped in an endless sleep.

Hendrix stiffened. "Y-you know her?"

Nzo giggled. "Titties, mimis. okie-okie?"

Hendrix frowned, confused, until it clicked—hanging around Parthena bars meant that sometimes athenas would pacify the channaks by letting them nurse him, even if they had no milk.

Hendrix swallowed hard. "Why are you doing this? I mean... helping me."

Nzo tilted his head, then tugged at Hendrix's hand. "Come, diner. Coffee. Okie-okie!?"

Hendrix hesitated. Then, when Nzo raised both arms, demanding to be carried, Hendrix sighed and lifted the toddler onto his shoulder. "A-alright."

12

Nzo The Channak

"Grandpa! You're here!" Lumen's voice rang out as soon as they stepped inside the coffee shop.

Hendrix froze for a moment before recognition struck. "C... Cathy?! Owww!"

Nzo yanked on his hair. "Lumen-Lumen, okie-okie!?"

Hendrix winced, rubbing his scalp as he looked at the young woman who approached them. She was the spitting image of Cathy, her resemblance almost eerie. He remembered her as baby and a preschooler —Jonathan and Cathy's bloodline finally producing a female heir after generations of grandsons. It was a huge deal back then.

A wave of guilt washed over him. He had drifted too far from his human friends, choosing instead to drown himself in the Isla de Parthena bars. It had been his refuge ever since he started drinking—though being around a perpetually drunk Nzo irritated the hell out of him.

Nzo, on the other hand, observed Hendrix carefully, tasting the air for any sign of danger. As expected, he sensed nothing threatening. But he couldn't help but wonder—was it because Lumen's critical days had already passed?

Unbeknownst to Hendrix, Nzo had secrets of his own.

<><><>

Lumen's birth had been both a miracle and a misfortune. For centuries, their family had only produced male heirs, making her arrival a rare and celebrated event. But she was born at the worst possible time—amid escalating city riots.

Bloodless sigbin, consumed by their jealousy of humans, had been wreaking havoc across Xego for decades, vandalizing the city and endangering human lives. To counter the chaos, Governor Hajji enforced strict lockdowns and began deporting violent sigbin to Zapad and Cintru, stripping them of their Xego citizenship and rights to live on the neutral continent.

Meanwhile, humans were encouraged to flee to Perlaz—especially the berhen, whose distinct scent could drive even the most composed sigbin into a frenzy.

Nzo's family had long practiced this exodus. Long before the sigbin turned into bloodless monsters. His ancestors had sent their Xego-born children to Perlaz, ensuring they were raised with the traditions and values of their Ati tribe.

It was a long-standing custom: his grandsons took wives from Vincot – a place for maidens waiting for their suitors. Granddaughters, if he had any, were to be sent to Perlaz to deepen their faith and preserve their heritage.

But Lumen had been born at a time when escaping to Perlaz was no longer an option. The riots had repeatedly destroyed Xego's only airport and train terminal, making mass travel impossible. Though alternative routes existed, they were treacherous, especially for fragile humans. The chances of reaching Perlaz—or returning from it—had become slim to none.

As the government struggled to restore the City of Ruinae to its former glory, new waves of riots would break out like clockwork, tearing down any progress made. With travel to Perlaz off the table, desperate families sought other means to protect their berhen daughters. Arranged marriages, deflowering clinics, and, in the case of Nzo's family—hiding Lumen.

At first, her parents hadn't been concerned about leaving Xego. But the moment she was born, Nzo and his grandson, Hugo, knew they were racing against time. Now, with Lumen nearing eighteen, her scent was growing stronger—more intoxicating. Sigbin around her were starting to lose control.

And so, for months after discovering Hendrix's secret, Nzo watched him closely. He invited Hendrix to the coffee shop regularly, making sure he spent time near Lumen, her scent lingering in the air between them. He was testing him. Pushing him. Provoking him. Because sooner or later, Hendrix would have to face the truth about his granddaughter. And Nzo needed to know —would he be Lumen's protector? Or her greatest threat?

◇◇◇

"Grandpa, are you sure about this?" Hugo asked again, his voice tight with worry. As a child, he had only fond memories of Hendrix. But now, as a father, he couldn't ignore the unease creeping into his gut. Hendrix wasn't just some old family friend—he was the only sigbin their family had ever asked him to treat as an uncle.

"No, Drix good sigbin. Very good, okie-okie!?" Nzo reassured him, his usual playful tone replaced with rare seriousness. His vocabulary might have been limited, but his conviction was unwavering. They needed help, and Hendrix was their best option to keep Lumen safe.

"Uncle Hendrix can help... how?" Augusta chimed in, concern etched on her face. She had met Hendrix a few times and heard stories about him after marrying into the family—a drunken yet peaceful sigbin, known for his kindness toward humans, especially those in Nzo's clan.

Nzo told them the truth.

He still remembered the blood-stained bib—the first clue that revealed Hendrix's secret. Instead of discarding it, he had soaked it in water, extracting the blood into a cheap plastic gun Augusta had bought for him. Then, the next time a sigbin lurked too close to their shop, drawn by Lumen's scent, Nzo cornered him behind the diner and fired.

It was a gamble. If his experiment failed, he had planned to act drunk, relying on his reputation to keep him safe. No sigbin in Xego would dare touch him—not when he was still known for his close ties to Mr. Hajji. Though, in truth, Nzo never fully trusted the governor. A sigbin who was also Kein's minion? That alone made him dangerous. Nzo's family believed in only one God - Adonai, and Kein would never be a god to them.

The sigbin stumbled upon impact, wavering for a moment before collapsing into a deep, unnatural sleep. Success. With Hugo's help, Nzo dragged the unconscious body to their basement. There was no longer any point in keeping the truth from his family—Hendrix's blood could put sigbin to sleep.

From that moment on, Nzo started thinking ahead. If blood-stained water was enough to knock a sigbin out cold, what would happen if he had Hendrix's pure blood in his arsenal? The possibilities were endless.

And so, Nzo took a calculated risk.

He invited Hendrix to Lumen's 18th birthday party—right when she would be at her most vulnerable. The timing wasn't a coincidence.

It was a test.

A couple of years later, what Nzo didn't know was that Hendrix was also testing Hiro, which was why he agreed to meet again at the arena.

<><><>

Back at the arena, Hiro had to admit—he hadn't expected this. Hendrix, a warrior, a survivor, now sat before him, sobbing uncontrollably. Vulnerable. Broken. For the first time, Hiro stopped struggling. He listened. Because whatever Hendrix had to say—whatever secret he had carried for so long—was enough to bring him to his knees.

And that terrified him.

Through ragged sobs, Hendrix managed to yank Hiro sideways, pulling him free from the trap. Under different circumstances, Hiro might have laughed at the absurdity of Hendrix's tear-streaked face—if he weren't also howling in agony from the deep gashes torn through his flesh.

For a while, they simply sat at the bottom of the pit—one sobbing, the other screaming, both drowning in pain.

Time blurred. Eventually, Hiro's body began to regenerate, his wounds closing as his strength returned. Hendrix, however, remained slumped beside him, shoulders trembling with every quiet sniffle.

Now, seated on their usual grassy spot in the center of the arena, the contrast between them couldn't have been starker. Hiro, fully healed, sat in awkward silence, watching as Hendrix wept like a child beside him.

It was strange.
Hendrix—brash, reckless, unshakable—was breaking right before his eyes.
And for the first time, Hiro didn't know what to say.

In that moment of vulnerability, Hendrix was ready to bare his soul—if he even had one -- much like when Nzo bared his.

<><><>

At first, it was awkward. But when Nzo began wailing like a baby, Hendrix instinctively pulled him into his arms. They sat together on the wet grass in Nzo's front yard, both drenched from the lingering drizzle.

Hendrix had needed air—needed space—after learning the truth about Nzo's secret and his true intentions for helping him. Betrayal burned at the edges of his thoughts, and he had every intention of confronting the channak. But when Nzo followed him outside, sobbing uncontrollably, Hendrix had no choice but to pacify the kid.

It was still Lumen's 18th birthday. He didn't want to be the one to ruin the celebration—not over something he hadn't fully processed yet.
Besides, he'd come to the party feeling… excited. For the first time in years, he felt like he belonged somewhere. It wasn't until much later, as he sat among them, that he realized he was the only guest.

"It's a family dinner, Uncle Hendrix, and you're family to us," Augusta had said, guiding his hand to her forehead in a traditional Perlazian gesture of respect. The sentiment caught him off guard. She looked so much like his mother, yet she—like the rest of them—still considered him their great-great uncle.

Hendrix had smiled then, brushing aside the nagging sense of unease. "Hmm... something smells delicious, Augusta! Now I'm starving," he had exclaimed as she ushered him inside.

Truth be told, with Nzo knowing his secret, a strange weight had lifted. He no longer had to drink himself into oblivion just to cope. A family dinner—being surrounded by warmth and familiarity—was a welcome change from his usual solitude.

But as the night wore on, something felt... off.

Despite the cheerful atmosphere, there was an underlying tension at the table. Nzo, who was usually mischievous and mean-spirited, ate his baby food in silence. Even Augusta and Hugo, who had greeted him so enthusiastically, had grown unusually quiet.

Lumen, however, was different. She remained as bright and bubbly as ever, effortlessly drawing Hendrix in with her breathtaking beauty and infectious charm. But there was something more—something about her that pulled at him in ways he couldn't explain.

The food was delicious, yet strangely unsatisfying. He found himself craving something... more. Something he couldn't quite name.

"Uncle Hendrix, I prepared the dessert! Did it taste good?" Lumen asked, beaming as she pointed at his empty plate.

Hendrix hesitated for a fraction of a second. He didn't even like sweets. But the flan had an oddly familiar taste—one that tugged at his senses, reminding him of something he had been smelling inside Nzo's house all night.

"Yes, it's actually my favorite," he admitted. But even as he spoke, his mind wandered. Was this it? The final dish Augusta had been preparing for hours? He had been expecting something else—something richer, something more... intoxicating.

"Yay! Here, let me give you another serving!"

Lumen leaned in, far too close, and in an instant, her scent hit him like a tidal wave.

It slammed into his senses—overwhelming, intoxicating, undeniable. A low, guttural growl rumbled from deep within his chest before he could stop it.

In a panic, Hugo yanked Lumen behind him, shielding her with his body. At the same moment, Nzo sprang onto Hendrix's lap, clasping both of his cheeks and forcing him to look away from Lumen—forcing him to stare into his wide, baby-like eyes.

"Easy, boy... easy," Nzo murmured, waiting. He expected the monster to come out—a scaly green beast, much like himself and the others.But nothing happened.

Confused, Nzo studied Hendrix carefully. He was certain that the growl would be followed by a violent transformation. Yet, not fully understanding the nature of arousal, the baby failed to recognize the monster that had already awakened—one that was very much alive between Hendrix's legs.

"K-kid...?!" Hendrix's voice was hoarse, almost unrecognizable. His face was turned toward Nzo, but his blazing eyes remained locked on Lumen, who peeked out from behind her parents.

A new kind of hunger twisted inside him—primal, maddening. A need so consuming that, for a terrifying moment, he imagined throwing Nzo across the yard, slaughtering Lumen's parents where they stood, and claiming the berhen for himself.

"Uncle Hendrix will not hurt me. R-right, Uncle?" Lumen's soft voice trembled with uncertainty. She looked so innocent. So beautiful. So weak and easy to—

AGHHHH! Hendrix gritted his teeth, his entire body shaking. He understood now. This was what Nzo had been intending all along.

"Out! Go, okie-okie!" Nzo barked, slapping Hendrix hard across the face. But it wasn't the slap that jolted him—it was Lumen's words.

"Y-yes!" Hendrix was out the door in an instant, running as if his life depended on it.

The farther he got from Lumen, the worse the pain became—an excruciating, twisting agony deep in his core. It felt like someone had kicked him hard in the groin, but worse.

The monster inside him raged. *Now! Two humans and a kid—darn it, Hendrix, get the berhen now! Kill the rest! Shut up. Shut the effing up.*

Outside, Hendrix gasped for air, gulping down the rain-scented night. But it was useless. Lumen's scent still clung to his tongue, tormenting him.

Behind him, Nzo's voice snapped through the doorway. "Lumen, bubble, go!" The door slammed shut. Footsteps squelched through the wet grass as Nzo followed him outside.

Hendrix spun on him, furious, grabbing the baby by his bib and lifting him effortlessly. "What the bloody freaking...crap, kid?!" he snarled, his voice raw. He wanted to rip Nzo apart. Wanted to shake the answers out of him. Why would he do this? Why would he torture him like this?

But Nzo just stared at him—calm, knowing. And that only made Hendrix angrier.

"I know! Help! Hendrix, help, okie-okie?!" Nzo dangled in the air like a rag doll, but somehow, being shaken seemed to help him string his words together. His cry was so raw, so desperate, that Hendrix felt his rage falter.

He had known Nzo for centuries, and never—not once—had he seen him like this. Hopeless. Desperate.

"Come see, look, come, please," Nzo begged between sobs. Hendrix finally put him down and followed the channak's lead.

<><><>

Back on the lawn, with the cool night air clearing their heads, Hugo handed them cans of beer. The short trip to Nzo's basement still haunted Hendrix—rows of sleeping sigbin, lined up like corpses, trapped in a slumber not of their choosing.

"H-how...?" Hendrix knocked back his beer in one go, desperate to dull the whirlwind in his mind.

Nzo explained. The tainted water gun.

"Slow down," Hendrix snapped. Nzo's baby-talk was always hard to follow, but when he got excited, it became pure gibberish.

With some effort, Hendrix pieced together the truth: Water mixed with his blood could put sigbin to sleep—but only for a few days. When they stirred, Hugo and Nzo forced more tainted water down their throats, keeping them sedated.

"Mouth better, skin no-no, Drix blood, you me want. Okie-okie?!" Nzo said, swigging beer from his milk bottle.

Hendrix narrowed his eyes. "So, you're saying you helped me because you need my blood?"

"No. Lumen. Help Lumen. Out Xego, okie-okie!" Nzo's determination was unwavering, his desperation growing.

Hendrix exhaled sharply. "Why don't you just marry her off? Or—heck—take her to a clinic, get someone to take her purity. Problem solved, right?" He regretted the words as soon as they left his mouth. His mind immediately conjured an image—himself doing both.

Darn it. Stop. He shook his head, trying to push the thought away. It was Beth all over again. And he knew exactly how that had ended.

Lumen was human. He was not. This was impossible. Carnage. To steady himself, he tried picturing Lumen as a little girl—innocent, untouchable. Not something to take. Not something to ruin.

"No!" Nzo snapped, cutting through his thoughts. "Help. Lumen go Perlaz, okie-okie!"

Hendrix knew about Nzo's beliefs. Lumen had to marry a man from Perlaz—someone from their tribe, someone who shared their faith. "Don't you know anyone from here who could be her husband?" Hendrix asked, gripping his beer tighter than necessary. "Hugo and his father found their wives here, right? They couldn't go to Vincot because of the riots."

The thought of Lumen marrying someone else stirred something dark inside him. But Hendrix recognized it now—it wasn't him. It was the monster. And the monster wanted Lumen.

"No... looking, but... no, no one." Nzo's voice wavered, his eyes welling up again.

"Scrap your tradition, kid! Just marry her off to any decent human you know. It's the only way to save Lumen!" Hendrix spoke so fast that he spit out some of his drink, his agitation boiling over.

"No. Can't do, okie-okie." Nzo sniffled, his tiny hands clenched into fists. His next words hit Hendrix like a punch to the gut—they would rather accept Lumen's fate.

"What?! You'd rather let her die?" Hendrix's voice was sharp with disbelief.

"Yswh go plan, okie-okie?!" Nzo said, wiping his nose. They'd rather lose Lumen's life than risk her soul.

"What PLAN?!" Hendrix thundered.

Nzo flinched, bracing himself as if expecting a slap. "Darn it, kid! That's bull—effing—crap!" Hendrix raked a hand through his hair, barely keeping his temper in check. "I respect your beliefs—hell, I used to have the same ones, remember?! But I don't buy it anymore. There's no heaven beyond this world, no life after death! If Lumen dies, that's it! She's gone!" His fists were clenched now, shaking with anger at Nzo's stubbornness. His stupidity.

"You, me—no heaven," Nzo mumbled. "Me, human family—yes. You... family... heaven, yes-yes?"

The words caught Hendrix off guard. His parents. Where are they now? For all his disbelief, did he still wish heaven was real? He suddenly realized—he did. He wanted to believe his parents had gone somewhere better. That they hadn't just... vanished.

They had been just like Nzo. Faithful. Devoted. Certain. His throat tightened, but he shoved the thought away.

"How the heck did I not realize Lumen was a berhen before?" Hendrix muttered, more to himself than to Nzo. Hadn't he known all along? Hadn't it been obvious? The way he wanted her from the moment he laid eyes on her—it wasn't just hunger, not like it had been with Beth. It was more. Deeper. Worse. And he had ignored every warning sign.

"Red cycle," Nzo said, his voice small. Hendrix frowned. Nzo explained in his usual broken words—Lumen's scent was strongest before and during her menstruation. For 14 days every month, she was locked inside her room, sealed in a plastic bubble with an oxygen and air-filtration system, preventing her scent from escaping. "Sigbin know...smell okie-okie?!" Nzo sighed.

The ones Hendrix saw in the basement—they had smelled something. Even from the coffee shop, they had sensed it. And their persistence had been dangerous.

Nzo had no choice but to put them down.

Hendrix let out a slow breath. Of course they knew. He knew, too. He almost tore Nzo's family apart trying to get to it.

Nzo continued, his expression dark. As Lumen matured, her scent became stronger. More intoxicating. More irresistible to sigbin. But not to Nzo—he wasn't like them. He had no craving for human flesh. No carnal desires. "Lumen... heat. Bad. Very bad," Nzo murmured.

Hendrix narrowed his eyes. "What do you mean, heat?"

Before Nzo could answer, Augusta returned, placing more alcohol on the table. She met Hendrix's gaze and answered for him.

"It's just a theory, but..." Augusta hesitated, her cheeks flushing. "I think that when Lumen is ovulating, she unconsciously seeks a mate—before and during her... um... red critical days. She's in heat, and her... her human desire smells good. Especially to your kind."

Her voice trailed off, and she quickly looked away.

"Yes, smell soooo good!" Nzo nodded enthusiastically, though he left out a dark truth—even he wasn't immune. Despite having no carnal desires for Lumen, there were times he caught himself imagining things he shouldn't.

—Like Lumen nursing him.

The first time the thought crossed his mind, he had drowned himself in alcohol, sickened by his own mind. Disgusted. "Yes, Lumen soul... very high. Life life— high too!" Nzo's voice cracked. "Me, Nzo fight! She not... she never harm...she...love Nzo love." Tears welled in his eyes, and he broke down before he could finish. Augusta reached out, gently rubbing his grandfather's back. Tears also flooded her eyes.

"You've heard the news, right?" Hugo spoke up, his tone grim. "Crimes against humans are rising—even with the government trying to step in. Grandpa thinks human berhen's are the main targets. Berhen who are trapped here in Xego, especially in the City of Ruinae."

Hendrix frowned. He didn't keep up with the news. Never cared to. "What makes you think berhen are the targets?" He turned to Nzo.

"Nano chips. Okie-okie?!" Nzo growled, his babyish face hardening with anger.

"Grandpa had me search the sleeping sigbin for weapons or tracking devices," Hugo explained. "We kept finding the same nano chips—like they all belonged to the same gang."

"Do you still have them?" Hendrix asked. He could dig into the chips, find out more.

"No. Grandpa told me to burn and toss them—so we couldn't be traced."

"Oh! But you took photos, remember?" Augusta perked up.

"Right. Let me get them." Hugo and Augusta hurried inside, leaving Hendrix alone with Nzo.

The baby looked up at him, eyes desperate. Pleading. "Gang... berhen kill... Lumen target. Hendrix, help!" Nzo crawled onto Hendrix's lap and clung to him, sobbing.

"K-kid... I just don't know how..." But before he could finish, Nzo wailed. And for the first time, Hendrix felt it. The sheer hopelessness. The desperation. The fear. The tiny body trembling against him wasn't just some annoying, talking baby. Nzo was terrified.

And Hendrix—he had no idea what to do. He was used to looking out for himself. Survival. Fighting his own inner demon.

But this?

Messing with someone else's problems? This was a whole new kind of nightmare.

"P-please, Hendrix! Save me family, pleaseeeee..." Nzo's scream ripped through the night, raw with agony, as if his very soul was being torn apart. Hendrix's heart pounded as he glanced at Augusta and Hugo watching from the window, their tear-streaked faces filled with silent horror. The desperation in his own voice made him feel exposed, ashamed.

"A-alright, I'll help you, I promise... but getting Lumen out of Xego— I-I don't know how. It's impossible..." The words tumbled out before he could stop them. He just needed Nzo to calm down.

"Me know...okie-okie?!" Relief softened Nzo's face, and before Hendrix could react, the boy lunged forward, pressing frantic kisses to his cheeks. The sheer desperation of it unsettled him.

"Okay, enough, Nzo... Enough!" Hendrix jerked back, wiping away the snot and the faint, sour scent of spoiled milk from his skin. But Nzo wasn't finished—he was practically vibrating with excitement, his joy overwhelming. Annoyed, Hendrix grabbed the boy by the shoulders and pushed him away.

"Me happy, Hendrix! Nzo happy!" The channak scrambled back onto Hendrix's lap, his gratitude nearly suffocating.

Hendrix exhaled sharply. "Nzo..."

Something shifted. The wild energy in Nzo's eyes dimmed, replaced by something solemn, something ancient. His childlike innocence faded as he spoke again, his voice quiet, but heavy with a lifetime of suffering.

"Me no memry. Me live bad kids. Nzo hurt many-many me hurt. Me no mama... no love-love. Stab drugs... me... Nzo."

Hendrix stiffened. He had heard rumors—whispers of vaccine experiments on street children. When he first met Nzo in Xego, he had looked up the term channak, but the pieces never fully clicked. Until now.

"No milk street... beer, blood, yes-yes. Nzo no-no blood! Yuck." Nzo's voice cracked, his wide eyes glistening. His memories bled into the present, spilling out in broken fragments.

Hendrix could see it now—the desolate streets of Zapad, a place abandoned by mercy. Where children were cast out like garbage. Where survival meant suffering. His stomach twisted as Nzo's words painted a nightmare too horrific to fully grasp.

"Nzo sick... and dead... lots lots me die. Okie-okie?!" The boy sniffled, rubbing his nose with a trembling hand. The weight of it all—years of torment, of dying and coming back only to suffer again—hung between them like a curse.

13

The Truce

Hendrix's chest tightened. He had seen cruelty before, but this? This was relentless. Beaten, tortured, bled, and discarded—Nzo had been forced to endure death over and over again. And for what? In Zapad, children weren't people. They were test subjects. The thought sent a chill down Hendrix's spine.

"In war... sigbin— nasty evil! Bad-bad evil, right-right?!" Nzo searched his face, his eyes pleading for confirmation. Hendrix, a self-centered nomad with no memory of the war, simply nodded, unwilling to shatter what little trust Nzo had in him. "sigbin... get Nzo home playing-playing... then poof, no more. Nzo trash-trash gone outside." His voice wavered, barely above a whisper.

The sobs came next—quiet, broken. The kind that never truly stops, only gets buried beneath time. Sigbin had once cared for him. But like everything else in Nzo's life, that, too, had ended. Leaving him abandoned. Again.

The pain in Nzo's voice was raw, woven into every word like an unshakable shadow. Hendrix felt it pressing against his chest, heavy and suffocating. He wished he could do more—say something, fix something—but all he had to offer was his ear and the promise of his help.

"Hah! That's because you've got some serious attitude, kid." Hendrix smirked, hoping to lift the weight between them.

Nzo blinked, then let out a small, hesitant laugh, sniffling as he wiped at the snot smeared across his face—only to spread it even more.

"If it were me, I wouldn't adopt your stinky ass!" Hendrix teased, grimacing as he glanced at the mess.

The baby giggled mischievously and, before Hendrix could react, wiped his boogers onto his arm.

"Gross! Nzo!" But Hendrix couldn't bring himself to be mad. The kid was trying, in his own way, to move past the pain.

Nzo appreciated the effort. It was hard—digging up his past, saying it out loud. Even with Hendrix, who had been nothing but kind, it felt like walking barefoot over broken glass. But somehow, Hendrix always knew how to make things feel... lighter.

"You Nzo... you me like!" Nzo shifted into an exaggerated baby pose, his eyes wide, his lips pursed in an over-the-top coo-coo.

Hendrix snorted. "What the heck was that?" Then it clicked—Nzo must have picked it up from the adoption center, where he had been placed after Kein's grand promise to rebuild the world, to make it better for sigbin.

Hendrix burst into laughter, a deep, genuine sound. It was the first time he'd seen this side of Nzo—goofy, playful, free. His way of charming sigbin or humans to adopt him, even temporarily.

Inside the house, Augusta and Hugo watched in silence. Their eyes were still red, their bodies still tense from everything that had happened. But as they saw the two sigbin laughing together, so carefree despite everything, something in them eased.

"They're drunk," Augusta murmured.

"Let them be," Hugo replied, his voice soft with something close to hope.

Outside, Nzo's laughter slowly faded. His expression shifted, something deeper settling into his features.

"Then Nzo—me—see human famly." His voice grew quiet. Serious.

Hendrix listened intently as Nzo spoke of Henrietta and Silas, the human couple who had shown him kindness even during the war. They had smuggled him into Perlaz as a refugee, offered him a home.

"Nzo love-love me. Me human son. Yes, okie-okie!" His face lit up with pride, even as silent tears slipped down his cheeks. They had other children after Nzo, but to keep suspicions at bay, they had introduced him as their grandfather.

Hendrix stilled. This was the first time he learned that Nzo had no blood relation to Lumen or anyone in his supposed family. The revelation hit him harder than he expected.

But looking at Nzo now, beaming despite his tears, Hendrix couldn't deny it—this was one of the happiest memories Nzo had.

"Then three world..." Nzo hesitated on the last word, struggling with the pronunciation.

Perlaz had been declared a human sanctuary. Nzo could no longer stay. His family had no choice but to send him beyond the border—either to join the channak warriors or migrate to Xego, the only place where humans and sigbin could live together.

And so, Nzo left. He could still remember the meeting, the way his family had gathered, nearly a thousand years ago, to decide his fate. A fate that had never truly been in his hands.

"Nzo—me go border—yes-yes?!" he had told Eka, Henrietta and Silas's great-great-granddaughter. He had long since grown used to being cast aside. But this time, it was different. This time, he wasn't being thrown away—he was choosing to leave. And yet, the years he had spent with his human family remained a gift he would always cherish.

"No, Grandpa! You can't live apart from us!" Martie, Eka's son, had protested, his voice breaking with desperation.

Nzo sniffled, his small hands gripping Hendrix's sleeve as if grounding himself in the memory. "Nzo family want, Hendrix... no more trash-trash Nzo, love-love!?" he whispered. His voice cracked, the words dissolving into a sob. But instead of grief, what followed was a quiet, trembling cry of happiness.

For the first time, he had been truly wanted.

Hendrix took a long swig of his beer, unsure of what to say. The weight of Nzo's emotions pressed against his chest, and for once, he didn't have some sarcastic remark to lighten the moment. A lump formed in his throat. He swallowed hard, but the heaviness remained.

Nzo kept talking, his words tumbling out between sniffles. He told Hendrix how his family had eventually decided to migrate to Xego—at least half of them—to stay by his side. They had accepted Mr. Hajji's offer of protection, using Nzo's existence as proof that humans and sigbin could build something together.

"Me, family... no Perlaz. Leave-leave coz me—Nzo. Love-love me," Nzo sobbed into Hendrix's shoulder, his body shaking with gratefulness that his family would leave Perlaz just to be with him.

Hendrix tightened his grip around the kid, holding him close. He had no words—just this. The quiet, unspoken comfort of being there. And somehow, in the midst of all that sorrow, they started laughing.

Nzo mimicked the voice of one of his grandsons, a voice Hendrix had never heard before. "No! You're family, Grandpa! We stay! Stop drinking!"

Hendrix chuckled, watching Nzo shift effortlessly between childlike innocence and perfect imitation. The kid spoke so clearly when mimicking the adults who had shaped his life.

"Family love Nzo. Me wipe drunk ass, love me scrap...crap diaper, me Nzo, love-love." His words were slurred but genuine, spoken with the conviction of someone who still couldn't quite believe he was loved.

Hendrix shook his head, laughing even as tears clung to his lashes. The absurdity of it all—crying, drinking, laughing—it was a mess. A beautiful, heartbreaking mess.

Then Nzo's expression crumpled again. "Crap, why? Famly? Why love-love Nzo? Okie-okie?!" His voice trembled, his small fists clenching in frustration. "Me trash-trash. Famly say me 'important'... me high... big value famly. But why? Why Nzo? Okie-okie?!" The question hung in the air, suffocating in its weight.

Hendrix exhaled slowly, gripping his bottle tighter. He didn't know the answer. He had no perfect words, no wisdom to offer. But he knew what it felt like—to question your worth, to feel like you weren't enough.

Nzo sniffed, his breath hitching as he spoke again, his voice barely above a whisper. "Lumen important... high big value. You see? I can't! Lumen no die. She me family...okie-okie?!" And then, like a dam breaking, it all came pouring out. "Me dead, yes. Save me family. Lumen important—big value! I give me life. Lumen! Okie-okie?!" His sobs came harder now, his small body trembling against Hendrix's.

Hendrix felt his own throat tighten. Because, despite the chaotic mess of words, he understood. More than he wanted to. Because deep down, no matter how much he tried to bury it, he knew—he'd do anything for his family too.

Even if it meant giving up everything.

<><><>

From that moment on, Hendrix's blood became the unspoken weapon in their fight to protect Lumen. It fueled Nzo's strength—both in defense and in attack. Side by side, they stalked the shadows, hunting down any sigbin who dared show even the slightest interest in Lumen.

The quiet hum of suspicion grew in Xego, and soon, rumors of missing sigbin began to circulate. But no one suspected where those missing sigbin had gone. They were resting in the basement of Hendrix and Nzo's hideaway, lying in an uneasy slumber.

The duo knew they had to act swiftly. Every moment brought them closer to discovery. A plan was forming, but time was slipping through their fingers. They had to smuggle Lumen out of Xego before anyone unearthed their carefully guarded secret.

Neither of them knew at the time that Hiro would play a crucial role in helping Lumen. Establishing that role was essential if only Hendrix could convince Hiro before they left the arena.

<><><>

Back at the arena, Hiro was no longer trapped in the pit. He was healed, his strength returned, and he could have easily lunged at Hendrix. But instead, he remained seated, his frame trembling with emotion. The once-proud alpha sigbin was now reduced to tears, sobbing uncontrollably, his shoulders wracked with pain.

"Please, my brother... help me... Zov... please," Hendrix pleaded, his voice breaking as tears streamed down his face. Hiro couldn't bear to witness his best friend in such a raw, vulnerable state.

"Enough! Stop crying, you're freaking me out!" Hiro snapped, the words sharp as he tried to choke back his own emotions. He clenched his fists, tempted to silence Hendrix's cries by force, but he stayed still, his internal battle raging.

"A truce... a real truce—for Lumen," Hendrix managed to say, his voice barely more than a whisper, but the weight of the request was undeniable.

Hiro exhaled deeply, his mind drifting to the scent of Lumen—her memory lingering in his thoughts. Was Hendrix pursuing her with the same intent he had? Hiro kept that question locked in his chest, unwilling to voice the suspicion.

"Why bother helping her at all?" Hiro asked, his tone feigning annoyance, though a flicker of curiosity betrayed him.

"Why do you?" Hendrix countered, his voice sharp, mirroring the same unspoken question. He stared at Hiro, searching for any hint of what truly motivated him.

◇◇◇

Hiro's mind wandered back to the first time he had returned to Nzo's coffee shop after centuries of absence. Since his falling out with Hendrix, he'd only returned to Xego for business, avoiding his former friend at every turn—whether they crossed paths in the office or around the City of Ruinae.

It was petty, perhaps, but Hendrix's refusal to fight him in the arena, despite Hiro's constant badgering, even begging, had cut deeper than he was willing to admit. Like most men, Hiro wasn't one to show the emotional storm brewing inside him, but the arena had always meant something more. It was a bond, a space where he wasn't alone. No matter what, Hendrix would always be there, standing by him.

The arena and Hendrix had once been his salvation, his anchor in a world full of chaos. But now, both had abandoned him.

That was the moment Hiro had truly accepted what he was—a bloodless sigbin with insatiable hunger for berhen. That was when he'd sworn, silently and resolutely, never to depend on anyone again, human or sigbin, for the next thousand years.

Yet, as he walked past the familiar coffee shop that day, the scent of roasted beans and warm spices hit him like a jolt of forgotten emotion. It was the smell of Cathy.

Nostalgia tugged at him, a force he couldn't ignore. Against his better judgment, he stepped inside, knowing he would be a stranger to everyone—except, perhaps, for Nzo.

"Mr. Hajji, it's been a long time."

Hiro hadn't expected anyone to recognize him. "H-Hello," he managed, his voice faltering at the warmth in the greeting.

The man introduced himself as Hugo. As Hiro studied him, he saw the same quiet strength in his eyes—the same fire that had always burned in Cathy's bloodline.

"I've seen your pictures in our old family albums," Hugo said with a smile. "And, of course, you and your father are pretty famous around here."

With a casual ease, Hugo led Hiro to the best seat in the house. For the first time in centuries, Hiro felt something stir within him—an unfamiliar warmth, an instant fondness.

But then, the door to the kitchen opened. Lumen stepped out, her presence like a sudden shift in the air. Hiro froze, his heart lurching in his chest. For the first time in an eternity, it felt as if his heart was truly beating again, though it ached with an intensity he hadn't known in centuries.

Cathy. She was standing before him.

Hugo, oblivious to the storm raging inside Hiro, introduced the young woman. "This is Lumen. People say she's the spitting image of our great-great-great-great-grandmother, Cathy."

But Hiro barely heard him. Because standing there, smiling, alive—was the woman who had once seen him as the hero he had always longed to be.

"Lumen, this is Uncle Hiro... a family friend," Hugo said with a calm confidence, introducing the stranger who had just stepped into their lives.

Hiro barely registered the words. Lumen was approaching, carrying his coffee, and his world stopped. Her presence was like an echo of a time he had long buried.

He had thought it was the coffee that had drawn him in when he passed by, but now he knew the truth. It wasn't the drink—it was her. This breathtaking berhen, standing before him, looked exactly like Cathy, the love of his life.

Lumen smiled, a soft and sweet expression that mirrored Cathy's in a way that made Hiro's chest tighten. "Oh, I k-know... I've seen pictures... with Grandma Cathy."

Hiro's breath hitched, and for a moment, his self-control teetered on the edge. The resemblance was striking, but it wasn't just her face. It was the scent—warm, intoxicating, unmistakably berhen. It filled the room, washing over him and eclipsing even the rich aroma of coffee.

He felt a surge of primal instinct, and for a split second, his body trembled as though he might transform right there, in the middle of the shop.

Even after Cathy had grown frail and old, Hiro had always returned to her side. She had been his refuge, the one person who knew him completely, the one person who never judged him. She had been his mother, his confidante—his heart.

But Cathy was gone. And here stood Lumen, an echo of a past he hadn't realized he'd mourned until now.

Hiro's heart thudded in his chest, erratic and unfamiliar. His fingers curled involuntarily, digging into his palm as he forced himself to remain still, to breathe through the storm of emotions threatening to drown him.

I want her.

The thought was raw, unbidden, and dangerous. His gaze followed Lumen as she moved behind the bar, and a flood of long-buried emotions surged up, nearly consuming him.

For the first time in centuries, Hiro felt something so deep, so raw, that it almost paralyzed him. An aching, undeniable longing. Just as he was teetering on the edge of something he didn't know how to handle, Nzo's entrance broke the moment.

It wasn't unusual for Nzo to stumble around drunk, but seeing him clutch a toy gun strapped to his diaper was absurd enough to draw a reluctant laugh from Hiro. Sure, the channak's RPG game had taken the market by storm and made him a fortune—but still... did the toddler really have to parade around like that? It was just pathetic.

"Hey, kid! Long time," Hiro chuckled, his eyes glinting with amusement as he looked at the ridiculous toy gun. The channak had never quite acted like a child before, and it was almost endearing in a way.

Nzo, half-lidded and unimpressed, simply stared back at him, his gaze blank. Hiro laughed again. As always, the little gremlin didn't give him the time of day.

He took a sip of his coffee, savoring the warmth as his attention returned to Lumen, though he remained careful not to draw attention to himself. Her scent lingered in the air, subtle but undeniable. Most sigbin wouldn't have noticed it, but Hiro had been around berhen long enough to understand their scent cycles—the fluctuations that marked their strongest periods.

And he knew, with a certainty that rattled him, exactly where on Lumen's body that scent would be most potent. He gripped the cup tighter, his knuckles white, fighting against the instincts threatening to take over.

Control yourself, boy. He forced himself to take another sip, allowing the heat of the coffee to ground him, to distract him from the rising tide of his emotions.

Then—

"Inside! Now!" Nzo's sudden snarl tore through the café, snapping Hiro to attention. Augusta immediately grabbed Lumen, her movements quick and decisive, ushering her into the kitchen and slamming the door behind them.

Hiro's gaze darted to the entrance. Elliad. And his men. Crap. Ehud's hellspawns. Hiro's instincts flared—Lumen was already marked. These bastards wouldn't stop until she was in Ehud's hands.

The atmosphere inside the café thickened with tension. Nzo, now fully sober, crouched on top of the bar, tiny hands gripping his toy gun.

"Get out!" one of the sigbin barked, his voice full of venom. The human customers scrambled, fear in their eyes as they fled the café.

Hiro remained seated, unmoving in the farthest corner, his eyes fixed on the door. Elliad took a slow step toward the bar.

THUNK.

A blade whizzed through the air, burying itself deep into Elliad's left eye. The sigbin let out a guttural scream, his body convulsing as he shifted into his monstrous form.

Nzo's rage ignited. An open attack—in his bar? The hellspawns had always been careful, lurking from a distance, but now they were getting reckless. Too bold. Where the hell was Hendrix?

"What the effing—KID!" One of Elliad's men lunged at Nzo.

Big mistake.

The channak leapt into the air, landing squarely on the sigbin's shoulders before dropping to the floor with a brutal grace. His tiny hands gripped a bread knife, and he didn't hesitate. A piercing scream cut through the air as the sigbin collapsed, clutching his groin, writhing in agony.

Another hellspawn charged from behind, but Nzo spun mid-air, his blade slashing through the sigbin's throat before delivering a flying kick that sent the body hurtling through the café doors.

Hiro raised an eyebrow, sipping his coffee as if this were an everyday occurrence. Brutal little bastard.

Nzo perched on a ceiling beam, eyes scanning the remaining three sigbin. His fingers tightened around his toy gun. He hated using it in broad daylight, but if these bastards didn't leave...

"Go get the girl. I'll deal with this little rodent," Elliad growled, his left eye already regenerating, though the damage was far from fixed.

Nzo aimed his gun just as one of the sigbin leaped over the bar, heading straight for the kitchen. "NO!" Nzo shouted, desperate to protect Lumen.

For a split second, he was distracted, and that was all Elliad needed. The bastard lunged, grabbing Nzo's leg and yanking him down with a brutal jerk.

THUD.

Nzo's gun slipped from his hand, skidding across the floor. Three sigbin pounced on him. Nzo struggled beneath their weight, his breaths quickening as panic began to rise.

No... Then— SPLAT.

Something smashed into two of the sigbin's heads with sickening force, sending them crashing to the ground.

"What the—?!" Elliad's eyes widened in horror as he took in the sight of his men—headless, twitching, still banging against the kitchen door like broken puppets. Their severed heads rolled across the floor, dragging with them strands of torn muscle and shredded vertebrae.

Nzo took his chance, stabbing Elliad in the kidney. The sigbin howled in pain, stumbling back. The channak scrambled for his fallen gun, but before he could reach it, someone grabbed him from behind and tossed him onto the bar. Nzo struggled, but when he looked up and saw who it was, he froze.

Hiro.

Elliad, still reeling from the attack, ripped the knife from his side, preparing for another strike. But then his gaze locked onto Hiro. His breath caught. "M-Mr. Hajji..." The words faltered in his throat.

Time seemed to slow as Elliad's eyes flickered between Hiro and the kitchen. He knew. He knew a berhen was hiding back there.

But Hiro didn't move. Instead, he tossed something at Elliad's feet. Two severed heads, rolling and stopping at his boots. "Leave. Now," Hiro commanded, his voice low and final.

Elliad blinked, momentarily stunned, before backing away. He glanced at his remaining men, but without another word, he and his crew turned and fled, vanishing into the streets of Xego.

The silence that followed was suffocating.
Then—
"What the heck, kid?! Why the heck are you keeping a berhen in Xego?!" Hiro's voice cut through the stillness, sharp and demanding.

Nzo, still catching his breath, glared up at him. He wasn't afraid, but the weight of Hiro's words made something shift inside him. He knew, without a doubt, Hiro was no longer just a bystander in this mess.

Hiro's mind was racing fast, liked it or not, he had to help Lumen—Ehud and his men would never leave a precious berhen like her in peace.

<><><>

1925 AB -- A gentle drizzle began as Hendrix and Hiro sat on the grassy field of the arena, each raindrop echoing the quiet tension between them.

Why are you helping Nzo's family? Hendrix's question echoed in Hero's mind. "Because I can," he replied, his voice calm and unwavering as he met Hendrix's gaze. It was a simple answer to a question far more complex.

Hiro had the power, the influence, and the means to make it happen. Hendrix knew it, and though it grated on him, he couldn't deny the advantage of having Hiro on their side, especially now that Hiro knew Nzo's secret.

The silence between them was thick, almost suffocating.

Finally, Hendrix spoke, his voice rough, edged with an emotion Hiro wasn't prepared for. "I'm helping them because they're family to me," he said, his words slow and weighted. "Just like you're my family."

The word hit Hiro like a physical blow. Family.

It felt like a sharp twist in his chest, an unexpected surge of something raw and painful. The walls he'd spent centuries building—walls of anger, distrust, detachment—began to crack, bit by bit. He had fought so hard to keep his distance, to hold on to his bitterness, but now... now, it was slipping through his fingers.

"I'm sorry I disappointed you," Hendrix continued, his voice faltering, the emotion thickening. "You're the only family I have left in this lifetime. You and Nzo. I'd do anything to protect both of you. I don't want to lose you, Zov."

Hiro's heart tightened as Hendrix took a shaky breath.

"I need your help." Hendrix's words hung in the air, heavy with the weight of everything unsaid. Hiro didn't respond immediately. He couldn't. The sight of Hendrix breaking down—his broad shoulders shaking, his face twisted in agony—left him speechless.

Hendrix had been living in this world alone. No immortal father to guide him. No hand to catch him when he stumbled. No safety net. He'd been forced to navigate everything, to carry the burden of his own existence without the comfort of a family. And Hiro... Hiro had expected him to always be there, always strong, always dependable, without ever offering the same in return.

Hendrix's voice trembled again, but this time, he shared something he had never spoken aloud before. "My father said my sister deserved the vaccine more than I did."

Hiro's breath hitched, the air around them suddenly heavier.

"As a nurse, she had more to offer the world than some useless gamer like me." Hendrix's voice cracked, his bitter laugh hanging in the air like smoke. "It hit me hard, Zov. I woke up that day not caring about anything. Just myself. My father looked at me like I was nothing. A waste of space. So I decided to live up to his expectations."

His hands curled into fists, his knuckles white as he remembered the pain. "That's why I didn't care about the wars –the humans dying.

The sigbin tearing each other apart. All I cared about was the game. My game. My own darn conveniences." The bitterness was raw, cutting through his voice like a knife. And for the first time, Hiro saw the depth of Hendrix's pain—the way it had scarred him, leaving marks that even time couldn't erase.

"I hated my father for making me feel like I was a monster." The words were a final crack, a release of years of buried hurt. Hendrix's face crumpled, his walls falling apart in front of Hiro. The sobs came suddenly, unrestrained, his body trembling with the force of them.

For the first time, Hiro truly understood.

14

The Marriage Proposal

Hiro understood because he, too, had lived with the weight of guilt. The guilt of the lives he had taken. The hearts he had torn apart. No matter how many centuries passed, no matter how many masks he wore, the guilt never faded. It was always there, lurking in the corners of his mind.

For the first time in centuries, Hiro's own tears threatened to escape. The walls around his heart, so carefully constructed, cracked under the weight of his own emotions.

He, too, felt like a monster. And in that moment, both of them were no longer just warriors, just survivors. They were two broken souls, trying to find their way in a world that had never been kind.

Before meeting Hendrix, Sofia was Hiro's everything—his lover, his mentor, and his confidant. Together, they had reveled in the forbidden, savoring the thrill of defying what others feared. They had shared countless berhen hearts, bonding over the carnage, over their shared hunger. Then Hendrix had entered his life, and everything shifted. With a simple introduction to gaming—and Cathy—Hiro's world began to change.

Hendrix's friendship reignited something deep within him. Hiro found himself rediscovering his humanity, realizing there was more to life than just destruction. He built his own empire and began to dream of making his father proud.

The same man who had once viewed humans as mere consumable commodities now found himself captivated by Cathy's kindness and humanity. For the first time in centuries, Hiro's heart shifted, learning to respect and value human lives again.

But Hiro never knew that Hendrix, with his innate goodness and kindness, was grappling with the same darkness. Hendrix saw himself as a monster, just as Hiro did.

When Hiro lost his blood and retreated into a cave of rage and confusion, he couldn't turn to Hendrix. Instead, he found his way back to Sofia's arms, to his old ways, to the comfort of his monstrous instincts. Without his blood, without Cathy's life to anchor him, and with Hendrix refusing to fight alongside him again, Hiro spiraled. He gave in to the monster, indulging in the pleasure of hunting innocent humans. His thirst for berhen hearts returned, and he blamed Hendrix for everything—how pathetic.

But deep down, Hiro knew the truth: he was the one who allowed himself to succumb to darkness. It was his own choices that led him here, no one else's.

When Hiro finally came to terms with it, it was as though a plank had been removed from his eyes. He finally saw Hendrix clearly—the pain, the loneliness, the bitterness they both shared. They weren't just friends; they were spirit-brothers, bound not by blood but by the experiences they had weathered together.

"Wh-what changed?" Hiro wiped his eyes quickly, not wanting Hendrix to see his tears.

Hendrix spoke softly, his voice rough with emotion. "I went home that day determined to stay out of Nzo's mess... but I found myself staring at old family photos. Ones I'd kept hidden for so long. I remembered my parents' faces, my sister's... and the last words my mom whispered to me before I lost consciousness. She told me she was proud of me." Hendrix sniffed quietly, the ache of lost love and family clear in his voice.

Hendrix didn't mention the old video he found, one that had been buried in his archive for years.

It was from a time when he was younger, playing games in his room while his father came home with dinner. Hendrix had forgotten to turn off the camera that had been set up to record his gameplay. What had started as a simple dinner had escalated into an argument about his future.

Hendrix had excused himself, unable to bear the weight of his father's constant push for him to become a doctor.

"What I'm trying to say is... I'm proud of the man you've become," his father's voice echoed in the video, unaware he was being recorded. "I wanted you to be a doctor, but I'm proud of you for standing up for yourself, for choosing your dream. I just want you to know... I'm proud of you, son."

Hendrix's father continued, his words filled with quiet emotion. "I'm sorry if I can't say this properly. I know you're helping people in your own way. Your games—those RPGs or whatever—they're teaching kids critical thinking. They're giving them hope in a world stuck in this endless pandemic. That's what you're doing, son. Helping people in your own way."

The video had been a turning point for Hendrix. It wasn't about Nzo's manipulation, or the secret Hendrix had to keep. It was about his family—his blood, his legacy—and the knowledge that helping others was part of who he was, part of the man his father had hoped he would become.

"I'm not just doing this for Nzo," Hendrix admitted, his voice steady. "I'm doing this because I can. Because helping others is in my blood. It's who I am, who my family was." He glanced at Hiro, his eyes softening. "That's why I'm here with you now, Zov."

Hiro stood up abruptly, shaking off the emotion that had begun to rise in him. "Fine. A truce then." Enough with the drama. He didn't want to drown in it. Not now, not anymore.

Hendrix stood beside him, his red-rimmed eyes still lingering with unshed tears, but a smile tugged at his lips. "...And a drink?" he asked, his tone lighter now, the weight of everything they had said hanging in the air between them.

Hiro grinned and pulled Hendrix into a tight hug. At that moment, it felt like coming home. He didn't need words. They both understood. The weight of their shared past was still there, but they were standing together, stronger than ever.

"Yeah, a drink," Hiro agreed, voice thick with emotion he didn't want to unpack just yet. But for the first time in a long while, he felt something like peace.

"...and a toast," Hendrix continued.

"For Lumen." "For Nzo's family." They spoke in unison. Hendrix pretended not to hear the longing thick in Hiro's voice, but a pang of jealousy struck him to the core.

It was confirmed then—they shared the same feelings for Lumen. Beyond the mission to save her, there was a deeper, unspoken motive: a desire to keep her alive for more than just duty.

"For Nzo's family..." Hiro corrected, as if downplaying what he truly felt.

Too late, Hendrix realized the truth. But what unsettled him more was the question lingering in his mind—what if...? What if Hiro discovered the secret he and Lumen had been keeping from everyone—even Nzo?

◇◇◇

Ehud entered the chaotic office, his gaze sweeping across the cluttered space. Gadgets lay haphazardly in piles, tangled electrical wires snaked across the floor, and empty food wrappers scattered on every available surface.

The stark contrast between the mess and the supposed workspace made him wrinkle his nose, but he had learned to overlook the disorder. As long as the job got done, he didn't mind the state of things.

"Hey, I have a job for you," Ehud called out, voice steady as he stepped further inside.

The woman didn't even glance up from her computer. "Alright, boss."

Ehud's eyes narrowed, his patience testing the limits of the situation. "W-wait, have you heard anything about Jared's boys? Lyndon's gang? Where are they?"

He tossed a crumpled food wrapper into the trash before claiming a chair for himself. He didn't expect an immediate answer, but he wanted to make sure she was focused.

"Still tracing their chips, boss. I'll call you once I have something," the woman responded without missing a beat, raising her hand in a gesture that suggested she was close to finishing whatever task was occupying her attention.

Ehud didn't have time for small talk. "Anyway, there's a berhen in Xego that I need," he said, tossing a file into the air and watching it land on her desk with a soft thud.

She skimmed through the file he had sent, then turned back to him with an eyebrow raised. "What do you want me to do?"

"Mr. Hajji will call you soon and give you the details," Ehud replied, his eyes inadvertently lingering on the woman's striking deep hazel eyes as she finally turned to face him. Despite her unkempt appearance, there was something undeniably attractive about her, though he wished she'd take a bit more care in her own presentation.

"Oh, which one? The father or the son?" she asked, her voice light, teasing.

"What do you think?" Ehud responded, a slight smile playing at the corners of his lips.

She gave him a knowing look, the edge of a smirk appearing. "Oh, the berhen. Right. Wasn't it him who orchestrated the destruction of the airport to trap all the berhen in Xego?"

Ehud let out a low laugh, shaking his head. "I don't know what you're talking about," he said with a wink, his tone playful despite the seriousness of their work.

She stretched lazily, then shrugged, "I guess it's harvest time, huh?"

"Maybe," Ehud replied, his tone turning businesslike once more. "Anyway, Hiro wants a very special berhen from Xego. Help him make it happen, alright?" He stood up, ready to leave.

Vahitna stood up as well, stretching her arms overhead. As she did, Ehud's eyes briefly flicked to her blouse, where a telltale milk stain spread across the fabric. She didn't seem to notice, or perhaps she didn't care. With a small sigh, she loosened her brassiere, and more milk spilled out, dripping onto her blouse.

"I'll clean up. Sorry, boss. I've just got a lot on my plate," she muttered, noticing the slight grimace on Ehud's face. Her tone carried an apologetic edge, but it was clear she wasn't overly concerned with her condition.

Ehud didn't respond immediately, his gaze fixed on her as she adjusted herself. The situation felt awkward, but he wasn't one to comment on personal matters. "Just get it done," he said curtly, turning to leave without another word.

<><><>

Meanwhile at Perlaz, the channaks, hukluvans, and brigada had gathered inside Bufe's cave for an emergency meeting, the air thick with urgency.

"Reeva... tell us what's happening?" Bufe's voice was steady but tense as he looked at Vhinoe, who was describing the presentation she was showing them.

Reeva projected her findings onto the screen, her expression serious. "We've discovered why some villagers refuse to send their berhen to Vincot. They're marrying them off through a marriage matching app called Bersig, found on the dark web."

The room fell into a stunned silence as the report flashed on the screen, outlining how the app could be accessed and downloaded. Bufe furrowed his brow, trying to make sense of the revelation.

"But the berhen aren't marrying humans in Xego or Perlaz," Reeva continued, advancing to the next slide. "They're marrying sigbin from Zapad."

Vhinoe's voice added gravity to the situation. "This is the key finding from Reeva's investigation."

A wave of violent gasps and growls echoed through the room. The elders and leaders—humans and sigbin alike—stared at the screen in disbelief.

"There must have been a leak in our security system," Bufe exclaimed, his voice low and dangerous.

"I can assure you, there's no issue with airport security," said the channak in charge of transportation security, standing firm. "No berhen can leave unless it's through Vincot, especially since Xego's airport and terminal are closed."

"Then it's a break in our border system," one hukluvan said, his voice edged with confusion. "But how? Flying is the safest way to leave Perlaz."

"Or we have traitors in our organization," another channak suggested, his tone laced with suspicion.

"This is a serious issue," one hukluvan added, his voice growing more urgent. "Not only are the berhen trapped in Xego, but now we have this situation with the app. We need to act fast."

Reeva raised her hand, signaling for calm. "I have a lead. A powerful individual in Zapad seems to be behind this."

Bufe's fists clenched. "It may lead back to Kein!" he said, slamming his cane against the floor with a sharp crack. The thought of that hellspawn filled him with fury. He had always suspected Kein's involvement. Pretending to protect humans was just a cover for whatever darker plot he was hatching.

"Maybe," Reeva said, her voice steady. "But we need evidence that this goes all the way to Cintru."

Vhinoe's eyes narrowed. "Who's your lead, then?"

"A sigbin hellspawn known in Zapad as Ehud." Reeva's words were grave, sending a chill through the room.

"What are these berhen thinking?! Marrying a Sigbin?! Don't they value their lives?" Vhinoe, who always led the protection of Berhens traveling to Vincot, couldn't comprehend why humans would fall for the monstrous schemes of the wicked Sigbin.

"Love," Bufe murmured, lost in thought. "The berhen believe that love has the power to turn hellspawns into angels." His gaze drifted as he searched his visions for a glimpse of what the future might hold.

<><><>

Hendrix's relief from the truce he had forged with Hiro in the arena was short lived. As he drank with Hiro at the Parthena, he couldn't shake the thought—Would their brotherhood fracture once again if Hiro ever discovered what had happened between him and Lumen before Hiro came into the picture to help out?

Hendrix stepped inside, expecting Lumen to be safely tucked away in her usual bubble. But the moment he entered Nzo's house, a familiar, mouthwatering scent flooded his senses, and he silently growled.

"Uncle Hendrix!" Lumen's voice was full of excitement, her bright smile cutting through his resolve. It was frustrating—every time he tried to distance himself, she only closed the gap.

"Stay right there," Hendrix said, his voice low but firm. He tried to keep his composure, but it was harder than ever. Lumen was too comfortable around him, too unaware of the danger she put herself in.

"Oh, don't be mean, please," Lumen protested, her voice playful as she continued to approach him.

"It's for your protection," Hendrix insisted, stepping back, his jaw tightening. The urge to pull away, to keep his distance, was stronger than ever.

"But you won't hurt me, Uncle Hendrix. I know you won't!" Lumen's arms wrapped around his neck in an innocent gesture that sent a spike of panic through him. She was too trusting, too innocent to understand how close she was to danger.

"See? My critical days are over, so I'm safe," she added, lifting her face toward him, her long neck exposed like an offering.

Hendrix stopped breathing, his pulse quickening. Her scent—sweet, intoxicating—made his control slip even further.

She didn't realize just how dangerously close she was to crossing a line.

With great care, he removed her arms from around him and stepped back, forcing himself to maintain some semblance of distance. "Where's your grandpa?" he asked, his voice rough.

His mind raced to regain control, to stay focused on anything but the temptation in front of him. They had plans—plans to clean out the basement to make more room for the incoming sigbin. The numbers had grown exponentially over time, and the space was already tight. Nzo's house had become more of a holding area, a place where the consequences of their actions gathered.

"I don't know. Probably buying more alcohol," Lumen said, trailing him further inside the house.

Hendrix's teeth gritted in frustration. "I'll wait outside," he muttered, irritation rising in him. He hated leaving Lumen alone in the house like this. It was Nzo's job to protect her, not to vanish off for a drink. *Darn it! You're killing me, kid.*

"Uncle, wait!" Lumen's hand grabbed his arm before he could step out. Hendrix's jaw clenched, his body tensing as her touch sent heat racing through him. The monster inside him screamed, but he fought it back, forcing his breath to remain steady.

"Look at this," Lumen said, pulling out her gadget with excitement in her eyes. She rattled off a list of things, but only one sentence registered in Hendrix's mind, jolting him from his thoughts.

"W-what?" He repeated, his voice almost hoarse as he tried to process the shock.

Lumen looked him dead in the eyes, her expression serious, and she spoke again, her voice unwavering. "I said—marry me, Uncle Hendrix, and take my virginity away."

Hendrix's world went still, the words echoing in his mind. Every part of him wanted to reject it, to pull away from her, but a sickening feeling settled in his stomach. The monster inside him stirred once again, darker and more dangerous than ever.

<><><>

Before their truce, Hendrix and Hiro had an argument about Lumen being safer among the Athenas of Isla De Parthena Bar. Nzo and his family had closed their diner and started managing the Parthena, which was owned by Hiro. Though Hugo and Augusta were initially uncomfortable with the idea, it began to make sense as time passed.

"They don't smell the same," Hendrix had argued during one of their early meetings, frustration evident in his voice.

"Yes, but at least berhen and athena scents are closely related. Lumen's fragrance is already saturating the diner. Soon, it'll overpower even the strongest coffee aroma," Hiro had countered, his logic undeniably sound.

"A-are you sure it's good for Lumen to be exposed to the athenas' lifestyle?" Augusta asked, clearly uneasy. She knew what athenas did for a living, and the thought of Lumen becoming part of that world unsettled her.

"She'll be in the kitchen most of the time anyway," Hugo had reassured his wife. "We'll also set up a more secure room for her in the basement."

Though reluctant at first, Hugo's words carried a weight of assurance, and the plan was set into motion.

Unbeknownst to them, it was during her time at the bar that Lumen discovered something about herself she hadn't quite understood before. The athenas' lifestyle—though puzzling and foreign—began to stir something within her. The energy, the allure, the atmosphere of the bar... It made her feel a longing, a desire she couldn't explain.

She watched the athenas as they danced and glamorously worked their way up the stage, their skimpy, glittering costumes leaving little to the imagination. Lumen couldn't help but wonder why she had always hidden her own body behind baggy clothes. She started to question the need to keep herself concealed, especially around Hendrix. It was hard to ignore the fact that she wanted him to look at her—really look at her—as a woman.

Her mind flashed back to childhood memories—simpler, yet now tinged with longing. She remembered how, as a small girl, she used to put her tiny hands inside Hendrix's shirt, tracing the colorful tattoos inked all over his skin. She'd follow their intricate patterns all the way to his neck and face.

"Uncle Hendrix, lookit!" she'd say, her voice filled with childish wonder. Hendrix would laugh as she proudly showed him her portraits of him—sometimes drawn in bright, childish colors, sometimes made to look like a buzzing insect.

"Lookit bug-bug!" Nzo would mock, laughing at Lumen's quirky drawings, teasing her until she cried. But Hendrix would always swoop in to comfort her, wiping away her tears and reassuring her.

"No, this is perfect... you're so talented, Lumen," he'd say, and her heart would swell with warmth, her tears forgotten in an instant.

Then one day, Hendrix disappeared from her life. He stopped visiting their house, stopped attending family gatherings at the diner. Lumen, though still young, had felt a pang of loss. When he finally returned just before her eighteenth birthday, her heart soared at the sight of her favorite uncle again.

<><><>

But for Hendrix, things had changed. He had watched Lumen grow from a baby into a young girl, though his memory of her remained hazy, blurred by constant drinking. He remembered holding her in his arms, watching her proudly present the drawings she'd made for him. But as the years went on and his alcoholism took deeper hold, he stopped visiting, drifting away from the family he had once been so close to.

When he finally stepped into the diner after a long absence, he was taken aback. The little girl he had once known had blossomed into a beautiful young woman.

He didn't recognize her at first, unsure of the charming lady who now greeted him with such eagerness and joy. He had never witnessed

Nzo's grandchildren grow into their teens—family tradition dictated they were sent off to Perlaz as children and only returned as adults, preferably married, to manage the diner.

For centuries, Hendrix had only known the male descendants of Nzo. Meeting Lumen as a young lady—a woman—was a revelation. She was no longer the child he had once comforted. She was someone else entirely, someone who, unbeknownst to Hendrix, would change the course of his seemingly meaningless life forever.

On the other hand, ever since Hendrix became one of Lumen's protectors, she made it a point to show him how grateful she was for all his help.

Before Hiro became involved, it was Hendrix and Nzo who took turns guarding Lumen. If Nzo was too drunk to stand, Hendrix ensured that Hugo had enough of his blood to protect her from anyone who might try to harm her.

When it was discovered that Hendrix's blood had no effect on humans, they found a way to extract and dilute it for protection. Lumen would always volunteer to handle the syringe, eager to be close to him. Hendrix, for his part, would stop breathing and brace himself, doing his best to remain still while Lumen did her work. Each time her fingers brushed against his skin, a wave of goosebumps would ripple across his body.

15

The Cursed Ink

Lumen would comfort him like a child after a painful needle shot, her gentle touch soothing his body, yet driving him to the brink of madness. He often found himself wondering what she'd think if she saw him bloodied and battered inside the arena where he used to fight.

He couldn't bring himself to refuse her care, even though every moment with her tested his limits. He liked having her close, perhaps too much. It took all his willpower to ignore the growing tension between them, the monster inside him hungering for her as much as he did.

After serving Hendrix coffee, Lumen would sit beside him, sometimes joining in the adult conversations when permitted. It was hard for Hendrix to watch as she frowned or cried when told to hide or remain in her room, especially during her critical days. He could sense her loneliness, the way she stopped going to school and withdrew from friends to protect her secret.

Lumen, in her own way, was just like him—different, a freak. She didn't deserve it, but it was her reality. Hendrix understood that isolation, that longing for someone to talk to, especially during her most vulnerable moments.

There were times when Hendrix, despite the pain it caused him, allowed himself to be near her. Too near, sometimes. When his body betrayed him, and the lust he kept buried began to rise, he would retreat, excusing himself to take a walk outside, away from her innocent touch and warm smile. It was an agonizing cycle he couldn't break.

Sometimes, when the atmosphere was safe, Lumen would bring out old photographs of Hendrix with her family, asking about his past.

"Here you are again, Uncle Hendrix. You look funny," she'd laugh, holding up a picture from his earlier years. Hendrix couldn't help but join in her laughter. The changing fashions, the eras—his appearance had certainly evolved, and not always for the better.

"That's your great-grandma, Cathy. She was the kindest soul I ever knew," Hendrix would say softly, tracing the photograph with his finger. He remembered the warmth of Cathy and Jonathan when they first welcomed him into Xego, their kindness still clear in his memories.

"You look just like her," Hendrix added, his gaze lingering on Lumen for a brief moment. Her emerald eyes, the freckles scattered across her face—it was uncanny. She resembled Cathy so much that it took Hendrix by surprise.

"She's very beautiful," Lumen said, her tone reflecting admiration as she touched the photo of her great-great-grandmother's long, silky, straight hair.

"Yes," Hendrix sighed, his thoughts clouded as Lumen leaned in closer to admire the photograph with him. Her scent, intoxicating and strong, enveloped him. The proximity was unbearable.

"Am I beautiful too, Uncle Hendrix?" Lumen's voice was soft, innocent, but there was something in the question that stirred something darker inside him. Hendrix recognized the subtle power in her words, the way she unknowingly rattled him with just a glance.

He knew Lumen wasn't playing games. She didn't understand the effect she had on him, how her innocent curiosity could set a sigbin like him on edge. But Hendrix had been with Beth, and he could distinguish seduction from innocence. This—what Lumen was doing—was unintentional. She simply didn't know.

With a forced smile, Hendrix would look away or invite her parents into the conversation, doing his best to regain his composure. It was the only way he could calm himself and suppress the monster clawing for freedom beneath his skin.

<><><>

One day, Lumen joined the argument between Nzo and Hendrix. They were at Nzo's house after putting another sleeping sigbin in the basement.

"No!" The channak growled, the sober mood only fueling his irritability. He had no choice though. He needed all his wits to protect Lumen.

"Come on, you owe me!" Hendrix insisted, chasing the baby outside.

"No owe-owe! Me you owe, okie-okie?" Nzo stomped his foot like a petulant child before sitting on the ground, patting his diaper for his missing pacifier.

They fell into an awkward silence when Lumen sat down next to them on the lawn. "What's up?" she asked, glancing between them. Hendrix was grateful for the open space; it softened Lumen's scent, making it easier to focus.

"I want to make your grandpa an avatar in my new game, but he's being stubborn," Hendrix explained, showing Lumen the sketches he'd made for Nzo's character. Now that Hendrix was sober, he felt inspired again. It was a long-time dream of his to create an RPG based on Nzo, ever since he first met him.

Instead of taking the gadget, Lumen moved closer to Hendrix, sitting near him to look at the sketches and read the game's storyline. The channak RPG featured a character wielding a water gun as a weapon, embarking on a quest to save his imprisoned mother from a dark lord.

"It's perfect, Grandpa, do it!" Lumen's excitement was palpable.

"No! You know no-no." Nzo muttered, sucking his thumb as he searched for his pacifier.

Lumen, feeling insulted, grabbed Nzo and placed him on the nearest outdoor side table.

"What-what?! You know no-no." Nzo struggled, his strength evident, but he held back, not wanting to hurt her. Lumen, undeterred, ripped off his diaper, causing Hendrix to gag from the smell.

"Ew, kid! What the hell! I thought the sigbin in your basement were rotting while they slept. Turns out it's you who smells like a corpse!" Hendrix stood up, stepping away, his face twisted in disgust.

"Eff-eff you! Me no smelly-smelly bad!" Nzo shouted, but he couldn't deny that he felt better after Lumen hosed him down.

"Language, Grandpa!" Lumen scolded. "Who knows nothing now, huh?"

Lumen finished cleaning him up, ignoring Nzo's protests as she dressed him. Nzo was never fond of wearing shirts; he preferred just a diaper, but Lumen insisted. She turned to Hendrix.

"Pin his hands, Uncle Hendrix," Lumen commanded.

"Frick you, bloody-blood freak!" Nzo spat, trying to hit Hendrix, but he ducked with ease, laughing as he avoided the spit. He'd seen that trick before and would never fall for it again.

"Don't piss off the berhen, kid," Hendrix winked at Lumen. She blushed, but Hendrix was too distracted by his banter with Nzo to notice how Lumen looked at him.

Once Lumen was done, Nzo sat fuming in his high chair, ready to throw a tantrum. But before he could, Lumen shoved a fresh pacifier into his mouth, instantly calming him. She gazed at him seriously, her demeanor no longer the playful child's—it was something more authoritative.

Hendrix swallowed hard, unnerved by the shift in Lumen's presence. She was no longer the little girl he once knew; she had blossomed into a woman. And though it disgusted him to admit it, it stirred something dark inside him. The tension was building again, his body reacting despite his will to suppress it. He forced himself to look away, desperately trying to maintain control.

"Listen, Grandpa," Lumen said, her tone firm. "This RPG is the perfect cover for you. Soon, people will wonder why you're always carrying a water gun. If Uncle Hendrix is working on a game about you, they'll think it's part of Hajji Inc.'s newest project, developed by the great Haruki. It'll also give him an excuse to always be around the coffee shop and our house. After all, he's doing research on you."

Lumen's gaze didn't waver from Nzo's, her words carrying weight and authority. Nzo, still sucking his pacifier, looked at her blankly. But Hendrix could only stare at Lumen, the girl who was now a woman, with a deadly combination of beauty and intelligence.

Crap, Hendrix thought to himself. *This is bad. Stop it, Hendrix. Don't think of her that way.* But he couldn't deny it. Lumen was smart, too smart for her own good. She knew how to manipulate a situation, how to make her point clear, and all of it made Hendrix want her more.

And worse yet, the monster inside him celebrated, knowing that soon, Hendrix might be pushed further than he ever expected.

<><><>

In the days that followed, Hendrix was overjoyed. After centuries of begging and persuading, Nzo had finally agreed to be the newest avatar in Hendrix's RPG. He owed it all to Lumen's ingenuity. Now, it was time to plot the story, design the levels, and settle on Nzo's quest as "The Channak Warrior."

Hendrix assembled his team to handle the research, graphics, and coding, but the toughest part was simulating the fights. That's when Nzo jumped on board, taking the lead during their meetings about the game.

The kid became incredibly enthusiastic when suggesting ideas for the ultimate battle simulations.

"Me like titty monster revenge?" Nzo asked, mispronouncing some of the words.

"No," Hendrix replied, puzzled by Nzo's odd choices of words.

"Nzo and boobsie stranglers?"

"No..."

"Mimi island? Me bathing, ocean swim breast milk, then me..." Nzo giggled, proud of his ideas.

"No..."

"Channak fight giant hooties?"

"No..."

"The kid and angry nipples?"

"No!!!" Lumen finally screamed, frustrated by her grandpa's obsession with breastmilk.

Through all this, Hendrix discovered Lumen's knack for digital art and design. Nzo and Hendrix both noticed how much happier and more engaged Lumen was now that she was part of the game development process.

While Hendrix's team worked on the technical side of things, Lumen and Nzo became the core of the fight simulations. They all knew that he bleeds anyway, he could join in on the physical aspect of the simulations.

Lumen was right—the game had become their perfect excuse to spend time together. Hendrix had found a secluded field in the province of Luzon, several miles south of the city of Ruinae.

"This is perfect. We've got all the elements we need here, just like in the arena," Hendrix said, surveying the vast forest he'd transformed into a private estate.

"Why me go forest? Fear-fear me! No! Me no like this!" Nzo grumbled, upset by Hendrix's idea.

"Don't you know your history? You're an abandoned baby. Channaks were cast out. This is the best place for you to live since no one else wants you," Hendrix teased, referencing Nzo's past.

"Effing-effing you, bleeding freak!" Nzo kicked Hendrix, but ended up injuring his own foot. He cried in pain while Hendrix doubled over in laughter, thoroughly enjoying the moment.

Hendrix was having too much fun designing ridiculous obstacle courses for Nzo to navigate during their fight simulations.

"The frick?! Me no want swim sink-sink hole! Me no get out!" Nzo protested after Hendrix described a scene where Nzo would be trapped in a bubbling, monster-infested pit of wet sand.

"The monster's ball-shaped, like your favorite titties," Hendrix explained, trying to keep a straight face as he continued. "You'll have to find a place to hide."

"Crap this!" Nzo grumbled but reluctantly sank into the sinking pit of mud.

Hendrix chuckled quietly, only to stop when Lumen shot him a suspicious look. He quickly straightened up and reminded her, "Just focus on your drawing."

"Okay, Uncle Hendrix, just don't be too obvious that you're pulling all these tricks with Grandpa," Lumen said, her sharp eyes catching on to Hendrix's antics.

Darn it, she's sharp! Hendrix swallowed hard, feeling a deeper attraction to Lumen as the days went on.

To keep up with Nzo's rapid movements during simulations, Hendrix often had to carry Lumen on his shoulder as they ran through the obstacle courses together. It was risky for her, but Lumen enjoyed every moment of it. In Hendrix's arms, she felt safe, happy, and loved.

<><><>

"Dang! Who's your new artist, boss? Why are we not hiring him full-time?" Joreel exclaimed when he saw Lumen's designs ready for coding.

Hendrix introduced Joreel and Lumen online, giving her the codename "Iluminato" and a male avatar so they could collaborate on Nzo's fight simulations.

"We're loving the simulations, boss. Can we join in?" Craig and Lane eagerly asked. They still missed the thrill of the arena and were excited to be part of the creative process.

Hendrix had a bit of fun with the simulations, bringing Nzo into the arena to fight Craig and Lane, who were dressed in costumes as two giant, angry pink nipples.

"What the freak, boss?!" Craig asked, confused by the bizarre simulation.

"Sorry, the kid's in charge of his fight scenes, or we lose him," Hendrix said, trying to keep his composure while stifling his laughter.

Craig and Lane found the simulation absurd, but Joreel, being a channak himself, was all for it. He even fought Nzo in one of the scenes, where the two of them began to bond.

"So, who's ready for the next simulation with Nzo?" Hendrix asked a week later.

"Oh, I have a date!" Craig quickly declared, hurrying off.

"M-me too," Lane followed suit, with Sandy just shaking her head, laughing. She watched as Joreel coded the simulation of the two angry nipples versus the channak, and couldn't stop herself from roaring with laughter.

Hendrix smiled as he watched Craig and Lane leave. Now, no one would question why Nzo and Hendrix were simulating outside the arena.

◇◇◇

After Nzo finished simulating his fight scenes with an invisible monster, Hendrix would follow through the same obstacle courses, playing the role of the monster, chasing and fighting Nzo. In these scenes, he had to die repeatedly, over and over again.

"Bad actor! You ugly-ugly!" Nzo would scream at him, as if he were the director. He would mock Hendrix's dramatic death pose, his body crushed under the trunk of a large tree.

"G-grandpa! Careful, the blood!" Lumen exclaimed, quickly pulling Nzo away and helping Hendrix towel off the spilled blood.

"It's fine, I can do it," Hendrix insisted, trying to take the towel from Lumen as she wiped him down.

She was so close—too close. Hendrix couldn't help but feel the warmth of her soft skin so near to him.

For a moment, he wondered if he should pull her closer, feel her warmth against him. Stop it, Hendrix. Get it together... his mind urged. But Oh, go ahead...the monster inside him whispered.

"It's okay, Uncle Hendrix. We need your blood in this towel so I can make diluted ammunition for my parents," Lumen said, meeting Hendrix's gaze as she carefully wiped blood off his bare skin.

Then she smiled sweetly at him, oblivious to the effect she was having. If it ever became too overwhelming for Hendrix, he would suddenly take off, flying away to clear his head.

That's when Nzo first noticed the strange inked marks lighting up across Hendrix's body. He didn't mention it immediately but began to watch closely.

For years, Nzo had been puzzled by the inked marks that seemed to appear and disappear on Hendrix's skin, especially when Nzo wasn't paying attention. He'd asked Hendrix about them before, but Hendrix always played ignorant.

"Hidden inked tattoos? How about I give your drunken ass one myself?" Hendrix would answer, ending the discussion. Nzo had let it slide, but he knew his grandchildren could see them too—at least, they used to. Lumen had told him she could no longer see them.

Every time Hendrix was in danger or about to die in the simulation, the inked marks would light up like invisible tattoos across his skin. Nzo observed this closely, especially now that he could see the colors illuminating Hendrix's body.

"You see? Lumen...see-see!?" Nzo asked Lumen, amazed by the bright lights.

"See what?" Lumen would ask, making Nzo feel like he was imagining things.

That's when Nzo realized that he and Joreel were the only ones who could see the light. Joreel had made a subtle remark about it once, but it didn't lead to anything significant. This cemented Nzo's belief that only children could see Hendrix's inked body marks. Grown up now, Lumen could no longer see them. So far, Nzo had discovered five distinct tattoos on Hendrix.

The first one was on Hendrix's back, shaped like burning wings, which would appear whenever Hendrix unknowingly flew or hovered midair. When Hendrix got trapped beneath the earth, trying to escape a hole, the ground would shift as if it were trying to expel him. That's when a sandstorm-shaped mark appeared on Hendrix's legs. When Hendrix was drowning, Nzo saw light emanating from his torso and spiraling up to his left neck, in the shape of a raging waterfall.

This sparked an idea in Nzo's mind: what if the elements were connected to Hendrix's inked marks—earth, wind, water, and fire? Although his vocabulary was limited, Nzo had existed for over a thousand years and had some understanding of the world's natural elements.

Hendrix was intrigued by the idea, but Nzo wasn't as thrilled. The thought of fire reminded him of the traumatic experience from his orphan days, but he was willing to endure it again to test if there was another mark on Hendrix's body.

True enough, it took longer for Hendrix to burn in the simulation. His right arm, all the way to his cheek, began to glow with sharp flames that seemed to protect his body, merging with the fire. What was strange was that Hendrix didn't seem to notice this self-preservation ability.

What are you? Nzo's thoughts were not that of a child. *You're bleeding and now this?* Nzo might have been young, but he knew Hendrix was no ordinary being.

The final mark would light up whenever Hendrix was near Lumen. Nzo didn't like it. The mark appeared on Hendrix's left chest and down his ribs, shaped like a long, sharp spear or an elongated scar from a deep wound.

"Lumen, away-away! Now! No close, not closing-closing!" Nzo would call out when he saw his granddaughter getting too close to Hendrix.

"But Grandpa, I'm close to you now," Lumen would say innocently as she helped Nzo with his diaper.

"Other sigbin," Nzo insisted, glancing over at Hendrix, who was working nearby. It was difficult to be Lumen's grandfather when she was wiping his backside.

"Uncle Hendrix won't hurt me. I even tried to be near him when I was having PMS..." Lumen said, trying to reassure him.

"Iluminata!" Nzo growled, his voice filled with frustration as he could clearly call out her name now.

"What?! He smelled me but just left and came back only when he was with you. He keeps me safe," Lumen replied firmly.

"You bad! Hendrix hurt! It hurt-hurt, okie-okie?" Nzo tried to explain, though he couldn't go into detail about the dangerous side of Hendrix, ripping her chest open to eat her heart.

"R-really?" Lumen stuttered, suddenly feeling guilty while offering Nzo his bottled milk.

"Yes, pain, Hendrix hurting," Nzo mumbled as he sucked on his bottle.

"O-oh," Lumen responded softly, feeling remorseful.

Nzo noticed that Lumen started being more careful around Hendrix, which was a relief. But there were still moments when Lumen naturally gravitated toward him. Whenever that happened, something in Hendrix's ribs would light up, and he would either pull away or, in some cases, fly off.

It was like an instinct—Hendrix knew when Lumen was in danger, even if she didn't understand it herself.

Nzo couldn't help but admire that part of Hendrix's character. He wasn't like the hellspawns he'd known before. *What are you, Drix?* Nzo wondered again, his mind racing with questions he couldn't answer.

It was doubtful, though, that Nzo would continue to admire Hendrix if he ever discovered what was truly happening between Hendrix and Lumen.

<><><>

Back at Lumen's house...

"You're my first love, Uncle Hendrix," Lumen said, her voice steady yet full of sincerity. "That's why I want to marry you and give you my virginity."

Hendrix snapped out of his reverie. Unsure of how to respond, he let the heavy silence settle between them.

"I love you, Uncle Hendrix," Lumen said, her voice steady yet full of sincerity. "Make me your wife, please." She repeated herself, her words hanging in the air, as Hendrix remained focused on the gadget in his hands.

He couldn't meet her gaze, not those beautiful emerald green eyes that seemed to see right through him. He knew that if he looked into them, he might lose control—might do something unforgivable.

How could this be? he thought. *A human marrying a sigbin, consummating their relationship... It was impossible. It was a thought he couldn't entertain.* "It's impossible," he whispered, barely audible, his heart racing as he slowly allowed his eyes to drift toward her. The moment he did, he could feel the shift—his monster stirring, waking up.

Eat her, Hendrix. Now! The monster's voice roared in his mind, an overpowering temptation that threatened to take over.

Hendrix's monster knew only hunger—it couldn't comprehend the overwhelming emotions that consumed Lumen's waking days and sleepless nights since Hendrix became her protector.

16

Impossible Love

Lumen knew that people, especially humans, would never truly understand the feeling she got from watching Hendrix. Even when he was completely absorbed in his work, coding away and barely acknowledging her presence, the sight of him brought an indescribable joy to her heart.

I could stay this way forever, Lumen often thought whenever Hendrix stayed at their house or in the diner to watch over her. Just being in the same space with him felt like enough.

There was something about Hendrix that had always drawn her in, even as a child. She remembered sitting on his lap, fighting with Grandpa Nzo for Hendrix's attention whenever he visited the coffee shop. Nzo, always drunk, would make her cry, demanding that Hendrix choose him over her.

Sometimes, Hendrix would play along, humorously picking her grandpa, but when Lumen cried, he would scoop her up and cradle her in his arms, soothing her tears away.

As Lumen grew older, she learned that this was a familiar pattern in her family. When Hendrix was around, everyone—her dad, grandpa, even Grandpa Nzo's mother—treated him as their favorite uncle or godfather. There was something magnetic about him that pulled them all in.

It was strange, though, for humans to be so physically close to a sigbin like Hendrix. From stories she heard growing up, some of her family members were fond of other sigbin—like Grandpa Nzo or Uncle Hiro—but they weren't as close to them physically when they were kids.

She was told that uncle Hiro, despite being kind in some ways, had a certain distance; the children could always sense that he didn't like them as much. Nzo, on the other hand, often played pranks or messed with their toys. Lumen didn't have clear memories of Uncle Hiro, as he had been absent for so long, but Hendrix—Hendrix was different. Her heart had always warmed to him in a way that was unlike any other.

Whenever Lumen was alone in her room, she would sift through old family pictures and drawings that had been passed down through generations. There was something familiar in the recurring patterns—drawings of Hendrix with wings, his body covered in glowing tattoos.

She remembered seeing Hendrix like that when she was younger, but those images had faded over time. Maybe her family's imagination had run wild when they were kids.

Inspired by those drawings, Lumen began sketching her own. It was meant to be a surprise gift for Hendrix. Unconsciously, her hand shaped an image of Hendrix—half-naked, fighting a dark-winged monster to save her. As he fought, he glowed with a radiant light, lifting her high into the sky. A vivid premonition of a distant future Lumen couldn't possibly foresee. At that moment, Lumen realized she had drawn Hendrix as an angel. A being long forgotten by humans. Angels were no longer part of human knowledge, relegated to myth and forgotten stories, especially in a world where Kein was considered the true god. To the older generation, Hendrix resembled the sigbin. But to children like Lumen... Hendrix was something else entirely.

When Lumen finished the drawing, she stared at it in awe. Her heart swelled as she took in the image of Hendrix—the glowing protector, the one who had always been there for her. But then, as her emotions surged, a heat radiated from her body. It was unlike anything she had ever felt before.

A flush of warmth spread across her skin, and she suddenly realized what was happening. Looking down at her undies, she sighed, a bit depressed. *It's that time again*, she thought. Her period had started. That meant she'd be confined to her room, stuck in the bubble she had created for herself, unable to leave for several days.

<><><>

Whenever Lumen saw Hendrix again, she couldn't contain the rush of excitement that surged through her. She would run to him, eager to be near him, even if it meant just watching him from a distance while he worked.

"What did I miss?" "Are we going on a road trip for a simulation?" "I have my drawings here..."

Uncle Hendrix... see me. Look at me. Be with me, Lumen longed to scream, feeling an intense desire to be held in his arms the way they were during the simulation fights in the forest. Those were the moments she treasured the most.

"So, did you talk to Joreel about the final design?" Hendrix asked, his voice bringing Lumen back to the present. She looked at him, feeling a little lost, as though her mind wandered again.

Lumen tried to focus. "Uh, yes, boss... I mean, Uncle Hendrix. Joreel always calls you 'boss' when we chat."

Hendrix flicked his fingers in the air to regain her attention. "Lumen, stop daydreaming!"

"Uh... yes, boss... I mean, Uncle Hendrix..." Lumen mumbled, still shaken by her errant thoughts. She was trying to ground herself, but a darker thought began to creep in—*I have to lose my virginity soon or else...*

Hendrix, sensing her distraction, asked seriously, "Where's your headspace? Are you okay?"

With a soft smile, Lumen replied, With you, but only nodded and smiled sweetly, trying to mask her true feelings.

Hendrix didn't miss the way her smile made something tighten in his chest. He felt a stir of desire that quickly turned into discomfort. His body betrayed him, but he couldn't help it. It was like an automatic response, one he couldn't control, and it only grew stronger when she smiled at him like that.

Stop it, Hendrix!, he thought. *Look away.*

"Oi you here, We go-go now, okie-okie?!" Nzo interrupted them, and Hendrix silently thanked him for breaking the tension.

<><><>

The next time they found themselves alone in the coffee shop, Hendrix sat in the quiet corner, working through the final stages of the RPG. The coffee shop had become his makeshift office—coding while keeping an eye on Nzo's family.

Lumen sat across from him, her eyes watching him carefully, a hint of sadness lingering on her face. It was hard for Hendrix to focus with her gaze on him, but he could tell she needed something.

"Talk to me," Lumen said, her voice serious.

Hendrix blinked, a little caught off guard, and looked up from his work. "Hmmm?" he muttered, distracted for a moment by the weight of her gaze.

"What's going on, Lumen?" he asked, genuinely concerned. She seemed different today, and it bothered him.

Lumen's gaze dropped to the napkin in front of her, her fingers fiddling with it. Hendrix could tell she was trying to gather her thoughts.

Usually, he didn't like to be interrupted when he was immersed in a project, especially not during the final stages of developing Nzo's RPG, but this felt different. He could feel that something was off with her.

"I had a nightmare last night," Lumen confessed, her voice barely above a whisper.

Hendrix's brow furrowed. He wasn't used to hearing Lumen talk about such things. "It's just a nightmare. It's probably from all the violence you've seen during the simulations."

Lumen shook her head, but her eyes locked onto his with quiet intensity. "No, it was... kind of nice. You were there."

Hendrix gave a half-laugh, trying to deflect the heaviness in her tone. "I was there and it's a nightmare? Wow, thanks for the insult," he joked, but he felt the weight of her words.

Lumen didn't smile. Her face remained serious, and she spoke again, her voice cracking with emotion. "You were leaving me."

"Oh," Hendrix replied, feeling a tightness in his chest. His heart ached at the vulnerability in her words. *Cathy...* he thought to himself. She looked so much like Cathy at that moment.

"I don't want to go to Perlaz," Lumen said, the words finally spilling out.

"You will be safe there," Hendrix tried to reassure her. "We're finding a way to…"

"I don't want to be away from you," Lumen cut him off, her voice soft but edged with something Hendrix couldn't ignore.

The intensity in her words was enough to make him freeze. She had confessed her feelings before, but now it was different. This time, there was anger behind the hurt.

Hendrix didn't know what to say. His body betrayed him again, and the monster inside him stirred, but he couldn't act on it. His mind raced with conflicting thoughts as his heart pounded. He forced himself to look away, trying to regain control.

Lumen's voice softened again, and she continued, "Do you remember when you competed with Grandpa to give me gifts when I was a kid?"

Hendrix blinked, his attention shifting. "Yeah, I remember," he said, although he was still a bit lost in the emotional current between them.

Lumen's eyes twinkled as she remembered. "Grandpa would always buy me the most expensive gifts, but you'd get me things I actually needed—crayons, drawing paper, colored pens. They weren't fancy or digital, but I treasured them every time."

Hendrix didn't know this about Lumen's childhood, but hearing it made his heart swell. He always valued the simplicity of what mattered to children. It reminded him of his own youth, before everything had changed. It was the small, pure things that made them happy.

"And then, when I was in grade school, you always protected me from Grandpa's mischief. You even brought me to one of your parties… and bought me ice cream afterward."

Hendrix smiled softly at the memory. He had always been fond of Lumen as a young child. But now, with the weight of her feelings for him, he didn't know how to navigate the path between family love and something darker that was pulling him in.

Hendrix's mind drifted back to that time – when he brought Lumen to a party.

Craig and Lane were working on an RPG game where players met through a dating app. During the launch, Hendrix had a feeling he was being set up. The guys assumed his reluctance to join the arena simulations stemmed from not having been laid in a while. Still haunted by what happened to Beth, Hendrix borrowed Lumen from Nzo and his family, telling them he planned to take the kid on a tour of the City of Ruinae during the Festival of Avlam.

Lumen ended up saving him from complete humiliation—Craig and Lane had tried to pair him with the most obnoxious drag queen he had ever met. The prank backfired. Hendrix gave them what they wanted—he returned to the arena, but not for a simulated match. He tore through them, piece by piece.

In the end, he learned the whole thing had been Hiro's idea. Despite their estrangement, his bond brother still refused to let go of his anger—for Hendrix denying him the arena fight he had long waited for.

Lumen's voice snapped him back to the present. "I dressed up like a princess that day, and you treated me like one. That day, you became my prince," she said, her tone serious.

Hendrix smiled softly, the memory of Lumen as a child easing the tension in his chest. His body relaxed, the discomfort between his legs subsiding naturally.

"That's why you're my first love," Lumen continued, her voice full of sincerity. Hendrix sighed, his gaze drifting. It was a simple girl's crush. Nothing more. He always brushed it off when she talked like this, telling himself it was just a phase.

"You'll find your prince in Perlaz soon enough, okay?" Hendrix said, trying to redirect the conversation. He finally regained control over his thoughts and the body's reactions. *Don't encourage it, Hendrix. You're being stupid if you think it means more than what it is.*

Lumen's expression shifted, and Hendrix saw a fire burning in her eyes—pain, anger, all mixed together.

"No!" Lumen suddenly slammed her hands on the table, startling the few customers nearby. Without another word, she stormed into the kitchen.

Hugo, who had been watching from a distance, shot Hendrix a puzzled look. Hendrix simply shrugged, scratching his head, unsure of what had just transpired.

Hendrix tried to brush off Lumen's obvious affection for him, convincing himself it was just a crush—a fleeting feeling that would eventually fade. But deep down, he knew that whatever attraction he felt toward her was complicated.

The monster inside him stirred every time she was near, an insatiable hunger for her innocence that he could not control. He shouldn't be thinking of her this way, and he couldn't allow himself to act on it.

He could not let himself believe that there was anything real between them, just as Lumen's feelings were driven by something naive and unformed.

With those thoughts in mind, Hendrix continued to keep his distance.

◇◇◇

But now, standing alone in Nzo's house, with Lumen confessing to him, everything was different.

"I want you to be my husband—the first man to claim my... my innocence." Lumen said, her eyes blazing with determination. She stood before him, vulnerable yet resolute.

Hendrix's heart skipped a beat, but his words came out in a whisper, laced with disbelief and deep seated desire. "Lumen, w-what are you saying?"

Lumen's gaze didn't waver. She was fierce now, her desire clear, and Hendrix's body reacted before he could stop it. The monster inside him reveled in her offer. "Look at the app! Humans and sigbin can be married. These couples found a way!" Lumen thrust her gadget toward him, showing him a page filled with testimonies and stories of unlikely unions.

Hendrix glanced at the screen, but his skepticism remained. It looked like a hoax—he could easily create the same kind of fake testimonies using his RPG programs.

"It's possible. Love made it happen. Love is love, so we shouldn't be forbidden to marry hellspawns. Love made my husband control himself, to stop himself from eating my heart. So, to all berhen out there, find your match..."

Hendrix couldn't believe what he was watching. This couldn't be real. "Where did you get the link for this?" he asked, trying to steady his breathing as he took the gadget from her hands. He searched through it, his mind racing.

"I don't know. I was bored, just messing around. Then this website popped up, and I clicked on it." Lumen was staring at him now, waiting impatiently, as if she couldn't understand why he was so focused on the details.

"This may not be legitimate," Hendrix said, a little more calmly, as he airdropped the link to himself, hoping to verify it later.

"That's not the point, Uncle," Lumen replied, her tone softer, but firm. She reached out and touched his arm, squeezing it gently.

Hendrix recoiled slightly, affected by her touch. His mind spun, unsure if the feeling in his chest was his own or if it was the hungry, maddened monster inside him trying to take control.

"The point is, I want you. I've wanted you since I was a child. You're my first love, and I want you to be my last. Please... take me as your wife... I want you to be the first to make love to me, and—"

"Let me check this first, okay? Please... don't do anything stupid, understand?" *Hendrix stood up quickly, grabbing his things, cutting off her desperate plea. His pulse was erratic, his thoughts jumbled. Where was Nzo? Why wasn't he back yet?*

Lumen's eyes filled with tears, and Hendrix's heart shattered. He wanted to pull her into his arms, tell her everything would be okay, but he couldn't. Not with the monster screaming for him to claim her. "Don't you want me too?" *Lumen's voice cracked with emotion, breaking Hendrix's resolve.*

Claim her. She's yours, the monster growled in his mind. She's offering herself to you. Look at her—she's not just beautiful; she's irresistible. She won't break like Beth. Take her. Just one kiss.

"No!" *Hendrix shouted, the sound coming from deep within him. He saw the pain flash in Lumen's eyes, and it tore him apart. He wanted to die.* "I mean... you're every man's dream, Lumen," *Hendrix admitted softly, his voice hopeless. He couldn't deny the truth. He was so deeply drawn to her, but he couldn't—he had to stop himself.*

"Including yours?" *Lumen asked, the tears halting as she looked at him, her gaze searching.*

Hendrix froze. Her words made something deep inside him ache. He wiped the tears from her cheek, trying to steady his shaking hands. He looked at her, wishing he could feel something other than the overwhelming desire that clouded his thoughts. He took a deep breath, but even that didn't seem enough. The inexplicable pull, the warmth, the heat—his body betrayed him.

That's my boy, the monster cheered, as Hendrix's carnal desire surged in response.

Lumen reached for his hand, but Hendrix pulled away quickly, terrified of what would happen if he allowed it to go further.

"Just… let me look at this first, okay?" he managed to say, his voice thick with tension.

He moved away from her, retreating into the safety of his own mind as he waited for Nzo to return. The silence between them felt like a weight that crushed him from all sides.

<><><>

Sofia was in full panic mode when Hiro stepped into her office. "Go to Xego and track the source of the leak. I want every trace of Bersig erased from any unsecured system—permanently!" she shouted, her voice sharp with urgency.

"Hey, calm down. What happened?" Hiro approached her, pulling her into a steadying embrace.

From across the room, Dimas—Sofia's latest fling—glowered at Hiro. As always, Hiro ignored him.

"Someone leaked our marriage app to the public," Sofia snapped. "For a brief moment, the website was accessible to anyone. Ehud's tech team managed to contain the breach, but now they're assessing how many unauthorized users accessed it."

"Oh…" Hiro tilted his head, "Should we prepare for the worst?"

Before he could brace himself, Sofia's fist collided with his jaw, sending a sharp jolt of pain through his face. With a sickening pop, his jaw dislocated. "This is your domain! How the hell did this happen?!" she yelled, panic creeping back into her voice.

Hiro took a deep breath, waiting for his accelerated healing to do its work. The pain dulled as his jaw reset itself. Same old Sofia—her punches still packed a hell of a punch. "I built the system," he said calmly. "But security and maintenance? That's your responsibility now." His focus had long shifted to the smuggling side of their operation—this wasn't his mess to clean up.

Sofia exhaled sharply, glancing at Dimas. Their eyes met in an unspoken exchange before she turned back to Hiro, her expression softening. "I'm sorry," she murmured, pressing a lingering kiss to the spot where she had struck him.

Hiro smirked, then kissed her lips, slow and deliberate. "What do you need me to do?"

Sofia's fury reignited. "First, we find the mole in our organization. And then?" Her eyes darkened with determination. "We make them regret it."

<><><>

"Me right-right! Okie-okie?!" Nzo exclaimed when Hendrix revealed the details about the app, excluding Lumen's connection to it.

He had already tried accessing it again—nothing. Even after enlisting Joreel and Sandy to hack into the link, they came up empty-handed.

"It's buried deep in the darkest AI internet portal, boss. What even is this link?" Craig asked, having also attempted to crack the system.

"If I knew, I wouldn't have asked for your help," Hendrix snapped, his patience wearing thin. Without access, he had no tangible proof to show Nzo, yet he couldn't shake the feeling that Nzo was right.

"You already knew about this?" Hendrix asked, narrowing his eyes.

"Yes-yes!" Nzo gestured for Hugo to explain.

"We've been hearing whispers in Perlaz," Hugo began. "Humans suddenly refusing to secure their berhen in Viscot, claiming they've already been matched for marriage in Xego. The thing is, they assume they're marrying other humans—not hellspawns." Hugo still had contacts among the human families in Perlaz, who helped him gather intel and arrange potential escape routes for Lumen.

"But how would humans even cross the borders without proper transportation?" Hendrix asked, frowning.

Kein had designed the world to limit travel between continents. Their technology allowed for strictly regulated flights, each departing from designated airports with fixed destinations. Planes from Zapad could never enter Perlaz, and vice versa. Only Cintru had access to three continents.

This system ensured that sigbin could never enter human territories undetected. Since there was no direct airport from Xego to Perlaz, there was no conceivable way for berhen from Perlaz to reach Xego alive and unnoticed. Any plane attempting to travel to a forbidden location would self-destruct before reaching its destination.

"I know," Hugo said grimly. "The border patrols are just as confused. There's a breach in their checkpoint system, and they're still investigating. Meanwhile, young girls are also disappearing from Xego."

Hendrix tensed. "What do you mean, disappearing?"

17

Sugar Rush

"They're being matched for marriage here," Hugo explained. "But after the wedding, their families never hear from them—or their so-called husbands—again."

Hendrix pulled out his gadget, scanning the news feeds. Nothing.

"No care news, okie-okie?!" Nzo scoffed. "Cops no-no care. Nzo, you-us fight-fight alone." In Xego, sigbin were treated better than humans, especially when it came to reporting crimes.

Hugo's expression darkened. "Some of our human friends are terrified. Their children are approaching puberty, and they're desperate. Some are even resorting to... preventing their daughters from being berhen—by any means necessary. Even marrying within the family."

Hendrix recoiled. "What?!"

Hugo nodded, disgusted. Lumen's parents formed a secret resistance group—humans facing the same nightmare. There's even an underground agency now, where men can be hired to sleep with the berhen if marriage is not an option.

Nzo's jaw tightened. He would never allow that to happen to Lumen.

Hendrix ran a hand through his hair, exhaling sharply. This was why he avoided politics—he hated knowing things like this.

"Me Nzo speak Mr. Hajji, okie-okie!?" Nzo said urgently. "Me no like this but—"

"Just don't mention Lumen," Hendrix warned.

Nzo nodded solemnly. "Okie-okie!?"

<><><>

The following day, Hiro stepped into the coffee shop for the first time in ages. Nzo barely knew how to react. He still hadn't arranged his meeting with Mr. Hajji—now, out of nowhere, Hajji's son had decided to show up at his diner.

Before Nzo could figure out what to do, trouble arrived. A group of thugs stormed in, targeting Lumen.

That's when Hiro intervened and saved the day.

By nightfall, Nzo called for an emergency meeting. In the coffee shop's kitchen, Hiro and Hendrix finally stood face to face after years apart.

"You told him?!" "He knew?!" Hendrix and Hiro glare locked in an unspoken challenge, years of tension crackling between them. Possibly deepening and becoming even more complicated due to their shared feelings for Lumen.

<><><>

With Hiro now involved, Nzo abandoned his plan to visit Mr. Hajji. But Hiro and Hendrix's reunion proved to be more of a headache than a relief—every conversation between them spiraled into contradiction.

First, they argued over whether Lumen should be moved to Isla de Parthena with the athenas. Then, it was about approaching Hiro's father.

"I don't know anything about the app Lumen saw, but I'll investigate," Lying through his teeth, Hiro began to grasp the full extent of the hacking Sofia had mentioned.

"Nzo thank-thank Hiro, okie-okie?!" Nzo replied, his voice unusually polite.

Hendrix shot a glare at the kid. Not long ago, Nzo had nothing but contempt for Hiro—mocking him behind his back, calling him a "privileged bloodhound full of diaper crap." Now? He was practically kissing Hiro's ass, and Hendrix hated it.

"As for my father," Hiro continued, "go easy on him. Let me feel my way around first. Like you said, if this goes all the way to the top, we need to tread carefully." His tone was persuasive, measured.

Nzo found it refreshing—Hiro wasn't acting like the daddy's boy he expected. So, he agreed.

Hendrix didn't —though he had to admit his judgment might be clouded by his past with Hiro and his possessiveness over other sigbin getting too close to Lumen.

"Be good. For Lumen. Be good to Hiro, okie-okie?!" Nzo nagged Hendrix relentlessly, trying to push him toward reconciliation.

"B-but... my secret," Hendrix stammered. It wasn't just pride or grudges—it was the other thing. The thing that made him refuse to face Hiro at the arena ever again.

"Yes, no tell Hiro. No, okie-okie?!" Nzo mumbled, sucking his thumb, agreeing that Hiro didn't need to know about Hendrix's blood. Not yet.

"You don't trust him?" Hendrix asked, handing Nzo the pacifier he was looking for.

Nzo shrugged. "Hiro you friend. Father, Mr. Hajji, friend. Kein... no... I dunno - okie-okie?"

Hendrix sighed. He knew Nzo had a complicated relationship with Mr. Hajji. The man was known to be sympathetic to humans, yet he remained one of Kein's closest allies. And Kein? Kein was a problem.

"You don't trust Kein," Hendrix stated, indifferent about the supposed god. He didn't care about divine politics.

"No trust evil, okie-okie?! Bad Kein, okie-okie?!" Nzo muttered, shaking his head.

And for once, Hendrix couldn't disagree.

"But you Hiro...love-love, okie-okie?! Brother...famly. No fighting-fighting, okie-okie?!" Nzo insisted. His wish finally came true when Hiro and Hendrix reached a truce in the arena.

<><>

With Hendrix having his brother back on board, he felt a sense of relief—at least for now. Whatever emotions they shared for Lumen, it would still serve their cause –save the woman they both cared for, no matter the cost.

"Uncle Hiro!" Lumen would beam whenever Hiro was around, her eyes bright with excitement.

Hendrix's heart ached every time he saw it—that same look of enthusiasm and warmth she gave him. If I say no, she'll ask Hiro—and with the way he looks at her, he'll probably say yes.

The thought tortured him. He knew how much Hiro had loved Cathy, and now he saw it—that same depth of longing, that same quiet devotion—whenever Hiro looked at Lumen.

<><>

"I don't like humans," Hiro had once confessed to him centuries ago.

Hendrix remembered it vividly. They had been at Nzo's family's coffee shop, the warm scent of roasted beans filling the air, when Hiro leaned in, voice low and certain. "But Cathy made me want to be with one forever. I think I'm in love with her."

Hendrix had dismissed it at the time—Hiro had been high, lost in a haze of whatever substance he was on. But he knew the truth: Hiro never truly hated humans.

His mother had been human. She had loved Mr. Hajji, and despite the difference in their races, they had been devoted to one another. Hiro had seen it firsthand. He had also felt the pain of losing her.

That was why he had sworn never to let another human into his heart. Because humans die. Because they leave.

And yet, Cathy made him break the very promise he swore to himself when he let her into his heart.

<><><>

Hendrix wasn't sure if Nzo had figured out how Hiro felt, but he noticed the kid watching Hiro closely, especially when Lumen was around.

"Uncle Hendrix." A soft whisper behind him.
Hendrix tensed, startled, his heart hammering.

Ahhhh, Lumen.

She wasn't through with her delusions of loving him. She teased him, danced at the edges of his resolve, made him feel something dangerous.

And yet, just when jealousy burned inside him—when he saw her smiling at Hiro, glowing with that same radiant light—she would look at him again, and for a brief, agonizing moment, make him feel like he was the only one in her world.

This is crap! Crap! Crap! Hendrix told himself. *No, it's not,* his monster whispered back.

Then she would do something like show him a picture. A dress—her wedding dress. "This will be my wedding dress," she'd say, lingering behind him, her voice low, teasing. "Promise me you'll be my husband," she would whisper, almost pleading.
"L-Lumen..." Hendrix would turn to her, breath catching—only to find her gone, already laughing, already talking to Hiro with that same glowing smile. And the rage—the hunger—would consume him.

Craaap! His mind screamed. His monster roared. He would flee, finding solace in Beth's sleeping body.
Beth—the one he had hurt, killed, ruined over and over again. Beth, who had never been more than an outlet for his darkest urges. What he had with Beth was nothing compared to what he felt with Lumen.
No, he told himself. *Yes,* his monster countered.

Then the memories would flood him—Lumen's soft, lingering touch whenever they were close, her whispers, her warmth...
"I'll draw my honeymoon dress next..."
"I trust you... you will not hurt me..."
"Please be my husband..."
"Sleep with me, Hendrix..."

She stopped calling him Uncle—except when others were listening.
"Lumen," was all he could ever say. Hendrix shook himself –heart pounding, painfully aroused. The basement was filled with the slow,

steady breathing of the sleeping sigbin around him. He clenched his fists.

Beth had been an indulgence. A mistake. A cycle of lust and destruction.

But Lumen? Lumen was something else.

I'm going crazy, Hendrix thought. And the worst part? He didn't want to stop going crazy for her.

<><><>

"Ahhhh! He's driving me crazy!" Hiro threw a punch into the air, his frustration boiling over.

Nzo was at it again—nagging them relentlessly during the meeting. Hiro had meticulously laid out his plan for Lumen's escape to Perlaz, but the kid kept circling back to the Bersig app and the missing berhen in Xego.

Hiro didn't care about the other berhen. He cared about Lumen. Lumen alone.

"Cool it, bro. Unless you want to face the kid in the arena," Hendrix said, smirking. He had already told Hiro about Craig and Lane's unfortunate run-in with Nzo. They had laughed about it for hours.

Hiro scoffed. "I'd rather die than be Nzo's titty monster."

They were still chuckling when their footsteps came to an abrupt halt.

Lumen.

She stood on the lawn outside Nzo's house, watering the plants, completely oblivious to her audience. Her soft giggle carried through the air as she spoke to the flowers, showering them with tenderness.

It was a scene so pure, so unguarded, that for a moment, neither man could move.

Hendrix and Hiro stood frozen, watching her.

Then, Lumen turned. Her bright, radiant smile lit up when she saw them, and she ran toward them, carefree and beautiful.

How can she be like this? Hendrix wondered, caught in the pull of her energy. How could she be so full of light, completely unaware of the danger looming over her?

"Are you done with your meeting?" Lumen asked, her voice light and playful.

Hendrix swallowed hard. Her dress clung to her, damp from the water, outlining the soft shape of her legs beneath the fabric.

"Y-yeah. Your grandpa is..." Hiro started, but his eyes had drifted lower, mirroring Hendrix's.

"In the mood, right?" Lumen finished for him, her smile turning mischievous.

Both men stared as she tilted her head, eyes gleaming with something wicked and seemingly dangerous.

"I have an idea," she gave a devilish grin.

<><><>

They were sitting around the wooden table near the garden when Nzo stomped outside, scowling like an old man woken from a nap. Being sober always made him grouchy.

"Iluminata! Inside! House, now! Okie-okie?!" Nzo bellowed the moment he saw his granddaughter hanging out with Hiro and Hendrix again. "You two! Out me Nzo house! Okie-okie?!" He stormed toward them, his tiny feet taking small but furious strides.

Lumen stood up quickly, holding up a brand-new bottle filled with milk like an offering of peace. "Hey, I bought your favorite breast milk online! Look—it even comes in this fancy new bottle," she said sweetly, presenting the gift.

Nzo's scowl instantly faded. He lifted his arms toward Hendrix, signaling for him to pick him up and place him on the table.

"Yuck, kid, what is that smell?!" Hiro asked, wrinkling his nose.

Nzo, wearing nothing but a sagging, stained diaper, ignored him. He grabbed his bottle, sprawled out on the table, and started sucking on it contentedly.

Hendrix and Hiro exchanged looks before turning their gaze to Lumen.

She just smiled. "Wait for it. I promise—it's gonna be fun." She winked.

The two sigbin shared another glance, feeling an odd mix of amusement and unease.

What Hendrix and Hiro didn't know was that sugar was both Nzo's best friend and worst enemy. And to get back at him for being a foul-tempered little tyrant lately, Lumen had let them in on a family secret.

"I'm not sure about this," Hendrix muttered, watching as Nzo drank his milk with increasing enthusiasm, eyes slightly glazed over.

"Oh, come on. It's just sugar. What harm could it do?" Hiro smirked, intrigued.

Then, without warning, Lumen burst into song. "Dance, Nzo! Dance, Nzo! Go! Go! Dance, Nzo!" She clapped loudly, her voice full of encouragement.

Nzo suddenly let out a giddy giggle. Then, to everyone's shock, he jumped onto the table and started dancing like a stripper.

Hendrix and Hiro collapsed onto the lawn, roaring with laughter as Lumen cheered him on.

The little channak was on fire—biting his lip, rolling his hips, grinding against the air like he was a performing athena. His diaper sagged dangerously, but that didn't stop him. He twerked with reckless abandon, sending shockwaves through the table, his tiny arms waving as if he were casting a seductive spell.

Hiro gasped between fits of laughter. *So this is how Ehud bribed his way past the channaks guarding the Berhen at Perlaz.* He clapped along with Lumen, egging Nzo on.

Hendrix, meanwhile, wiped tears from his eyes as he secretly recorded the entire performance. *Future reference for Channak warrior dance simulations,* he thought smugly.

Despite everything—the danger Lumen was in, the chaos surrounding them—this moment felt right. As he watched Lumen, Hiro, and even a delirious, half-naked Nzo, a warmth spread through Hendrix's chest. *I wish this day never ends.*

Then, the spell was broken.

"LUMEN! WHAT HAVE YOU DONE?!" Augusta's horrified shriek cut through the music.

They turned to see Lumen's parents standing in the doorway, fresh from work—only to find them in the middle of an all-out sugar-fueled party.

Nzo, completely naked now, was splashing water everywhere like an unhinged garden fountain, still grinding his hips as if possessed.

Hendrix, Hiro, and Lumen froze.

Then, Nzo turned, lip still caught between his teeth, and blew Augusta a kiss.

"S-sorry, Mom," Lumen mumbled as she hurried over to help Augusta with her bags.

"We were just having fun, Augusta. No big deal," Hiro grinned, completely unfazed.

Meanwhile, Nzo was still at it—dancing and giggling like a sugar-fueled hellspawn.

Augusta's eyes narrowed.

"Alright, boys. No big deal," Hugo said, stepping in with a smirk. "But you're staying with him until his sugar crashes. We're not cleaning up this mess."

True to their word, Hiro and Hendrix stayed behind. For hours, the family played an unusual game of catch—Nzo being the ball.

"More! More!" Nzo shrieked in delight as Hendrix hurled him toward Hiro.

Hiro kicked him back, sending the little terror soaring through the air.

Hugo caught Nzo mid-flight and tossed him effortlessly back to Hendrix, who, with a deadpan look, sent him bouncing onto the grass like a ragdoll.

From the porch, Augusta and Lumen watched in mild horror as the men continued their impromptu sport, launching Nzo in all directions until he was black and blue—but still laughing like a maniac.

The garden was wrecked. The lawn was in ruins. And Nzo? Still going strong, bouncing off the ground like an indestructible goblin.

"Why did you do this?" Augusta sighed for the nth time, glaring at her daughter.

"W-we just wanted to have fun, Mom. Come on. What if I die tomorrow?" Lumen countered dramatically.

Augusta groaned. "Oh, Lumen..." She was too exhausted to argue anymore.

Suddenly—

"Enough!" Hiro growled.

Nzo had climbed onto his back, riding him like a champion equestrian, tiny fists yanking at Hiro's hair. "NO! MORE! MOVE, SLAVE!" Nzo screamed in his ear, kicking Hiro's ribs like he was urging a racehorse forward.

It had been days, and Augusta refused to let anyone leave the house until Nzo finally calmed down.

"You started it, boys. You finish it," Hugo said sternly. There was no way he was taking responsibility for his sugar-crazed grandpa.

"How long is this supposed to last?" Hendrix groaned, sprawled out on the dirt, filthy and utterly exhausted.

Augusta shrugged. "Depends. Could be days. Weeks. Years." She smirked, enjoying their suffering. "Depends on how much sugar you put in his milk."

CRAP!

Hendrix's mind reeled. Lumen had wanted to add only one cube of sugar—but Hiro had dumped in more while she wasn't looking. Hiro glanced at Hendrix, miserable and regretful.

Nzo, however, was still thriving. The kid had now latched onto Hiro's face—chewing on his chin, sucking on his nose, and drooling all over him like a teething baby from hell.

Hiro tried to pry him off, but Nzo clung to him with superhuman strength.

Hendrix died laughing at the sight of Hiro struggling, completely defeated.

Then— THUMP!

Nzo launched himself onto Hendrix's face, landing with a victorious squelch.

Hendrix barely had time to register what was happening before—

Nzo sat down. Diaperless. Right on his face.

Hiro howled with laughter, rolling across the dirty lawn, clutching his sides.

"Move, SLAVE! MOVE!" Nzo cackled, pulling Hendrix's hair while rubbing his bare little ass all over his face.

Hendrix's muffled scream of horror rang through the air.

And then— The baby farted. Long. Loud. Directly into Hendrix's screaming mouth.

Hiro completely lost it. He collapsed onto the grass, howling with laughter, tears streaming down his face. In his entire immortal life, he had never laughed this hard.

Hendrix, however, was not laughing. He was gagging. "Hirooooo!" he screamed in rage.

And Nzo? Nzo just giggled, completely unbothered, bouncing happily on his human fart cushion.

<><><>

"It's Hiro," Sofia announced as she stepped into Ehud's office, uninvited.

Ehud blinked, momentarily thrown off. "Hiro is our mole?" He could hardly believe it. But more shocking than the accusation itself was who had come to deliver it. Sofia.

A royalty from Cintru. One of the original sigbin created by Kein. And now, here she was, standing in his grimy warehouse in Zapad, among dust, crates, and the stench of old blood.

Sofia was breathtaking—as she always was. Ever since Hiro had introduced them, she had been his ultimate fantasy, lingering in the darkest corners of his mind. Their partnership in the berhen-smuggling trade was purely business, but that never stopped Ehud from imagining otherwise.

"Show him," Sofia ordered, motioning for someone behind her.

Vahitna stepped forward.

Ehud's eyes widened. Vahitna? She had always worked for him. She handed him a tablet with a set of collated reports. His frown deepened. He had always assumed Vahitna was loyal to Mr. Hajji. And yet, here she was, standing beside Sofia. Interesting.

As far as he knew, she had been working with Hiro on his precious berhen from Xego. All the while, she had also been investigating him? Huh. The eternal pregnant sigbin was proving to be more formidable than he had ever given her credit for.

"He's planning to smuggle a berhen from Xego—using our usual route in reverse," Sofia explained as Ehud flipped through the files. That made him pause. Doing that would trigger the security towers in Cintru.

"I paid them a lot," Sofia continued, "but this won't slip past them. If Hiro goes through with it, it'll expose everything. And that means—our whole operation is eff up."

Ehud's stomach twisted. This was Hiro's plan?

"We needed to be certain before telling you," Sofia added, watching him closely. "That's why I told Vahitna to report directly to me. I had to know who I could trust."

Ehud leaned back, exhaling slowly. The association between these two women was unexpected—but it made sense now. What he didn't know was that Sofia had a soft spot for pregnant women.

For Sofia, it was something she would never experience herself. A lost possibility. And that fascinated her. The moment she had met Vahitna, she had felt an instinctive kinship—one that she had also experienced not too long ago.

"So," Ehud finally said, recovering from his shock. "What do we do?"

Sofia's expression darkened. "Stop Hiro at all costs." Her voice was grave. "If Kein or Caiphaiz ever find out about our operation..." she trailed off, her lips pressing into a thin line. The look in her eyes wasn't just anger—it was fear.

Ehud considered that for a moment. He had built something profitable. Very profitable. Not only was he drowning in koine, but his hunger was also satisfied in ways no other business could provide. He wasn't about to lose that. "Alright," he finally said, smirking. "I'm on board."

Sofia nodded and turned to Vahitna. Without a word, Vahitna brought up the detailed plan to trap Hiro.

Ehud leaned in, eyes glinting with intrigue. This was about to get interesting.

After his meeting with Sofia and Vahitna, Ehud didn't waste time—he called Hiro on a secure line. And he told him everything. He replayed their conversation in his mind.

"The berhen from Xego is just a decoy. I want to know who leaked the app. There's a mole in our organization," Hiro had said.

That was the real reason Ehud had reached out. Why hadn't Sofia mentioned anything about the app leak? That was where the sabotage had begun. If she truly wanted to stop Hiro, wouldn't she have focused on the root of the problem? Instead, she was hyper-fixated on the berhen smuggling plan—something that, to Hiro, seemed personal.

But the app leak? That was business. "How can you be sure it's not me?" Ehud had asked bluntly.

"Because you have nothing to gain and everything to lose if you sabotage our scheme." Hiro's voice had been steady, calculating. "Besides, if this leaks out, you'll be the first to take the fall. You're practically running the whole operation."

Ehud had gritted his teeth. He hated to admit it, but Hiro was right. "So, are you saying the berhen from Xego isn't going to Perlaz?" Ehud had asked, needing clarity. There had been a sigh on the other end of the line.

"Just stick to my plan." And then Hiro had hung up.

Ehud clenched his jaw, staring at the phone in his hand. Now, he had to decide whose game he was really playing.

<><><>

"You promised me!" Lumen's voice trembled with anger as she cornered Hendrix after their meeting. She wasn't allowed in the dungeon, but she had found a way to listen. The echoes had carried through the walls, faint yet clear enough for her to piece together their conversation. She had listened intently, heart pounding, disbelief creeping in with every word.

For months, they had been happy. And now? Hendrix had betrayed her.

"What the heck are you doing outside?! Are you crazy?" Hendrix's voice was harsh, but his panic was worse. The scent of Lumen overwhelmed him instantly—sweet, intoxicating, dangerous. He knew her cycle well, knew she was nearing her critical dates.

She had been waiting for him in the back alley—the one he always used when coming and going from Parthena. "I don't care," she snapped. "I'd rather die than go to Perlaz!" She stepped in front of him, blocking his path.

"Lumen!" Hendrix's heart pounded. She heard everything.

"You promised you'd marry me! Why am I leaving for Perlaz tomorrow?!" Tears welled in her eyes as she pounded her fists against his chest. The impact was nothing to him, but the pain in her voice nearly shattered him.

"This... this is the only way," Hendrix muttered, gripping her shoulders, forcing himself to meet her tear-filled gaze.

"I don't want to marry anyone! I want you! I love you!" Lumen's voice cracked as she stared at him, pleading.

Hendrix felt his resolve slipping—felt himself drowning in the raw truth in her eyes. "You're young... you don't even know what you are—"

"I'm turning twenty! That's older than half the girls getting married in Perlaz!" she shot back, refusing to let him finish.

"Lumen... please." His voice wavered. He could feel himself losing the battle.

"I won't go!" she declared. "If you try to send me away, I'll run—"

"No! No, please, Lumen... I can't—don't!" Hendrix crushed her against his chest, silencing her threat with a desperate embrace.

Lumen froze, her breath hitching. The way he was holding her—the way his arms trembled around her—she knew. Despite his distance, despite his resistance, despite all the walls he had built around himself...

"I..." His voice broke against her hair. "I want you too. But—"

Lumen clung to him, pressing her face into his chest. "That's enough," she whispered. "That you want me too."

The anger melted from her body, replaced by quiet tears—this time, of relief.

Hendrix swallowed hard, torn between guilt and longing. He needed to get her inside before— Before they noticed.

–But. They weren't alone.

Loitering nearby, several sigbin hellspawns had caught her scent. They weren't part of Ehud's team—just low-level, hungry hellspawns. They had been prowling for something, something they had never expected to find near Parthena. And now, as they lurked in the shadows, watching the scene unfold in the alley, realization dawned.

"Tell the boss." One of them murmured into his phone. "The berhen is moving out soon. We need to make our move—fast."

And with that, the hunt began.

18

The Chase

Everything was set.

Augusta and Hugo had their assignments. Hendrix had mobilized his most trusted allies without directly meeting Lumen—except for Joreel, the only one both Nzo and Hendrix trusted without question.

Still, something gnawed at Hendrix. "Do we have to do this now? Lumen is ovulating. She smells like both heaven and hell right now," Hendrix muttered, glancing at Hiro.

"This is the perfect time," Hiro countered, his tone firm. "My contact says there's already a koine bounty on her head. The club could be raided anytime." There was truth in Hiro's urgency—some truth, at least.

Joreel, being too young, couldn't smell Lumen, so Hendrix had arranged their first meeting. Upon seeing her, Joreel tilted his head, unimpressed. "You're way too girly to be a boy, Iluminato."

Lumen blinked, then laughed. "Sorry about that." She liked Joreel. They had already spent hours working together on Nzo's RPG, and despite his sharp tongue, he was fun to be around.

Meanwhile, the escape plan was moving into place.

Hendrix had armed Hugo, Augusta, and Nzo with water guns filled with his diluted blood—a desperate contingency in case things went sideways. Craig and the rest of their team were positioned along the escape route, ensuring that no unexpected obstacles arose between Parthena and Hiro's house, where the X-helion SkyRaptor (AI operated chopper) was waiting to take Lumen to Perlaz.

Hendrix raised an eyebrow when Hiro mentioned the aircraft. "You have a runway at your house?"

"It's an X-helion SkyRaptor, not a plane," Hiro corrected. "It will make several stops before we reach the boundary of Perlaz safely. The trip will take days, and it's going to be risky as hell because the X-helion SkyRaptor is only authorized to fly to Cintru, not anywhere else." His voice was smooth, confident.

Hendrix narrowed his eyes. Something felt off.

Hiro leaned in slightly, lowering his voice. "It's my father's aircraft. I'm hijacking it for a day." That, of course, was a lie. But Hendrix didn't need to know everything. Some details were better left in the dark.

"Yes! Save lots-lots berhen! Okie-okie?!" Nzo chimed in, already imagining a grand rescue mission.

Hiro smirked, shaking his head. "Easy, kid. Let's focus on Lumen's safety first, alright?"

Meanwhile, Hendrix had his own battle to fight. He had learned about the ambush only recently—overheard the murmured plans of sigbin lurking in the shadows, waiting on the rooftops when he and Lumen had spoken in the alley. He had even listened in on their hushed conversations when he'd gone to check on her later that night.

They were coming for her. And he would be ready. While Hiro prepped the X-helion SkyRaptor, Lumen would be traveling with her family. Hendrix would be waiting, intercepting any threat before it could touch her.

Between Parthena and Hiro's house, Lumen had to arrive safely. With everything in place, Hiro gave Ehud the signal. The plan was in motion. There was no turning back now.

<><><>

"Are you there?" Sofia's voice was crisp over the phone.

"Yes," Ehud replied, lounging comfortably in Hiro's lavish estate. Aldred, Hiro's ever-efficient butler, had just escorted him inside.

"Good. I want you to catch Hiro red-handed," Sofia commanded.

"No problem." Ehud ended the call without hesitation. He turned to Aldred. "Is the X-helion SkyRaptor here?"

"Yes, Ehud. It just landed," the butler confirmed, already leading the way. Ehud followed him to the rooftop helipad, where the X-helion SkyRaptor was settling on its skids. As the blades slowed, the passengers inside became visible—fresh berhen from Perlaz. Their faces were filled with excitement, each of them believing they were moments away from meeting their Prince Charming.

It was all part of Hiro's brilliant plan.

First, they had eliminated the airport—the only official means of transporting berhen from Xego to Perlaz. Then, they had introduced the Bersig marriage agency, offering an escape to trapped berhen in Xego. A fairy-tale dream.

Except, for many, the dream ended in a nightmare.

For those who refused arranged marriages, Hiro's men waited. They stalked their targets, sometimes for months, even years, until they found the perfect moment to strike. A quiet night. An unguarded step. A locked door that was suddenly not locked.

"Just keep it nice and discreet," Hiro always reminded Ehud.

It was Ehud's job to keep his men in line. To make sure they stayed in the shadows.

When things got too heated in Xego, Hiro would shift operations toward the border of Perlaz. They had discovered a backdoor pass near Cintru—an area where the channaks were easily deceived and the humans were too ignorant of the true ways of the sigbin.

Koine. A better life overseas. The same lies. The same promises. The humans walked willingly into the hands of the coyotes—only to be hunted like prey the moment they left Perlaz's protective territory.

Another one of Hiro's genius ideas was the use of a rendezvous X-helion SkyRaptor and the construction of his own helipad. A faster, cleaner way to move berhen between Perlaz, Xego, and Zapad.

The system was nearly perfect. The X-helion SkyRaptor would land in Cintru for a few hours—or a day—to validate its travel pass. This allowed it to legally fly between Perlaz and Xego under the guise of a sanctioned route.

Sofia made sure the right people at the Cintru airport were well compensated—with fresh berhen for their dinner. Moving berhen from Xego to Zapad had never been an issue.

The only challenge? Humans could not survive in Cintru for more than a few minutes. The cold would kill them instantly.

Hiro had used his knowledge and connections to develop a specialized temperature-controlled system inside the X-helion SkyRaptor, ensuring human survival for a day at most. The initial runs had been disastrous. But after refining the technology, they managed several glitch-free trips.

Ehud watched as the berhen stepped off the X-helion SkyRaptor, wide-eyed and hopeful.

"Welcome!" Abigail greeted them with a practiced smile, her voice warm and inviting.

Ehud studied her carefully.

Abigail was Hiro's longest-surviving bride. Most of Hiro's wives never lasted this long. Now that Hiro had a new berhen from Xego—the one he was obsessed with—Ehud knew Abigail's time was running out.

Soon, she would become dinner.

Ehud's attention shifted when a young channak emerged from the X-helion SkyRaptor alongside the berhen. His brow furrowed. "Who's this?" he asked the pilot.

The girl stepped forward. "I'm Reeva. Turing sent me to make sure everything's in order."

A channak. Interesting. Ehud examined her with curiosity.

At twelve years old, Reeva was at the delicate cusp of womanhood when she had been turned into a sigbin.

"Make arrangements for our guests," Ehud instructed Aldred and Abigail. "We'll transfer them to their fiancés as soon as my trucks arrive."

He then turned to Vahitna. "You—go with them. Make sure they're gone before Hiro arrives with his girl."

"Understood," Vahitna said, nodding toward Reeva and the others before following Aldred.

Ehud took one last glance at the berhen before shifting his gaze toward the darkening sky. Everything was in motion. And soon, the real game would begin.

<><><>

Hiro had no intention of bringing Lumen to his house. The risk was far greater than he had anticipated.

"Why would you schedule the transfer of your berhen to Perlaz when I have a new delivery coming in?" Ehud asked, frowning. It didn't make sense. Their X-helion SkyRaptor would be flagged in Cintru for an unscheduled trip.

"Who said I was taking the berhen to Perlaz?" Hiro's lips curled into a wicked smile.

Ehud chuckled knowingly. *So, Abigail's time is finally up.*

But Hiro had a different plan. He was taking Lumen to his father's house instead. There, another X-helion SkyRaptor waited—one that could pilot itself under any radar. It was the only way to bypass all the red tape in Cintru.

To make sure his father was distracted, he had arranged a meeting between Mr. Hajji and Nzo—his father's favorite channak. With Hajji preoccupied, Hiro would hijack the X-helion SkyRaptor without a hitch.

He had spent weeks weighing his options. Cathy would never have approved of him hurting Lumen. Losing her had been painful enough—he wouldn't lose his brother again, too. And Nzo... Nzo had made him feel like family. For the first time in his life, Hiro belonged somewhere.

Just like Hendrix, he was determined to get Lumen to Perlaz safely—to let her live the life of a human, marry, and have children. This time, Hiro was proud of himself. He had chosen to betray Sofia again. Sofia always brought out the monster in him. But Hendrix?

Hendrix saw the good in his heart. And that was all that mattered now.

Nzo would meet with Mr. Hajji. Joreel would protect Lumen and her family from possible attacks. All Hiro had to do was wait—and get the X-helion SkyRaptor ready.

<><><>

Hendrix gritted his teeth as he followed three sigbin-occupied cars tailing Joreel. He was starting to doubt himself. He had never anticipated that his driving skills would be so outmatched.

He might have excelled in simulated battles, but car chases? That was a whole different beast. "Craig," Hendrix called, gripping his phone.

"Yes, boss," Craig answered quickly.

"Take care of the two cars behind me. I'll handle the third." He floored the accelerator. If he couldn't shake them, he would force a confrontation.

"Copy, boss," Craig responded.

Hendrix saw his car overtake a cluster of vehicles ahead. But in his focus, Hendrix missed something. Another car. It had been trailing Joreel from a distance—its passengers weren't part of the original ambush. They had accidentally picked up Lumen's scent when Nzo stepped out to meet Mr. Hajji.

And now? They were hungry—just like the others.

<><><>

Hiro pulled into his father's estate, his eyes immediately locking onto the X-helion SkyRaptor. It was there. Secured. Untouched. But as he approached the mansion, his stomach twisted.

The front door swung open. Sofia stepped out. And right beside her—

"Father." Hiro froze.

Mr. Hajji hurried toward him, his expression filled with a mix of relief and concern. "H-Hiro... Is it true?" His father's voice trembled.

Sofia stood at his side, smiling wickedly.

Hiro's fists clenched. The plan had just become a hell of a lot more complicated.

<><><>

"Hiro, not now!" Hendrix roared into the phone, gripping the steering wheel so tightly his knuckles turned white. His entire focus was on the road—until a car slammed into his side out of nowhere. His tires screeched, the impact jolting him into the ditch. He spun out of control, losing sight of the car tailing Joreel. "What?!?" Hendrix could barely hear Hiro screaming on the other end of the line.

He swerved, fighting for control, but the pursuit had turned chaotic. Three new vehicles had joined the chase. Above them, flying cars hovered, their drivers likely reporting the reckless pursuit. They had chosen traditional cars for a reason—to avoid detection.

But now?

They had failed at staying discreet. Hendrix barely had time to react as another car cut across his path—

Then, impact.

The sickening sound of metal crumpling. The world tilted, and suddenly—he was rolling. Car after car. On and off the road.

Until everything— Went still.

<><><>

With Hendrix out of the picture, Joreel was alone --and surrounded.

Five full-grown sigbin closed in around him. Hugo's car was totaled, its doors crushed inward. Inside, the family screamed in terror. Joreel assessed the battlefield. He could take three of them, but the remaining two were dangerously close to breaking into the car—and once they got inside, it would be over.

Hugo had a weapon, but it wouldn't be enough. No human could survive fighting them.

Joreel tightened his grip. He wouldn't let them take Hendrix's friends. No matter what. The largest sigbin shifted into a monstrous green form and advanced.

From atop the car, Joreel stayed high, his position giving him a strategic advantage. His mind calculated angles, attack points, escape routes—his simulated battles had prepared him for this moment.

The kid smirked. Come at me, then. In a blur, Joreel launched forward— His flying kick struck dead center, blades snapping from his forearms in one fluid motion. By the time his feet hit the ground, two sigbin had been cleaved in half.

The battlefield stilled for a breath. Joreel barely spared them a glance. They would regenerate—but not quickly enough.

Hendrix will be here soon. I just have to hold them off. He squared up against the next two, fully prepared to take them down. But he missed the one crawling beneath the wreckage.

Metal groaned. The car door wrenched open—right where Lumen was sitting.

"Lumen!" Joreel spun toward her, but the giant sigbin seized him from behind.

Lumen screamed.

Hugo raised his water gun—a desperate, last-ditch effort to protect his daughter. The blast missed. The weapon clattered to the ground, useless. The sigbin lunged— And was ripped away from behind.

Joreel caught the blur of motion before he was sent flying—the giant sigbin had kicked him with inhuman force. Joreel barely had time to register the impact before he was airborne. Crap!

The wind roared in his ears as he tumbled through the air. He'd land miles away if not for— A car. He collided with an unfamiliar car, abruptly halting his acceleration. Joreel landed several meters away from the wreckage, missing it at first—until he saw

—Hendrix. His boss' grip on the bloodhound was unrelenting. The sigbin struggled against him, its movements wild, erratic. Then—a blade. Joreel saw it before Hendrix did.

The sigbin's clawed fingers wrapped around the hilt, bringing it up, straight for Hendrix's throat—

Hendrix didn't stop it. Instead, he let the blade cut him. Dark, thick blood gushed over the sigbin's body.

"W-what the f—" The hellspawn collapsed.

Joreel stared, not fully understanding what was happening—Hendrix's back was turned to him.

"Get them out of here!" Hendrix barked, shoving the car—the whole darn car— with the humans inside, toward Joreel, who was scrambling back from his crash landing.

Joreel clutched his arm—his shoulder was definitely broken, but regenerating as expected. But there was no time.

"Go!" Hendrix shouted, not wanting the channak to see that he was bleeding everywhere.

Joreel ran to save the humans inside the car.

◇◇◇

Hiro waited on the deserted road. The meeting point was eerily quiet. He had barely managed to escape from Sofia and his father, but he knew it wouldn't take them long to follow.

Then— Two cars pulled up. Both wrecked.

Hendrix climbed out first, no traces of blood anywhere. One vehicle was packed with unconscious snoring sigbin—Hugo's car. The other belonged to the attackers, now being driven by Hugo with his family. Hendrix had taken all the sigbin down—one by one, methodically, until only his team remained.

He had switched vehicles, transferred Joreel and the humans to a safer car, and cleaned up after himself before meeting Hiro.

Hiro exhaled. "What the hell happened?"
"What's going on?" Hendrix asked.
They spoke in unison while trying to understand what was happening.
Hiro explained his failed plan B.

"Joreel," Hendrix turned to the kid. "Call Nzo. Tell him what happened. He's still waiting for Mr. Hajji. Tell him Craig is picking him up to meet us."

Joreel quickly dialed. Nzo answered almost immediately.
"Me...Nzo here, okie-okie?!" Nzo said, his voice sharp.
"Back to plan A –my house." Hiro interjected, thinking fast. "But my b-business partners are there. My father knows it's the last place I'd hide. Let me go there first—make them leave. I'll call you when it's safe to sneak Lumen in."

The plan was shaky. But Hiro was running out of time. "Wait here."
"No!" Hendrix snapped.

Hiro clenched his jaw. They didn't have time to argue. "Wh-what? Why?" Hiro's voice wavered, confusion gripping him. His mind raced—he had to warn Ehud, tell him to leave before it was too late. But he couldn't use his phone. Ehud was likely waiting for him, believing he was part of his plan all along. He wasn't.

But there was no time to explain.

"I can handle your guests," Hendrix said, his tone firm. "It'll be faster if I deal with them. Let me go to your house instead." Hendrix knew that the sigbin they had shaken off earlier would eventually pick up Lumen's scent again. They would catch up. And he had an idea. Gather them all at Hiro's house. Put everyone to sleep.

Then, once Lumen was safe in Perlaz, he would tell Hiro the truth – about his blood.

"You have to take Lumen far from here," Hendrix continued. "They'll follow us to your house, thinking she's still in my car. Your car doesn't carry her scent yet."

"No!" Hiro shot back instinctively. "I can't... be with her." He wanted to say yes. He wanted to protect her. But he couldn't let Hendrix see what was inside his house.

"Hendrix fast, yes. Go! Okie-okie?!" Nzo cut in, joining in the conversation through video call.

Hiro gritted his teeth. "Then let me and Hendrix go to my house. Joreel can take Lumen somewhere safe."

"I can be with her," Joreel volunteered.

But Hendrix hesitated.

Joreel was strong—but barely managed against five sigbin in their last fight. If another attack came, Hiro's presence alone could deter them.

"Hendrix, you okie-okie? Hiro know now?" Nzo asked meaningfully. It wasn't just about strategy. Nzo was really asking—was Hendrix ready to reveal himself to Hiro?

Hendrix's jaw clenched. "Yes," he said at last. "Hiro can come with me." He had no choice but to trust Joreel with Hugo's family again.

—but just then.

Craig had reported four more cars still tracking Lumen's scent. The sigbin had caught her trail where Hendrix had fought them earlier—it was impossible to lose them now. Nzo had to wait for them to pick him up. Craig and Lane would try their best to intercept or slow them down, but it was only a matter of time before they reached them.

Then—another problem.

"HELP! HELP! MY MOM!" Lumen's voice shattered the moment. Hugo was shaking. "I have to take her to the hospital!"
"GO!" Nzo barked over the phone, his voice tight with worry.
Lumen jumped out of the car, panic in her eyes.
"Hiro, go with them!" Hendrix ordered. "They might be chased—a sigbin needs to escort them."
Hiro froze.
"Hendrix," he muttered. "I can smell Augusta's blood."

Silence.

"Joreel go-go, okie-okie?" Nzo interjected. "He - channak - no blood like." Nzo acknowledged Hiro with a rare sense of respect, grateful that he had the courage to admit his weakness.

Now, it was just them as Joreel left for the hospital helping Hugo and his wife. Three sigbin –one on the phone Two cars. And no plan. They were back to square one.

Who would take care of Lumen while they handled the sigbin at Hiro's house? Hiro could do it, while Hendrix stayed with Lumen. However, if he had to fight off four cars full of sigbin chasing them, Lumen could be put in harm's way.

Craig's voice cut through the comms. "We can't shake them off! They're heading straight for you!"

Hendrix clenched his fists. There was only one way to end this. He would lure the sigbin to Hiro's house, as he originally planned. Take them all in one go. His blood would do the rest.

Likewise, Hiro's mind spun. Ehud needs to get the berhen out. Now. If he didn't—Hendrix would find out everything.

Hendrix turned to Hiro. "Take Lumen."

Nzo echoed the same command. "Yes Lumen Hiro. Okie-okie?! GO!"

The plan was final.

Hiro looked at Lumen. Her frightened eyes met his. And he lost his resolve. Saving Lumen... This was his redemption. His final chance to undo the sins of his past. Whatever Hendrix would find in his house—whatever truths came to light—Hiro only hoped he could be forgiven. By saving Lumen. That would have to be enough.

"U-Uncle..."

Hiro and Hendrix turned to Lumen at the same time. Her voice was small, trembling. There was dried blood on her clothes—her mother's blood. She looked lost, her emotions tangled in fear and uncertainty. She was worried about Augusta. She was terrified for her own life. And now... Hendrix was leaving her.

Hendrix stepped forward, removing his jacket and gently draping it over her shoulders to cover the bloodstains. "Uncle Hiro will protect you," Hendrix assured her. The words felt thick in his mouth.

Lumen's scent was getting stronger, richer—and even Hendrix had to take a moment to suppress the instinct clawing at the back of his throat.

Lumen's lips parted. "...But you said..." She trailed off, her voice barely a whisper. She liked Hiro—she really did. But she wanted to be with Hendrix.

"Shhh... I'll be with you soon, promise," Hendrix whispered as he pulled her into a hug. His grip was warm, steady, reassuring. "We just have to make sure everything is safe first, okay?"

Lumen clung to him, nodding weakly.

Hiro watched. A pang of jealousy twisted in his chest. Their closeness—the way Lumen melted into Hendrix's embrace—hurt. How was Hendrix able to do this? Why did Lumen allow him to touch her like that?

Lumen was always pleasant around Hiro, but there was something guarded about her. A quiet caution. But with Hendrix? She trusted him completely. And Hiro knew why.

She senses it. She knows. You're a predator. And Hendrix is not. "Stop it," Hiro snapped at himself internally. "Lumen, I will protect you. I promise," he said aloud, his voice steady. And he meant every word.

Hiro needed to earn her trust—the same way Hendrix had. He had done it before with his berhen brides. All it took was patience. He could do it again, clutching the vial of blood – Caiphaiz's – discreetly chained around his neck. Self control. He can save Lumen, he must!

Hendrix stood still as he watched them drive away.

Then— "I love you," Soft. Barely audible. But Hendrix heard it. It sent a sharp ache through his chest. And he regretted not answering her back.

"Kid, are you still there?" Hendrix asked, still looking at the moving car Hiro was driving to take Lumen away from him.

"Yes, boss" Craig answered instead. "We got Nzo. We have four cars behind us though."

Hendrix's grip on the wheel tightened. The urge to toss his sleeping passengers out gnawed at him, but he couldn't risk leaving a trace. Time was slipping away.

He exhaled sharply. "Here's the plan."

19

The Vial

Hiro and Lumen drove in silence. The air inside the car was thick, charged with something unspoken. *"I love you,"* he heard—soft, almost a whisper. But... no, it couldn't be. *I must have misheard it.*

Hiro couldn't allow himself to believe that Lumen had feelings for Hendrix. Not like the brides he once had—brides he had feasted on. "Don't worry, Lumen," He murmured, stealing a glance at her. But reassuring her wasn't the problem—her scent was making his head spin.

If he had known he'd end up alone with her like this, he would have married Abigail first. Eaten her first. Satisfied himself before facing this. Stay in control. His grip on the wheel tightened.

To calm himself, he pulled out a small vial and took a sip of Caiphaiz's blood. It worked—for now. Hiro glanced at Lumen again when she didn't respond.

She was asleep. It was past midnight. They were halfway to the water reservoir, where they had agreed to wait for Hendrix's call, when—

A soft moan.

Hiro's head snapped toward her. "Lumen? What's wrong? Are you alright?" Concern flared inside him. He pulled the car over, choosing an abandoned tunnel that cut through the reservoir. The area had thick vegetation—trees, tall grass—enough to scatter Lumen's scent and confuse any sigbin still tracking her.

No one would suspect his car.

A government-issued vehicle, owned by his father. The nearest, most convenient escape route when he had fled his father's house. Hiro got out and rushed to Lumen's side, opening her door. She collapsed into his arms.
"Lumen!"
She was barely conscious, her breath shallow.

Panic clawed at Hiro's chest. He carried her to the grassy ground near the water, laying her down gently. The fresh air helps dilute her scent—finally giving him room to think. "Don't die on me... what's wrong?" He splashed cool water onto her face.
She moaned, weakly, and touched her side.
Hiro lifted her blouse. His stomach dropped. A dark bruise—deep, almost black—spread across her ribs. The car crash. A rib must have broken. She was bleeding inside.
"No!" His mind raced. He had to get her to a hospital.

But—

That would expose her. Every sigbin in the area would smell her. His phone was in the car. But there was no one to call. No one to trust. Not even his father.

Then—

Lumen gasped. A sharp, rattling sound. Then—nothing.

"No!" Hiro pressed his fingers to her neck. Her pulse was fading. "Lumen—!" Without thinking, he pressed his lips to hers, forcing air into her lungs.

Her scent hit him like a drug. A mistake. His body reacted. He shifted instantly, his fangs lengthening, his hands gripping her too tightly. Her blood. Her soft flesh. And the scent from between her legs.

His mouth watered. His vision blurred. "NO!" Hiro wrenched himself back, shaking his head violently. *You're disgusting. Get it together.* His fingers trembled as he grabbed the vial again, drinking more of Caiphaiz's blood.

The hunger dulled. He was himself again. He turned back to resuscitating Lumen. "Come on, Lumen. Wake up." He pressed his hands to her chest, carefully—so carefully—massaging her heart, making sure he didn't break her.

Again. And again. Then—

A cough. Lumen gasped, sucking in a desperate breath. Her heartbeat stabilized.

Hiro exhaled, his body sagging with relief as he cradled her, pressing his forehead against hers. "Lumen... you're bleeding inside. I have to—" His words died in his throat.

Lumen's eyes fluttered open. And something about them was different. She smiled. "Hi."

Hiro blinked, caught off guard. "A-are you okay?" He leaned in, listening to her heartbeat. It was different. Steady. Stronger. Changed.

Then—

Lumen reached up. Gripped his collar. And pulled him down. Her lips crashed into his. A deep, desperate kiss.

<><><>

Reeva had finally uncovered how their border had been breached. The channaks stationed on the Cintru side were too young, too naïve, and far too easy to deceive. It was their fault.

They had grown careless, assuming no one would dare cross the sacred lands of Kein, their god. No sigbin in their right mind would defy his order to leave the humans of Perlaz untouched.

And yet—someone had.

And now, the borders were compromised. Reeva had recently learned that it wasn't just Cintru—the other border outposts were also falling apart. Why? Because the channaks were being bribed. Fed a steady supply of sweets—making them lazy, complacent, and easily manipulated.

With Vhinoe's help, they had tracked down the humans involved in the scheme. Those who could be dealt with—were.

But there was still more to uncover.

Reeva had gotten critical intel from Turing, one of the channaks tricked at the Cintru border. Using his information, she had infiltrated the next berhen delivery—coming along under the guise of an observer.

Now, she was here. She needed to understand how the entire operation worked. Rescuing the berhen was her ultimate goal. But first—she had to find the culprits. The traitors. And she was close.

The AI operated helicopter carrying the berhen landed on a massive estate—one of the many properties under Hajji Inc. Reeva's stomach twisted. She was beginning to see the full scope of this. Who was truly behind it. How deep this corruption ran. How high up the operation really went.

If her suspicions were correct, this could be the start of something far worse—something that could lead to another war between humans and sigbin. And Perlaz would be caught in the middle.

Inside the mansion, the berhen were seated comfortably in an opulent receiving area, their faces alight with excitement and wonder. They thought they were stepping into their new lives. They had no idea what awaited them.

Reeva clenched her fists. She needed answers. She needed to dig deeper. As she turned to leave and begin her search, she heard a commotion outside. Her ears perked up.

She moved toward the window— And what she saw stunned her. They were under attack. By a baby channak. Armed with a water gun.

Reeva blinked.

What. The. Heck?

<><><>

Hiro was stunned. Lumen's lips pressed against his—soft, urgent, needy. For a brief moment, his mind blacked out. Then instinct took over. He kissed her back.

Her sweetness melted into him, her soft tongue tangling with his. A deep growl rumbled from his chest as his body reacted—heat pulsing, his restraint slipping.

Hiro, stop! He tried to control himself, tried to fight the transformation clawing at his insides. But how could he?

Lumen was on top of him now, pressing into him, her movements urgent, desperate. She was kissing him—devouring him.

And he—

He growled in ecstasy. Lumen answered him with a moan, breathless, wanting. "L-Lumen... wait—" Hiro struggled to rein himself in. He was careful not to crush her, but she was relentless, her hands sliding against his chest, her fingers gripping him tightly.

He forced himself to pull back—just enough to breathe. Then he saw it. He lifted her blouse slightly, expecting to see the bruise from earlier. There was nothing. His stomach dropped.

Her ribs—completely healed. How? Lumen was human. She had no ability to regenerate. "Lumen...?"

She leaned in, her lips brushing against his ear. "I want you, Hiro." Her voice was a whisper, thick with longing, and it sent shivers down his spine.

Hiro swallowed hard.

Lumen straddled him, her arms locking around his neck, pulling him into the softness of her chest.

Her scent—thick, intoxicating, overwhelming. It was driving him insane. The monster inside him clawed at the surface.

Then—

A sharp ringing shattered the moment. Hiro froze. The burner phone Hendrix handed to him. Lumen barely reacted, still wrapped around him. "Wait here," he muttered, untangling himself from her grip. It took him a moment to pry himself away. His body was still burning when he reached the car.

Hendrix.

Hiro hesitated, staring at the name flashing on the screen. Then he looked back.

Lumen was laughing, playing in the water reservoir, carefree. Alive.

Something inside him clenched. Without a second thought, he threw the phone into the water. "Come on, Lumen! We have to go!" Hiro called out.

Lumen turned, smiling—glowing. She ran to him and hugged him tightly, pressing her warmth against him like she never wanted to let go.

Hiro's chest ached. "Where do you want to go?" he asked, waiting, expecting her to say Hendrix's name.

Lumen smiled softly. "Anywhere you want." Then she reached for his lips again.

Hiro's heart swelled. "What about Hendrix? Your grandpa? Your mom—" His words were muffled as Lumen kissed him again.

"I don't care!" she breathed between kisses. "I want you! Only you!" And for the first time in his immortal life—

Hiro felt pure joy.

<><><>

Nzo, small and fast, darted past Hiro's guards before they even had a chance to react. A quick blast from his water gun—one down. Another splash—two more crumpled to the ground. With the entrance cleared, Nzo signaled for the others to move in. Several trucks were parked in Hiro's driveway.

Odd.

Hendrix noted them but had no time to investigate. His priority was handling the cars chasing them before they reached Hiro's mansion.

"Help Nzo inside. I'll deal with these guys," Hendrix ordered Craig and Lane. Headlights appeared in the distance—incoming vehicles.

Hendrix clenched his fists. He would meet them head-on. "This isn't a simulation," Hendrix reminded his team, his voice low and firm. "We aim to cut them up—fast. No drawn-out fights. They should take hours to heal, buying us enough time for Hiro to get Lumen out on the X-helion SkyRaptor."

Craig and Lane nodded.

"Attack and go. No distractions. We're not here for fun—we're here to empty this house. Move quietly around the trucks. No unnecessary noise."

The two sigbin still didn't understand exactly what was going on, but if both Hiro and Hendrix were involved, they were in.

Nzo and the rest rushed toward the main house. Hendrix turned toward the approaching cars.

Inside Hiro's Mansion, Nzo darted through the dimly lit hallway. Then—

"W-what the fu—" Ehud's chair scraped against the floor as he whipped around, spotting Nzo's reflection on his computer screen. Before he could react, splash! A jet of water hit him square in the face. Ehud staggered, choking. Before his partner could even stand

—THUMP!

Nzo landed on the second man's shoulders, spraying water directly into his mouth. Both sigbin dropped instantly, unconscious. Nzo grinned.

Then—

A gasp from behind him. Nzo's ears twitched. Someone's still inside. Moving silently, he tiptoed to the corner, following the familiar layout of Hiro's mansion. He had been here before. He knew the hallways.

A shadow flickered in the dim light. Nzo pressed himself against the wall, waiting.

The figure passed—

He leaped, gun aimed. "Stop!" The woman froze, arms raising in surrender. "Turn around!" Nzo commanded, stepping forward cautiously. Slowly, she did.

Vahitna's breath hitched. The room was filled with unconscious sigbin, their bodies sprawled across the floor, glistening with reddish liquid.

A channak baby stood in the center, his tiny frame dominant, his weapon lethal.

Before she could react, she turned and ran. She needed to hide. Whatever that liquid was—her instinct screamed at her to stay away from it.

Then—

She stopped. Nzo stood in the middle of the hallway, gasping. Their eyes met.

And Vahitna froze. Her heart slammed against her ribs. She had never seen a child more beautiful in her life. He looked exactly like her son, Jordan. Tears burned at the edges of her eyes. She had lost him long ago. And now, standing in front of her was—

Nzo.

The baby stared back, his face softening, his mouth slightly open. His nostrils flared, drinking in her scent. His lips parted. His gaze dropped— To the milk dripping from her leaking breasts. A hunger unlike anything she had ever seen flickered in his eyes.

Vahitna's breath shuddered. Her body responded—heart pounding, emotions crashing over her.

Nzo licked his lips.

Vahitna trembled—and in that moment, they both discovered what they had been searching for their entire immortal lives.

<><><>

Hiro had nowhere to take Lumen. Not without his father's help. Not without his friends. He was too well-known to risk seeking aid from other sigbin. That left him with only one option.

A place Hendrix wouldn't look for them—at least not for a while. By the time they reached the quiet safehouse, the sun was already rising. Lumen was still asleep.

Hiro didn't place her on the bed. She would look too much like food to him. But for some strange reason, he no longer wanted her heart. He wanted—something else.

Instead, he laid her on the couch near the fireplace and watched her. He had ditched the car. Destroyed anything traceable. No gadgets. No GPS. Nothing that could lead anyone to them.

And yet—

His mind raced. "Crap, Hiro. What are you doing?!" The question echoed in his head, over and over. But the answer was always the same— "I don't know." He had saved Lumen. He was sure of it.

She had been dead. He had felt her fading pulse beneath his fingers before he pressed his lips to hers, breathing life back into her.

And yet—

She had come back—not just alive, but healed. He had expected her to be weak, but instead, she was stronger. Her eyes were different. Her scent had changed. Still delicious. Still intoxicating.

But not the same.

It had to be Caiphaiz's blood. But how? Lumen hadn't tasted it—he had.

Then—

You tried to resuscitate her. His breath caught. Was that it? Hiro had seen humans ingest Kein and Caiphaiz's blood before. He had seen their effects. A sensual bond. An intoxication.

But this— This was different.

Something else was happening to Lumen. Would the high wear off? Would she go back to her old self, just like the others who had been stoned on a god's blood?

Somehow, Hiro doubted it. He watched her as she slept, and the more he looked, the more he wanted her. His body tensed. He turned away, staring at the darkening sky, trying to think. He had already betrayed his friends—

First, with Sofia. Then, with Ehud and his team. Then, with his father. And now— Hendrix. His brother. And Nzo's entire family.

The weight of it crashed over him. Panic coiled in his chest. He grabbed the vial and drank from it again, feeling the burn of the blood coat his throat. A few drops lingered on his lips.

Then—

Arms wrapped around him from behind. His body froze. The warmth. The softness. A scent so achingly familiar that for a moment— He thought it was her.
Ahhh, heaven... It was like Cathy all over again. Like he was human again. Like nothing had changed.

He turned.

Lumen's eyes were heavy-lidded. Her breath was hot against his skin. Then she kissed him. Hungrily. Desperately. With a passion that threatened to undo him.

<><>

Lumen woke to the intoxicating scent of something delicious. Her eyes fluttered open, and she saw Hiro standing near the window, bathed in the soft evening light. He smelled so good. Before she could even think, she rushed toward him, wrapping her arms tightly around his body.

Hiro turned—

The concentrated fragrance of his presence hit her like a drug. Lumen's lips parted. She didn't hesitate. Her mouth crashed into his. Hiro's lips set her on fire. A part of her screamed to stop—whispers of her family, of Hendrix, of the girl she had once been.
This isn't who you are. But something stronger—something primal—drowned out the doubt. It was liberating. It was right.

Hiro groaned into the kiss, but his body reacted on its own. His skin shifted— Scales. Green. Monstrous. A deep growl rumbled through him as his transformation overtook him. No—

Hiro clenched his fists, fighting it, not wanting her to see his ugliness.

But then— Lumen touched his face, her fingers tracing his transformed features with something close to reverence. She looked deeply into his eyes.

And then—

She smiled. "Beautiful." She leaned in, pressing a gentle kiss to his monstrous face. Hiro's breath hitched. Then—

"Ahhh!" Lumen crumpled, clutching her stomach in pain.

"Lumen—!" Hiro dropped to his knees, eyes scanning her frantically. Her skin was perfect. No wounds, no bruises. "What's wrong?!"

Lumen gasped, her body trembling. "I-it's hot… burning hot."

Hiro grabbed a glass of cold water, pressing it to her lips.

She drank, panting.

Then—

She laughed. A sweet, playful sound as she splashed the water over her face, drenching herself.

Before Hiro could process what was happening, Lumen was peeling off her clothes, heading straight for the bathroom. Hiro hesitated. His mind was still spinning from the moment before.

Was she okay? Was this another effect of Caiphaiz's blood? His concern overpowered his hesitation. He followed her.

Lumen lay in the bathtub, fully submerged in the icy water.

"This is too cold," Hiro muttered, dipping his hand into the water.

"It's perfect."

Before he could react, she grabbed his wrist and pulled him in. Hiro stumbled, his clothes soaking instantly.

"Lumen, do you even understand what's happening to you?" Hiro asked, trying to anchor himself in reason, trying to fight the way her bare skin felt against his beneath the water. "Do you even know who I am?"

Lumen grinned, pressing her lips to his jaw. "Yes." Then she kissed him—again. And again.

Hiro growled, losing himself in the feeling of her.

The sensation of her soft, wet skin. The way she fit against him. The pull of something forbidden.

"W-what about your family?" Hiro gasped between kisses. "They'll be looking for you—"

"We'll see them after." She giggled when he kissed the side of her neck, her laughter sending shivers through his body.

"They won't approve of this—" Hiro barely finished the sentence before she pulled away. His heart sank.

But when he met her gaze, he froze. There was something new in her eyes— Something unchanging.

"Then I choose you," Lumen said stubbornly.

Hiro's breath caught. "You're high on Caiphaiz's blood," he murmured, pulling away slightly. He held up the vial, showing her the small remnants of the liquid that had changed everything. "You might change your mind."

Lumen didn't flinch. "Then don't let me." Her voice was fierce. She clung to him tighter. "I want you, Hiro. Please… Uncl—" She stopped herself. "Hiro." The name left her lips like a declaration. "Don't give up on me. Not like Uncle Hendrix did."

Hiro stared.

Whatever feelings she had once held for Hendrix— They were gone. I'm Lumen. I'm Still her — Yet something changed. She heard the small voice inside her, screaming at her to stop, to think, to remember who she was. But she couldn't. She didn't want to.

And for the first time— She loved the new Lumen she was becoming.

Hiro's chest tightened. His heart was pounding. He had been with so many berhen before.

But Lumen— Lumen wrecked him.

She was electrifying. Intoxicating. Something he couldn't resist.

"I'm yours," Lumen whispered, her lips trailing down his jaw. "Say it." She bit his lip.

Hiro groaned, shuddering at the sensation. "You're mine," he breathed, savoring the words. It wasn't just something he said. It was something he felt. Something he knew. "You're mine!" Hiro's voice rose, filled with something deeper—something undeniable.

And this time— He believed it.

It took some convincing, but eventually, Lumen climbed out of the water.

Hiro had already prepared food for her, and the moment she sat down, she devoured it with unrestrained hunger. He watched her, mesmerized.

Her wet hair clung to her shoulders, strands curling down her back. The oversized white T-shirt—something he had pulled from the laundry basket—draped over her body, slipping slightly off one shoulder.

She looked effortless. Beautiful.

Hiro himself wore nothing but loose pants, his chest bare, his damp skin still cooling from the water. For a fleeting moment, they felt like a couple on a honeymoon, sharing a midnight snack in the stillness of the night. "Are you satisfied with my cooking?" Hiro asked, pushing yet another glass of cold water toward her. She must have consumed liters by now.

Lumen licked her lips, finishing her last bite, then flashed him a mischievous smile. "Not yet."

Before he could react, she jumped onto his lap, straddling him right there at the dining table. Hiro inhaled sharply, his hands instinctively gripping her waist to steady her. "Lumen— I want to do this right."

Her breath was warm against his ear, her fingers tracing his shoulders, her hips pressing into him.

His pulse hammered. His grip tightened. And yet— He forced himself to pull away. Gently. Firmly.

Lumen's brows knitted together, her lips parting in frustration. "Why?" She hated the rejection.

Hiro swallowed hard.

"In the bedroom, then?" she asked, her voice softer this time—realizing he wasn't rejecting her, but redirecting her.

"No!" The word came out too fast, too sharp.

Lumen blinked.

Hiro exhaled, rubbing a hand down his face. *Bedroom is my kitchen.* That was where he ate. Where he consumed the ones who came before her. And he would not take her there.

Instead, Hiro lifted her effortlessly and carried her into the living room. There, he pressed her gently against the wall, their bodies entangled, their eyes locked. "Don't move." His voice was low, commanding, as if she were a child testing her limits.

Lumen laughed, giddy, her fingers trailing over his shoulders. But she nodded—knowing full well she would probably disobey him.

"Are you sure you want me?" Hiro asked again, searching her eyes. The haze was gone. Her pupils were clear—a soft, light green. She was no longer high. This was her choice.

And yet—

There was hunger in her gaze. Hiro saw it. Felt it. And it broke him. His restraint shattered. A low growl rumbled through him as he claimed her mouth, his lips moving against hers with undeniable need. His kisses trailed downward, almost devouring her skin—her neck, her shoulders—

And then—

His mouth hovered dangerously over her berhen heart. Much like the countless wives he had taken before, he knew exactly how to lead Lumen to the edge. To make her crave him. To pull her deeper, until she would willingly give him what he needed.

He expertly teased, navigating her body with the precise knowledge of a man who had done this a thousand times before. Every touch. Every whisper. Every slow, deliberate movement— Timed perfectly to seduce, to weaken, to destroy her defenses.

And all the while—

He was suffering. His monster roared beneath his skin, starving, held back by nothing but the slow anticipation of the feast to come. When he finally devoured her berhen heart, it would be worth it.

A wicked smile curled Hiro's lips as he kissed every inch of her soft, warm skin. Hiro owned this moment.

And soon— He would own her.

No! Hiro growled, his mouth splitting open, fangs elongating—a cavern of razor-sharp teeth poised to sink into Lumen's bare chest.

Lumen was lost in her delirium – completely unaware of her imminent demise. Her body was trembling uncontrollably —not from fear, but from pleasure Hiro was generously opening her eyes to feel.
What's wrong?! The monster inside him snarled, frustrated. *You know the routine. Take her! You can still have her— After I've fed.* A dark, familiar laughter echoed through his mind, slithering through his veins like poison.
No! Yes! No! Please... not... yet... NOW!
Hiro's body shook with conflict. The hunger. The primal urge. The routine—it was all so familiar.

And yet—

His body refused. With a roar, Hiro tore himself away, his chest heaving. He dropped to his knees before her, his forehead pressed against her stomach, trembling as if in worship. He felt her. Tasted her joy in the air—so raw, so pure, so alive. Her body didn't lie. She was his. She had given herself to him, fully.

And Hiro knew—

20

Hiro Her Hero

Lumen had already taken more than enough from him. He had been generous to her. Too generous. Lumen should have died hours ago. Yet here she was—glowing beneath him, her heartbeat strong, her warmth intoxicating.

Hiro clenched his fists, his fangs retracting, his breath shuddering with restraint. *What the hell is happening to me? Embrace your true self, Hiro... You are no hero. By now, Hendrix knows what you really are. There's no coming back from that. No redemption arc for you. They'll hate you anyway... So make the most of it.*

Yes. The monster won.

Hiro's lips traversing every inch of Lumen's skin, his hands roaming as he slowly rose to his feet, avoiding her gaze—focusing instead on the steady, rhythmic beat of her berhen heart.

The sweetest taste awaited him. The ultimate satisfaction. The insatiable hunger clawed at his insides, no longer willing to be controlled.

Lumen reached for him, her fingers grazing his jaw, attempting to lift his face—wanting to kiss him. To show him her gratitude. For opening her eyes. For revealing what the world truly was. For giving her what she never knew she had been missing.

Hiro's growl rumbled low and dangerous. His lips never met hers. Instead, he buried his face in the curve of her neck, kissing a path down to her collarbone, down to the soft, vulnerable flesh of her chest.

Where her heart beat for him. *I'll have you after.* Hiro assured himself, his resolve solidifying. His monster would be fed. Another berhen heart. One more. Just one more. Then—

"I love you, Hiro... My hero."

Hiro froze. It was so soft—so fragile—that he almost didn't hear it. Hiro's jaws were seconds from tearing into Lumen's chest, from ripping out the berhen heart that would finally sate his hunger.

Then— "I love you."

His fangs halted. His breath hitched. His hands—poised to claw through her flesh—trembled. A shudder ran through him as he forced his mouth closed.

His body shifted. The scales receded, his monstrous form melting away, leaving behind the man—the handsome, broken man—who now stood before her, exposed.

Hiro straightened, his gaze locking onto Lumen's. Her crying eyes burned into his soul. They held so much. So much emotion. So much trust. So much love.

For me? He couldn't read it – couldn't believe it. But he understood.

"I love you." Her voice was steady, filled with something so pure it unraveled him.

Hiro's breath came out shaky. His chest tightened. A single tear slid down his face before he could stop it. "I love you, Lumen." The words left his lips, raw and real, and as they did— The monster inside him shattered.

Its grip on him—on his soul—was obliterated. Hiro no longer hungered for her heart. He craved something else. To be one with her. Not as a predator. But as a man. He took her—gently, at first.

No! The monster inside screamed, thrashing in agony. Lumen's heart—her precious berhen heart—was lost to it forever. No feast. No satisfaction. Lumen is now tainted. No! "Hiro! Stop!"

But Hiro's own scream drowned it out— "Yes!" He embraced Lumen fully, becoming one with her—body, heart, and soul... if he even had one left to give. The ecstasy was unlike anything he had ever known.

Then—

His fangs sank into her neck. Her blood rushed over his tongue, warm, intoxicating—pure. Lumen cried out, but not in pain. In rapture.

Her fingers tore at his skin, her nails scraping against his neck— And then she found it.

The vial.

The last drop of Caiphaiz's blood. She ripped it from him, her breath ragged, her lips parted. And then— She drank it all. A final shudder passed between them.

And in the house, in the middle of nowhere, their voices rose together. A howl— A primal, unearthly, and exultant symphony.

<><><>

Despite sitting peacefully across from each other, the tension in the room was palpable. Everyone was inside Hiro's main house now. Hendrix had secured the sleeping sigbin, stuffing their bodies into Ehud's trucks, which had proven useful in hiding them. Craig and Lane patrolled the perimeter, assisting Nzo in rescuing the berhen.

And yet, no one fully trusted one another. Hendrix's sharp eyes remained locked on Reeva. Nzo, seated beside him, was glued to Vahitna. A handful of berhen huddled in the corner, clueless about what was happening, their expressions shifting between confusion and unease.

Craig and Lane, meanwhile, were outside, keeping their distance. The scent of the berhen inside was too much for them to bear. They had all briefed each other, but alliances were still uncertain.

Vahitna, the mole within the organization, was responsible for leaking the Bersig app to the authorities. Reeva was an undercover agent, investigating the smuggling of berhen from Perlaz. Hendrix and Nzo had one mission: smuggling one berhen—Lumen—out of Xego.

But trust? Trust was still a luxury no one could afford.

"T-thanks... for back there..." Reeva hesitated, directing her words at Hendrix. She had been seconds away from being dismembered by Hiro's butler, Aldred, when she was gathering the berhen back to the X-helion SkyRaptor.

Hendrix had silently intervened—slitting Aldred's throat before discreetly putting him to sleep. "No problem," Hendrix muttered, brushing it off. He had no interest in small talk.

Reeva's gaze flickered to Nzo's water gun. Her lips parted— "H-how did... what's in your...?" She couldn't finish. She had seen what it could do. She was curious.

Nzo's expression darkened. "No! Nzo no tell, okie-okie?!" he snapped. He might trust that she was from Perlaz, but that didn't mean he trusted her intentions.

She had openly admitted that she was here to investigate berhen smuggling—but what if she was here to take them all down?

"Why not? We have a right to protect ourselves too," Vahitna interjected, equally curious.

Nzo, however, had completely switched modes. His baby-like innocence resurfaced in front of Vahitna. "Oh, Nzo protect you, okie-okie?!" he cooed, flashing his wide, adoring eyes at her.

Vahitna melted, her laughter spilling out giddily. For her, Nzo was Jordan—the baby she had lost. And in her eyes, he could do no wrong.

Hendrix and Reeva exchanged looks, both annoyed.

"What's going on?" Abigail, Hiro's fiancée, finally spoke up. She and the other berhen had been ordered to sit and wait.

For what? And who were all these people inside her fiancé's house? She needed answers. Where was Hiro? Why wasn't he here to sort this out?

Vahitna turned to her. "Your marriage match is a fraud." Her voice was calm. "You're here to be eaten."

The words hit like a shockwave. "No—!" Abigail gasped, as did the other berhen. Disbelief. Fear.

"It's true." Reeva confirmed it, relieved that, at least for now, no one had been harmed.

"You'll be back in Perlaz soon," Hendrix assured them.

"Why betray your own group?" Hendrix's gaze bore into Vahitna.

She had risked everything by exposing the operation. The Bersig app had been the core of their scheme. Why had she turned on them, knowing how powerful they were?

Vahitna hesitated—then decided to trust them. "I was promised citizenship in Xego," she admitted. "To live among humans." She took a deep breath, her voice softening. "And to be around... babies." Her cheeks burned at the confession. She wanted to say it— I want to be with you. She nearly blurted it to Nzo.

"Really?" Nzo beamed, his excitement pure and childlike.

"Don't pregnant sigbin eat babies?" Reeva's voice cut through the moment, cold and analytical.

Nzo's eyes widened—"You do!? Okie-okie?!" he giggled in fascination.

Then—

"Ouch!" A smack to the head from Hendrix. "What's wrong with you?" Hendrix snapped.

"Effing you, Drix, okie-okie?!" Nzo yelled.

"Language, dear," Vahitna scolded gently.

"Sorry, Mimi—er... Mama—ouch!"

Another smack from Hendrix.

Reeva smirked despite herself.

"Stop it!" Vahitna chided, her maternal instinct kicking in.

Nzo huffed, standing up—his small frame shifting, his aura changing. He was preparing to attack Hendrix. His body tensed, slowly shifting into—

"Enough!" Vahitna's voice snapped through the room.

Instantly, Nzo froze. Then, pouting, he sat back down, obedient.

Then—

"Oh." Vahitna's blouse was soaked. Again. Her milk leaked through the fabric. Her instincts screamed to bite Nzo, to cradle him.

And Nzo— His mouth watered. His ears twitched, hearing the soft patter of dripping milk.

"What are we waiting for?" Reeva, frustrated, finally spoke up.

Hendrix glanced at his phone, agitated. "The pilot. And another berhen." His grip tightened around the device. He had been calling Hiro. Texting him. But there was no response. Hours had passed. And Hendrix was growing restless.

–Just then.

The phone rang. The sharp sound cut through the room like a blade. Everyone jumped.

Nzo grabbed it first. "Okie-okie?!" he said into the receiver.

Hendrix leaned forward. "What?" He was hoping—praying—that it was Hiro.

"Augusta okie-okie!" Nzo let out a relieved sigh.

Hendrix barely had time to process the information before making a decision. "I'm going to find them," he announced, already moving. "I can trace Lumen's scent." He turned toward the door—

Only to have it open before he could take a step. A heavy presence filled the doorway. A familiar face.

"Mr. Hajji." Vahitna stiffened. Her true boss had arrived.

<><><>

Hiro had lost count of how many times he had taken Lumen into his arms. She met him with the same hunger, the same eagerness, never once recoiling from his monstrous form. The beast inside him—once relentless, insatiable—was now silent.

Satisfied.

No longer regretful that it had been denied the taste of Lumen's berhen heart. Because Lumen was no longer a berhen. She was safe.

And as long as she was his, no one would dare harm her—unless they were foolish enough to face his wrath.

"Come here." Hiro reached for her, pulling her up from where she knelt before him—her worship of him as divine as it was carnal.

She couldn't seem to get enough of him. Just as he couldn't of her. Hiro's fingers skimmed over her skin, tracing the places where his fangs had pierced her. The wounds were already closing. She was healing. Faster than any athena he had ever encountered.

Yet Lumen was not like them.

She was something else. Something more. Hiro's mind struggled to grasp it, his instincts screaming that he knew— That he had seen this before. A memory, buried in the depths of time. Lumen wasn't just transformed. She was becoming.

But what?

His golden eyes flickered as he studied her, searching for the truth. And then— It hit him. It wasn't just the vial of Caiphaiz's blood that had changed her.

That wasn't enough.

She had tasted the purest blood of a god— And she hated it. Her body had rejected it. She had nearly vomited the precious last drop of the sacred liquid he had risked everything to acquire from Cintru.

But he hadn't let her. He couldn't. Not a single drop could be wasted. So before she could spit it out, Hiro had captured her lips. A quick, desperate transfer. A kiss laced with divinity. A kiss that sealed her fate.

That's when Hiro noticed the change. His saliva—mixed with the blood from Lumen's mouth—tastes sickly sweet. That was it. That had to be it. The answer struck him like lightning. *This is why she's different.*

Hiro had no way to test his theory, but deep down, he knew— This was the only explanation. The only thing that made sense. And to think— He had been moments away from ripping her heart out. He had been starving.

Freaking romance! He had intended to end her life.

Then she whispered— "I love you, Hiro... my hero."

And in that instant, everything had changed. Not only had he spared her, but— She had enslaved his heart. He was hers. As much as she was his.

It wasn't just love. It was something deeper. Something binding.

A sire bond.

He had heard of this before— Of how Caiphaiz loved Kein because he was sired through his blood. It was an unbreakable tether—a connection to Kein's heart and soul that would never fade. All sigbin feared Kein, but not all were sired in this way. The immortal creations forged through vaccine inoculations were nothing compared to the ones created by pure blood.

And now—

Lumen was one of them. A bond unlike any other. A bond that would never break. With his love for Lumen consuming him, Hiro was ready to face the wrath of Hendrix and Nzo. They could curse him. They could fight him. It didn't matter. Because in the end—

Lumen was already dead.

But now— She was alive. And she was his. *I brought her back.* He had resurrected her— Given her new life. They had no choice but to accept it. Either way, Lumen would always be safe with him now. Now that she was no longer a berhen. She belonged only to him.

Then—

Lumen was kissing him. Fiercely. Passionately. Whispering against his lips, confessing how much she adored him, how deeply she loved him.

Hiro's heart ached— So full, so overwhelmed with joy he thought it might burst.

How could someone like Lumen—so pure, so radiant—want him this way? He didn't deserve her. Didn't deserve this happiness. But heck if he was going to let it slip away. He would take it. Hold it. And never let anyone come between them.

A new surge of desire ripped through him. He took over—guiding Lumen, pleasuring her, starting the seduction over again. He was tireless. He could go on for eternity. And if he had his way— He would.

Lumen shuddered beneath him, breathless, her fingers clawing at his back. "More. I want more." She was begging— As if for her life.

Then—

She flipped him over, impatient, claiming him this time. Hiro chuckled, surprised at her boldness.

But then—

They struggled. Playfully, at first— But there was strength in Lumen that he hadn't expected. It reminded him of his battles in the arena. For the first time— Hiro felt the weight of her power. He could hurt her. She could bleed. She could break.

And yet—

She was far from fragile. She was ferocious. Supernatural. Her strength—it amazed him. And before he even realized it—

He was defeated.

Lumen took him, as if he were her slave. Their bodies moved together, as if dancing— At first to a slow, delicate melody— Then to the wild, untamed rhythm of a storm. Electricity ripped through Hiro's body. His muscles tensed. His skin shifted. He could feel himself changing again—

But he held it back.

He wanted to savor this. Wanted to devour every second. Wanted to let Lumen have him, fully— Again. And again. And again.

Then—

Lumen screamed, her body arching, going rigid beneath him. That was when Hiro bit into her skin, bathing in the warmth of her blood. She shuddered beneath him, gasping—

Yet she welcomed it.

She laughed, the sound light, breathless— As if he was tickling her, even as his teeth sank deeper. She didn't flinch. Didn't fight. Instead, she clung to him— Desperate for more.

Hiro, bloodless at that, had nothing left to give her— But Lumen didn't need anything else. She seemed satisfied with any part of him— His sweat. His saliva. Even his tears.

She wanted him completely. And that—that was terrifying. And yet— Hiro took pleasure in watching her. The way her bite marks healed instantly before his eyes.

It was unnatural. It was impossible. *What are you?* Hiro's mind whispered the question even as he finished what Lumen had started.

They collapsed together, spent, their bodies tangled in each other. The bed—the same bed he once saw as a kitchen— Was now soaked in dried blood and other remnants of their love.

<><><>

"Mr. Hajji." Vahitna stood as Hiro's father entered, her posture stiff but composed.

"Well done, Vahitna." Mr. Hajji shook the pregnant sigbin's hand firmly, his voice carrying both authority and approval.

"And Sofia?" Vahitna asked, needing confirmation.

Mr. Hajji's expression darkened. "She's being dealt with." Sofia had assumed they would pursue Hiro when she accompanied Mr. Hajji. She had learned—too late—that he had other plans for her.

Vahitna hadn't set out to betray the organization. She was good at what she did—online research, covering tracks, creating false realities. She had even designed the program that kept berhen alive in the eyes of their families in Perlaz, embedding it deep within the Bersig app. She had known, on some level, that she was killing them too. But they had never appealed to her.

Until now.

Because no matter how she tried to justify it, she was part of this operation. She was guilty. But then— She saw the news. Sigbin in Xego were now able to adopt babies.

Human babies.

The thought alone made her stomach flutter— And inside her, she swore her own unborn child reacted too, as if happy. But she couldn't transfer to Xego if she didn't know how to value human lives.

She wanted out— But leaving Ehud's organization meant death. That's when she made her move. She leaked the link to the Bersig app, hoping it would catch the attention of the authorities. And it did. She had stumbled upon a secret investigation—

One led by Mr. Hajji himself, tracking the missing berhen across Perlaz and Xego. She had contacted him directly. From there, they began exchanging information. And through Vahitna, Mr. Hajji had learned that his own son was trying to save a berhen.

But Sofia—

She had been working to sabotage him. That's why Mr. Hajji had never shown up to his meeting with Nzo. He had to protect Hiro. Vahitna had warned him about the trap Sofia had set— A plan meant to frame Hiro for the very crimes he was trying to stop.

Still—

She had held back. She hadn't told Mr. Hajji everything about Hiro's other involvements. Not yet. If she spoke too soon, it could turn against her.

And now—

Now she had another reason to hesitate. Because she had met Hiro's friends. She had seen Nzo. And she no longer doubted Hiro's sincerity. Maybe— Maybe he had changed. If she deserved redemption— Then maybe Hiro did too.

"I'll take care of your transfer back to Perlaz, Reeva," Mr. Hajji assured. He had already promised the channaks and hukluvans of Perlaz full cooperation. Justice would be served. The system would change. This would never happen again.

"Thanks, Mr. Hajji. Bufe will be happy." Reeva shook his hand. She had done her part. And Perlaz would finally get its answers.

"Tell him Kein had no hand in this." Mr. Hajji's voice was firm. Kein would handle Sofia himself.

Reeva nodded. Satisfied. For now. But Kein would always remain their enemy.

"Where Is My Son?" Mr. Hajji's gaze swept the room. "What about my son? Where is he?"

Nzo—who had been watching him closely—finally spoke. "Yes. Me - Drix Nzo - wait Hiro, okie-okie?!" He studied Mr. Hajji—the man he hadn't seen in a long time. A friend once. And maybe still.

Mr. Hajji knelt slightly, offering his hand. "Nzo, my friend. I'm glad we are on the same side."

Nzo hesitated— Then placed his small hand in Mr. Hajji's. "Nzo human side." His voice was quiet. But the words carried weight.

Mr. Hajji's expression softened—as if understanding something deeper.

Then—

"Mr. Hajji?" A hesitant voice broke through the conversation. It was Abigail.

Mr. Hajji turned. "Yes?" His eyes landed on the berhen. His body tensed. For a split second, he froze.

She— She resembled her. His dead wife. Too much. The same beauty. The same face. Her scent hit him next— Pure. Dangerous. He stepped back before he could lose control. He prided himself on self-restraint, but with so many berhen in the room—

With her—

He couldn't afford a moment of weakness.

Then Abigail's next words stunned him. "H-Hiro Hajji... Is your son?" Abigail took a step closer, her face tight with confusion.

"Yes." The confirmation was like a bomb dropping in the room.

Abigail's breath hitched. "He... is my fiancé." The words hung in the air. "I met him online... We were supposed to be married any day now. A-are you saying that...-Hiro...my fiance was planning to eat me too?"

A cold silence settled over the room. Reeva. Nzo. Vahitna. Mr. Hajji. All of them stared at Abigail— Speechless.

Then—

"NO!" A voice shouted. A voice filled with pure disbelief. Hendrix. No! Hiro would never...!

21

Her Second Life

As the morning sun spilled through the window, Hiro held Lumen close against his chest. She fell asleep instantly. He sighed, watching her. He was jealous. He wished he could sleep like her—so they could meet in their dreams. But he never could.

"Definitely not a sigbin," Hiro murmured, brushing a strand of hair from her face. Sigbin don't sleep. That alone told him she was something else.

He slid out of bed and stretched. She'd be famished when she woke up later. He needed to prepare food -- she preferred her meat fresh and uncooked.

This had become their new routine. Lumen slept all day. She woke at sunset. She ate.

And then—

She made sweet, sweet love to him all night. Over. And over. And over. *Ahhh*, Hiro exhaled. This is paradise. My own version of heaven.

But—

When he opened the fridge, he stared into the empty shelves. No food. He'd have to leave her—just for a little while. He had to be careful. He wasn't ready to face Hendrix and Nzo's wrath. Not yet. He wanted more time. More of her. He would deal with everything later. He scribbled a note for Lumen, hesitating before he left—then hurried off to complete his errand.

<><><>

He returned later than expected. He couldn't risk leaving any trace that might lead the search party to them—he wasn't ready to share Lumen with the others just yet.

But with no food... her insatiable appetite was becoming more than he could keep up with.

CRASH.

A noise from somewhere in the house. Hiro froze. His breath hitched. His instincts flared. *They found us.* Panic shot through his veins.

Hiro hadn't expected to be home late for dinner. He had been careful—meticulous in avoiding every street camera, keeping his head down, blending into the crowd. He had even walked far from the house before hitching a ride, then retraced his steps on foot to ensure he wasn't followed.

By the time he arrived, the house was dark and silent. A frown crept onto his face. Lumen should still be asleep. She had been snoring loudly when he left— A sound he had come to find endearing. Even the way her snoring would shift into strange, almost inhuman tones, like a chorus of voices inside one body, hadn't unsettled him.

Not at first. At one point, he had even thought Hendrix and Nzo had found them, only to realize it was just Lumen's bizarre sleep sounds.

But now—

Now, the house was too quiet. As he stepped inside, a sudden gust of freezing air hit him in the face. Hiro stiffened. The house should've been warm. Had Lumen left the lawn window open again? She loved the cold.

Still, something felt wrong.

He reached for the window, gripping the frame— And then— He froze. His breath hitched. His heart stopped. Because in the glass reflection— Behind him— There was something. Something standing there. Hiro whipped around.

And there it was. A naked, half-body—standing on its own. No head. No torso. No arms.

Only hips and two feet. And the worst part? The intestines inside— They weren't lifeless. They were writhing. Boiling in a pool of blood. A sickening realization hit him.
He had kissed those legs. Had worshipped them. Had taken pleasure in what lay between them. He knew those legs. He knew who they belonged to.

Lumen.

His mind spun. His stomach churned. He stumbled backward, crashing into the wall. And then— He ran. Not away. To the bathroom. Where he collapsed to his knees—

And vomited.

<><><>

Earlier that evening, Lumen woke up starving. Her stomach twisted, the hunger an ache that throbbed deep in her bones. She was alone. The bed beside her was cold. Hiro was gone. Her eyes narrowed, irritation bubbling beneath her skin. She wanted him. She needed him. And he had left her?

Her gaze flicked to the note on the bedside table— *Grocery shopping. Be back soon.* Lumen huffed, crumpling the paper in her fist. She wished she had gone with him. She wished he hadn't left her alone. Her body burned—not just with hunger, but with an unnameable need.

She stormed to the fridge, yanking it open. Empty. Nothing inside could satisfy her. Her body knew what it craved—

Meat. Fresh. Bloody. Raw. But there was none. Her hands trembled. Her skin burned hotter. The heat spread from her core to her limbs, an excruciating fever that made her gasp. She needed to cool down.

Lumen staggered to the bathroom, twisting the knob to full cold. Water rushed over her body— But it wasn't enough. The heat remained.

Then—

A sharp, stabbing pain exploded inside her. A twisting in her gut. She doubled over, clutching her stomach. And then she vomited. A thick, green, oily substance splattered onto the floor. Sticky. Unnatural.

Instinct took over.

Before she could think, her hands moved— Scooping up the slime and rubbing it over her body. Her breath hitched— And then—

Relief.

The fever broke. The pain faded. She felt lighter. Better. Lumen stepped out of the shower, her skin glistening, her body coated in the green substance. And then— It happened.

A blistering pain shot through her midsection— Like an invisible blade slicing her in two. Her eyes widened. Her breath stopped.

Then—

"AHHHHH!" A scream ripped from her throat as her body was cut in half at the waist. She almost collapsed, her fingers digging into the walls for support. Her hair frizzed wildly, her pupils darkened, shifting into black voids. A sharp, inhuman grin stretched across her lips— Her teeth growing long, jagged, razor-sharp.

Then—

A new pain erupted from her spine. She screamed again— As thorny, black wings burst from her back, tearing through skin and bone, unfolding with an ancient, monstrous power. For the first time in over a thousand years,

A new azhuang was born.

The blood of Caiphaiz, mixed with the saliva of a sigbin, had created something forbidden. Something long thought to be extinct. Lumen breathed in deeply— And smelled it.

Food.

Human blood. Human hearts. A primal hunger—ravenous, uncontrollable—seized her completely. Without hesitation, she leapt forward— Her wings spread— And she flew out the window.

Leaving behind her lower body, still standing, for Hiro to find.

<><><>

Hendrix and Nzo secured the sleeping sigbin deep within Nzo's basement—including Ehud, the leader of the berhen kidnapping group from Zapad, and Hiro's butler, Aldred.

The air was heavy. Neither spoke. The weight of what had just happened pressed down on them like a vice. Hendrix couldn't stop shaking.

Then— A quiet sniffle. A ragged breath. And then— Nzo broke. He sobbed, the sound raw and heart-wrenching, echoing in the dimly lit basement. They had searched everywhere. Followed Lumen's scent as far as the water reservoir—

And then— it vanished. Without a trace.

"I... I'm sorry, kid." Hendrix's voice was strained. His own chest ached, but he had to be strong— For Nzo. For his family. "We will find them, I promise."

But Nzo only shook his head, his tiny hands clutching Hendrix's shirt. "I-it's me fault! Nzo... Nzo not take care Lumen! Okie-okie?!" His body shuddered with grief.

"It's my fault too," Hendrix admitted. He lifted Nzo into his arms, holding him tight. Trying to shield him from the truth they were both afraid to face.

"Augusta -Hugo, no... Lumen... can't see famly! Me fail, okie-okie?!" Nzo buried his face in Hendrix's shoulder, wailing.

Hendrix clenched his jaw, his fingers digging into Nzo's back. "We will find them." Even if it killed him. Even if it meant hunting Hiro down.

"What if... what if?!?" Nzo suddenly pulled back, his wide, bloodshot eyes filled with horror. "Hiro... Hiro eat Lumen heart. Okie-okie!?"

Hendrix froze. A cold shiver ran down his spine. Then— "NO!" The word ripped from his throat. But the doubt had already sunk in. His last moment with Lumen replayed in his mind. Her voice— "I love you."

And he had said... Nothing. He hadn't said it back. Now— She was gone. And he hated himself for it.

<><><>

With Abigail's revelation, Vahitna had no choice but to finally reveal what she had known all along. Still, she needed proof. She hacked into Ehud's files, pulling every piece of evidence she could find. And there it was.

Everything.

When Mr. Hajji saw the files— When he read the reports— When he watched the footage— His heart shattered. "No..." He stared at the screen, disbelieving.

His son. His own blood. A monster. He had spent years investigating the missing berhen in Perlaz and Xego. But Hiro— Hiro had been there all along.

"Guys... ahm... I think you have to see this." Craig's voice cut through the tension.

Hendrix turned.

Outside, Lane was digging. In Hiro's backyard. A graveyard. A shallow mass grave of berhen carcasses. Bones. Flesh.

The rotting remains of the girls Hiro and his butler, Aldred, had devoured. Their bodies had been discarded like garbage. Hendrix's stomach turned. And then— The videos. They hacked into the security system. And they saw it.

Hiro. Aldred. Feasting. Hiro's fiancées— His brides. One after another. Used. Slaughtered. Devoured. Hendrix couldn't take it anymore. He stumbled back. Turned his head. And vomited.

<><><>

"I... I've been investigating this since the war." Mr. Hajji's voice was a whisper. "How... how did I miss that my own son was involved?" His fingers trembled. His face paled. Hiro had started this.

With Sofia. The two of them had built the berhen smuggling empire.

And yet—

Something had changed. The investigation had begun, and Hiro had stopped. For a while. But now— He had relapsed. Or maybe— He had never stopped at all.

<><><>

Moving Forward, the berhen were secured. Reeva left for Perlaz, aided by Mr. Hajji.

Vahitna, despite her ties to Hiro, continued assisting the investigation. But Nzo— He lingered. He and Vahitna were drawn to each other. A connection that shouldn't exist.

And yet— Nzo had to deny himself what he wanted most. Because he had to find Hiro. Had to save Lumen.

Whatever the cost.

<><>

Hiro stood in the bathroom, carefully washing the blood and dirt off Lumen's naked body. The water ran crimson, spiraling down the drain as he gently worked shampoo into her long, tangled hair.

"Are you careful to hide your victims before leaving them?" His tone was calm, almost casual, as if discussing dinner plans.
Instead of answering, Lumen reached for his lips— And kissed him. Soft at first— Then hungry.
Hiro sighed against her, giving in, tasting the sweetness of human blood lingering on her tongue.

She was full. Satisfied. Her latest victim hadn't been a berhen— But it had been a yummy heart nonetheless.
"Alright," Hiro murmured as he pulled away. "I'll bury them later." He had to be careful. There could be no more reports of heartless corpses showing up all over Xego. The authorities were too focused on the airport reopening, easing human transfers to Perlaz—
But if the bodies kept piling up, they would start asking questions.

"Thank you, my love," Lumen whispered. She kissed him again, her lips still stained red from her feast. Then, she rose from the tub, water glistening over her smooth skin. "I'm all clean. Come."
She stepped toward him, her fingers hooking into the waistband of his clothes. One by one— She peeled them off.

Hiro had to admit— Lumen's blood tasted divine after a hunt. Especially when her victim was a berhen. It made him stronger. It made him lose control.

They had both decided—

There was no going back. They would abandon their families. Disappear into the shadows of the world. Somewhere no one could find them. Hiro was already arranging for their escape—

But they had to wait. The city was still dangerous for them.

Lumen had finally reconciled with what she was. She had accepted what she had become.

An azhuang.

But Hiro's main concern wasn't her soul— It was her safety. She wouldn't be allowed to exist. Not after how many she had already killed. And it wasn't just the hunters or the authorities he feared—

It was his father.

By now, Mr. Hajji had to know. And Hiro knew exactly what that meant. His father had always been an advocate for humans. A man who loved Hiro's mother, a human woman, until the day she grew old and died. His father had never wavered in his loyalty to humanity. And if he discovered that Hiro and Lumen were feeding on them—

There would be no mercy. Not even for his own son.

Lumen sighed as she pressed her palm against her bare stomach. Then, without hesitation— She sliced herself open. A deep gash, right below her ribs. Fresh, warm blood spilled onto Hiro's fingers.

His breath hitched. His body tensed. And then— He tasted it. The moment Lumen's blood touched his tongue, Hiro's bones cracked. His skin split. Scales rippled over his flesh— His body twisting into its true form. A green, scaly monster—

Hunger blazing in his eyes. Hiro wasn't gentle anymore. Not with her. Not after this. Not after everything he knew.

And Lumen—

She loved it. She craved it. The violence. The pain. The torture. She welcomed it as Hiro claimed her again and again, their bodies twisting together in a union of monstrous desire.

He wasn't trying to be human anymore. And Lumen had already lost her soul.

There was remorse, self-disgust, and a fleeting desire to die after the initial shock of what she had done. When Hiro was away, even for a brief moment, she had given in.

At first, it was freeing—the burning sensation was gone as she soared through the night, searching for food. But the relief was short-lived. Guilt wrapped around her like a vice, only to dissolve the moment Hiro touched her—violently.

"Ohhh," Lumen moaned, caught between pain and pleasure as Hiro took not just her blood but her body, consuming her with a ferocity that nearly tore her apart. His lips devoured her neck, his hunger insatiable. Their passion burned, raw and destructive, nearly wrecking their bedroom in its wake.

As dawn broke, Hiro gazed at the rising sun, jealousy simmering in his chest. Lumen slept soundly, oblivious to the world. He lifted her delicate frame from the bloodstained floor and laid her on the sofa, marveling at how she remained untouched by exhaustion.

Unlike him, who once knew the burden of fatigue, Lumen would not wake as long as the sun ruled the sky. She would stir, moan, even snore, but never fully wake. She was as lifeless as the azhuang he had once despised—those creatures he had seen staked through the heart and left to burn.

But Lumen was different. She was radiant, beautiful even in her unnatural existence. He traced a hand over her soft cheek, and she smiled in her sleep. Hiro exhaled deeply. How had he been so lucky? To have someone like her—bleeding, soft, warm—yet eternal and unyielding. They were perfect together.

He pressed a gentle kiss to her forehead, but the love surging inside him overwhelmed him. Without warning, tears spilled down his face. He had never felt this before—not even when Cathy died. The sheer impossibility of their love crushed him—paired with the suffocating fear of losing Lumen.

"No... No... No..." Hiro sobbed, cradling her sleeping form. He kissed every inch of her warm skin, his voice breaking. "I love you. I love you. I can't live without you." His tears fell onto her chest as he clung to her.

Cathy had once spoken of a God— Adonai -- a BEING who redeemed even the most wicked, as long as their hearts were sincere. Hiro found himself wanting to believe. Could such a God exist? Could He give their love a chance?

He lay there for what felt like hours until Lumen's loud snore startled him. Hiro chuckled, wiping his damp face before kissing her lips. He couldn't wait for her to wake, to lose himself in her again.

Then, a noise.

His amusement faded instantly. Hiro's sharp ears picked up on something—a sound not from Lumen. His entire body tensed. They weren't alone.

What the heck? Silently, he pulled on his pants and listened, pinpointing the faint disturbances. He followed them, tracing them to the kitchen. A hidden door. A basement. He descended cautiously, his eyes adjusting to the dim space below. Then he froze.

SIGBIN.

Piles of them, all asleep. And among them—Beth. The one he thought had fled to Zapad. Hiro's pulse quickened. He had chosen this house because it belonged to Hendrix. Hendrix, who never returned home when preoccupied. It was the safest place for Lumen.

But this—this was a secret Hiro hadn't anticipated. *What the bloody heck is Hendrix hiding? Lumen can't stay here.* He needed to get her out. Now.

As he turned to leave, he collided—hard—into another body.

Hendrix.

His old friend stood there, arms wrapped around yet another unconscious sigbin. Ingrid. Hiro's butler. The one he had tasked with securing their escape.

Both men stared at each other, equally shocked.

<><>

Nzo was in shock too. He'd expected to find an empty villa—instead, he found Lumen, fast asleep on the couch, completely untouched.

Hendrix's plan had seemed foolproof—until they arrived at one of Hiro's possible hideouts and were met with unexpected resistance from the butler. He refused to answer any question about Hiro. What they hadn't expected was for the butler to fight back—unaware that Hiro had already anticipated their move. He had warned his butler in advance, instructing him to fend off any sigbin who came snooping and to alert him immediately.

But before the butler could send word—Nzo shot him.

"K-kid, what the fu—" Hendrix muttered, staring at the unconscious sigbin sprawled at his feet. "Enough putting them to sleep! We have no room left in your basement!"

"No, okie-okie! Your house... me Nzo go. You go, okie-okie?" Nzo replied with a shrug, completely unfazed.

With their plan derailed, the duo had no choice but to use Hendrix's basement instead. What they never expected... was to find exactly what they were searching for waiting there.

<><>

Hiro shoved past Hendrix, his desperation overriding all reason. The force sent Hendrix stumbling backward, the unconscious sigbin slipping from his grasp as he hit the ground. Hiro barely noticed—his only thought was Lumen.
But Nzo was already there, standing between him and her.
"You!" Hiro growled.
Nzo lifted his gun, aiming directly at Hiro's chest.

"No!" Hendrix lunged, shielding Hiro just as the trigger nearly clicked. He couldn't let Hiro be harmed—not yet.

Hiro staggered back, his breath ragged as he stumbled onto the porch. "I have to be with her, Hendrix! She's mine!" His voice cracked, raw with anguish. He tried to push past, but Hendrix was unyielding. With one shove, Hiro was sent sprawling off the porch, landing hard on the driveway.

"Kid, is Lumen alright?" Hendrix shouted over his shoulder, never taking his eyes off Hiro.

"Yes, but..." Nzo's voice trailed off.

Hendrix turned sharply, catching the troubled look on Nzo's face. Something was wrong, but Nzo wouldn't—or couldn't—say what. That uncertainty sent a fresh wave of fury through Hendrix.

"What did you do to her?!" Hendrix was on Hiro in an instant, pinning him down. His hands twitched, the temptation to pour his own blood into Hiro's mouth overwhelming. He needed answers, and he needed them now.

Gritting his teeth, Hiro struggled beneath him. "It was an accident, Hendrix. She was dying—I saved her!" His voice was frantic, desperate. "I did what I had to do!"

"Lies!" Hendrix raised his hand, ready to strike—ready to end it.

But Hiro was faster. Fueled by Lumen's blood, he kicked Hendrix with inhuman force, sending him hurtling backward. Hendrix crashed into the house, splintering the wooden wall on impact.

Hiro was on his feet instantly, his hands trembling. "Give her to me, Hendrix. You can't protect her anymore!" His voice broke. He wasn't just demanding—he was pleading. And then, he did something Hendrix never expected.

Hiro wept.

Tears fell freely down Hiro's face as he sobbed, his body shaking. "Once, you called me brother," Hiro whispered, his voice thick with emotion. "Once, you asked for my help. I'm begging you now—don't take Lumen away from me. I love her. I'd die without her… my brother, please."

The sheer agony in Hiro's voice rattled Hendrix. This wasn't the Hiro he knew. This wasn't the fighter, the cold strategist. This was a man undone, a man terrified of losing the one thing keeping him alive.

Behind them, Nzo worked frantically, trying to wake Lumen. He was dressing her, shaking her shoulders—but something was wrong. "What you do Lumen?! No lying! Okie-okie?!" Nzo's furious scream shattered the moment.

22

The Water Vessel

Hendrix snapped out of his hesitation. The rage returned, overtaking his sympathy. He attacked. Strike after strike, he came at Hiro, but something was different. Hiro was faster, stronger—unstoppable. Blow after blow, he dodged, countered. It was nothing like their old fights in the arena.

Before Hendrix could register what happened, he was on the ground, face pressed into the dirt. Hiro had him pinned. Arms twisted, legs locked down—Hendrix could feel his bones straining, moments from snapping.

"Listen to me! Listen!" Hiro's voice was raw, almost unrecognizable. He was screaming into Hendrix's ear, his grip tightening. "Once, brother, you begged me to listen. Do you remember?"

There it was. That voice. Something in Hiro's tone—sincerity, desperation—cut through Hendrix's rage. He was torn. Lumen was alive. That was undeniable.

But Hiro...

Hendrix had never seen him like this before. And that terrified him more than anything.

"I must protect Lumen. I'm the only one who can." Hiro's voice was no longer frantic or desperate. It was firm, unwavering.

Hendrix stopped struggling. He could hear it—the tremble in Hiro's voice, the suppressed sobs. Just like before, in the arena, when Hiro had cried to him before they made a truce.

"I love her, and she loves me," Hiro continued. "We are meant to be together. Please, let's wait for her to wake up so we can all talk. I will marry her, Haru. She's my life now."

Hiro's sincerity was disarming.

Seeing an opening, Hendrix acted. He blew hard at the ground, sending a cloud of dust and sand into Hiro's eyes.

Hiro stumbled back, momentarily blinded, but still managed to block Hendrix's strike. They locked eyes, muscles tensed, breaths ragged. Hiro could see it.

Hendrix was listening. There was hope. Hiro was counting on it—Hendrix was still his brother, after all.

But Hendrix was torn. Lumen didn't love Hiro. She never had.

And yet... there was something disturbingly truthful in Hiro's voice, and that terrified Hendrix. What if—when she woke up—she chose Hiro over him? A knot of emotions twisted inside him, ones he had never fully acknowledged.

He had felt her absence like an ache, like something vital had been torn from him. And now, faced with the reality of Lumen being alive but possibly choosing Hiro, that ache turned into something else—something deeper.

Would he be allowed to stay by her side, even if she chose Hiro? Was that enough? Would she even want him there? Hendrix's thoughts swirled, making it impossible to focus on the fight.

And Hiro saw it.

"What about the ones you killed?" Hendrix suddenly spat, snapping himself back to the present. "The berhen? Do they deserve no justice for what you've done?"

Hiro froze. His eyes widened, a flicker of realization cutting through the haze of his obsession. He had forgotten—forgotten what he had done. The blood on his hands. The lives he had taken. Even if he had Lumen, he could never escape the consequences. Even if she chose him, he would still face Kein's judgment. And there was only one way out.

His expression darkened.

No more talking. He would tear Hendrix apart, limb by limb, and escape with Lumen—no matter where they had to run, no matter what he had to do.

Hendrix barely had time to react. The moment he registered the sharp glint of metal embedded in Hiro's wrist, it was already too late. The hidden blade shot forward, aiming straight for Hendrix's throat.

With inhuman reflexes, Hendrix managed to jerk back just in time, avoiding a fatal strike—but not entirely. The blade sliced his neck, a shallow but deep enough wound, and blood spilled out.

Hiro froze.

His eyes locked onto the crimson liquid seeping from Hendrix's wound. sigbin didn't bleed. Not for decades. Yet here it was—Hendrix's blood. Dripping. Real. Impossible.

Hiro's gaze darted between the weapon still protruding from his wrist and the wound on Hendrix's throat. His mind raced, piecing together the horrifying realization. "Y-you..." Hiro stammered. "Blood... sigbin... sleeping..." His breath hitched as the truth clicked into place.

Lumen's blood was powerful. But Hendrix's blood— His eyes widened as a single drop of Hendrix's blood fell from the blade, landing on Hiro's open wound. Before he could react, before he could wipe it away—

The blood moved.

It slithered. It crawled inside his dry veins. Hendrix's blood was alive. A surge of heat exploded through Hiro's body, his limbs growing heavy. His vision blurred. Then—darkness.

"NOOOOO!" Hendrix's scream echoed as he lunged toward Hiro, who collapsed onto his knees, succumbing to the creeping pull of sleep.

Hiro's head spun, his vision swimming in and out of focus. A crushing weight settled over him, dragging him down like an anchor in deep water. His limbs felt like lead. He hadn't felt this way since— Since he was human.

"Haru...?" His voice was barely a whisper, heavy with confusion and fading strength.

Hendrix caught him just before he collapsed, his grip firm yet trembling. His own chest tightened, his breath hitching. This wasn't how it was supposed to be. "Zov, my brother..." Hendrix murmured, his voice breaking. Tears burned in his eyes. He had wanted to stop Hiro, to make him answer for what he had done. But not like this. Never like this.

Hiro's fingers twitched against Hendrix's sleeve, his lips parting in one last effort to speak. "Lumen... protect her for me... Lumen is az..."

His words faded into nothing as his body finally gave in. His eyes fluttered shut. He was gone. Deep in sleep.

"NO!!!" Hendrix's scream tore through the night, raw and unrestrained, echoing into the void. It was the only thing he could do.

<><>

Then, as the last ray of sunlight kissed her skin, Lumen's eyes snapped open—wide, wild, and filled with something primal. And she screamed.

<><>

PRESENT DAY - **2025 AB** (Anno Bhiasti - The Year Of The Beast)

One Hundred Years after Hendrix put his brother, Hiro, to a deep slumber,

the world had changed, reshaped by time, war, and forgotten legends. What was once myth had now become reality, and the whispers of the past echoed in the bones of the present.

Yet, some things remained—unfinished stories, lingering debts, and a destiny waiting to be claimed.

In Cintru, after a harrowing encounter with the serpent Velial, Kein regained his strength and prepared to journey to Xego for the Festival of Avlam, determined to find a child—his child—the last sigbin who still bleeds.

Six years ago in Perlaz, Luminaria woke early to prepare for their long journey to Vincot.

"I'm scared, Naria. I've heard the stories—whispers of berhen dying in Vincot. I don't want to go," Grace, her young sister-in-law, admitted, her voice filled with apprehension as she sat on the edge of her bed.

"That was long before our time. Vincot is a stronghold now. You'll be fine," Naria reassured her, though deep inside, she wasn't entirely sure. Grace was a free spirit—restless, adventurous, and unaccustomed to confinement. If anything, it's Vincot that should be worried about her arrival—not the other way around.

"How was it when you were there?" Grace asked, her curiosity endless.

"...G-great," Naria hesitated. Her time in Vincot had been restrictive, but it had also kept her safe, especially during a vulnerable period in her life.

"How long did you stay there?"

"Until I married your brother—not for long." Naria counted on her fingers, recalling the time.

"I miss *kuya* Gab. I wish he's the one taking me," Grace sniffed, her heart heavy.

"I miss him too," Naria murmured, reaching over to ruffle Grace's golden hair. She was the spitting image of Gabriel.

Naria had married Gabriel when she was eighteen, but their time together was fleeting. Barely a year into their marriage, he was gone, leaving Naria a widow at just nineteen.

"Ugh! Why?! Why do I have to leave?" Grace flopped onto her bed dramatically, shutting her eyes as if to block out reality.

"Because you're a woman now," Naria said softly. "You'll bleed every month from now on."

Grace opened her striking emerald eyes and scowled. "And sigbin will eat my heart," she added sarcastically.

"Yes," Naria replied, her tone serious.

"Unless I get married," Grace pouted. The thought of marriage at her age was utterly unappealing.

"Yes," Naria nodded, understanding her reluctance. She, too, had been uneasy about the idea of marrying young.

"Ugh! I hate being a girl. Boys have it easy," Grace huffed.

Naria smiled, remembering Gabriel. No, sometimes, boys have it rough too. A light knock interrupted their conversation.

"Are you, guys, ready?" Eze, Grace's father, peeked inside.

"Yes, Father," Naria zipped up Grace's bag and gently pulled the girl off the bed.

◇◇◇

From their village in Zalem, twenty young girls, all berhen, were set to travel to Vincot. Their journey would be grueling—seventeen hours by water, followed by another ten by land. A convoy of brigada soldiers would escort them, ensuring their safety.

Vincot, a city at the heart of Perlaz, is more than just a sanctuary—it's a boarding school, a place where young berhen learn not only academic subjects but also the sacred divinity of womanhood. No sigbin, hukluvans, or channaks were allowed inside, making it one of the safest places for young women.

Despite its security, the tradition of sending berhen to Vincot was rooted in deep-seated fear—fear that another war might break out, and that sigbin would once again hunt them for their hearts.

Before departure, Naria was given a water vessel by her mother-in-law. "Naria, here... take this," Sariah said, handing over the worn but priceless heirloom. The vessel, though stained and patched, held an almost mystical significance.

Naria blinked in surprise. "A-Are you sure, Mother?"

Traditionally, the vessel was passed down to the eldest child. Grace, being Sariah's biological daughter, should have been the rightful recipient.

"G-Grace should have this," Naria hesitated, honored yet uncertain.

"No, my child. The tradition is to pass it to the eldest," Sariah insisted, stroking the vessel lovingly. "Gabby may be gone, but you are our daughter—our real daughter nonetheless."

Touched, Naria clutched the vessel tightly. "I'll take good care of it, Mother."

"Keep it full," Sariah reminded her. "No matter how hot it gets, the water inside will always stay cold and refreshing."

Eze stepped forward, handing her two copper goblets. "Don't drink from anyone else's cups. Be careful of viruses and bacteria," he warned.

Though it had been two thousand years since the RPTR21 virus wiped out five billion people, the cautionary lessons had been deeply ingrained in human society. Humanity had survived not only a devastating pandemic but also centuries of war with sigbin.

"Are the berhen ready?" A brigada soldier called from the transport.

"Yes, we are!" The girls responded in unison before boarding their assigned vehicles.

Naria and Grace waved goodbye as they departed. Eze and Sariah remained at the roadside, watching until the convoy disappeared into the horizon.

"Stop crying, she'll be fine," Eze whispered, comforting his wife.

"Why do we have to do this to Grace?" Sariah buried her face in his shoulder.

"It's tradition," Eze reminded her. "Besides, we never know when another war will break out. A berhen's heart will always be at risk. Grace must stay in Vincot until she's ready for marriage."

Vincot was also known as Ciudad de Berhen, a city where only the most esteemed warriors and noblemen were allowed to seek brides. Now that Grace had come of age, she would remain there until a suitable husband was chosen for her.

Sariah wiped her tears. "Let's find a good husband for her soon, promise?"

Eze nodded. Their ATI tribe, a devout and conservative people, believed strongly in preserving their faith and heritage. They allowed inter-tribal marriages, but only within the boundaries of their faith in Yswh –the begotten son of Adonai.

<><><>

Inside the moving vehicle, Naria held the vessel close, unaware that someone was watching her intently. A pair of eyes flickered toward the vessel, then to the drawing in his hands.

*It's the same one...*Rhailey thought to himself, thinking about his great-great hukluvan grandfather Bufe's vision decades ago. Their bloodline—from his father Vhinoe, his grandfather Melvin, and great-great grandfather Miguel—had long searched for a particular vessel. It seemed that he had been chosen to find it.

The woman carrying the bag with the vessel was unmistakably a widow—her black scarf marking her grief—so Rhailey eyed the berhen beside her: Grace.

23

The Blinding Light

PRESENT DAY - **2025 AB** (Anno Bhiasti).

Days after Kein and Velial reunited to hunt the bleeding sigbin—an event that triggered the unified transformation of all sigbin into green, scaly monsters—Hendrix, in another part of the world, had laid the perfect trap. He'd been tracking the wild boar for days—an elusive creature long believed to be extinct.

"I know you're supposed to be protected," he muttered, his voice barely above a whisper. "But sorry—I'm hungry." Talking to himself had become a habit, a tribute of sorts to the prey he hunted, since there was no one else to talk to.

Then, suddenly, the boar stiffened. Its body tensed, ears flicking as if sensing something unseen.

"No, no, no!" Hendrix hissed under his breath, frustration curling in his chest.

The boar bolted. He could have chased it down, could have easily ended it with a well-placed strike, but he wanted it to die a certain way—he needed to test his trap. The anticipation, the precision of the setup—it all had to be perfect.

And then he heard them.

Darn it! What now? Annoyed, Hendrix abandoned his pursuit and scaled his treehouse in a fluid motion, seeking cover from whoever was intruding on his solitude.

Perched above, he scanned the area. His beard had grown thick, his disheveled hair falling over his half-hidden face. His muscular frame, tanned from years under the sun, was an intimidating sight—half-naked, rugged, and hardened by survival. But despite his fierce aura, there was still kindness in his eyes, the last trace of a man who once knew love and family.

How long had it been since he left Xego? He had lost track of time, and honestly, he didn't care. All he knew was that after dealing with the fallout between him and Hiro, he had found himself caught between two impossible choices—erasing the life he once had or fulfilling the promise he made to Nzo. A promise not to fail Lumen again.

But there was one loose thread he could never quite shake.

Nzo didn't know the truth—didn't know that Hendrix had lost Hiro. If he was still a wanted man, he had no idea, nor did he want to risk Nzo and his family being dragged into the chaos he left behind. They had already been through too much.

When Nzo's family traveled back to Perlaz with Lumen in tow, Reeva left no trace of their migration, smuggling them in secrecy.

"Stay... stay with me, please," Vahitna had begged Nzo.

But Hendrix knew Nzo would sacrifice everything for his human family—even if it meant turning his back on the perfect mother he had longed for his entire life.

"I'll clean up this mess first," Hendrix had promised. "Vahitna and I will find a way to visit you."

"We save Lumen. We must! Okie-okie?!" Nzo had sobbed into Hendrix's shoulder.

"I will. I promise. As soon as I find the answers, I'll come looking for you," Hendrix had sworn, his own voice breaking. He meant every word.

But now, alone in exile, he had no idea how to make good on that promise. And for that, he hated himself. Hendrix had intended to stay in Xego for a few decades, keeping a low profile while waiting for any fallout about Hiro's disappearance. If there were whispers of missing sigbin, especially one as prominent as Hiro, he needed to hear them first.

It took multiple trips to move the sleeping sigbin from their various hiding places into Hiro's own basement—a perfect place to bury the evidence of their crimes. After all, Hiro was already a known serial killer. One more atrocity wouldn't make much of a difference to his reputation.

Hendrix wiped every trace of security footage—every digital record that might lead back to him. But when he checked in on Hiro one last time... he was gone. Panic settled in his gut like a stone.

A missing sigbin of Hiro's status? His father would stop at nothing to uncover the truth.

Realizing time was against him, Hendrix erased every digital footprint he had left as Hendrix Mercado, shedding his past identity like old skin. And with that, Haruki's alter was dead.

But instead of heading straight for Perlaz as he had promised Nzo, Hendrix chose another path. He wandered—through jungles, deserts, and forgotten lands—living the life of a nomad. A man without a home, without a name, without an identity.

It was the life he deserved.

Punishment for everything he had done wrong.

But some punishments never truly end.

Hendrix could still hear her voice—Lumen's screams, her cries, her hatred.

I hate you, Hendrix!
I want Hiro! What did you do to him?!
I love him! I will never forgive you if you hurt him!
Every word had been a dagger to his heart.
I can't live without him. He is my life. Let me go!

He had lost her to Hiro. How? He still didn't know. But her words, her eyes—the way she looked at him—told him everything.

She despised him. Even now, the memories of her rage and despair haunted him like a nightmare, though he never slept. She had fought them with an inhuman strength that neither he nor Nzo could explain.

Hiro had been right. Lumen belonged to him now.

"She's alive," Hugo had told him. "That's what matters most."

But was it? As Nzo and Hendrix parted ways, both desperate to forget the past, neither had any certainty of the future.

Hendrix forced himself to snap back to the present. From the top of his treehouse, he spotted movement near the river below—a shallow but treacherous current where travelers occasionally attempted to cross.

This time, it was a small group: two Channaks, barely ten years old, carrying a baby and an unconscious woman. A widow—easily identified by the black shawl wrapped around her shoulder—struggled to drag a goat that stubbornly refused to move.

"Come on! Move!" the widow cried, yanking the rope. "You're going to drown! Do you want to die here?!"

The goat brayed in protest, digging its hooves into the riverbed.

Hendrix sighed. If he didn't intervene, these strangers would end up disturbing his entire plan for the day. And for once, he wasn't sure if he was more irritated... or intrigued.

<><><>

"Leave it!" Maharlika barked at Naria. Despite being only five feet tall with a stocky frame, her presence commanded authority. Hendrix could tell she was the leader of the group.

"No! The baby has no food," Naria shot back, gripping the rope tightly. She knew the child's mother was too sick to feed her.

"That's her problem, not ours," Blake, the blonde, taller, and leaner channak, sided with Maharlika.

"I said no!" Naria was determined to bring the goat across the riverbank despite also struggling with her wet black shawl, drenched from the relentless waters.

"Then you feed the baby," Blake countered with a smirk.

"How?!" Naria turned to him, hoping for another solution.

Maharlika shrugged. "Use your nipples."

The channaks burst into laughter.

"You—! I'm gonna kill you both!" Naria growled in frustration, nearly losing her grip on the rope.

"Go ahead, try!" Blake taunted.

"Bring it on!" Maharlika chimed in, grinning as they continued to mess with her.

Then—a sudden splash.

Water erupted around them, and before they could react, Hendrix was already wading through the river, lifting the goat with ease.

"Stop!" Maharlika commanded, but Hendrix ignored her and kept moving. Her eyes narrowed. Crack! She fired a shot. The dart hit him squarely in the arm.

Hendrix didn't even flinch. He walked on as if nothing had happened, the goat still securely in his grip.

Maharlika and Blake exchanged uneasy glances. They both knew what was in that dart—A potent liquid sedative designed for unwelcome sigbin. Yet, the stranger barely acknowledged the hit.

Reaching the riverbank, Hendrix set the goat down, yanked the dart from his arm, and flicked it at the raging river away like it was nothing.

The channaks fell silent. For the first time, uncertainty flickered in Maharlika's eyes as she caught sight of Hendrix's punctured wound. *Who the heck is this man?*

"Just get out of here and be on your way!" Hendrix snapped, turning to face the passersby trailing behind him.

"Oh, you're human! Wow! I've never seen a human in this part of the forest," Naria exclaimed, stepping closer. Her expression flickered between fear and curiosity, but when she saw the stranger bleed, she looked... relieved.

"No need to thank me. Just leave." Hendrix instinctively stepped back from the widow. It had been too long since he'd been around humans—or anyone, for that matter. Their presence infuriated him.

"I... er... my family actually owns this land," Naria said. Her voice held certainty. This wasn't just an excuse—she meant it.

"That's right, so you should leave then," Blake muttered, his tone carrying an edge of nervousness. Hendrix's overpowering presence unsettled him. He reminded the boy of Reeva—a male version. Maharlika remained silent, observing closely.

Hendrix clenched his jaw. *Darn it.* He was the trespasser now.

"Now that's settled," Naria continued, kneeling beside the unconscious mother slumped against Blake's back, "we're resting here—whether you want us to or not."

Hendrix's fingers twitched with restraint. "What's wrong with her?" he asked, unable to do anything to make them leave.

"Oh, we don't know yet. We found her and the baby on the other side of the river, miles from here. She's probably sick, but I haven't had a chance to check." Then, without warning, Naria reached for his arm.

"What the heck are you doing?!" Hendrix jerked back, startled by the unexpected contact. He hadn't been touched by another human in years.

"You're bleeding. See?" Naria wiped a piece of cloth over his skin, revealing a smear of blood.

Hendrix yanked his arm away before she could inspect further. The wound was already gone. He waited—braced himself—for Naria to freak out at what she had just seen.

But she didn't. Instead, she shrugged and turned her attention elsewhere, completely unfazed.

"Wow! A treehouse!" Blake shouted excitedly. "Did you build this? We pass through this part of the forest all the time, and I've never seen it before!" He set the unconscious woman down carefully before racing toward the wooden structure.

Hendrix sighed, irritated beyond belief.

"Great! So, you're housing us for the night, right?" Naria grinned and tapped Hendrix's bare chest like they were old friends.

Hendrix scowled. *Clearly, I misjudged her. It wasn't the channaks who were in charge—it was her.*

"What about food? I'm starving." Maharlika asked, still trying to soothe the baby.

Before Hendrix could respond, a sharp snap echoed through the forest. His trap.

Without a second thought, he bolted toward the sound—his unwanted visitors following close behind.

"Whoa! A wild boar!" Blake exclaimed. "A house and a feast? This is great!" He crouched down, examining the animal with interest.

"That's mine!" Hendrix barked, stepping forward.

Blake merely smirked. "Our land, our food, sir."

Hendrix's jaw tightened as Naria casually ascended the stairs to his treehouse. "Bring the mother up here, please," she ordered. "You're stronger than the rest of us."

"No." Hendrix's refusal was immediate. Why the heck would he let himself be bossed around by a brown-eyed brunette so small he could easily put her to sleep? Or... something more permanent.

Naria, completely unfazed, glanced at Maharlika. "You know what? With the way he's welcoming us, we might just stay for a week. What do you guys think?"

Maharlika smirked. "Plenty of food here. Sure, why not?" She winked at Blake, who had already started chewing on a fresh chunk of the boar's raw meat. Channaks craved flesh and blood—animal, not human.

Hendrix's eye twitched. "Fine," he growled through clenched teeth. He had no choice. He liked this part of the forest. He wasn't ready to move—not yet. His treehouse was newly built, and he had enjoyed every moment of crafting it. With a sharp exhale, he reluctantly lifted the unconscious mother into his arms and carried her inside.

"Good boy," Naria quipped sarcastically.

It took everything in Hendrix not to hurl the snoring woman straight onto the widow's head.

◇◇◇

As night fell and a thick fog settled over the area, the group gathered around the fire pit, feasting on the wild boar that Hendrix's unexpected guests had cooked. To his surprise, Naria—the widow, as she had introduced herself—had prepared a hot soup using herbs and spices she had gathered from the forest.

He had to admit—it was a very good meal. Home-cooked, no doubt about it. If it were up to him, he would have just tossed the entire beast into the fire and eaten it as it was.

"I thought humans and sigbin didn't mingle here in Perlaz," Hendrix said, keeping his tone casual. He had told them he was from Xego, just passing through to see a friend.

"In the inner part of Perlaz, yes," Blake said between bites, gnawing on a bone. "But we're on the border. Relationships still need to be built between us. We help each other, send messages across both races—especially when humans need assistance, and vice versa."

Hendrix frowned. "Sigbin needing human help? That's new."

"Sometimes," Naria answered, her expression unreadable. "Why? Haven't you ever helped a sigbin before?" She handed him another serving of soup. "We're not as weak as you humans from Xego seem to think."

Oh, they think I'm human. Hendrix mused. *Of course they do.* His beard obscured his philtrum, and unlike most sigbin, he still bled. It was better this way. No need to explain what he was or why he was different.

After dinner, Hendrix noticed Blake fiddling with an old RPG console. He smirked. *Nzo's game.* The device was practically ancient, and yet Blake seemed completely absorbed in it. Unable to resist, Hendrix leaned over and effortlessly showed him a few advanced moves and secret mechanics—techniques to clear a level faster and move on to the next.

"Whoa! I didn't know you could do that!" Blake's eyes widened in awe.

Hendrix chuckled. He had almost forgotten what it was like to have company after spending so many years alone. "It's a trick not everyone knows about," he said, handing the console back.

"Cool." Blake grinned and held out a fist.

Without thinking, Hendrix bumped it—the same way Nzo used to whenever he won a match. A flicker of nostalgia hit him as Blake laughed like the kid he still was.

"Guys, the mom's awake," Maharlika called from above.

The group quickly made their way up to the treehouse, which was sturdy and spacious enough to hold them all.

The woman—Mayumi, as she introduced herself—looked disoriented, her eyes darting around as if struggling to piece together what had happened.

"W-We were attacked," she stammered. "Something—a big black animal—it took my husband..." She paused, pressing a shaking hand against her temple as if the memory pained her. "I tried to save him, but... but I was shoved back—by its... something—a black thorny thing." Her words tumbled out in a frantic, incoherent mess.

Hendrix's eyes flicked to Naria, who was watching the woman closely.

The wound on Mayumi's back—about three inches long, but deep—had bled more than Naria had initially realized. The woman's clothes had been soaked through when she was first brought in. Now, Mayumi was scratching at the bandage furiously.

"Stop that! You'll infect it," Naria said, reaching out to restrain her.

Mayumi growled.

Naria froze, startled by the sudden shift in her demeanor.

"It wanted my baby..." Mayumi's voice cracked. "Then my husband... He blocked it... He saved us..." Her eyes locked onto Maharlika, her gaze desperate. She reached out, gesturing for the baby. The channak reluctantly handed her the child. "With my husband... gone... I ran... then I slept... so tired..."

She cradled the baby tightly, squeezing him against her chest. Then—she inhaled. Deeply. Her nose pressed against the baby's neck. The child let out a sharp, panicked cry.

"Here, let me," Maharlika said gently, reaching for the baby. But Mayumi snarled—low and primal—refusing to let go.

"Do you want to eat?" Naria asked Mayumi softly.

The mother froze. Her grip on Maharlika loosened, and she finally released the baby.

<><><>

"Good thing we brought that goat, huh?" Naria muttered to Maharlika, who was now rocking the child back to sleep. Mayumi was in no condition to care for her baby—she was far too weak.

The group made their way down to the fire pit, serving Mayumi a portion of their meal. But instead of taking the cooked food, she lunged at the raw meat, tearing into it hungrily.

Hendrix watched as Blake and Naria exchanged a look—one filled with silent concern. "What's wrong with her?" Hendrix asked, lowering his voice, though he already had a good idea.

After leaving Mayumi by the fire and discreetly instructing Maharlika to protect the baby by staying inside the treehouse, the three of them stepped away for a quiet discussion.

"There have been other attacks like this in the area recently," Naria admitted.

"Have you noticed anything strange around here?" Blake asked Hendrix.

Hendrix shook his head.

Then—Blake's eyes darted to the fire. Mayumi was gone. "Where is she?" he muttered, scanning the darkness. Without hesitation, he disappeared into the trees to look for her.

"Stay here," Naria warned Hendrix while carefully concealing the rope ladder beneath the treehouse. "You don't know what we're dealing with."

Crap! Hendrix clenched his jaw. He didn't need another mess to deal with, yet something about Naria's protectiveness caught him off guard. He decided to follow her as she made her way in search of Blake. But before he could move—he saw Mayumi.

She was creeping below the treehouse, searching for a way in. Her movements eerily silent. "H-Hey, where have you—" He didn't get to finish In an instant, Mayumi lunged.

She crashed into Hendrix, slamming him to the ground with unnatural force. Pinned beneath her, he struggled as she growled, feral and unrecognizable. Her wild, disheveled hair. Her darkened, vacant eyes. The way her mouth dripped with saliva, lips curling back to reveal sharp teeth.

She looked exactly like Lumen had when she attacked.

She's sick... just like Lumen. Hendrix's theory had been right all along.

Mayumi's nails raked across his skin—deep, but not fatal. She was strong, stronger than she should be, and she wouldn't stop until she tore his throat open.

"No!" Naria yanked at Mayumi, trying to pull her off Hendrix.

Mayumi snarled, her nails slicing through Hendrix's shirt, drawing more blood.

Instinctively, Naria pressed her hand against his chest to stop the bleeding—only for Mayumi to snap her head toward her, eyes locking on her next target. With a guttural growl, Mayumi lunged for Naria's throat. Reacting on pure instinct, Naria raised her hand—and then it happened.

A blinding burst of light exploded from her palm. The force sent Mayumi flying, her body crashing several feet away.

Silence.

Then, Mayumi writhed on the ground, violently convulsing.

Hendrix's breath hitched. He looked down—his blood had splattered across Mayumi's skin. And it was reacting.
Mayumi screamed. Her body spasmed as if it was rejecting something—something inside her.
"What the heck are you?!" Naria gasped, staring at Hendrix in shock.
Hendrix, just as stunned, met her gaze. "What the heck was that?"

They lay motionless on the ground, eyes locked on Mayumi as her body convulsed, her screams echoing into the night like a haunting cry.

<><><>

Blake had his weapon raised before Naria and Hendrix could even get up. He hadn't seen much—just heard the screaming, the growling—and when he returned, Mayumi had been thrown several feet away, thrashing violently. Between her, Hendrix, and Naria, Blake didn't hesitate. Mayumi was the threat. He had to protect Naria.

Naria found herself sprawled on top of Hendrix. Hendrix found himself holding her—his arms locked tightly around her body.

The moment he had seen the blinding light, his instincts had kicked in. He had shielded Naria without thinking, using his own body as a barrier.

Naria, however, was focused on the blood –Hendrix's.

The moment her hand—covered in Hendrix's blood—had touched Mayumi, the woman had convulsed and been thrown backward.

And now... Mayumi lay still.

Naria's eyes drifted downward. More of Hendrix's blood had splattered across Mayumi's face. Not noticing that the wound on Hendrix's chest had already begun to heal – fascinated – she instinctively leaned in, her fingers brushing the torn fabric of his shirt—

In a blur, Hendrix moved. He pushed himself upright, instinctively creating space between him and the mysterious widow.

"What are you?" Naria whispered, breathless.

"What was that?" Hendrix muttered as he helped Naria to her feet.

Their eyes locked—both searching for answers in the other's gaze—until realization hit them at once.

At that moment, Blake made his move.

"Blake, wait!" Naria shouted, scrambling to her feet just as Blake aimed his weapon. She stepped forward, Hendrix still steadying her, as she inspected Mayumi.

The woman was unconscious, her body limp and unmoving, her face... normal again. Naria frowned. *No. Something had changed. Just for a moment, I saw it...*

Then, Mayumi stirred. Her eyes fluttered open, disoriented and unfocused. "W-What happened?" she whispered hoarsely. "Where's my baby?"

Naria watched carefully as Mayumi sat up. The wound on her back—the deep gash she had treated just hours ago—was now completely healed.

Mayumi looked better. Stronger. More... herself.

But Naria wasn't convinced. She still needed to observe her. They offered her more food, and this time, she ate the cooked meat and broth without hesitation.

Still, as Mayumi ate, Naria's mind spun. Her gaze flickered toward Hendrix, deep in thought across the fire, occasionally glancing back at Mayumi.

Hendrix's blood.

Naria had noticed how quickly he changed into a new shirt—how he concealed the wound before she could insist on treating it.

"It's just a scratch," Hendrix had claimed, brushing her off. In reality, he was already healed—and he intended to keep up the illusion of being just human in their eyes.

But Naria wasn't convinced. She needed to inspect him. Maybe even test his blood.

Hendrix was preoccupied with something else—the light. A blinding flash. Intense. Unmistakable. It had appeared in an instant, but its presence lingered in his mind, demanding answers.

Did it come from her? Did she do that? The mother seemed cured. Could Lumen be cured? But how? His blood never harmed Lumen— stung and knocked her unconscious for a short time, yes... but never reversing her condition. He was certain his blood had nothing to do with what happened to the mother.

Maybe it was the light. But where did it come from? Hers? Hendrix clenched his fists. He would have to see Nzo sooner than expected—if this truly was a cure.

24

Princess Sofia

That night, as Mayumi settled into the treehouse with her baby, Naria made a decision. "Maybe we should stay another night. Just to observe her," she said.

Hendrix didn't argue. He wanted the same thing – for Naria to stay much longer so he could observe her.

"She seems fine," Maharlika commented as she prepared to keep an eye on the mother throughout the night.

But both Hendrix and Naria remained unconvinced.

By morning, Mayumi was awake and… alive. She stepped out into the sunlight with her baby in her arms.

Hendrix stiffened. She's not afraid of the sun. Lumen had slept all day, hiding from the light. She became violent when even the slightest beam touched her skin.

Hendrix and Nzo had learned this the hard way.

The memory flickered in his mind—Lumen growling, fighting them as they tried to move her from his house. She had seen Hiro's motionless body on the ground and lost control, lashing out with terrifying strength. Hendrix still bore the emotional scars from that night.

But now, standing before him, Mayumi was out in the sun—completely unaffected. *That's a good sign, right?* But Hendrix wasn't sure anymore.

"Whoa! What is this?" Maharlika exclaimed. She had discovered the obstacle course Hendrix had built within the forest.

Hendrix smirked, explaining how he had designed it using natural resources—traps, snares, and various challenges. It was his way of keeping himself sharp, a replacement for the arena he secretly missed.

The two channaks wasted no time. They spent the entire day attempting to conquer the course, testing themselves against each level of difficulty.

Hendrix watched from the sidelines. His mind was still elsewhere. *If Mayumi could be cured, then maybe... just maybe... Lumen could too.* And for the first time in years, Hendrix felt something he had long forgotten.

Hope.

Hope... that Naria and everyone will stay a bit longer, and he has found a way to make it happen.

Hendrix had always been a programmer, designing digital worlds and challenges. Now, the forest itself had become his new arena.

His obstacle courses weren't just for survival—they were training grounds. He needed to master fighting without shedding blood, especially if his goal was only to defend himself rather than attack. He had no desire to leave behind more sleeping sigbin as he carved his way through this new life.

"This is cool!" Blake exclaimed, panting as he recovered from a particularly brutal section of the course. His body regenerated and healed, his wounds vanishing like they were never there. "We could use this idea to ward off unwanted visitors at the boundary."

Hendrix smirked. Some of the courses were meant to be hard to navigate. That was the point.

But then Blake and Maharlika took it up a notch. They started designing their own obstacle courses—for him. And for the first time in years... Hendrix found himself having fun.

It was different from the ones he built for himself. He knew all the traps in his own designs—how to anticipate, how to counter. But with their courses? It was a fresh challenge, unpredictable and exhilarating.

One course was so difficult that Hendrix had no choice but to fly. Without thinking, he leaped—pushing off the ground, soaring above the treetops, landing effortlessly on the roof of the treehouse before dropping smoothly to the ground.

Silence.

Naria's mouth fell open. She had seen many strange things in Perlaz, but this...

Angel --like those mentioned in their tribe's Sacred Book Of Adonai's Words. He moved like an angel with invisible wings.

Blake and Maharlika stood frozen, wide-eyed in awe. "How the heck did you do that?" Blake asked, the start of a bromance moment forming between them.

Hendrix just shrugged. "You just have to jump high... and walk in the air." He meant it as a joke. But the truth was—he didn't know. To him, it felt like a normal movement. He had no idea that what he had just done wasn't normal at all.

By the time they returned to the fire pit, famished from their training, Naria and Mayumi had prepared a feast. The smell of cooked meat and herbs filled the air, a comforting contrast to the chaos of the day.

"Ohhh, this is life," Blake groaned after stuffing himself full, leaning against a tree in the shade. He burped, looking like he wanted to sleep but couldn't.

As the sun dipped below the horizon, two choices hung in the air. Two decisions had to be made.

And then—

"Would you like to stay another night?" "Would you like to come with us?" They had spoken in unison.

Eyes met.

And in that fleeting moment, both Naria and Hendrix knew—whatever happened next, their fates were now intertwined.

<><>

Meanwhile, a silence stretched between Caiphaiz and Kein as the latter plucked a fruit from one of the cloned trees. The immortal god turned it over in his hand, bringing it to his nose. Then—his expression darkened.

The fruit was rotting. Again. He sighed, annoyed at the failure, just as a scream erupted from his office nearby.

Caiphaiz flinched. He knew that voice. Sofia. Trapped within the Abyss, she was begging—pleading. Her words were garbled, incomprehensible. Had she not returned the vial of blood he had given her, Caiphaiz knew he would be in the Abyss with her right now.

He still wasn't certain if it was his blood that had turned Hiro and Sofia—his two most prized sigbin—into creatures addicted to hunting and devouring berhen. But he regretted supplying them with such an indulgence.

Decades ago, when he learned of Hiro's involvement in berhen smuggling, he traced the vials he had gifted him. Each one had been embedded with a nano-tracking system, designed for emergency retrieval. Disguised, he traveled to Xego himself. He found the mansion.

And he found Hiro—asleep. A sigbin, in deep slumber along with the others at the basement. He wasted no time shipping him and the rest to Cintru's lab for study, reporting the discovery to Kein.

"Mr. Hajji found him and requested our help, my Lord," Caiphaiz had told Kein at the time, lying without hesitation.

Kein had merely chuckled. "A sleeping sigbin. Hah! Perhaps Adonai had something to do with this." Unlike most of his hellspawns, Kein and Caiphaiz still slept. Rest was necessary. If Hiro's condition allowed him a reprieve from the blood craze, it might actually benefit him.

"May we proceed with our research?" Caiphaiz asked, hoping this new development would distract Hajji's team from further investigating Hiro's crimes—or worse, discovering Caiphaiz's role in them.

Kein had been too fixated on his quest for the bleeding sigbin to notice. And that suited Caiphaiz just fine. As long as Sofia remained silent, his betrayal would remain hidden.

"I want to see him," Kein interrupted his thoughts.

Caiphaiz nodded. "He's in the lab, my lord. More tests are being conducted."

Kein twirled a green fruit between his fingers, his expression unreadable. "And his father?"

"As always, he refuses to leave his son's side."

Kein smirked. "Is he investigating what happened?"

Caiphaiz hesitated. "He's searching for Hiro's two long-time sigbin friends. He believes they might have answers."

"Or they might be sleeping as well," Kein mused.

Caiphaiz felt a chill run down his spine as Kein started toward the lab, still turning the fruit over in his hands. Then, his gaze sharpened—because he had heard it, too.

The whisper. "Find the bleeding one." Velial had spoken.

Caiphaiz understood all too well—Kein had no real intention of healing Hiro. His interest was driven purely by curiosity, not compassion. Everything hinged on the mission Velial had entrusted to his master and lord. And though Caiphaiz remained loyal, he couldn't shake his unease over this growing obsession with a bleeding sigbin.

Before following Kein to the lab, he took a brief detour—toward Kein's altar. He leaned in close, lowering his voice. "Sofia, are you listening? Stop screaming. It's me, Caiphaiz."

A shuddering breath. Then— "Caiphaiz!" Sofia's voice cracked. "Dimas—is he safe? Please, take care of him."

"I will. Just don't say a word."

Kein could never find out how deep his loyalties truly ran. Not yet. And certainly not before he figured out what the heck was happening to Hiro— And why Kein was obsessed with this Angelo Markado.

◇◇◇

Sofia, the first-generation sigbin, took immense pride in what she had become. The initial shock of turning into a hellspawn had long since faded, replaced by a deep acceptance—even admiration—for her new nature.

Yes, she killed. Yes, she devoured humans. But that was survival. That was life. And so, she reconciled herself to it.

When Kein abolished the monarchy, she was left with nothing—a princess without a kingdom to rule, without a purpose to serve.

But she was Kein's favorite girl. They had feasted on each other's blood and bodies, tangled in an intoxicating, eternal paradise. It was perfect.

Until everything changed.

When the mutation began—when they all became bloodless—Sofia was among the first to experience the shift.

And Kein? He turned cold. Indifferent.

Sofia, once adored, was now discarded. So she turned to the only two who hadn't abandoned her—Caiphaiz and Hiro. Hiro, her friend... her lover. Decades passed, dragging them through the misery of being bloodless hellspawns. Weak. Empty. Desperate.

Until they came up with a plan.

They wouldn't just survive. They would thrive. Smuggling berhen across the border wasn't just lucrative—it was a game. Hunting. Devouring. Breaking them.

Feeding wasn't just necessary—it was fun.

Then there was that night. Among one of their shipments, a human male had the nerve to lay with the berhen—thinking his compassion could somehow save them from their fate.

Pathetic. He died, of course. Torn apart—mouth first—by Ehud, just like the rest of the "damaged" goods.

Except one.

Sofia had been about to kill her when a scent—different, richer, intoxicating—caught her attention.
"She smells... wonderful," Sofia murmured, circling the trembling girl. "What is that?" Sparing her for later, Sofia discovered the truth—the girl was pregnant. Pregnant... after just losing her purity. The idea of feasting on a newborn sent a thrill down Sofia's spine. So she took the girl—Dolores—back to her mansion in Xego and waited.

But something unexpected happened. Sofia got... attached. Dolores became the sister she had never had, the one person who felt real in a world of endless indulgence. But the moment the baby was born, that attachment shifted. Her love for Dolores faded—transferred to the newborn in her arms.
Dimas.
"Sofia, where is my baby?! I want to see him!" Dolores' screams echoed through the chamber.
Sofia barely heard her. She gazed down at the infant she had delivered herself—his tiny, writhing body still slick with blood. Slowly, deliberately, she licked him clean.
"No! Please don't eat him! Please!" Dolores' pleas barely registered.
Sofia simply laughed—wicked, amused, detached. Then she left. And let Ehud feast. From that moment on, Dimas was hers.

Dimas became the love of her life. First, she was his mother. Then, his sister. Then, his equal. She could never get enough of him—his smooth, charcoal skin, his thick, curled black hair, his boyish smile that masked a devil's charm.

<><><>

Sofia ensured that Dimas learned the ways of the sigbin more than the ways of humans. He was an eager student, quick to grasp their teachings, and even quicker to embrace danger.

Dimas had an adventurous spirit—he lived as though he were indestructible. Until the night his luck ran out. A racing accident nearly claimed his life.

Sofia had rushed to his side, trembling as she pressed her lips to the scar that now ran across his forehead and eyebrow—a painful reminder of how close she had come to losing him.

But fate had been cruelly kind. The surgery had been so flawless that instead of leaving him grotesque, the scar only made Dimas even more striking. It gave him an edge—a rugged, masculine appeal that Sofia couldn't help but admire.

From that moment, her obsession with him deepened. She became overprotective, possessive, relentless. Because Dimas would grow old. He would wither. He would die.

And she would remain—forever without him.

Sofia still had distant family who had survived the virus, but they were all estranged. Dimas was the only family she had left.

Between Xego, Cintru, and Zapad, Sofia built her empire—but no matter how busy she was, she always had time to worry about Dimas.

Her solution?

A castle.

A gilded prison. Somewhere impossible for a human to escape. She had trapped him, just like the fairy tales she had once read as a human princess. Dimas—the vulnerable prince, locked away for his own protection.

"Let me out! This is boring," Dimas grumbled. "You're never around... Can I go out, please?" He was in his early thirties now—a man, not a boy.

But to Sofia, he was still her most precious possession. "You will," she soothed, stroking his hair. "After your recovery."

It was a lie.

"I've been 'recovering' for years!" Dimas snapped, his frustration seeping through. "I'm fine now! I swear, I'll never risk my life again." His voice softened as he turned on the charm, giving her that boyish look she could never resist.

Sofia smiled knowingly. He was lying. She kissed the scar on his forehead. She knew him too well. The moment he left this castle, he would run toward danger again.

"I'm lonely here," Dimas muttered, his voice bitter. He stood, moving away from her, dodging her motherly kiss.

"I'm here now," Sofia whispered, eager to make it up to him. She reached for him, smiling. "What do you want to do?"

"I want to go out!" His fist slammed against the table, his control snapping.

"No!" Sofia blocked him, her body a barrier between him and the small window—her only entrance and exit.

It was too tight, barely big enough for her to slip through. She had broken bones just to squeeze inside.

Dimas knew it was impossible for him to escape. He was just mocking her. Showing her how frustrated he was.

Then—he snapped.

Infuriated, Dimas shoved her. Sofia staggered back, stunned. He had never raised a hand against her before. No matter how controlling she had been, no matter how many demands she placed on him, he had always been gentle.

Not this time.

Something inside her snapped, too. With a growl, she lunged—wrestling him to the ground. If he wanted to fight, then she would show him what she really was. Dimas had always seen her as sweet, devoted, loving.
Maybe it was time he finally saw the monster she truly was.

Sofia, though, was surprised by Dimas' strength. For a mere human, he had become formidable—his blows landing with raw fury, his body moving with an animalistic edge.
And for some twisted reason, she liked it. Though she held back, careful not to let her full hellspawn strength break him, she relished the physical fight between them.

Dimas, on the other hand, fought with everything he had—unleashing years of pent-up rage, frustration, and resentment.
He didn't just attack her. He killed her. Again. And again. And again. But Sofia always came back.
No matter how many times he snapped her neck, crushed her ribs, or left her lifeless, she would simply regenerate, her laughter echoing through the chamber as she rose to face him again.

Until, finally, Dimas collapsed—exhausted, drained, and defeated.

He lay sprawled on the floor, breathing hard, his body shaking from exertion.

Sofia crawled over to him, her lips ghosting over his forehead, just as she had when he was a baby. The way she had kissed him when he was still a wicked, mischievous child. Her touch was meant to comfort.

But Dimas' reaction wasn't that of a child. His body tensed—then ignited.

Before she could react, he flipped her over, pinning her beneath him, tearing at her clothes with raw desperation. Sofia froze, her mind struggling to catch up with what was happening.

Dimas' hands were rough, urgent, his body still humming with adrenaline and lingering fury. Her clothes shredded beneath his grasp, the heat between them turning volatile, dangerous, and—

No. A sharp wave of disgust shot through Sofia. *No. No. No.*

This wasn't happening. She had never—would never—sleep with a human. It was beneath her. She had slept with gods—Kein. She had taken demigods to her bed—Caiphaiz, Hiro.

But humans?

They were just food. And who the heck sleeps with their food? Her stomach churned. She started to struggle.

"No! Dimas, STOP!" Her panic was real now, a rare thing for Sofia to feel.

Dimas wasn't just human— He was her son. Not by blood. Not by human logic. But in the way that mattered most. She had raised him, loved him, protected him. And there were some lines even she refused to cross.

Killing humans? Fine.
Destroying empires? Sure.

But this?
Never.

"NO!" She struggled beneath him, but she couldn't bring herself to hurt him—not in the way she should.

And Dimas didn't stop. His rage and lustful hunger consumed him. And Sofia's body—betrayed her. She felt it. The pleasure. The explosions they made. The way her body responded in ways she never expected.

And as her screams filled the chamber, she hated herself for the part of her that— enjoyed it.

"D-Dimas?!?" Sofia's breath hitched. Her mind struggled to process what had just happened. The man before her—her Dimas—had transformed into someone she desired. She couldn't think straight.

His scent...

The same intoxicating fragrance he had carried since the day she cradled him as a baby. But now, his touch was different. Stronger. Dominant. Claiming. A flicker of hesitation crossed her mind. If she revealed her true form, if she let go completely, she might break him.

And she couldn't risk hurting him. So she let Dimas take the lead. In his arms, she became fragile, human, his.

With Dimas spent and fully satisfied, it was her turn. She unleashed herself upon him. Their bodies clashed, collided, consumed each other—so violently that the castle itself trembled, stone walls cracking beneath the force of their passion.

If Dimas had any doubt before, it was gone now. "We were made for each other," Sofia whispered, refusing to let go. Dimas, barely conscious, smiled against her skin. "I love you."

And for the first time in her existence, Sofia's heart ached. She had been desired before. Worshiped. Used. But never... loved. She watched him sleep, her fingers trembling as tears fell freely, her body wracked with silent sobs.

<><><>

Dimas was no longer restless in his gilded cage. His hunger for freedom had been replaced by a hunger for her. Every time Sofia visited, he craved more—more of her touch, her scent, her presence.

But Sofia knew their passion was dangerous. Dimas was still human, and each violent, ecstatic encounter between them risked shattering him. She had to protect him—even from herself. And so, she ensured that Caiphaiz's blood flowed through her veins before every meeting.

Even before Hiro and Lumen's sire bond, she had already sealed Dimas' fate—transforming him into an azhuang through her tainted blood, mixed in her kiss.

He was hers. Forever.

<><><>

"Help! Help me!" A fresh berhen, just delivered to Sofia's home, screamed from the dungeon below.

Dimas' eyes snapped open at the sound. His body stirred, muscles tightening with anticipation. "For me?" His voice was still husky from sleep, but his excitement was unmistakable.

Sofia's lips curled into a satisfied smile. "Yes. Your wife. Your BerSig match. Enjoy, my love."

She had watched him sleep all day, waiting for this moment—waiting to give him his gift. Dimas was no longer her prisoner, but she still forbade him from hunting on his own. If the world discovered what he was—an unwanted, unnatural being—he would be annihilated.

She would not allow it. So instead, she provided for him—only the best. Only high-grade berhen—fresh, untouched, perfect. Dimas disappeared into the dungeon for his feast.

The silence that followed was only broken by the sound of screams.

When the sunset faded and the moon rose high, Dimas returned to her. Blood-stained, sated, feral, but still hers. He climbed into bed beside her, wrapped his arms around her, and devoured her in a different way. Untiring. Unrelenting. Unbreakable. Sofia could never wish for anything more. Her life was perfect.

And she would never let it change.

<><><>

That fateful day, Sofia tightened her robe and stepped out onto the driveway, where Ehud waited.

"I just came from Hiro's house," he said, kissing her hand with the grace of a knight greeting his princess. "Delivered him his new bride."

Sofia's lips curled into a pleased smile. "And Dimas' new bride?" she asked eagerly. All she ever wanted was to make Dimas happy.

Ehud chuckled, motioning to the truck parked behind him. "She's inside—excited, nervous, the usual." He smirked. "Told her she's marrying someone way better and richer than Mr. Hajji."

Sofia laughed softly. "Of course. She's marrying a human bachelor, after all."

Like Hiro, Dimas enjoyed playing with his food before devouring it. Days of indulgence, pleasure, and torment—a show Sofia loved to watch and enjoy. Her perfect world had never been more complete.

She never imagined it would all come crashing down so soon.

25

Illuminaria

"I promised Sofia I'd protect you." Caiphaiz's voice was calm, but Dimas barely heard it. He was losing his mind. Without Sofia, he didn't know how to function—how to breathe. His rage and hunger consumed him, twisting inside his gut, turning him into something feral.

He had become something unnatural, and Sofia had warned him never to let Kein's closest confidant find out. So when Caiphaiz unexpectedly appeared at his home, Dimas masked his turmoil with careful suspicion.

"What can I do to free her?"

Caiphaiz sighed, watching him closely. "Nothing."

He walked through Dimas' house, his sharp gaze scanning every corner—until he found what he came for. The remaining vials of his blood that he needed to retrieve back. It was the last loose end—the last trace of his involvement in Sofia and Hiro's crimes. He had no reason to stay.

But Dimas' desperation was palpable. "There has to be a way."

Caiphaiz tilted his head, amusement flickering in his golden eyes. "Well," he mused, "Kein is looking for a bleeding sigbin." Dimas stilled.

"Find him," Caiphaiz continued smoothly, "and take him to Kein. In exchange, Sofia will be free."

It was a lie. Sofia was never going to be freed. But Caiphaiz didn't care. Dimas was just a human—one who would grow old and die. He just needed to be kept occupied until then. Satisfied, Caiphaiz turned on his heel and left, convinced that his role in Sofia's downfall was now neatly erased.

As soon as Caiphaiz was gone, Dimas headed straight to the dungeon.

His body trembled—not with fear, but purpose. He tore off his clothes. His stomach convulsed.

Then, he vomited. Thick, sticky green fluid oozed from his lips, pooling into his hands. He dipped his fingers into the sickly substance, then slathered it across his bare skin, coating himself in the grotesque mixture.

His heart pounded. His vision blurred. His body shifted, adapted, prepared.

Then, without hesitation— Dimas disappeared into the night, ready to hunt for the bleeding sigbin.

◇◇◇

"We're here!" Naria called out excitedly, barely containing her excitement as she approached the gate of their home.

"Naria!" Grace rushed out of the house, her face lighting up at the sight of her sister.

"Careful! Goodness, you're huge!" Naria laughed as she ran toward her, meeting her in a tight embrace.

Grace, now nineteen, was set to give birth any day now—her belly round and full with life. She had spent the last few years in Vincot, the village of berhen, before being courted and married to Arnel, a man from their tribe.

"Are you delivering my baby?" Grace asked eagerly, already shouting to their mother that Naria was home.

"Of course! That's why I'm here." Naria grinned before glancing toward the house. "How's my clinic?"

"Good! Aunt Marie and Uncle Aaron have been taking care of your patients," Grace replied, ushering their guests inside.

"Naria, welcome back!" Sariah emerged from the kitchen, her face beaming with warmth.

"Mother!" Naria rushed forward, embracing the old woman who had become a real mother to her.

Sariah's eyes curiously scanned their guests before settling on Mayumi, who was holding her baby close while Grace gently played with the smiling child. "And who do we have here?"

Naria introduced Mayumi, explaining how she was recovering well.

Sariah nodded approvingly before turning her gaze to Hendrix. "Welcome to our village. Your husband is very handsome."

Mayumi's cheeks flushed pink. "Oh—no! He's not my husband," she corrected quickly, offering a shy smile.

Naria had already arranged for Mayumi to be picked up by relatives in a nearby village, hoping they could help her find her missing husband.

"Hello... My name is Hendrix." He placed his right hand over his chest and offered a slight bow, mimicking the traditional greeting of the Perlaz people—one he had observed even back in Xego.

Sariah raised an eyebrow in curiosity and mild amusement. Before she could ask anything, Naria quickly jumped in. "H-he's training to be a doctor! To assist me!" she announced, winking discreetly at Hendrix.

Hendrix blinked but said nothing, catching on quickly. Naria hated lying to her family—but she had no choice. She wanted Hendrix close.

For now.

<><><>

Just yesterday, Naria swallowed hard at Hendrix's invitation for them to stay longer. She wanted to. If it meant having more time to study him, she would gladly accept—but how?

She couldn't just experiment on his blood without him questioning her intentions. What she needed was to bring him to her clinic in Zalem, the village of her in-laws—where she had the proper tools to study him discreetly.

Hendrix, on the other hand, was caught off guard by Naria's invitation. Accompany her to the village? It was unexpected—but then again, what was his plan, really?

Lock her inside the treehouse and observe her like some caged specimen, trying to determine if she was the source of the light that cured Mayumi?

Her offer made more sense. Even if it meant risking everything. He was forbidden from entering the innermost part of Perlaz, yet here he was—choosing to do it anyway. Because in the end, none of it mattered—not the rules, not the risks.

All that mattered was Lumen.

And if Naria was the key to saving her, then Hendrix would follow wherever this path led.

That morning, as the group prepared to depart, Maharlika and Blake stepped back, their expressions unreadable. "This is where we part, Naria! So long!" Blake called out, waving lazily.

As sigbin, they were not permitted beyond the village boundary.

"Alright! Tell Bufe I'll visit him soon." Naria smiled, waving at them.

"When?" Blake asked, raising an eyebrow.

Naria sighed, already walking ahead. "I don't know. Ask him."

Blake chuckled. She didn't need to explain—Bufe's visions of the future were always an uncertain mystery to her. She just hoped, this time, he saw something she actually wanted to hear.

<><><>

Naria had met Bufe years ago—though not directly. On her journey to bring Grace to Vincot, a young man in charge of their security had introduced himself.

Tall and lean, with a warm face and kind, deep-dark eyes, he seemed far too easy going to be a high-ranking brigada general. His name was Rhailey, Vhinoe's great-great-great grandson. And despite his casual charm, he carried the weight of command.

"Would you like to learn medicine?" Rhailey asked her during the journey. He even offered to secure the fragile clay vessel she had been carefully holding. It was cracked and ancient, but within seconds, Rhailey had woven a holder of knotted rope, wrapping it securely so it wouldn't shatter if dropped.

Naria blinked in confusion. "M-Medicine?"

"Yes," Rhailey nodded. "We heard you cared for your husband... and your parents before they..." He hesitated, choosing his words carefully. "Before they passed on."

Naria lowered her gaze.

"You must already have some knowledge of patient care." Rhailey always sat with Naria and Grace, ensuring their comfort throughout the long journey to Vincot.

Now, he was offering her something she had never considered. He explained that on the outskirts of Perlaz, a hermit hukluvan trained humans in medicine and patient care. These human doctors would provide healing, treatment, and even basic medical procedures—skills that were necessary in a land where death was rare, but suffering was not.

The hukluvans and channaks had long since decided they could not depend on Kein to protect Perlaz. So they made a choice. They would become self-sufficient. This meant reviving old knowledge—medicine, engineering, agriculture—all disciplines that had been pushed aside after the global inoculation of the KSi22 vaccine.

Perlaz had to stand on its own. After all, to those who could not die, healthcare had never been a priority. The humans of Perlaz, however, still bled. And they needed healers.

<><><>

Naria had no words. She didn't know what to say—until Rhailey brought the conversation home. After their journey, he personally visited her in-laws to discuss the matter.

Eze, the head of the family, immediately welcomed Rhailey into their home, recognizing the significance of his visit. "Yes, I know who Bufe is," Eze said, clearly pleased by the conversation. "He is legendary."

Naria tilted her head, curious. "Who is Bufe, Father?"

Eze's expression turned solemn. "He saved the berhen long ago... and he was also one of the hukluvans who guarded humans during the wars."

"I don't remember the wars," Sariah admitted, "but I do remember the berhen kidnappings." She shuddered. "My mother told me stories about it. Berhen were recruited for marriage—promised new lives in Xego—but instead, they were eaten by the evil sigbin." A shadow crossed her face. Naira was aware of that ancient story, all the maidens were told that as bedtime stories. "My great-grandmother, Abby, had signed up and left the village—but she was rescued just in time. If she hadn't been, I wouldn't be here today."

"The famous Bufe and Reeva discovered the truth," Rhailey added. "They found the captives at the border and rescued the berhen before they could be taken to Zapad."

Eze regarded Rhailey with a raised brow. "You are too young to know this history."

Rhailey smirked. "Yes... but our bloodline serves Bufe. We're family."

Eze nodded in approval, visibly impressed.

Sariah's eyes softened as she turned back to Naria. "Bufe was also the one who developed the medicine to ease your husband's pain."

Naria stiffened. She remembered the herbal mixtures she had used to put Gabby to sleep—effective, powerful remedies she had never fully understood. Now, she knew where they had come from.

Sariah turned to Rhailey. "Are you sure she is qualified to be Bufe's apprentice?"

Rhailey nodded without hesitation. "Yes. Unless..." He paused, then spoke bluntly. "Unless you have other plans for her. Are you marrying her off to another family?"

Naria's face burned. Her heart sank. She had no say in her own fate. She belonged to the ATI tribe now. Their laws and customs dictated her future. If they chose to marry her off, she would have no choice but to obey.

"No. Not yet, anyway." Eze's voice was slow, measured. "But Bufe is offering her a greater opportunity, so..." He weighed the decision, his expression unreadable.

Sariah turned to Naria. "What do you think?"

Naria fidgeted, her heart racing. Then, without hesitation— "YES! Please—let me study medicine, Mother, Father!" She clasped her hands together, eyes wide, begging.

She had seen too much death, too much suffering—the weight of caring for the sick had nearly broken her. But the thought of marriage—of being sold off for a dowry like livestock

—terrified her even more.

<><><>

That was how Naria, along with other selected humans from across Perlaz, became apprentices under Bufe's mentorship—training to be the next village doctors, tending to the medical needs of both humans and sigbin alike.

Despite their immortality, hukluvans suffered from chronic diseases. Many of them had pre-existing conditions before contracting the RPTR20 virus. When the vaccine was introduced, it cured the virus, but not the comorbidities.

Now, the undying were trapped in a state of suffering—forced to endure the torments of aging diseases for eternity.

That was why Bufe was determined to defeat Kein. He wanted to reclaim mortality—to die in peace, finally free from pain and disease.

With thousands of years of wisdom and medical knowledge, Bufe's teachings were priceless to the doctors he trained and to the new generation of apprentices.

And yet—

He watched Naria more closely than the others. Not just her, but also the vessel she always carried with her. He trained her harder, longer, more thoroughly than anyone else.

◇◇◇

"Are you sure she's a maiden? She's a widow, Grandpa." Rhailey's words were casual. At first, he assumed the vessel belonged to Grace—one of the maidens he had escorted to Vincot. But that changed the moment he learned the truth. The ancient, worn-out vase from his grandfather's vision didn't belong to Grace. It was Naria's.

Between the berhen and the relic, Rhailey chose to introduce Bufe to the one who truly held its secrets—

"In my dreams, she is." Bufe's response was anything but casual. He took a slow bite of the sandwich Rhailey had brought him. "She is the key." His voice was steady, but his eyes burned. "The key to unlocking the mystery of the bleeding sigbin."

"And the end of Kein." Rhailey raised an eyebrow. "You know... I could just ask her." He casually placed a drink in Bufe's hand.

Bufe took a sip before narrowing his eyes. "Ask her what?"

"If she's still a berh—Ouch!"

Bufe whacked Rhailey on the head—with the same sandwich he had been eating.

"Grandpa!" Rhailey groaned, brushing crumbs from his hair.

Bufe scowled. "Get out! You're not my blood relative, you fool!"

"You have no blood, Grandpa." Rhailey smirked. "But you do have me as family." He turned to leave—only to slam directly into Bufe's chest at the cave entrance. Rhailey winced.

Bufe grinned. "I may be blind, but I'm not a cripple."

Rhailey – just like his brigada general ancestors who came before him to be Bufe's second in command – suffered a good spanking that day.

Outside of Bufe's cave, Rhailey was a respected Brigada general. But inside? Alone with Bufe? The hukluvan treated him like a child. And Rhailey didn't mind. His father—and his father's father—had endured worse under Bufe's infamous temper.

Blood or no blood, Bufe was family—and they would always respect and obey him. Just like Bufe, Rhailey kept an eye on Naria too. As she studied medicine, she lived near the boundary, alongside other students.

At times, Rhailey would escort them into hukluvan territory, where they treated ancient sigbin—some who had been suffering for over 2,000 years.

<><><>

Naria was treating a patient when she finally understood the true horrors of immortality.

Santi, a former world leader –a president, claimed to have met Kein himself at a global convention in Cintru—two thousand years ago. Now, he wasted away, trapped in an agonizing eternity, his body riddled with colon cancer that could never kill him.

Naria listened to his stories as she worked, intrigued despite his obvious suffering. "I never imagined sigbin could be in so much pain." She murmured the words under her breath, stunned.

Rhailey clenched his jaw. "That vaccine is a curse, not a miracle." His voice was sharp with anger.

Naria met his gaze. "This should end."

"It will." Rhailey's voice was steady, certain—but there was something deeper in his tone.

Naria frowned. "How?"

Rhailey hesitated—then locked eyes with her. "You should talk to Bufe."

<><><>

"What do you mean?" Naria found Bufe after their seminar at the hospital, where doctors from Xego had given lectures. The facility lacked the advanced technology of Xego, but human doctors donated tools and medical equipment, ensuring that Perlaz's hospitals could still function.

Now, as the other students left, Naria finally asked Bufe what Rhailey had implied. His response was as cryptic as ever.

"People are supposed to die, Naria. We can't stay in this fallen world forever." Bufe watched her closely, contemplating whether she was ready to know the truth.

"Life and death are Yswh's greatest gifts to humankind," he continued. "We are meant to be passersby in this world. Not prisoners. Not immortals." His fists clenched. "But Kein—Kein defied Adonai. He corrupted the grand design." His voice shook with fury. "This must end."

Naria hesitated. "But some humans wish for immortality," she admitted. She was one of them. She had lost too much. Her parents. Her husband. Her past life. Had she been immortal, she wouldn't have suffered such pain.

If humans could become like the sigbin, maybe they would never have to fear loss. She had thought of it often—of what she would have given to keep her loved ones alive.

Bufe's voice was like a slap against her thoughts. "Then those humans are fools." His tone was unforgiving. "They believe immortality is a gift—but if they lived long enough, they'd see it for what it truly is: a curse."

His eyes darkened. "It may be appealing at first. But when your body is rotting from the inside—when your soul is trapped in a decaying shell—you will beg for death." Bufe's conviction was unshakable.

Naria, for the first time, began to see the truth. That day, Naria learned the full extent of Kein's corruption. Without him, the world would heal. Without him, souls could return to Yswh—just as they were meant to.

Whenever Naria spent time with Bufe, their conversations always led to the same conclusion.

Kein must fall.

Yet, Bufe never revealed what he had seen in his visions. He never told Naria of her role in Kein's downfall.

Not yet.

Soon—very soon—she would learn the truth. Until then, Bufe watched and waited for another vision to come. A clearer, more definite one –the one that eventually happened years later, in 2025 AB to be exact.

In the years that followed, Naria devoted herself to medicine, becoming one of the most trusted doctors in the village— And a beloved healer to the suffering Hukluvans who lived in the shadows of eternity.

<><>

Naria often attempted to remove the cataracts clouding Bufe's eyes. Each time, he allowed it—but the moment she scraped them away, they would simply return. Still, he welcomed these moments alone with her. Because they gave him time— Time to teach her more.

"If there's really life after death... does that mean I'll see my parents again?" Her voice was soft, uncertain.

Bufe's response was steady. "And your husband too." He smiled gently, his blind eyes unfocused. "And if not—there will be no more pain where we are going."

Hope swelled in Naria's chest. "That's... nice." She had always believed in Adonai—the unseen God of their tribes in Perlaz. But being with Bufe, hearing his convictions, strengthened her faith like never before.

After her lessons with Bufe, Rhailey would escort Naria back to her dorm. The path home was peaceful, surrounded by lush greenery—a reminder of why Perlaz was called the green continent.

The road was gentle, easy for humans to travel by foot, but Rhailey's mood was anything but light. "You must have really loved your husband, huh?"

Naria glanced at him.

"Not willing to marry again and all."

She smiled softly, eyes on the path ahead. "Yes. But I'll see him again someday."

Rhailey sighed. "And until then?"

"Until then, I just want to be the best doctor I can be. I want to help." Her purpose filled her—left no room for anything else.

Some people were meant to have partners. Naria had settled into a life where she could be happy—even alone.

Rhailey exhaled deeply. "But what about... after?"

Naria glanced at him, confused. "After?"

"When you become a doctor. When you achieve your goal. Have you ever considered..." Rhailey hesitated, his voice quieter, "someday... marrying again?"

She laughed lightly, missing the weight of his words. "I don't know." She shrugged. "As Bufe always says—leave it to Yswh! Whatever His plan is, I'll follow." She meant it.

But the truth—the one she never admitted, not even to herself—was that the thought of losing someone again terrified her. The idea of being left behind once more was something she never wanted to endure again.

And if Bufe was right— If there was a place beyond this world where her loved ones waited for her— Then that was the future she longed for most.

◇◇◇

"Grandpa!" Rhailey, after taking Naria home, rushed into Bufe's cave, panting.

Inside, the old Hukluvan sat in deep meditation, waiting for another vision. Bufe's eyes snapped open at the urgency in his grandson's voice. "W-What?! What happened?! Is something wrong? Tell me!" For a moment, panic gripped him—had something happened to Naria?

But the young brigada General's face wasn't filled with fear—it was filled with excitement. "What if Naria isn't the chosen berhen we are looking for?" Rhailey blurted. "What if her daughter is?"

Bufe's entire body stiffened. "W-What? Did you have a vision, my child? Tell me!" For the first time in years, he took a long, careful look at his great-great-grandson.

But then—

"N-No," Rhailey admitted, hesitating under Bufe's piercing gaze.

Bufe's face darkened. "Then why are you saying this? Naria has no daughter." His mind was already spiraling—his meditation shattered.

"Soon, she will," Rhailey said confidently.

Bufe's heart pounded. Was this a sign? Was Rhailey experiencing a vision of his own? For years, Bufe had hoped—prayed—that someone from his bloodline would inherit his gift.

And now—

"How?" Bufe demanded.

Rhailey grinned. "I'll marry her and make her pregnant with our daug—" Before Rhailey could finish his sentence, his body was airborne. One second, he was standing inside the cave. The next— He was flying through the air, soaring straight toward the river.

SPLASH!

Rhailey crashed into the water, gasping and sputtering, barely registering what had just happened. Bufe wasn't finished. By the time Rhailey crawled to shore, the old hukluvan was already waiting.

And that day—

Rhailey learned what a serious beating felt like.

26

Doctor To The Barrio

"Wow! You're our new doctor?" Grace blurted out in surprise. She had overheard what Naria told her mother.

"A doctor-in-training," Naria corrected quickly. "For now, he'll be my assistant."

It was a brilliant idea—one she had come up with on their way to the village. As for why Hendrix had agreed so easily to accompany her, she had yet to figure that out. But for now, she just wanted him close. She needed to observe him, study him, and—please, please—get a sample of his blood.

There had to be something in Hendrix's blood—an antigen, an antidote, something that made him cure this unknown disease plaguing the villages. Naria's mind raced with possibilities.

Hendrix, though wary of Naria's true intentions, played along. If it meant staying close to her, perhaps he could uncover the secret she was keeping.

As they sat down for lunch, Grace suddenly turned to Hendrix. "So... you're going to help deliver my baby?"

A chorus of voices erupted at once.

"Grace!"

"You!"

"No!" Even her husband, Arnel, joined in, his eyes wide with alarm.

Grace rolled her eyes. "W-what? It's not like I asked him to sleep with me—gosh! You people have such dirty minds." She smirked before adding, "I was joking. Obviously, Naria is the only one who can see where my baby will come out!"

She laughed so hard that she ended up peeing a little. That was all it took—everyone burst into laughter, even Hendrix, despite himself.

<><><>

"Dr. Hendrix, I'm Marie, your nurse, and this is my husband, Aaron. He helps out at the clinic when Dr. Naria is away," Marie introduced herself with a warm smile.

She was in her late forties, with a round face and prominent cheekbones that made her look like a child when she smiled. Aaron, her husband, was older and noticeably more subdued.

Hendrix shook Aaron's hand, but before he could react, Marie pulled him into a hug. He stiffened. Proximity with humans—especially the kind who liked hugging—was awkward for him. But they couldn't help it. They truly believed he was one of them.

"Ohlala! Your body is mwah! Been working out to stay sexy—I mean, healthy, huh, doc?" Marie teased, giving him a playful squeeze in places he had never been squeezed by a human before.

Hendrix's eyes darted to Naria in silent plea. She simply chuckled, clearly amused by his discomfort.

"Marie!" Aaron pulled his wife away, chuckling uneasily. He knew she was only teasing the new doctor.

Hendrix was reminded of Cathy and Jonathan when he first met them—Marie and Aaron carried the same warmth. After so long without human connection, these strange yet familiar interactions intrigued him.

Likewise, touring the small clinic was unexpectedly nostalgic. Since becoming immortal, Hendrix had never needed to step into a hospital again. Yet here he was, surrounded by white sheets, surgical tools, and the distinct antiseptic scent—fragments of his past life.

His parents had been in the medical field. Hospitals were once a second home to him. *Well, Dad, I guess your dream came true. Apparently, I'm a doctor now.* The thought nearly made him laugh. It was absurd. But underneath the amusement, a pang of guilt surfaced. These people trusted him. He was deceiving them. *But I have to*, he reminded himself. *For Nzo. And especially for Lumen.*

If he found the answers he needed, he would tell Naria everything. Maybe he would even introduce himself to this famous sigbin, Bufe. Perhaps Bufe could help him find Reeva—and through her, Nzo.

For now, he had to play along.

The clinic had only a few patients that day. Hendrix observed as Naria tended to them, assisting as expected. "Can you get me the—" Before she finished her sentence, Hendrix handed her the tenotomy scissors. "And also the—" Again, he passed her the exact scalpel and size she needed before she could say it.

When she asked him to assist in stitching a wound, he instinctively knew where to place his hands and what to do. Marie and Naria exchanged looks.

"Well, doc... do you really need training?" Marie asked, impressed as she dressed the wound.

Naria narrowed her eyes. "H-how did you learn to...?"

"I grew up in a hospital. My father was a doctor," Hendrix replied. Saying it out loud made him feel slightly less guilty for hiding the full truth. *I didn't lie*, he reasoned. *Naria just assumed I was human.*

Naria nodded, absorbing the information. But something still didn't add up. *Maybe—just maybe—Hendrix had been part of some kind of medical experiment. Perhaps that was why his blood held the key to a cure. Gosh, I can't wait to get my hands on you—I mean, your blood,* she thought, glancing at him.

Hendrix caught her staring. Her cheeks flushed, and she quickly averted her eyes. *She suspects something,* he concluded. *I need to be cautious. She must know I'm not to be trusted.*

<><><>

As they prepared to leave the clinic, Hendrix overheard Naria speaking with Marie and Aaron. "You've heard about the attacks?"

Marie's face darkened. "Yes. It's getting worse. They're even attacking their own families now. Some of them are restrained—sleeping all day but turning violent at night. Do you think it's another virus?"

Aaron nodded grimly. "You said Mayumi was like that too?"

Naria had asked Aaron earlier to help Mayumi and her family find transport to the next village. "Yes," she confirmed, a thought forming in her mind.

"And now she's cured?" Marie pressed.

Naria glanced at Hendrix. "I hope so."

Hendrix met her gaze. He understood.

"Do we have the same case here in our village?" Naria asked.

Marie and Aaron exchanged glances. "Yes. Anilaz's son. He's been confined to their house," Marie said. Aaron nodded in agreement.

Naria turned to Hendrix with a knowing smile. "Hey, doc... you want to help me cure the sick?"

The bleeding sigbin nodded. *I'll see what your blood can do.* Naria's thoughts raced.

This time, I'll check if your light can really cure Lumen. Hendrix eyed Naria meaningfully.

Both were lost in their own calculations, their own secrets. But soon, the truth would surface.

◇◇◇

Dimas was enjoying his vacation in Perlaz. The air here was intoxicating—pure, crisp, and rich with the scent of life. It reminded him of the fresh, untouched aroma of a berhen's skin. He found himself salivating non-stop.

The only problem was the people. The villagers were deeply bonded, like threads woven tightly into a single cloth. You couldn't attack just one without the whole family rising to defend them.

To supply Goran—the human smuggler from Zapad—he needed several kills each time he transformed, whenever the full moon loomed high in the sky. But the tribal structure of Perlaz made things complicated. Families lived in tight-knit, shared housing, making discreet hunts nearly impossible. A messy massacre? Out of the question. Too risky. Too obvious.

One night, he hovered outside a bedroom window, drawn by the sound of a baby's wailing. A perfect target. Vulnerable. Alone. Or so he thought. As he tried to slip inside, his massive wings wouldn't fit through the narrow opening. The frustration barely settled when—

SHNK!

A blade came hurtling toward him. The baby's father, wielding a massive butcher's knife, lunged. Dimas reacted instantly. With a savage swipe, he ripped open the man's chest, tearing through flesh and bone. He devoured the still-beating heart, its warmth spreading through him like fire.

Then, a searing pain exploded in his right wing. The baby's mother had struck him with an axe. Snarling, Dimas slammed her hard against the wall, injuring her in the process. Saliva dripped from his mouth—some of it landing on the open wound, unknowingly infecting the mother.

She crumpled to the floor, unconscious. He wanted to finish her off, but there was no time. He couldn't fit through the entrance, and the sounds of movement were already rising from the surrounding homes.

Grabbing the man's lifeless body, he soared into the night, disappearing into the mountains where no one would find the remains. He swore he would return for the baby. But dawn came too soon, forcing him back to his hidden body before the first rays of sunlight could destroy him.

The following night, under the full moon's glow, he returned. The house was empty. Fury coursed through him. The mother and child were gone. Someone had warned them. He couldn't leave empty-handed. His eyes landed on an old farmer sleeping in an open shed outside his house. It wasn't ideal, but it would do.

The farmer never woke up.

Dimas made quick work of his meal before returning to his hiding place, ensuring not a trace of blood remained. As the sun began its descent, he emerged clean and composed—blending into the evening like any ordinary man.

"Mr. Gunder... good evening," the receptionist greeted as he strolled through the lobby.

"Good evening, Lariza," Dimas responded smoothly, flashing his practiced smile.

Lariza was a known gossip. She knew everyone's business. "I heard you're off to Vincot to meet with your fiancée," she said with a teasing lilt.

Dimas nodded. "Yes."

Lariza sighed dramatically. "Too bad. I got married last year. I should have waited for you." A flirtatious smile played on her lips.

Dimas returned it, his interest piqued for a different reason. Beneath her perfume and powder, he could smell it—the baby growing inside her. His stomach clenched. The scent was mouthwatering. "Too bad, indeed," he murmured, his smile widening.

An invitation. A promise. And soon, another hunt.

<><><>

Reeva tossed the struggling wild pig into the steel cage, deep within the darkest part of the cave.

The pig squealed in terror, its cries cutting through the cold, damp air. Then came the sound of flesh tearing, bones crunching, and sickening, wet chewing—followed by a scream so horrifying it sent shivers down Reeva's spine.

Even after a century of feeding Lumen, that wailing never failed to unnerve her. She turned and walked out of the cave, where Nzo was waiting under the dim glow of the moon.

"How-how she? Okie-okie?!" the boy asked.

"A monster," Reeva said bluntly, making no effort to hide her disgust. She knew the words would sting, but Nzo had to hear them. He was getting emotional again. "Stop it! Crybaby!" Reeva snapped, her tone harsh but necessary. She had to be the tough one for both of them.

Nzo sniffled, trying to hold back his emotions. "Me see Lumen... when... if... she good... she better. Okie-okie?!" His voice was small, but his burden was enormous. Though frozen in time, he looked older, the weight of Lumen's sickness aging him in ways immortality couldn't prevent.

"We've accepted it, Grandpa." Augusta's voice was frail, her body barely clinging to life.

"Come back to us. Adonai will take care of Lumen." Hugo held his dying wife close, pleading with Nzo one last time.

Lumen's parents are long gone now. They had never blamed Nzo for what happened, yet he could never face them—or the rest of his human family. Instead, he had chosen exile, watching from a distance, taking care of Lumen alone.

Still, he dreamed of returning home one day, with Lumen by his side -- cured.

Reeva exhaled sharply. "You better check on her and clean up in there too. Ugh. Remind me again why I'm helping you?"

Nzo smirked, knowing full well that behind Reeva's sharp tongue and hardened exterior, she cared deeply for both him and Lumen. "Coz me cute-cutie pie...oki –" he teased.

PAK!

Reeva smacked the back of his head, a familiar routine.

Nzo just laughed, scratching his head. "Nzo save berhen, huh? Me 'n' Drix. Okie-okie?!"

Reeva crossed her arms. "And where is your friend, by the way?"

Nzo's expression faltered. "He come-come... he be here soon...okie-okie..." His voice trailed off. It had been many decades—close to a century, in fact—since he'd seen Hendrix. A part of him still believed Hendrix would keep his promise, but doubt had begun creeping in.

Reeva sighed. "I don't know how much longer I can keep this from the hukluvans, especially Bufe. He has the gift of vision, you know." She had no hesitation in helping Nzo—he wasn't just an ally from

Xego, he was like a younger brother to her. But deep down, she wondered if Bufe could actually help them. She was also baffled that the hukluvan hadn't uncovered her secret by now—some seer he was.

Nzo shook his head firmly. "No! Bufe no like Kein, no Lumen enemy. Okie-okie?!" He had never met Bufe, but he knew he was a great sigbin. Still, Nzo wasn't ready to involve anyone else in Lumen's condition.

Reeva's gaze hardened. "We are partners in guarding the border, Nzo. This... whatever this is with Lumen... he needs to know."

Nzo's lips trembled before he pulled out his secret weapon—big, blinking baby eyes. "Nzo wait Hendrix, pleeease? Wait –okie-okie?!"

Reeva groaned, rolling her eyes. "Fine!" She stomped off, leaving him at the mouth of the cave.

Nzo waited until just before sunrise to step inside the cave. The smell hit him immediately—rotten, metallic, unbearable. No matter how many times Reeva helped him clean, the stench remained.

Lumen constantly slathered herself in vomit, and Nzo had to fight the urge to gag every time.

Even now, as he approached, he felt his stomach twist like it did the first time he saw her transformation. Nzo could transform too, but he was still... somewhat cute in his monster form. Lumen, however—Lumen was something else entirely. She was a purity of ugliness. A being of pure evil.

"G-Grandpa... is that you?" Her voice was weak, almost delicate. She was whole again, her naked body covered in dried blood. Despite the horror of what she had become, Nzo made sure her cage was as comfortable as possible.

His voice trembled. "Yes."

Lumen crawled closer. "Grandpa, please… let me go. I need to find Hiro. Please." Her tone was sweet, manipulative. But Nzo had long since learned to resist her angelic deception.

"No. You hurt out. Lumen no safe. Okie-okie?!" His baby-like voice was steady, unwavering.

Lumen's soft expression twisted with impatience. "No. I will not hurt anyone, promise! Hiro will protect me!" She slammed her fists against the steel bars, making them rattle.

Nzo sighed. "Hiro no more. Gone. Sleep. Okie-okie?!" He had repeated this truth to her countless times.

"NOOOO!!!" Lumen's shriek was inhuman—a sound so high-pitched it physically hurt.

Nzo winced, his ears ringing. There were nights when her tantrums were so intense that his eardrums burst. He adjusted the cloth soaked in Hendrix's blood—the only thing that kept Lumen from breaking free. The blood made her weak, burning her on contact.

But it was drying. And running low. *Hendrix, Nzo need you. Come now, please.* Nzo pleaded in his thoughts.

Lumen thrashed inside, destroying everything in her cage. Nzo sighed, knowing he'd have to ask Reeva for help cleaning again. She was going to kill him for this.

Nzo remembered the first time he saw Lumen in Hendrix's house, he knew something was wrong. She no longer smelled the same. But it was more than that.

He remembered the pain in Hendrix's eyes when he put Hiro to sleep. A necessary tragedy. Nzo was always grateful for it. They were moving Lumen to the car when she woke up.

She went mad.

The sunlight made her wild, feral. She kicked Nzo away as if he weighed nothing.

"HIRO! I NEED HIRO!" She lunged at Hendrix, clawing at him. But then— She recoiled. As soon as Hendrix's blood spilled from his wounds, she backed away in horror.

She threw a shattered windowpane at him, making him bleed even more. She shrieked in pain and disgust, as if his blood were poison.

That's when they knew—she had changed.

As soon as they trapped her in darkness, she collapsed. They wrapped her in thick blankets, soaked in Hendrix's blood, and loaded her into the car.

<><><>

"How can we travel to Perlaz like this?" Augusta whispered as she cleaned Lumen's unconscious body.

"Reeva. Me ask help, okie-okie?!" Nzo said.

"Travel during daytime. She's lethal at night," Hendrix agreed with Nzo's plan -- Mr. Hajji was not an option.

The last thing they needed was for Mr. Hajji to find out. He had been searching for Hiro ever since the berhen corpses were discovered in his son's mansion. If he found Lumen, there would be questions—especially with Hiro's connection to Nzo's granddaughter. And if they had to explain what really happened to Hiro... everything would unravel against them.

"Come...Drix, come. Me Lumen Nzo, okie-okie?!" Nzo had begged Hendrix.

Hendrix had promised. "I will follow. I just need time to clean up our tracks."

That was decades ago. Now, Nzo wasn't sure if Hendrix was coming at all –and he was running out of Hendrix's blood.

<><><>

In the early years after putting Hiro to sleep, while waiting for Reeva's signal to transport Lumen to Perlaz, they locked her in the dungeon, surrounding her with Hendrix's blood as a barrier. Meanwhile, they desperately searched for answers.

"What is she?"

"What did Hiro do to her?"

"What should we do?"

They had no answers.

Neither Hendrix nor Nzo had ever encountered an azhuang before.

Hendrix had been a nomad during the war, never staying in one place long enough to learn about them. Nzo had been too young—a street-raised channak, barely surviving, let alone worrying about ancient horrors.

Any recorded knowledge of the azhuangs had been systematically destroyed—wiped from history, erased from digital archives. The only ones who still remembered them were sigbin who had lived alongside them.

But who could they trust? Not even Vahitna—despite how close she and Nzo had grown since their first meeting.

"I don't know what she is," Hendrix admitted. "But I'll find a cure. There must be one!" He had promised Lumen's family that he would not give up.

At a private airstrip, just before sunrise, Hendrix pulled Nzo and the others into a tight embrace. Tears. Long, lingering hugs. The kind that felt like permanent goodbyes. Then, after making sure Lumen was sound asleep, Reeva smuggled Nzo's family to Perlaz.

<><><>

Now, Nzo desperately ached to be reunited with Hendrix. But lately, he also longed for Vahitna. He wanted—needed—to see her again. But it was impossible.

Leaving Perlaz for an extended time meant leaving Lumen vulnerable. Vahitna wasn't allowed in Perlaz—not even near its borders. And worst of all, Nzo had to remain digitally untraceable. Using any form of modern communication was out of the question.

Driiiiix, where you?! Nzo exhaled heavily, his frustration mounting.

Inside her personal hell, Lumen was finally quiet. The sun was up. She was asleep.

Nzo cautiously stepped inside her cell. The stench hit him first—raw, metallic, thick with decay.

Lumen lay naked on the cold stone floor, her body smeared with animal blood. In the corner, the carcass of a freshly devoured wild boar lay in ruins, bones shattered, flesh stripped clean.

Nzo's throat tightened. His chest ached. *This is not living.* Kneeling beside her, he carefully draped a blanket over her battered body, swallowing back tears.

Lumen's condition was inhumane. And yet, he didn't know what to do anymore. With a heavy heart, he stepped out and locked the cell door securely behind him. Had Nzo thought to check underneath Lumen's bed, he would have seen it—freshly dug earth, barely concealing a large, deep hole.

<><><>

Back in the barrio, Naria and Hendrix paid a visit to a house near their baranggay.

"He sleeps all day and becomes violent at night. That's why we have to shackle him," Anilaz explained, her voice laced with exhaustion as she glanced at her 16-year-old son, Thomas.

Naria kneeled beside the bed, carefully inspecting the fresh wound on the boy's back. The injury was deep—unnatural. "How did this happen?" she asked.

Hendrix and Naria had come for a house visit early that morning, hoping to understand what was happening to the boy.

Anilaz swallowed hard. "He told me he was walking home when he felt... something. A cold wind. Then he looked up and saw something flying above him. He ran for cover, but before he could hide, he felt a sharp stab in his back. He ducked and fell into a manhole. Since then, the wound hasn't healed, no matter what I do." Her voice broke. "It doesn't dry out. It won't close." Tears welled in her eyes. She had fought for so long to keep her son alive, and now, with two doctors standing before her, she felt the first sliver of hope in a long time.

"Maybe we should keep him at the clinic for observation," Naria offered.

Anilaz's face lit up. "Yes! Please, yes! Thank you!" She sobbed as she gripped Naria's hands in gratitude. Naria embraced the distressed mother while Hendrix prepared to carry Thomas' unconscious body.

He wrapped the boy in a thick blanket before lifting him with ease. Naria shot him a questioning look. Hendrix merely shrugged. Better safe than sorry. He had a strong suspicion about what would happen if sunlight touched the boy's skin.

"Whoa! Look at you, Hercules," Marie teased, squeezing Hendrix's bicep with a playful smirk.

Hendrix exhaled through his nose, getting used to her antics. Marie was nearly his mother's age, but that didn't make her teasing any less embarrassing—especially when her husband, Aaron, was around.

As expected, Naria just laughed.

<><><>

At the Clinic, they secured Thomas in one of the beds, making sure no other patients were around.

"Go home, you two," Naria told Marie and Aaron as she extracted blood from the boy. "I'll take care of him. Just come back tomorrow to assist me with the outpatient check-ups."

Aaron hesitated before turning to Hendrix. "What about you, Doc? Want to grab a drink?"

Hendrix, who had been watching Naria from across the room, shook his head. "I'll stay." His mind was already racing with too many thoughts—he needed clarity, not alcohol.

Naria's ears perked up. "Really? Great!" This was exactly what she had planned. She needed him here. Especially tonight.

Marie wiggled her eyebrows. "Oh, you two have fun," she teased.

Naria rolled her eyes and promptly shoved both Marie and Aaron out the door before Marie's imagination could run wild.

Once the two were gone, Hendrix grabbed some rope and tied Thomas' wrists securely to the bedposts, cursing himself for not bringing the shackles from Anilaz's house.

Naria raised an eyebrow. "Is that necessary?"

Hendrix shot her a look. Of course, it is! Had she forgotten how Mayumi attacked them? Instead of responding, he simply tightened the knots and stepped back.

"How about I take the first few hours to observe him, then I'll wake you up later so I can rest?" Naria suggested.

Hendrix nodded. That was the best arrangement. The boy might be relatively calm while the sun was up, but once night fell, he would become a different creature entirely. Naria was far too fragile to handle him alone. Besides, Hendrix still had too much to think about.

Lumen. Naria's light. How it worked. How it could cure the boy. How Naria was somehow involved. With a sigh, he made his way to the other side of the room, separated only by a thin wooden wall. He climbed onto the bed and pretended to sleep—just like every night.

Eze and Sariah had been so welcoming, offering him a spare room. But the nights here were dull, the air filled with the sound of soft snoring. It reminded him of his home in Xego, where sleeping sigbin crowded the space.

He endured it, just as he always did. To them, he was human. And he had to keep it that way.

<><><>

Naria waited. For hours. She listened carefully, ensuring Hendrix was asleep. Just to be sure, she had even given him water from her magic vessel, laced with a mild sleeping potion.

Hendrix had taken a sip and hummed in approval. "This water tastes... hmmm."

"Weird?" Naria asked, watching him carefully.

"Sweet. Delicious, actually." He drank some more.

27

The Cure

Naria exhaled in relief. He didn't seem to notice anything strange. "I was told this vessel is magic. My in-laws gave it to me," she said, staring at the ancient clay container.

"Magic?" Hendrix's eyes flickered with curiosity.

"The clay keeps the water sweet and cold," she explained. The vessel could hold a liter of water despite its delicate, fragile appearance.

"Hmm... nice. Ugly vessel, but refreshing water."

Naria gasped in mock offense. "Please don't insult my vessel! It's older than you—have some respect."

Hendrix chuckled. If only she knew. He was nearly 2,000 years old—but he let her have that one.

Satisfied that the potion was working, Naria picked up the syringe and tiptoed toward his bed. She moved slowly, carefully, barely breathing as she lowered herself onto the mattress beside him.

Hendrix's arm was draped over his eyes, his chest rising and falling in steady, rhythmic breaths.

Naria placed her head gently against his chest, listening to the slow, powerful thrum of his heartbeat. Then, she hesitated. Her gaze drifted across his body. Broad shoulders. Chiseled form. Strong arms.

Despite herself, her mind wandered. *What does he look like under all that facial hair?* She knew his hazel eyes were deep and intense, but what if— *Naria, focus!* She shook her head, pushed aside the intrusive thoughts, and lightly tapped the spot on his arm where she would draw blood.

She pressed the needle against his skin, ready to

— "AYYYY!"

In a flash, Naria found herself pinned to the bed, her wrists locked above her head, the syringe knocked to the floor. And Hendrix was on top of her.

Her breath hitched. She stared up at him, heart hammering in her chest. "You're a-awake!"

Hendrix's hazel eyes bore into hers, sharp and alert. He hadn't been asleep at all.

<><><>

On the other side of the room, Thomas's eyes snapped open. At first, he was dazed—confused—his instincts primed to attack his prey: his mother. But then a scent hit him—rich, intoxicating, mouthwatering. It flooded his senses, pulling his focus. Hunger surged through him like a wave.

Instinctively, he tried to move but found himself tightly bound to the bed. The coarse rope dug into his skin. A low growl rumbled in his throat, but he forced it down. Noise would only alert his prey.

Stay still. Wait. His breathing slowed as he listened. There was a commotion nearby—voices, movement. They were distracted.

Good.

He twisted his wrists against the restraints, muscles flexing. The fibers strained. He pulled again—harder. The rope snapped. Thomas grinned. The moment his hands were free, his fingers curled, nails sharpening into something inhuman.

His eyes darkened, turning pure black. A sickly green hue briefly pulsed across the wound on his back—an ugly, festering mark of something unnatural. His wicked smile widened.

The hunt was on.

<><><>

Hendrix knew it was Naria the moment she entered the room. He had been listening to Thomas's breathing from the other side, waiting for any sign of wakefulness, ready to spring into action. But then, he smelled her. Maybe it was because he wasn't used to human scents anymore, but hers stood out. It had imprinted on him the moment they met, embedding itself deep in his senses.

And it was getting stronger. Stronger in a way that made him uneasy. It wasn't unlike what happened with Lumen. But Naria was different.

She was experienced, a widow. That alone should have made her safe from the monster inside him. He had been around married humans before—their scents were pleasant, but he could control himself around them.

At first, it had been easy with Naria too. But each day around her, it became harder. Then—a sudden rush of her scent hit his nostrils. Too close.

Way too freaking close.

A deep hunger stirred inside him. He hated it. His body responded against his will, muscles tightening, something primal clawing to the surface. A low growl nearly escaped his throat, but he bit it back.

Then her fingers brushed against his skin. His heart stuttered. Something about her touch—the warmth, the softness—stilled the monster inside him. Silenced it. For the first time in two thousand years, Hendrix felt something human.

But the moment the needle pressed into his skin, his mind snapped back to reality. *She wants my blood.* He had seen this before. Nzo had tried the same trick on him.

How does she know?
What does she know?
Why?

Without hesitation, he moved. Before Naria could inject him, Hendrix flipped her. Now he was on top of her.

"H-Hendrix?!? You're a-awake!" Naria's breath hitched in shock. How the heck did he move so fast?

"What the heck are you doing?!" Hendrix growled, eyes locked onto hers. For a moment, they just stared at each other.

Naria should be terrified. But she wasn't. Instead, she felt guilt.

Hendrix should be furious. But he wasn't. Instead, he felt something else. Something dangerously pleasurable. His chest tightened, heartbeat pounding like a war drum. Louder. Faster. Too fast. If he didn't move away now, he was going to—

Then she touched his face.

A featherlight caress. Curious. Testing. His breath shuddered. Naria wasn't thinking about danger. She was thinking about him. What would he look like without his facial hair? The thought sent a shiver down her spine.

The monster snapped awake. Hendrix jerked away. And that's when Thomas attacked.

"No!" Naria gasped, struggling to sit up. Thomas didn't care about Hendrix. He was after her.

But Hendrix was faster. Stronger. He slammed Thomas against the wall, pinning him there. The boy thrashed violently, growling like a rabid beast.

"Cure him!" Hendrix snapped.

Naria froze. "W-what? No! You cure him!"

Hendrix's grip tightened on the boy, but his eyes shot toward her. "What?"

"Your blood, Hendrix! It's the cure!" Naria lunged for the discarded syringe, her hands shaking as she fumbled for it.

Hendrix's jaw clenched. *No. That's not the cure.* "No! Your light is the cure!"

Thomas snarled and twisted, nearly breaking free from Hendrix's grip. His strength was unnatural.

Naria could barely hear Hendrix over the commotion. "L-light? What light?!"

Hendrix didn't answer. Because he wasn't sure how to explain it himself.

The argument between Hendrix and Naria was cut short when Thomas's hand shot out, fingers wrapping tightly around her arm ready to draw Hendrix's blood with the syringe Pain exploded through her. She let out a sharp scream, struggling against the inhuman strength that crushed her wrist like a vice.

Hendrix reacted instantly, trying to pry Thomas's fingers off her, all while still keeping the boy pinned against the wall. In the chaos, Naria's syringe found its mark—Hendrix's arm.

But the struggle was too intense. The needle slipped free, tumbling to the ground, leaving nothing behind but a single bleeding injection mark.

Their eyes met. A moment of realization flickered between them. Then, without thinking, Naria dipped her fingers into Hendrix's blood and smeared it onto Thomas's hand.

And then it happened.

A blinding light burst into existence—searing, intense, and all-consuming. Hendrix flinched at the sight, the same inexplicable glow that had appeared once before. At the same time, Naria gasped. Hendrix's blood wasn't just burning Thomas—it was being absorbed.

The boy's body convulsed violently, his back arching as if struck by lightning. Then, with an inhuman scream, he shoved both of them away. Hendrix was sent flying backward, his shoulder slamming against the wall. He gritted his teeth, shaking his head as pain ricocheted through his skull.

Naria wasn't so lucky—she hit the metal bed railing hard before crumpling to the ground, barely conscious.

Thomas collapsed, his body going still, sliding down the wall like a ragdoll. For a moment, everything was silent.

Hendrix was the first to move. Ignoring the dull throb in his head, he pushed himself up and stumbled toward Naria.

There it was again. That feeling. That same protectiveness he used to feel for Lumen. His hands reached for her before his thoughts could catch up. "A-Are you hurt anywhere?" His voice was tight with worry.

Naria blinked up at him, disoriented but conscious. "No, I—I'm okay... ouch!" Her hand instinctively clutched her right shoulder.

Hendrix's jaw tightened. He could already see the damage. Dislocated. Darn it! He hesitated for a split second before reaching for her blouse. "M-May I?"

Naria gave him a small nod. "Just do it."

Hendrix swallowed hard, trying to ignore the heat rising in his chest as he carefully slid the fabric off her shoulder. Her skin was warm beneath his fingers. He clenched his jaw, inhaling deeply before focusing on the injury.

"It's dislocated," he muttered, feeling the misaligned joint beneath his fingertips.

Naria bit her lip. "C-Can you fix it?"

Hendrix nodded. Broken a million times over—both inside and outside the arena—of course he could. Naria was human, though. He had to do it the old way. "I can, but it's going to hurt like hell."

"It already hurts," she gritted out.

Hendrix didn't like seeing her in pain. But he had to do it. Taking another breath, he tightened his grip and did exactly what his father had taught him.

A sharp crack filled the air.

Naria screamed, instinctively throwing her good arm around Hendrix's neck, burying her face in his chest as the pain peaked—then faded almost instantly.

The joint was back in place. Relief flooded her immediately. Hendrix let out a breath, his pulse slamming against his ribcage at the unexpected closeness.

"Whew... where did you learn that?" Naria panted as he helped her sit on the bed, carefully placing her arm in a sling.

Hendrix hesitated. "Like I said...my dad was a doctor. I helped him sometimes." The memory washed over him—his father's hands, steady and precise, his voice calm as he worked on saving lives. It left a bittersweet ache in his chest.

Then he looked at Naria. She reminded him of his father. She had the same quiet strength, the same unwavering dedication to helping others. His mother once told him that's why she fell in love with his father.

And now...

Hendrix's breath hitched. His thoughts were starting to go places they shouldn't.

Naria, still adjusting her sling, noticed his fingers trembling slightly. "You're shaking, Doc. You okay?" She was smiling—but nervously. Because the truth was, she was shaking too. Strangely enough, she felt both scared and safe at the same time.

Before either of them could process what had just happened, a groan pulled their attention. Thomas. The boy stirred.

Naria ignored her aching shoulder and rushed to his side.

"Careful, Naria," Hendrix said, his voice laced with quiet protectiveness.

Naria was already kneeling next to the boy. "Thomas?" She called gently.

Thomas' eyelids fluttered open, dazed and unfocused. Then— "M-Ma?" His voice was hoarse. He struggled to sit up, looking around in confusion. "Where am I? Where's my mom?"

Hendrix and Naria froze. He sounded... normal. Naria quickly checked his wound. It was gone. The once-festering injury had dried up completely.

Naria locked eyes with Hendrix, her mind racing. *It was his blood.* She was certain now—100% sure.

Hendrix felt the weight of her realization settle between them. It worked. Relief crashed over him like a tidal wave. *Nzo, I found the cure*

—Naria's light. The thought pulsed through his mind, resonating deep in his bones.

<><><>

In the days that followed, Hendrix, Naria, and her team traveled from village to village, treating patients afflicted by the same mysterious condition. The work was exhausting—long days, endless miles, and little rest. But every life saved made it worth it.

Sometimes, they forgot to eat, surviving on nothing but determination. Yet, the water from Naria's vessel seemed to sustain them, keeping their strength from failing.

They stood at the side of a dusty road, waiting for their transport to the next clinic when Marie groaned.

"Water, please..." she sighed, fanning herself against the scorching heat.

"Where's your cup?" Naria asked.

Marie waved a dismissive hand. "It's with Aaron. Just let me borrow yours." She reached for Naria's goblet, half-joking, half-serious.

Naria immediately snatched it away. "No!" she scolded, stepping back. "Get your own cup. I'll share the water, but not the goblet. Doctor's orders."

Marie rolled her eyes but grabbed Aaron's cup from his pack. Naria poured the water, smirking. Marie took a sip, then smirked right back. "Germaphobe."

"Thank you!" Naria grinned and winked at Hendrix.

Hendrix blinked. *So that's why she got me my own cup... Crap! Where did he even put it?*

Aaron also took a deep drink, then suddenly hugged Marie from behind. "Whoaa... super nice! I love you, my wife!" He kissed her right on the lips. Marie gasped, then laughed like a schoolgirl before kissing him back—deeply.

Right there. In the middle of a dusty road. Under the blazing summer sun. Naria and Hendrix both turned away, embarrassed. "Ugh."

"Naria, I think the water in your vessel is an aphrodisiac," Marie teased between giggles as Aaron kept showering her with affection. He wasn't exactly sexual, but the way he embraced Marie was far too intimate for public display.

"Enough, you two!" Naria groaned. Thankfully, their car finally arrived.

The next village was even farther than the last. The journey stretched late into the evening, and despite their exhaustion, the cramped space forced them close.

Too close.

Hendrix felt Naria's head gradually lean against his shoulder as she drifted off to sleep. Aaron and Marie, equally worn out, had curled up together in the backseat.

Hendrix, however, wasn't asleep. He barely breathed, trying not to inhale too deeply. Because Naria's scent was... too darn intoxicating.

Too darn good.

◇◇◇

Word of Naria's treatment spread swiftly from village to village. Soon, countless patients came to them, all sharing eerily similar stories.

They had been attacked.

By a flying creature. Yet, the details never aligned. Some claimed it was a large black bird. Others swore it was white, gold, or blood-red. The size, the shape, the wingspan—every description changed depending on the victim.

But one thing remained the same— The cold wind. The same cold wind that touched Thomas before he was attacked. And Hendrix had a very bad feeling about what it meant.

<><><>

"It's a virus." "Or a bacteria." Hendrix and Naria never agreed. Their debates had become a routine, one that neither seemed willing to concede.

Still, Hendrix allowed Naria to study his blood. Because, deep down, he needed answers too. For centuries, he had bled like a mortal. Considering that the sigbin mutated, stripped of blood—yet he was still bleeding. And if Naria discovered why—then, and only then, he would tell her the truth. He hated lying to her anyway.

"There's something in their blood, alright," Naria murmured, examining her latest samples. "But I need better facilities and more advanced tools to dig deeper into this." She had been studying each patient's blood before treating them, hoping to uncover the root cause of their affliction. But so far, nothing made sense.

Then came Hendrix's sample.

Naria leaned over her microscope—a relic so ancient Hendrix swore it came from the Jurassic period. He watched her closely, tension knotting in his chest. This was the first time in centuries he had been examined by a doctor. For the first time since becoming a sigbin, he was being studied. He braced himself for the worst.

Naria squinted at the sample. Her brows furrowed. She adjusted the microscope, checked the slide again—then exhaled sharply. "It's... normal. Type O...for ordinary." Naria teased, she's type +A, adorable as she claimed.

Hendrix blinked. "What?"

"It's just... normal human blood." She sounded a bit disappointed. She had expected something extraordinary.

Hendrix stiffened. He should have been relieved. But instead, a cold wave of uncertainty washed over him. "Oh." That was all he could say. Because, for the first time in a very, very long time... He didn't know what he was.

<><><>

"Tell Bufe about this. And tell him I'll be back soon," Naria instructed Maharlika and Blake, who had met her at the boundary. She explained the situation—her patients, the mysterious illness, and why she couldn't leave just yet.

Maharlika sighed dramatically. "Alright, alright! A flying animal or bird... something... and a disease that you can cure. Got it!" She sounded irritated, as if Naria had asked her to repeat it one too many times.

Meanwhile, Blake was engaged in yet another conversation with Hendrix—talking about computer games and obstacle courses as if the fate of an entire village wasn't hanging in the balance.

"Be back in a week to pick me up," Naria said, waving them off. "Hopefully, I can go back with you soon."

"Okay. Blake! Let's go!"

And just like that, the two channaks vanished as swiftly as they had arrived.

<><><>

As Naria and Hendrix made their way back to the village, their conversation picked up right where it left off.

"So, it's not your blood," Naria started, glancing at him. "Because you, my friend, are pretty... ordinary." She dragged out the word ordinary as if it were some contagious disease.

Hendrix shot her a flat look. "I told you—it's not my blood. It's energy. A light. A bright light coming from you."

"I still have no idea what you're talking about." Naria folded her arms. "I saw your blood getting absorbed into their skin. That's all."

They walked slowly, side by side.

Hendrix remained stubborn. "Yet you said my blood is ordinary. I applied it to the patients. Marie applied it too. Nothing happened. But when you applied it, they were cured."

That part still bothered him. It wasn't just about the reaction to his blood. When anyone else used it, the patient's body rejected it violently. But with Naria...

Naria sighed. "True." She had been mixing Hendrix's blood with herbal oil—masking it as part of their clinic's traditional treatments. It helped conceal the truth from Marie and the others.

The strangest part? The remedy only worked when Naria administered it herself. Even Hendrix couldn't replicate the effect. And that fact unnerved them both.

"Fine," Naria finally conceded. "But there's no freaking light like you're saying. Even Marie saw nothing."

Hendrix held back a sigh. He still saw it. Every single time Naria treated a patient, a blinding light erupted from her hands. She just didn't realize it. "Yet you have to admit—my blood does nothing without you." Hendrix held her gaze. "So you are the cure."

Naria squared her shoulders. "Yet my touch does nothing without your blood." She smirked. "So you are the cure."

They locked eyes. For a split second, they both understood the gravity of their discovery. It meant only one thing— They couldn't be apart. They had to stay together. Then, as if the same thought struck them at the same time—they both looked away.

Unbeknownst to them, they were both right. And yet, they were both wrong. The truth was—it wasn't just Naria's touch. It wasn't just Hendrix's blood. The patients weren't actually transforming into Azhuangs.

Not yet.

The infection only turned a person into an azhuang if they consumed human flesh—particularly when shared with an already infected Azhuang. It was their saliva that triggered the transformation.

But every time Naria treated a patient, something inside Hendrix stirred. The inked mark on his ribs would ignite, flooding his body with light—so blinding that only he could see it. The first time, it was driven by fear—fear for Naria's life. Then it became something else.

Now, it was admiration. It happened every time he watched her. Every time she healed someone. And that light—not his blood, not her touch—was what actually cured them.

Because of this, they had to be together. But they could never truly be together. Because destiny had its own plans.

<><><>

"Naria!" Grace's excited waving caught their attention as they neared the house.

Naria immediately tensed. "What? Are you feeling something? A contraction?" Without hesitation, she hurried through the gate, stopping Grace before she could break into a run.

Grace rolled her eyes. "No, calm down! I'm fine!" Then, without pausing for breath, she launched into conversation. "Remember Faith? My best friend from Vincot? Hi, Doc. H!"

She barely spared Hendrix a glance before rushing on. Hendrix, still amused by being called a doctor, simply nodded.

"Yes, yes... now breathe. You might give birth right here," Naria quipped, giving Grace's bulging belly a quick check.

"Doc H, are you hungry?" Sariah appeared on the porch, calling him with the same pet name --her expression warm and welcoming. "Come taste the dinner I prepared for the party tonight."

Hendrix wasn't hungry—at all. But he agreed, if only to avoid getting caught in more girl talk. As Naria stayed back with Grace, Sariah led Hendrix toward the dining area.

"Her fiancé is here tonight," Grace continued excitedly as they followed Hendrix inside.

"Fiancé?" Naria arched an eyebrow.

"Yeah! He heard about our victory party—celebrating you guys curing that mysterious disease and all. Anyway, he remembered Faith telling him about me, so he decided to visit."

Naria nodded absently. "Really?" Truth be told, she could barely recall who Faith was.

That was when Hendrix nearly collided with someone. As he stepped inside the house, a tall, dark-skinned man with a scar on his eyebrow was coming out.

Their eyes met. Hendrix stiffened. The energy around this man was off. Before he could analyze it, Grace's voice cut in. "Dimas, this is Doc

Naria and Doc H. They're the duo who cured the unknown virus we were talking about."

28

Child Birth

Dimas smiled at Hendrix, who simply nodded in return. Then, without hesitation, Dimas stepped toward Naria. Instead of shaking her hand, he took it. Not just to hold it—but to kiss it. Hendrix's eyes narrowed.

Dimas took his time. Savoring the contact. Savoring her scent. Then, finally, he released her hand. "I hope you don't mind," Dimas said smoothly. "I just wanted to meet you both. And, well... I ended up getting invited to your party." His voice dripped with charm. Too much charm.

Naria, keeping her composure, gave him a polite smile and gently pulled her hand away. "It's okay. Nice to meet you."

Dimas turned to Grace next. "And you, pregnant lady," he said playfully, placing a hand on her belly. "You should get inside. The evening mist isn't good for you." Then, to everyone's surprise, he leaned down and kissed her stomach.

Hendrix and Naria exchanged glances. *What the freaking heck!?*

"Faith and I are going to be godparents to this little one, right?" Dimas added smoothly. "So take care of yourself. Give us a healthy baby."

Hendrix's fingers twitched at his sides. Something about Dimas felt wrong. And from the look on Naria's face, she felt it too.

<><><>

Meanwhile, on the other side of the world… the memory of the day she met him—decades ago—still stung.

"They are here, my lord," Caiphaiz announced, ushering Mr. Hajji and his companion into Kein's office.

Kein looked up from his altar, where he had been immersed in quiet reflection. As his gaze settled on them, he offered a slow, knowing smile. "Mr. Hajji, good to see you again."

Mr. Hajji bowed deeply. "As promised, my lord, I am here to introduce someone who once helped us resolve the kidnapping crisis. She is highly skilled in computer hacking and may be of use in your research." His voice was laced with reverence, as was expected when addressing their god.

Kein's sharp eyes immediately focused on the woman beside Hajji. He took in her confident stance, the unmistakable intelligence in her gaze, and—most notably—the bulge of pregnancy that made her bowing slightly awkward.

Intrigued, he stepped forward, gently taking her hand—not for a handshake, but to kiss it. "I've heard great things about you," Kein said smoothly.

Vahitna met his gaze, carefully measuring her response. "I was already briefed on your requirements, sir—I mean… my lord," she corrected herself, mimicking Hajji's bow despite how ridiculous it felt with her heavily pregnant belly.

Kein chuckled. "Call me Kein." He gestured toward the conference table as Caiphaiz quickly pulled out a chair for him. Once seated, Kein leaned back slightly, his voice soft yet commanding. "Mr. Hajji, I'm truly sorry about your son. We will find a cure soon."

Hajji had been thrilled by her discovery. Especially when they found the sigbin she had mentioned— A man who truly remembered nothing of what had happened to him. Nzo is safe. Vahitna thought to herself.

"You are very good with what you do, Vahitna," *Hajji had told her.* "This means Hiro will wake up someday, too." *Then he made her an offer.* "Would you like me to introduce you to Kein?"

Vahitna had smiled. Her plan had worked. "It would be my honor."

<><><>

When the two men left, Vahitna found herself –alone, sitting across the very man she had loathed all her miserable and lonely life. The architect of her suffering.

She could still remember it clearly—Kein's hellspawn armies dragging her sleeping husband into the sunlight, along with the Azhuangs they had captured. Kein had given the order to destroy them all. And now, here she was. Face to face with the man who had taken everything from her.

"Do you think you can help me?" *Kein finally broke the silence.*

Vahitna forced her voice to stay steady. "Yes, sir." *She activated the gadget implanted in her arm; a virtual screen flickered to life, displaying what she had uncovered so far.* "Two thousand years ago, you ordered that all our DNA be registered in the World Statistics Office." *Vahitna's voice was clinical, controlled.* "That was when we were still bleeding."

Kein gave a small nod, intrigued.

"I developed an application that carries the DNA metadata of all registered sigbins," *she continued.* "It uses an algorithm that tracks movements through their Koine accounts whenever they make a purchase."

Kein raised an eyebrow.

Vahitna tapped on her screen. "Since the Koine purse is embedded in the skin of sigbins worldwide, I can use data analytics to detect if a new DNA sequence appears in my app."

Kein leaned forward slightly. "Meaning?"

"Meaning," Vahitna explained, "only if you're still bleeding will the gadget you embedded in our skin detect movement in the bloodstream. If a demon is bloodless, my database won't register anything."

Kein's lips curled into a smile. "But if they're still bleeding…" He exhaled slowly, his excitement growing. "This is brilliant."

Vahitna nodded. "All I need is access to the DNA records from 2,000 years ago. I assume your office still has them." Of course, she already knew that Hendrix had never registered his DNA.

The Koine purse technology –their cryptocurrency had only been embedded in sigbin after they lost their blood. Hendrix, being different, still used Koine tokens, the currency of humans. She pieced it together—Hendrix, a bleeding sigbin, would never allow weapons or gadgets to be embedded in his flesh.

Kein stood, setting aside the fruit he had been holding. "I'll give you anything you need. And so much more." Kein slit his wrist with a single razor-sharp nail, and let his blood spill, seducing Vahitna.

Vahitna swallowed hard. "N-No need, my… my lord…" Her voice faltered upon realizing where the mouthwatering odor was coming from.

Kein walked toward her, his presence commanding. The rich scent of his blood filled the air.

Vahitna froze. Her body betrayed her. She felt her skin tighten, stretch, harden. *No! Vahitna! Don't!* she screamed inside her own mind. But the moment the smell hit her, her body transformed. Green scales erupted across her skin.

Her baby kicked wildly. Excited. Hungry. *No. No. No.* But she couldn't resist. With unnatural speed, she lunged forward, grabbing Kein's arm and sinking her fangs into his bleeding wrist.

Kein chuckled, watching her lose control. "Easy, my child. We have plenty of time." His voice was soothing, almost affectionate—but his eyes held something far more dangerous. His excitement wasn't just from her obedience.

It was her scent. Pregnant. Pregnant and monstrous. Kein had almost forgotten about the eternal pregnant ones. Virgins and the unborn had a scent that drove him mad. But pregnant ones—ones like Vahitna—were rarities.

And Kein wanted her.

Vahitna hated him, but then again...No! No! Vahitna wanted to stop. She needed to stop. But Kein's blood flowed through her, flooding her veins with power. More than power. Obedience. Submission. Devotion.

She felt herself slipping. She didn't just drink Kein's blood—she craved it now. She would do anything for him. Even betray the ones she loved most. The thought horrified her.

But when Kein pulled his wrist away, she let out a desperate whimper.

No. No. No. But in her mind— Yes. Yes. Yes. She was high. Drunk. And completely under his control.

"Beautiful." Kein's voice was a mixture of reverence and hunger as he stripped away Vahitna's worn maternity dress, exposing the bulging, restless belly beneath. His fingers trailed over her stretched skin, feeling the shifting movements inside. The baby, already high on his blood, responded eagerly.

Kein laid her on his altar. His touch was possessive—exploring her, tracing the life he had corrupted.

Vahitna had long since abandoned fleshly desires. Losing her blood had helped. She had been loyal to James, resisting the monstrous men who lusted after pregnant creatures like her. She had once been a sinner, devouring innocents, but what remained now was regret—a fragile hope that she might redeem her soul.

Yet with Kein, remorse dissolved.

All that existed was hunger. Lust. And the feeling of him draining her of milk. Vahitna's mind flickered to Nzo, the monster baby she had breastfed so many times before they said goodbye.

The violent thrashing inside her belly pulled her back to reality. Pain coiled around her spine, but Kein's blood made it bearable. Droplet after sweet, intoxicating droplet, he fed her as she fed him. Kein burped, satisfied, then laughed, and—somehow—Vahitna laughed too. Laughed with the monster she despised most.

Then she felt it. Kein's fingers pressing, feeling. His lips curled as he whispered to her womb. "Sweet darling, I can feel your head." And then—he pushed deeper.

Vahitna gasped. Moaned. The pain was agonizing, but Kein was ready. His blood silenced her cries. Suddenly, a new agony tore through her.

She was in labor.

Her body seized, and Kein's demeanor shifted—from lover to doctor, tormentor, executioner.

"Push, Vahitna. You can do it!" His voice was mocking, twisted with delight.

"No... please... I can't! The baby is not—AAAH!" The channak kicked violently, demanding more blood, which Kein happily supplied—this time, with a kiss, his lips cut and bleeding.

"Thank... you... ohhh..." Vahitna felt herself surrender to the numbness...

Until Kein pressed down on her belly. Hard.

"AHHHH!" The excruciating pain came crashing back, drowning her in white-hot agony. "No! STOP!" Vahitna sobbed, begging, clawing at the altar beneath her.

But the blood had lost its mercy. Kein ignored her screams. Instead, he forced her legs wider, pushed his entire hand inside her womb— And ripped something free. "Push, my girl... push!" He drove his full weight against her belly, his other arm buried deep inside her.

Her bones cracked. Her pelvis splintered. She screamed. And then— A sound. A beautiful sound. Her channak was crying.

Kein laughed in pure, ecstatic glee. He lifted the newborn, pressing it to his wrist, letting it drink his blood.

"Give her to me... please... give her to me!" Vahitna reached out, desperate.

But Kein didn't answer. Instead, he pressed a button. A dark hole opened beneath them. Vahitna's heart stopped. And then—he let go. The channak fell.

"NOOOOOO!" Vahitna lunged, but she was too late.

Kein peeked into the hole, his voice gentle, soothing. "Eat, my child. Eat." A scream echoed from the abyss.

Vahitna felt her baby being ripped apart. The umbilical cord jerked, yanking her insides down into the darkness. The baby's final cry was cut short.

And all Vahitna could do was sob. Her body convulsed in grief, but then— She felt it. A pulling. A reversal. Her belly swelled again. Her milk-filled breasts throbbed. Her baby was back inside her.

Whole. Waiting.

Kein wiped the blood from his lips, smiling down at her. "Don't cry, my love. Daddy is still here." He fed her another dose of his blood.

Vahitna wanted to scratch his beautiful face, rip him apart, tear him limb from limb. But the blood was too powerful. Instead, she moaned, helpless against its spell. And then it happened again.

And again.

And again.

Vahitna had lost count of the number of times she had given birth. She had lost count of the number of times she had begged for death. But death never came. Only Kein. And the hell he had created for her.

Today, despite knowing the encounter would be torturous, Vahitna needed Kein's blood once more. The moment she painfully transformed out of nowhere in her room, she knew— how desperately hooked she was on the devil's blood. Hopeless. A cursed addiction she wished she had never tasted.

She hated that she had ever laid eyes on the devil himself. But there was no turning back.

"Hold on, Vahitna... everything is for a good cause. Just hold on." She whispered the words to herself, forcing her legs to move, forcing herself to breathe. With steadied resolve, she made her way to Kein where she would know pleasure and excruciating pain.

<><><>

In Perlaz, the thanksgiving dinner was simple but lively, attended by many of the villagers who had been cured, along with their families. As expected, the conversation revolved around the mysterious attacks—whispers of a giant bird preying on humans at night.

Each person had a different version of the story, blending fear, superstition, and speculation into a web of uncertainty.

"Maybe it's another mutation of the sigbin demons," someone suggested.

"Or the channaks and hukluvans did something," another added.

"*Mananaggal yun! Sa umaga tao, sa gabi demonyo. Kaingat tayo, lalo sa gabi,*" one of the eldest guests claimed in a language only few understood.

Hendrix tuned out. He had heard enough. Stepping onto the terrace for fresh air, he leaned against the railing, inhaling deeply. Yet the moment he exhaled, he noticed something... off. Or rather, someone.

Naria.

She was getting more and more... Her scent was... different. Hendrix couldn't explain it. Couldn't understand why it affected him this way. He sighed, frustrated with his own confusion.
"Hey, you."
Hendrix turned, already knowing who it was.

She was standing there, bathed in the soft glow of lantern light—and for once, She wasn't in scrubs or overalls, nor was she draped in a widow's shawl. She was dressed up. Just a little. But it was enough.
Enough for Hendrix to feel his chest tighten. His hands clenched into fists. His body betrayed him. He brought his glass to his lips, drank, hoping to drown whatever unwanted thoughts were creeping into his mind.
But the moment he swallowed, he choked. Spitting water over the railing, he coughed as Naria laughed. "T-This water tastes different," he said between breaths.

"Hmmm... you just want water from my vessel, don't you?" Naria smirked, lifting the clay vessel she carried. She noticed Hendrix slip away earlier and had followed him—making sure she had a reason to.
She picked up the vessel from the dinner table, and now, it worked. They had something to talk about.
"Oh no, isn't it...?" Hendrix started to protest as she took his glass.
"Mine is empty," Naria cut him off with a playful shrug.
"W-Why are you carrying an empty—"

"Shhh... watch and learn." Naria smiled as she poured the remaining water from his glass back into the vessel. Then, she poured it out again into two glasses—one for her, one for him.

Hendrix stared. He took a sip, and his eyes widened. It was the same water. And yet... it wasn't. "H-How did that...?" He drained the rest of his glass, still dumbfounded.

"See? Magic, huh?" Naria grinned, bringing a finger to her lips. "Now, shhh. It's our secret."

Hendrix eyed her in wonder, wanting more from her than just a glass of water. "It's the clay... I know it is. Don't pull my leg."

Naria chuckled. Hendrix avoided her eyes to clear his head of her. Soon they were laughing together. For a moment, it was easy—simple, light.

Then, the mood shifted.

"Finally! The famous doctors --Doc Hache and my dear Naria." The voice cut through the moment. Dimas didn't know that Doc. H was only a pet name give by Grace to Hendrix.

Hendrix's laughter faded. Turning, he found Dimas approaching—his stance casual, his expression unreadable.

Naria greeted him first. "Hi! Are you enjoying the party?"

"Immensely." *What a joy—to be in a room full of my former victims.* Dimas though sarcastically as he leaned against the wall, settling far from Hendrix but still close to Naria.

Too close.

Hendrix's jaw tightened. Something about this man was off. He was too familiar. Too assuming.

"Great!" Naria smiled, glancing at Hendrix—as if reading his unease.

"I have to leave soon, though," Dimas continued, his voice smooth. "A bit tired from my travels."

Naria nodded, relieved. "Oh, when will you be in Vincot then?"

"Maybe next week or so." His gaze flickered to her. "I might stay here for a bit, though… this place is simply magical." His tone was different now. Lower. Slower.

Too sensual.

Naria felt the shift. Her smile faded. Something about the way he spoke unsettled her.

Hendrix took a step forward. "Dimas." He extended a hand, forcing a firm handshake. Dimas accepted it, his grip tight.

But then—

Instead of shaking Naria's hand, he hugged her.

Hendrix bristled. Dimas held on too long. Too close. Hendrix moved. He didn't think—he just stepped between them, forcing a subtle separation as he pretended to check something on the other side of the porch.

Dimas exhaled, deeply—his face buried near Naria's hair before he finally let go. "Goodbye, Naria," Dimas murmured.

"Bye, Dimas." "Farewell," Naria and Hendrix said in unison.

Dimas left without another word.

"That guy gives me the creeps," Naria muttered, rubbing her hand from which he kissed her.

Hendrix was thinking the same thing. Yet, he had no real reason to suspect anything. No basis for his unease. Maybe he just didn't like how invasive Dimas was. How familiar he had been. How he had hugged Naria.

The voice in his head laughed, *You're the creep*, it taunted. *Oh, shut up.* "He's too familiar," Hendrix finally said, staring at the gate where Dimas had disappeared. "I don't like it either."

◇◇◇

For the rest of the night, Hendrix kept his distance from Naria—because that was the only way being around her was bearable. She smelled too good. With each passing day, it became harder to ignore. And for a married woman, she seemed so... pure.

"...Grace, like she's something to be desired..." Naria's voice trailed off as she spoke.

Hendrix snapped out of his thoughts, realizing he had barely been listening. "Hey, doc... are you even listening to me?" Naria clapped her hands, forcing his attention back to her.

"Y-yes," Hendrix forced a smile, struggling to concentrate—to control himself.

"Can you even hear me? You're so far away."

They were cleaning up the kitchen, and Naria had been talking about Dimas and Grace. The guests had long been gone.

"I can hear you... it's about Grace," Hendrix said, grabbing a towel to dry his hands. He gathered the trash, making sure everything was ready to go.

"Yes. That Dimas guy looks at her like she's... sexy or something. Cringe!"

Hendrix glanced at Naria, watching as she swept the floor with her good hand. Then he quickly looked away. What if... he was the same? Because sometimes, when he got too close to her, his body reacted, his long hidden monster inside was hard to control. Every day they were together, it became worse.

"Guys, what are you doing? I'll clean those," Eze walked into the kitchen.

"It's okay, Father. We'll finish up and head back to the clinic anyway," Naria said, setting the broom aside.

Hendrix immediately corrected her. "I will head back to the clinic. You should stay here." He didn't trust himself around her tonight. Until he figured out why his body and instincts were reacting so strangely, he needed space.

"But I still want to look into the bacteria I'm cultivat—"

AHHHHHH! A piercing scream shattered the air.

29

Another Child Birth

"N-Naria!" It was Saraiah. The three of them rushed into the living area and found Grace—bleeding. Arnel, her husband, stood frozen, pale.

"D-Don't push, Gracie! Wait... wait for me." Naria, still with her injured arm in a sling, quickly assessed Grace's condition.

She motioned to Hendrix. "Carry her to the sofa."

He didn't hesitate, lifting Grace and laying her down gently.

"Should we take her to the clinic?" Saraiah asked, holding Grace's hand.

"There's no time. Father, get Arnel out of here! Mom, boil some water, please."

Eze took Arnel outside—the shock on his face was making Grace more anxious.

Naria turned to Hendrix. "Give me a hand... Can you do this?" She quickly demonstrated how to guide Grace's belly, controlling the contractions.

Hendrix nodded, immediately following her lead. Blood was everywhere.

Naria was on the verge of panic. "Grace... no! Don't push yet!"

"It hurts! It hurts!" Grace screamed, gripping onto the cushions.

"The baby is in a breech position... I can't... he's too—" She reached inside Grace, but panic set in. She looked at Hendrix, searching for an answer.

"Let me try something." Hendrix placed both hands on Grace's belly—massaging, twisting, and shifting.

"AHHHH!" Grace writhed in pain, trying to push his hands away. "STOP IT! IT HURTS!"

"H-Hendrix...?!" Naria was shocked. What was he doing?

"Shhh." Hendrix focused. Somewhere in his memories, his father's voice surfaced. "Son, do this." His hands moved instinctively, massaging in an ancient rhythm. Then—a shift. A collective gasp.

Silence.

Then Naria's eyes widened.

"I CAN SEE IT! I CAN SEE THE HEAD!" Relief washed over her.

"Grace, can you push now?" Hendrix asked.

Grace, now exhausted from all the screaming, shook her head. "No... I can't... too tired..." She was drifting.

"Grace, one push, okay? Just one. For your baby." Hendrix touched Grace's face, waking her.

"T-The baby..." Grace whispered weakly.

"Yes. One more, and it's over." Hendrix assured her.

"Come on, Gracie girl! Come on, sister!" Naria cheered.

"Fine..." Grace exhaled.

"Now, Grace!" Hendrix urged, feeling another contraction.

Grace lifted her head, gave one final push—

And then—

"WAAAAAH!" The baby's cry filled the room.

Hendrix and Naria laughed—nervously, breathlessly.

Grace's eyes shot open. "My baby! Give me my baby!"

"Ahm... help?" Naria reminded Hendrix of her one working hand.

Hendrix stepped in. He gently wrapped the newborn in a clean towel and placed the baby in Grace's arms. The room filled with relief, joy, exhaustion.

And as everyone gathered, Hendrix slipped out. He stepped into the cool night air, his chest rising and falling with deep breaths.

Then, without warning—

Tears rolled down his cheeks. The moment had pulled him back. Back to a time so long ago, it felt like another life. His father's hands on his own. *"Son, do this." His father had always wanted him to be a doctor. Had taught him everything -- even about a traditional massage known as hilot. Hendrix had never wanted it.*

But now— Tonight—

It had mattered. He had held a human baby in his hands. And it had been spectacular. His heart swelled with joy—

And then—

A tap on his shoulder. Hendrix turned. Naria stood there, smiling. Tears in her eyes. "You are... what are you?" she whispered. "You're good at everything." Her voice cracked with so much emotion as she hugged the sigbin.

Hendrix welcomed the warm embrace as he cleared his throat, discreetly wiping his own tears away. She had come just in time—before he started crying like a baby himself. "Y-You're the one with the hands that heal," he said, smiling back, and fighting the urge to hug her tightly and never let go.

"Where did you learn to do that?" Naria asked, teary eyes filled with curiosity as she pushed Hendrix gently to look at his beautiful bearded face.

"My father was a doctor," Hendrix replied. "I told you that... for the nth time." He stepped back, trying not to push his luck and provoking the monster within. They both laughed, relief washed over them.

"I bet he was famous in Xego," Naria mused. "Wait... Bufe must've known him," she added. "Oh...! Are you visiting Perlaz to—"

Hendrix was about to respond when—

"Doc H!" Saraiah came running from the house, tears in her eyes. She threw her arms around him.

Hendrix felt awkward—but also happy. And scared. Because if he had made the wrong move— Grace or the baby could have... He didn't want to think about it.

"Mom, you're scaring him," Naria teased, pulling Saraiah away.

"I'm just glad you are here," Saraiah whispered.

Naria met Hendrix's gaze.

"She would have bled to death." Saraiah sobbed again, and Naria hugged her.

Hendrix swallowed, unsure why—yet tonight, he had never felt so happy.

<><><>

Not far from Eze's house, Dimas seethed. His naked, oil-slicked body glistened under the faint moonlight, his rage palpable.

Grace had already given birth. Too soon. He wanted to devour the baby inside her womb, where it was still raw, untouched. Now, the newborn was out, its scent tainted by the world. Less appetizing.

But still... not entirely off the table.

Dimas had been watching Grace from the moment he left the house. He had listened. He had waited. And then, he heard the perfect opportunity. The tall, bearded man—Doc Hache—would be at the clinic after the party.

Good.

That one was big. Capable. The rest? Weak. They would be easy to maneuver around. Dimas had lingered, circling the house under the cover of night. Through the kitchen window, he spotted Grace. Her mother entered, placing a gentle hand over Grace's belly.

Dimas could hear it. Could smell it. The baby's heartbeat drummed in his ears, intoxicating. His body shivered in anticipation. He slipped deeper into the shadows, finding a secluded spot in the backyard.

He shed his clothes.

Then—the purge began. A thick, black oil oozed from his throat, coating his skin, seeping into the dirt beneath him. His naked body convulsed as the oil saturated his pores, his limbs elongating in unnatural ways. His jaw cracked open wider than humanly possible, his eyes sharpening into blackened slits.

Now, he was ready. He would have his feast. And no one would stop him.

<><><>

Near the border of Perlaz, Bufe sat in his dark cave, lost in another daydream. But this time—it was different. This time, the vision was clear. For the first time, he knew exactly what to do.

"I found you..." he murmured, his voice trembling with revelation.

"Grandpa?" Rhailey's voice echoed through the cave as he stepped inside, catching sight of Bufe.

The old man's eyes were distant, unfocused. He wasn't speaking to him.

"Shhh..." Bufe raised a shaking hand, silencing the boy.

The vision was intensifying. A sleeping man appeared in the vision, encased in a glass casket. Then—

Blood.

It seeped into the man's pale skin, bringing color, life... power. Huh... The bleeding demon. The glass casket shattered with a thunderous crash, shards flying in all directions.

Behind the rain of broken glass, stood Naria. She clutched the vessel tightly, her gaze locked onto the awakening hellspawn. With steady hands, she tilted the vessel, pouring water into the sleeping sigbin's mouth.

And then—

His eyes snapped open.

"Grandpa!" Rhailey grabbed onto Bufe just as his body convulsed, violently crashing off the bed onto the ground.

His limbs shook uncontrollably, his vision blurring as the final piece of the prophecy fell into place. Through his seizure-stricken gasps, he forced out the only words that mattered. "I FOUND HIM! I FOUND ANGELO MARKADO!!!"

<><><>

Hendrix was ready to transfer Grace and the baby to the clinic—But Naria was nowhere to be found.

"Look for her at the shed. She's probably there," Eze suggested.

At the back of the house, Hendrix approached the small room he had once mistaken for a bathroom. It was nothing more than a simple study, furnished only with books, a small lamp, a fan, and seat pillows. He hadn't understood its purpose the first time he saw it.

But now—he did. As he drew near, he saw a soft glow.

And then—he heard Naria sobbing. "Thank you for guiding me tonight, Yswh. Grace could have… but You didn't let it happen. This is Your plan for my life—to help others. And I'm so grateful. Use my life, Adonai… Make me a better person—one who follows and obeys Your command…"

Hendrix froze. He knew exactly what she was doing. His mother used to do the same. She would lock herself in a dark, quiet space and cry while praying. He took a step back, turning away to give Naria her privacy.

Hendrix stood there, gripped by an emotion he couldn't define. His chest tightened, his breath uneven—and yet, he had no name for the feeling stirring inside him. What he failed to notice was the source of the soft glow surrounding the shed.

It wasn't from a lamp. Naria had none. She was praying in complete darkness. And yet—Hendrix saw a glowing light. He had assumed, once again, that the brightness belonged to her. That the glow was hers alone. But the truth was far more unsettling. The light had been emanating from inked body marks—still invisible to his eyes.

As he waited in the shadows, giving Naria her privacy, Hendrix's thoughts drifted— To his mother. To her prayers. To the nights he would wake up to her touch, her hand resting gently on his forehead, whispering words meant to protect him.

Back then, he had dismissed it. Brushed it off as superstition—something that made sense when he was a child but felt uncomfortable as he grew older. Yet now, standing here in the silence of the night, hearing Naria's soft cries and whispered pleas to Yswh...

He realized— He missed his mother. And for the first time, he truly understood what she had been doing all along, appreciating now every single one of those prayers.

And then—after what seemed like forever— The shed door creaked open. Naria stepped out, her eyes swollen from tears, her expression calm, resolute.

Hendrix straightened, exhaling slowly. Finally. He took a step forward. "Naria!"

She turned, startled at first, then smiled—a tired but genuine smile. "Hey, let's go?" Naria changed direction, heading toward him.

Then—

A gust of wind slammed into Hendrix, nearly knocking him down. His instincts flared. Both of them looked up— And saw something massive, black, flying overhead. Its wings were so wide, so dark that they swallowed the moonlight above them.

No. NO! Hendrix's blood ran cold. The shadow dived toward Naria. She screamed. The house erupted in chaos.

People rushed outside, their eyes widening in horror. They all saw it—

Naria was being taken. Her body yanked upward into the sky— Her screams echoing in the night.

Hendrix's breath caught in his throat. Then, he saw it clearly. The creature. The hairy, winged, demonic figure. Its sharp teeth gleamed, its black, hollow eyes burned with hunger.

Its claws dug into Naria's arms as it carried her higher, higher...

"NARIA!!!" Hendrix ran.

"NARIA!!!" The others screamed her name, helpless.

"NO!" Hendrix sprinted toward the disappearing shadow, his heart pounding. His rage overtook him. His instincts roared to life.

And he chased after Dimas— Determined to rip him apart.

The entire household and nearby neighbors rushed after Hendrix, but only he was able to keep up. The terrain was rough, uneven, and the flying beast was too fast. One by one, the others fell behind, struggling to navigate through the fields in the dark.

But Hendrix never slowed down. He would not let Naria be taken.

<><><>

High above the ground, Dimas clutched Naria tightly, his clawed, hairy arms wrapped around her like a cage. Her wrists were pinned to her sides, trapped against his oily, burning skin. She kicked, thrashed, screamed—but it was useless.

"Ohhh... you smell sooo good!" Dimas growled, dragging his tongue across her cheek.

Naria cried out, her entire body recoiling in disgust. *Let me die. Just let me fall and die.* She wanted to vanish, to be anywhere but here—but all she could see were massive, scaly wings, thorny flesh, and claws as sharp as daggers.

"HELP! AHHH!" Her scream pierced the night, but the only one still chasing was Hendrix.

Dimas glanced down, and his expression twisted in shock. Hendrix was still running. Still tracking them. *Impossible!* A sneer crept across Dimas' face. *Fine. Let's see you follow me now.* Veering sharply, he shifted course, heading toward the raging river below—a cliff so high, so steep, that no human could survive the fall.

Hendrix was so focused on Naria's screams, he never saw the edge. His foot slipped— And he plummeted.

Dimas let out a satisfied laugh, already anticipating the splash below. *That fool's body will be found miles away from here.* He turned his attention back to his prize. "Now, you're all mine." He buried his face into Naria's neck, inhaling deeply.

Then—

Dimas snapped his head up, his eyes widening in horror. Hendrix was floating. Not falling. Floating. His entire body glowed, and from the mark on his back, it was as if invisible wings had erupted.

Hendrix himself was stunned. He had willed himself toward them— And his body had obeyed. In one swift motion, he snatched Naria away from Dimas' grasp.

"WHAT THE...?!" Dimas roared, lunging after them—

But Hendrix simply lifted his hand. The air shifted. A howling gust of wind slammed into Dimas, forcing his wings against his own momentum.

SNAP! Dimas screamed, his wings breaking under the force.

Naria's wide eyes locked onto Hendrix, her mind spinning. "H-Hendrix?"

He pulled her close to his chest, his heart pounding violently against hers. "Hold on tight," he murmured. Then, without thinking, he leaned down— And pressed a kiss to her forehead. It was instinct. It was relief. It was everything he shouldn't have done.

Naria clung to him, burying her face in his shoulder. *Much like Lumen's drawing from a century ago, Naria looked as if she were being carried away by a mythical angel.*

Hendrix's entire body tensed. A shiver crawled up his spine—not from fear, but from something far more dangerous. He had almost lost her. And now—she was in his arms.

For a moment, nothing else existed. Then, shaking himself back to reality, Hendrix searched for a safe place to land. Spotting a large tree, he gently lowered her beneath its cover, ensuring Dimas wouldn't reach her again.

"Are you okay?" His hands ghosted over her arms, her shoulders, her face—checking for wounds, scratches, anything.

"Hendrix... what is happening? I don't understand." Naria's voice shook. Her hands reached for his face, touching him as if trying to confirm he was real.

Hendrix froze. Her fingers traced his jaw, her gaze searching his. A surge of something raw twisted inside him.

"W-Who are you?" Her whisper was barely audible, her fingers trembling against his skin. "What are you?"

He cannot be a sigbin. Hellspawns of Kein don't bleed. She had treated too many of them to know that. Hendrix tried to form words—

Then— AGONY.

A sharp, searing pain ripped through his back. His flesh tore open. His body jerked forward. And as his vision blurred, he saw— A clawed hand— Drenched in his own blood.

"AHHHH!" Hendrix's scream ripped through the night as searing pain exploded through his back. He staggered, his body failing him, yet he managed to push Naria away—gently, but firmly.

"No! Hendrix!" Naria barely caught herself as she collided against the rough trunks of the surrounding trees. She struggled to regain her balance, her eyes locked onto Hendrix.

"Go! H-hide!" His voice was ragged, wet with blood. A choking cough followed—a fresh stream of crimson spilling from his lips. Then, without hesitation, Hendrix turned back to face Dimas, who seemed to have lost his footing as well—just from touching Hendrix's blood.

Hendrix positioned himself between her and the monster. A shield. A barrier.

But Naria could see the damage. Hendrix's back—torn apart. Dimas' claws had ripped deep, too deep. The wounds were fatal. There was too much blood.

Hendrix was losing too much blood.

No, no, no! Panic choked Naria. She had seen death before. She had lost people before. And now, Hendrix. The thought of losing him— It made her want to die, too. *Take me with you. Don't leave me, Hendrix.* Tears streamed down her face as she sobbed uncontrollably, watching him stand—wounded, broken—but unrelenting.

And then—

Hendrix grabbed Dimas. And they shot into the sky.

Naria's breath hitched as she craned her neck, watching the two figures disappear into the swirling darkness above. The wind howled, the trees bent, and the air thickened with the scent of blood.

Then, from above— The sounds began.

Slashing. Tearing. Pounding. It was brutal. It was merciless. And Hendrix—Hendrix was being torn apart. She could do nothing but pray. *Please, Abba... No! Please, Yswh, save him!*

<><><>

Far above, Hendrix's marks ignited, his body radiating an ethereal light as he fought through the pain. But he did not defend himself.

Instead—

He let Dimas attack. Let him claw. Let him bite. Because every time Hendrix's blood touched the azhuang's skin

Dimas screamed.

The monster howled in agony, thrashing as Hendrix's blood burned through his flesh like fire. Yet—Dimas did not stop fighting. And Hendrix knew—he had to end this.

Now.
Ignoring the sharp thorns piercing his hands, he gripped one of Dimas' massive wings— And ripped it off.
"AAAARGH!" Dimas' screech was deafening, his body convulsing violently. The severed wing plummeted to the earth below. Hendrix reached for the second—

But Dimas, in a final, desperate act, lunged— And sank his teeth into Hendrix's face. Tearing. Ripping. Chewing. His nose. His mouth. His chin. Gone.
A garbled cry of agony escaped Hendrix's throat, his body reeling from the unbearable pain. But even through the torment— He did not stop. With one final grasp, he dismantled Dimas' last wing.

And then— They both fell.

"AHHHH!" "AAAAAH!" The two plummeted, screaming, their bodies twisting wildly through the air. The wind rushed past them, the ground racing up to meet them.

Hendrix could no longer control the fall. He had lost too much blood. The world blurred.

Then— Everything went dark.

<><><>

Naria sprinted toward Hendrix, desperation fueling her every step— But before she could reach him, Dimas—wingless but relentless—lurched forward. His clawed hands slammed into her legs, tripping her to the ground.

A sharp gasp escaped her lips as she hit the dirt, dazed but conscious.

Then—

He was on top of her. A growl rumbled deep in Dimas' chest, his eyes wild with hunger. He pinned her down, his claws pressing into her shoulders.

His mouth stretched into a gruesome grin, revealing rows of jagged teeth. "Time to feast..."

Naria's breath caught in her throat. She couldn't move. Dimas' fingers dug deeper, ready to tear her open— To devour her heart. Just as Dimas prepared to strike, A shadow moved.

Then—

a sudden force enveloped Naria as Hendrix threw himself over her, shielding her body with his own. In that instant, a blinding light erupted from his marks.

It was pure, electric—violent and divine.

It struck Dimas like a thousand bolts of lightning, sending waves of crackling energy through his monstrous form. "AAAAAARGHHH!" Dimas' scream shattered the air as his body convulsed uncontrollably, paralyzed by the searing power surging through him.

His skin smoldered, burned, and finally— He collapsed. Seemingly lifeless.

For the first time, Naria saw it. The light Hendrix always spoke about. It had been real all along. Her breath hitched as she looked at Hendrix. Or what was left of him.
His face—his beautiful, gentle face—was gone. There was nothing left but blood, the bone beneath exposed, his lips torn, his nose missing.

And yet—

His eyes. His kind, unwavering eyes still looked at her lovingly.
"H-Hendrix..." Naria's voice broke, her sobs racking her chest as she reached for him— Only to realize— There was nothing to touch. His cheeks were gone. Her fingers hovered helplessly, unable to comfort him, unable to do anything but weep.

Then—

Her eyes widened. Before her very eyes, Hendrix's face began to heal. The torn flesh stitched itself back together. His bones shifted, re-shaping. His mouth formed anew. His skin grew back—smooth, unscarred.

And this time— There was no beard.

30

The Reunion

For the first time, Naria saw Hendrix's true face. And it was breathtaking. His features were flawless, otherworldly—but something was missing. Her breath caught in her throat as her eyes locked onto the absence of one thing.

No philtrum.

Her stomach dropped. "Y-You're a... sigbin?!" Her voice was barely a whisper, but her heart screamed. She had seen too many hellspawns of Kein to mistake what stood before her.

The truth was undeniable. And yet—

Hendrix looked just as shocked as she was. His lips parted in disbelief as he stared back at her. Then he asked—his voice raw, hesitant. "Y-You're a berhen?!?"

What?! At first Hendrix couldn't believe his ears. Dimas' words echoed in Hendrix's mind. He had told him as they fought midair.
"What do you want from her?!" Hendrix had demanded.

"Her berhen heart!" Dimas' voice had been distorted, his sharp teeth making his words difficult to understand.

But Hendrix had heard him clearly. "She was married..." Hendrix had argued, his voice trailing off, unsure.

Yet—Dimas had laughed. Salivating, his lips curled into a wicked grin as he taunted— "She may be... but her body is not." Dimas' breath had been thick with hunger, dripping with dark green saliva, "His monstrous eyes scanned below, hunting for Naria like a predator stalking its prize.

Hendrix's mind was spinning. The pieces finally fell into place. Naria was pure. Unmarked. Untouched. Lost in his own thoughts, the weight of realization crashing down on him like a tidal wave. Naria... is a berhen?!

His jaw tightened, his hands clenching into fists. The mere thought of Dimas laying a single claw on her—of his filthy hands even grazing a strand of her hair— Rage ignited in Hendrix's chest.

Both torn and bleeding, the battle was far from over – both of them were craving for Naria's berhen heart.

◇◇◇

A berhen widow. Illuminaria - Naria came from a small tribe in Jamin. Her people were poor farmers, but they lived with dignity and happiness. When her parents fell ill, she cared for them until their last breath. At thirteen, with no family left, she was sent to Viscot in hopes of finding a husband who could provide for her.

Gabriel, her childhood friend, wept when she left. Years later, when Naria became of marriageable age, he arrived in Vincot with his parents to ask for her hand.

"Naria, you're the only one who knows the truth about me. Will you accept this arrangement, even if I can't be a real husband to you?"

Gabby asked, his voice hesitant. He wanted her to understand before making the proposal official.

Naria smiled softly. "Gab, you coming here already saved me. I don't want to marry a stranger—someone I don't love. I love you. You're my best friend."

Unlike the other girls in Vincot, Naria wasn't eager to be married. She was still young, still growing into herself. But she trusted Gabby, and that was enough.

"...But I love Ivan," he confessed, needing her to fully grasp what she was agreeing to.

"I don't care. We can all have fun together," she said, wrapping her arms around him in a hug.

And they did. Gabby was a good husband, kind and protective. Through their marriage, Naria became part of the Ati tribe, welcomed warmly by his family—especially his sister, Grace.

Though their union lacked intimacy, Gabby was everything a husband should be. His heart, however, belonged to his business partner, Ivan. The three of them spent so much time together that people hardly questioned it. Naria flourished in their unconventional household, free from societal pressures to conform to the expectations of a traditional wife.

"Hey, when are you two giving us a grandchild?" Gabby's mother, Sariah, would often tease when they visited.

"S-soon, Mom... soon," Gabby would promise with a nervous chuckle.

"We can try... I can try, Naria," he once told her after another round of parental pressure.

"No, Gabby. You don't have to," she reassured him. "We're happy just like this."

They hadn't thought this far ahead when they made their arrangement, but Naria had no regrets. She was grateful to be free from the fate of an unmarried maiden in Vincot, and Gabby was relieved to live without the burden of pretending to be someone he wasn't.

"Thank you, Naria," Ivan would say whenever the three of them spent time together. He and Gabby had never crossed the line into physical intimacy, out of respect for Naria and for each other. Their love was understood, deep and unspoken, bound by something greater than the need to be lovers.

Years passed in quiet contentment—until Gabby fell ill.

Naria cared for him as she had once cared for her parents, refusing to leave his side. And when he finally passed, he left behind two grieving hearts.

Yes, Naria had once been a wife. Now, she was a berhen widow—her secret hidden from everyone... until now.

<><><>

"You're a sigbin!?" "You're a berhen!?" Naria and Hendrix asked in unison.

Naria didn't need to answer—Hendrix didn't need one. It clicked. He knew all along because the truth was staring him in the face. Everything made sense now.

Naria was a virgin. That's why he could smell her so strongly. That's why she was so... A piercing scream shattered his thoughts.

Dimas howled as the sunlight struck him.

Naria and Hendrix sprang to their feet, watching in horror as the azhuang's monstrous form flickered and shifted, revealing Dimas's true face beneath. "Y-you...?! Hendrix, the bleeding sigbin... I've been looking for y—" Dimas choked on his words before another scream tore from his throat, his body convulsing in agony.

Somewhere in Naria's backyard, Sariah shrieked in terror. She had found the lower half of Dimas's body lying on the ground—severed and burning under the unforgiving sun.

Hendrix's gaze remained fixed on the writhing remains. If Dimas was like Lumen, then he would die. And if Lumen couldn't be saved, neither could Dimas. Not even with Naria's help.

What Hendrix didn't know—what no one knew—was that Dimas could have been cured. A fusion of Hendrix's blood and his light might have saved him, if only his body had not been separated before sunrise.

But it was too late. The sun's rays consumed Dimas's severed torso, turning it to ash.

Naria watched, trembling, still reeling from the horror of it all. She had been attacked. She had nearly been killed by a monster. And now, another truth had been revealed—Hendrix wasn't just some ordinary man.

He was a sigbin – a bleeding one.

A painful realization settled in her chest. *I can never be with him.* The same way she could never truly be with her husband. The same way she wanted to be with him. Her heart ached with the thought. Because she did want Hendrix. She knew they were good together.

We could be village doctors... she thought desperately. *If he wanted to be. If he wanted me, too. I hope he wants me.* This had been her silent prayer in the shed, after thanking Yswh for saving Grace.

She had prayed for Hendrix. Not just for his safety, but for his heart. She had asked Yswh to give him to her, because— She was falling in love with him. Tears welled in her eyes as she faced the bittersweet truth.

What she didn't know—what she couldn't know—was just how much Hendrix wanted her, too.

Oh, he wanted her. Not just literally. Figuratively. He wanted her berhen heart, not to eat, but to love, treasure, and cherish for as long as his immortal existence.

As Dimas's remains melted into nothing, Hendrix and Naria turned to each other. Neither spoke, but they were thinking the same thing. Hendrix longed to touch her face, to wipe away her tears.

But deep down, he knew—this was already the end of something that had never been allowed to begin.

"Naria!!!" A voice cut through the air. Maharlika. Naria's head snapped up. They were at the border. Hendrix followed her gaze to where Blake and Maharlika stood, waving frantically. "Bufe needs you now!" Blake shouted as he ran toward them.

Naria took a deep breath, steadying herself. "All right!" she called back. She turned to where Hendrix had been standing.

But he was already gone.

<><><>

"May I go now?" Vahitna's voice was barely a whisper. She sat astride Kein in his office chair, pain lanced through her as he was draining her of milk while obsessing on her bloated belly. The position was excruciating—her condition made it unbearable, but the agony was familiar now. She had endured it countless times over the past decades.

Kein had done this before. Over and over. And each time, he had forced her to watch as her channak got snatched away from her and offered at altar hole where Sofia waited. She had seen it. She knew now what had happened to her.

"Do you want to join her?" Kein's voice was mocking, teasing.

Sometimes, she wondered if he knew. If he had discovered what she had done. If this was her punishment for betraying Sofia.

"No," Vahitna forced herself to answer. She hid her fear as best as she could, doing everything he asked—anything to keep him pleased. Because if not for Kein's blood... Ohhh... Kein allowed her to bite him.

It was his way of keeping her hooked, his way of chaining her to Cintru. Pleasure warred with pain as she reached another high –addicted to Kein's blood.

She didn't want this. Because she knew what would come next. Kein would open her again. The anticipation of it terrified her. The uncertainty of how he would do it this time made her shudder. But her body betrayed her, shattering in release against him. And she screamed in unbearable pain and pleasure.

Vahitna's grip on the office table tightened. In the throes of her forced ecstasy, she accidentally bumped the table, causing a single fruit—carefully placed on a rack above—to tumble forward.

She barely had time to process what happened before she was airborne. Kein had shoved her. Violently. Her body slammed into the wall, face-first. She collapsed onto the cold floor, belly torn open.

Kein caught the falling fruit before it hit the ground. His fingers curled around it, his entire frame trembling with fury. Without a second glance at her, he strode forward, ripped her ruined body, and tossed another one into Sofia's abyss.

"Get up and get out!" Kein roared.

Vahitna trembled. But the command was a blessing. Despite the pain, despite the horror, she felt a twisted sense of relief. She could leave. As soon as her body mended itself—her wounds sealing, her form replenishing, her womb full again—she rose and fled.

Kein didn't watch her go. Instead, his eyes locked onto the fruit in his hands. Its color was changing. A strange flicker crossed his face. Then, softly, like a child speaking to something greater than himself, he whispered: "Yes, Father. I'm doing everything I can... I will find him. I promise."

Vahitna had seen everything. She had heard everything. Instead of leaving, she lingered outside, peeking through the doorway. Because she needed to know. *Why was that fruit so important to Kein?*

◇◇◇

Finding the channaks' lair was easy for Hendrix. Getting there, however, was another story. The dense northern forest was riddled with obstacle courses, each one an intricate snare designed to deter intruders. Some traps were simple, others were familiar, but all of them were ingeniously crafted.

And then there were the new ones—complex, unpredictable, and utterly amusing to navigate.

Blake.

Hendrix smirked. Some of these traps bore his friend's signature style, subtle yet unmistakable. Each obstacle kept his mind occupied, offering a welcome distraction from thoughts of Naria.

It's right that you left, he reminded himself. *You're no good around berhen. You'd only ruin her life. And you don't want what happened to Lumen to happen to Naria... all because you got too close.*

But another voice inside him whispered—*Naria is not Lumen. She was special. Which is exactly why I need to stay away. I deserve the pain of being apart from her.* Hendrix clenched his jaw as he moved through another snare, his body responding to the challenge even as his mind battled itself.

I stayed too long with Lumen. I wanted to be her hero, and I destroyed her anyway. My selfishness wrecked her life. If I truly care about Naria, I must—

A sudden whirr filled the air. Then, thousands of flying daggers pierced through his body. Hendrix barely had time to react before he was surrounded. Channaks of all shapes, sizes, and ages emerged from the shadows, their eyes gleaming with curiosity and hostility.

One of them—a young boy—stepped forward.

"No! Stay back!" Hendrix warned, his voice sharp with panic. If the kid got too close, if he so much as touched him—he'd put him to sleep. Forever.

But the boy only laughed smugly, unfazed. "Strangers aren't allowed here, you know," he said, stooping to pick up a fallen dagger as he continued his slow approach.

Hendrix gritted his teeth. He didn't dare pull the blades from his body—his blood was too dangerous. If it splattered, if even a drop landed on the boy—

But the child was stubborn. His small fingers reached for one of the knives embedded in Hendrix's flesh.

"STOP!" A sharp voice cut through the air. A figure dropped down from above, landing with effortless grace.

Hendrix exhaled in relief. Reeva.

She took one sweeping look at the scene before barking out her command. "Step away from him! All of you!"

The channaks hesitated, glancing at each other. But her authority was absolute. Slowly, they backed away. Hendrix remained still, his chest rising and falling with controlled breaths. At least for now, the worst was over.

"Where in the bloody heck have you been, freak?" Reeva's voice was sharp, cutting through the night.

Hendrix, no longer bleeding, ran a hand through his hair as he watched her carefully handle the blood-soaked towel. She used a stick to drop it into a large bag before sealing it tightly. With a nod, she handed it off to a group of channaks, who hurried away to store it somewhere safe.

Nearby, the young channak boy—Rebel, the one who had nearly touched Hendrix's blood—watched with wide eyes. "So he's the source of our magical blood... a bleeding sigbin," Rebel murmured in awe.

Reeva smirked. "Yes. The very blood you lot use to put intruders to sleep."

Hendrix's brow furrowed. "They're doing that?" He tested his footing, relieved to find that now that he had stopped bleeding, he could move without pain.

Reeva shrugged. "Only for trespassers. Since we can't kill them—we discard their sleeping bodies beyond the border. When they wake up, they don't remember much." She gestured for the other channaks to return to their posts.

"Your blood, when diluted in water, isn't as potent," she continued. "Just enough to make them inactive for a few days... or sometimes months."

"Thanks for the towel," Rebel piped up, still hovering close. "We can make more ammunition from it."

Another channak, voice full of wonder, muttered, "Maybe we should get a bucket next time. That way, we can collect more."

Hendrix tensed. The way they talked about his blood—as if he were some kind of endless supply—made his skin crawl.

Reeva must have noticed because her tone turned deadly serious. "Back off, kid," she warned. "Touch him, and you'll sleep forever. I guarantee you that."

Some of the younger channaks hesitated, but Rebel only grinned. "Sorry, bleeder," he said, but he didn't move far.

Hendrix just nodded, shifting uncomfortably. Being surrounded by a pack of curious kids in the middle of a dark forest was unsettling, to say the least.

Finally, when the channaks had dispersed, Hendrix turned to Reeva. "Reeva…" he started.

She sighed before he could finish. "I know." Her expression darkened, her usual tough exterior slipping for just a moment. "He's been waiting for you. Come with me."

It was about time.

<><><>

Nzo cried like a baby the moment he saw Hendrix. And then, without warning, he leaped at him.

They were deep in the heart of the forest, the journey more grueling than Hendrix had anticipated. But seeing Nzo again made it worth it.

"I'm sick and tired of hiding and babysitting him. I'm glad you came." Reeva muttered, exasperated.

Then—

PAK!

Nzo smacked Hendrix across the face. Then again. And again. Even as Hendrix still held him, Nzo pummeled him, raining down blows on his head and shoulders.

"YOU! So long coming-coming! BLOODY HECK! Me wait and wait! Okie-okie?!" Nzo shrieked, his voice escalating into full-blown rage.

Hendrix didn't stop him. "I'm sorry," he said simply, letting Nzo land as many hits as he needed. He deserved this.

Eventually, Nzo exhausted himself and stilled. Breathless, he clung to Hendrix, his small frame trembling. When he finally calmed down, Hendrix told him everything—about his journey, his discoveries.

Everything except Naria. Instead, he focused on Dimas. "Is Lumen the same? Is her body and belly..." Hendrix hesitated, unable to finish the sentence.

Nzo's expression crumpled. "Yes," he whispered, tears brimming in his eyes again.

Hendrix swallowed hard. "How is she? I want to see her."

A lie.

He didn't want to see Lumen. Because deep down, he knew—Lumen would never forgive him.

Reeva exhaled sharply. "That's the problem."

Nzo glanced away, hesitant. Then, finally, he said the words that made Hendrix's blood run cold. "She gone." The channak howled again, a heartbreaking cry. – Followed by...

Silence.

Hendrix's heartbeat pounded in his ears. Nzo explained in between sobbing. He had discovered a hole in the ground beneath Lumen's bed. When he crawled inside, it led him straight to the border between Xego and Perlaz—outside of sigbin territory.

Reeva crossed her arms. "Where do you think she went?"

A beat of silence. Then

"Perlaz." "Xego." Hendrix and Nzo spoke at the same time.

Hendrix's jaw clenched. "She could be hunting berhen. Perlaz has plenty of them." His stomach twisted. *Naria... is she safe?*

But Nzo shook his head. "No. She look Hiro. She want him see. Okie-okie?"

Lumen's obsession with Hiro had never wavered. Their answer came soon enough. They found out the truth when they heard the world news.

31

The Fab Five

"Again?" Naria's voice was barely above a whisper as she stared at Bufe, struggling to process everything he had just told her.

After returning home to assure her family she was safe, she had checked on Grace's condition. She made sure Marie and Aaron knew how to care for her while she was away.

"Where is Doc H? I haven't thanked him yet," Grace asked once she had settled into the clinic, and Naria had checked her stats.

Naria hesitated before forcing a smile. "H-he was called away for work... somewhere." The lie felt heavy on her tongue. She was still reeling from everything that had happened—still confused, still shaken—but she had to be strong. For her family.

Saraiah was still terrified after witnessing the attack, so Naria put on a brave face, assuring everyone there was no longer a giant flying beast to fear.

The sigbin at the border had taken care of it. Or rather... Hendrix had taken care of it. But she couldn't bring herself to tell them the truth --not even to Bufe.

Then Blake and Maharlika had practically dragged her to Bufe's cave, urging her to hurry. Now, standing before the hukluvan elder, she felt like the ground beneath her was slipping away.

"We are going to Xego." Bufe repeated, as if she hadn't heard him the first time.

"W-why?" She stammered. She had come to discuss the winged monster plaguing the villages, but Bufe seemed distracted—especially after learning it had been destroyed by the sun, just as the channaks had briefly witnessed.

Bufe's gaze was steady. "Remember when we first met? I told you the truth about your vessel. About the purpose of our search—to find a cure for Kein's curse."

Naria did remember. She had seen the suffering of the hukluvans firsthand—those who were sick, those bedridden, those waiting for a cure that never came. She had tended to them herself.

"If we become mortal again, then we can die. We just want to die and be with Yswh." Bufe's voice carried the weight of centuries. A desperation she had heard before—from every hukluvan she had cared for. Their suffering would only end when Kein's curse was lifted.

"You and your water vessel, Naria, are the key to Kein's death." His words sent a shiver down her spine.

She tried to wrap her mind around what he was saying. Tried to process the enormity of it all. "I'm... supposed to kill Kein?" The memory of the monstrous being that had nearly killed her flashed through her mind. She shuddered.

Kein wasn't just a monster—he was the monster. The god of hellspawns himself.

Bufe shook his head. "No. I've found the one who can kill Kein. And I finally understand your role in making it happen." His voice had shifted—no longer heavy with sorrow, but charged with something else. Excitement.

"What?" Naria asked, still trying to make sense of how she could possibly help.

Bufe's gaze locked onto her. "The vessel and the berhen. It all makes sense now."

Naria's breath caught.

"Tell me, Naria... are you a maiden –untouch and pure?"

"Grandpa!" Rhailey, flustered, turned red as he scolded Bufe. He didn't want Naria involved in whatever his grandfather was planning. But what could he do to stop it?

Naria hesitated, then nodded, though she quickly clarified. "Yes. But... I was married."

Bufe's face lit up with something close to joy. "Yswh has answered our prayers!" He clapped his hands together, his excitement barely contained. "You must feed him water from the vessel. It has to be you. Just like the Samaritan woman Yswh met at the well... but you are different. You are a berhen—pure, just like Yswh's mother."

Naria's heart pounded in her chest. "Why would I need to give him water?"

Bufe smiled patiently. "So he can wake up."

A lump formed in Naria's throat. "Who?"

Bufe's expression turned radiant. "Angelo Markado... the one who will kill Kein."

Naria felt the weight of those words settle over her. She could barely breathe. "And... he's sleeping?"

Bufe nodded, then turned to Rhailey.

Rhailey hesitated, then silently held out his device. On the screen, a video played.

Kein.

Addressing the world. "We will be in the city of Ruinae for the festival of Avlam. Be there and witness history. Now, my dear children... you may finally rest. For I bring you the first ever sleeping sigbin."

The footage shifted. A glass casket. Inside, a breathtakingly beautiful sigbin hellspawn lay still, asleep in an unnatural, eerie peace.

Naria's stomach twisted.

Bufe's voice was gentle, but firm. "You must wake him up, Naria. He will kill Kein. This is your destiny." He reached out, taking her hands in his. "Will you accept Yswh's calling? Will you help humankind?"

Naria swallowed, overwhelmed, remembering her prayer at the shed. *Yswh, use me according to your purpose.* Looks like her prayer was answered. She looked at Rhailey, searching for answers in his eyes.

But he had none to give. Because how could anyone tell her what to do with a destiny like this?

<><><>

Lumen moved through the crowd, blending in effortlessly. She was starving. But she forced herself to walk past the humans, ignoring the scent of warm blood pumping beneath their skin. She couldn't afford the risk—not until she found a safe lair to hide in.

Instead, she had hunted animals in the forest, barely satisfying her hunger. Her grandfather wouldn't stop hunting her. She knew that. So she had to be careful. Cover her tracks. Plan her next move.

The plan she had been thinking about for so long. *But where is he?* she thought.

Her body ached from the endless nights of wandering. She had been sleeping on the cold, hard ground during the day and walking aimlessly at night. Sometimes, she sneaked into houses—just long enough to clean herself, steal fresh clothes, and disappear before dawn.

Tonight was no different. She stumbled upon a bustling restaurant, drawn not by the scent of food but by something else. Something stronger. The people inside. Their voices, their laughter. The clinking of glasses. The rhythmic pounding of human hearts.

Lumen's hunger sharpened. She forced herself to ignore it. She walked to the counter. "Ahmm... do you have water?"

The waitress, barely looking up, handed her a glass. "*May bayad ang refill.*"

Lumen reached for it, not understanding a word she said, her fingers trembling from exhaustion. "Thank you."

Then— CRASH!

The glass slipped from her grip, shattering against the floor. The waitress gasped, spinning around. "*Ayyy yayamo! Anong problema mo, teh?!*"

But Lumen didn't move. She didn't even hear the commotion. Her eyes were locked on the large projected screen above the restaurant.

Hiro's face filled the screen while Kein's voice playing over the speakers. Her breath hitched. Her hunger vanished. Energy surged through her veins, replacing the exhaustion in an instant. She knew where to go. She had found him.

And nothing in the world was going to stop her now.

<><><>

Hendrix remained silent throughout the flight. He hadn't told Nzo about the failed cure. Or about Naria. Surrounded by technology once again, all he wanted was to drown himself in alcohol and lose himself in mindless games. Anything to escape his thoughts.

Then Hiro's face appeared on the news again. His brother. His best friend. The one he betrayed. The one who betrayed him. A sharp tension coiled in his chest, but he forced himself to stay still, his fingers gripping the armrest tighter.

"We will land in five minutes," Reeva's voice crackled through the intercom as she checked in from the cockpit.

Both Hendrix and Nzo were grateful for her help.

Reeva had unrestricted access between Xego and Perlaz, a privilege few possessed. She was assigned to monitor flights, ensuring berhen—those with pure blood—could be transported safely from Xego to Perlaz.

But no berhen could leave Perlaz. Not ever.

Mr. Hajji had made sure of it, placing Reeva in charge of the operation to prevent history from repeating itself. A century ago, the kidnapping of the berhen had changed everything. And now, history was dangerously close to repeating itself in another way.

Because when Hendrix and Nzo saw the news about the sleeping sigbin, they knew— Lumen was headed straight for it.

<><><>

Bufe requested a meeting with Kein. Surprised but intrigued, the god he loathed wasted no time in arranging their travel. Bufe and his team were invited to the City of Ruinae to attend the grand festival of Avlam. Now, seated comfortably in a private jet bound for Xego, they were on their way.

Naria slept soundly, her backpack securely holding the vessel. Even now, she still couldn't fully grasp how easily she had said yes to this journey. But perhaps... it wasn't so much choosing as it was escaping.

Leaving Perlaz, if only for a while, meant leaving behind the weight of Hendrix. The memory of him. The life she had known. And now, she was stepping into an unknown future—placing her trust in Bufe and Yswh to lead the way.

Across from her, Rhailey sat in quiet contemplation, watching her sleep. His chest felt heavy. Of all people, she was the truly the berhen Bufe had been searching for. His heart ached at the thought.

Then, Naria stirred slightly, a soft smile tugging at her lips even in slumber. Rhailey's heart skipped a beat. She was dreaming.

In her mind, she was back in Hendrix's treehouse, searching for him. *Where are you? Will I ever see you again?* The words drifted through her subconscious, unanswered.

And as the jet soared through the skies, carrying her toward destiny, she dreamed of the man she thought she had left behind.

<><><>

"Hey, looking for a good time?" Lumen's voice was low, sultry, as she peeked into the dimly lit train compartment. She had been traveling for days, slipping past borders, moving through the shadows. The journey had left her filthy and starving.

After sneaking into an empty compartment to clean herself, she set out in search of something else— Food. Shelter. And two unwitting souls to take it from.

Inside, two older men sat hunched over a small table, a deck of cards between them. Smoke curled in the air, the scent of tobacco clinging to their clothes.

She needed their boarding passes. Their hearts. A warm place to rest.Both looked up at the doorway— And froze. One dropped his cards. The other, his cigarette.

Lumen stepped inside, her movements slow and deliberate. Then she slid onto the table across from them— And spread her legs wide.

<><><>

Vahitna was ecstatic. Finally, Kein had given her permission to return to Xego. "May I attend the festival, please? You're going anyway, so I'll just see you there," she murmured between breaths, kissing him.
Kein barely reacted, only releasing a satisfied sigh as he finished. "Sure. Go," he said simply, as if dismissing an afterthought.

She swallowed hard — relief flooded her. *He's done with me. Finally.* She noticed how distant and preoccupied he had become after the agonizing transformation—when sigbin across the world writhed in unified torment, forced into their monstrous true forms.

Mr. Hajji had assured her the last time they saw each other, "Kein can be obsessive at times. You're his favorite for now. Just bear with it. He'll be bored with you eventually."
Vahitna couldn't wait for that to happen. She's done!
"Don't you like his blood?" Hajji would ask during his occasional visits to the office where Kein kept her, forcing her to work on her task—tracking down the bleeding sigbin.
"I do," she would answer. But what she really wanted to say was—But I hate him to the core. And worse... she hated herself for allowing him to toy with her –for being with the man who had destroyed her husband's life –for allowing the man who had ripped her baby from her time and time again to continue.

"Enjoy yourself for now," Hajji would say dismissively, before casually inquiring about Hiro.

"How long will his obsession with me last?" Vahitna asked once, her voice laced with quiet desperation.

Mr. Hajji didn't even blink. "Weeks... or hundreds of years. It depends."

Hundreds. Of. Years. A lifetime of this. Her channak dying over and over again. Her body used and abused over and over again. She wanted to scream. Kill me. Just kill me. Throw me into the altar hole with Sofia and end this.

***

"I need to renew my citizenship in the City of Ruinae during the festival," she had told Kein once, before the fruit incident.

"No. Let Mr. Hajji handle it," he said, dismissing her as usual.

Vahitna clenched her fists. "Aren't you going?"

"Yes." Kein barely looked up, distracted as he pressed a hand to her belly, listening to the baby inside her.

"Can I go with you?" Please. Please. Please.

"No. You have to be here and feed Sofia."

Kein smiled as the baby shifted, running his fingers over the small protrusion of an elbow pressing against her skin.

Vahitna snapped. "The heck with Sofia!" The words spilled from her lips before she could stop them.

BLAG!

Pain exploded through her body as she was hurled to the floor. Kein had punched her—square in the stomach. She gasped, eyes wide as she felt the familiar, sickening stillness inside her. Her channak had stopped moving. A sob tore from her throat, but she swallowed it down. She always cried when her baby died.

Kein loomed over her. His voice was cold. "Just do as I say... or you'll join her in the dark hole." Then the kicks came. Again and again, until she was black and blue..

And then—

He turned her over onto her stomach and took her. Vahitna screamed, but no one would hear her. Kein knew exactly how to make it worse. Flat on her belly, crushed against the cold stone floor, unable to move beneath his weight—he knew the position was unbearable for her.

And he loved it. Kein could go on for days without stopping. And he did. By the time he was done, she was bruised, battered, dying—and only then would he offer her his blood.

She took it. Not because she wanted to. Because she had to. The intoxication dulled the pain, but never the horror. Enough. Stop. I don't want this anymore. She screamed the words in her mind, but her lips never moved.

Instead, she sobbed silently, her gaze locking onto the fruit resting nearby. She had no idea what it was or why it was so important to Kein. But after the fruit incident, everything changed.

Kein had lost interest in her. And when he publicly announced the display of the sleeping Hiro, his mind was elsewhere. The next time she asked about leaving for Xego and the festival—

"Go. Leave." That was all he said. And just like that, she was free. Or at least, as free as someone like her could ever be.

<><><>

At the airport, Vahitna walked toward the restroom, her mind preoccupied. She barely noticed the man who passed her by on the other side of the aisle—

A man holding a beautiful baby girl.

At a nearby gate, Reeva stood arranging the flight back to Perlaz. She waved at Hendrix and Nzo, briefly glancing at Vahitna's retreating figure but not recognizing her. "I'm heading to the other side to pick up the berhen, then straight back to Perlaz," Reeva said, adjusting Nzo's dress and messing with the baby's already sour mood. "Call me if you need anything, alright?"

Hendrix smirked as Nzo squirmed in Reeva's hands, the frown on his tiny face deepening. "Thanks, Reeva. We owe you a lot," Hendrix said, tapping the child's head.

Reeva grinned. "You paid me with blood, so we're even."

"Sucker!" Nzo pouted. "Me - girl, no like. Nzo hate me - okie-okie?!"

With a playful smirk, Reeva pinched Nzo's chubby cheeks—hard. The baby wailed in protest.

"Anyway, good luck! May Yswh be with you," Reeva called as she turned toward the train tarmac, where a new batch of berhen from various parts of Xego were waiting to be transported to Perlaz.

Exiting the airport gate, Nzo was still protesting "Me not like girl dress! Hate-hate this! Okie-okie?!" Nzo complained, tugging at the pink ribbon in his hair.

Hendrix sighed. "Because you were once famous here, and Mr. Hajji might be looking for us," he reminded the baby for the nth time.

Nzo huffed. "Vahitna no like-like nzo dress this! No! Okie-okie?!"

Hendrix chuckled. "She won't care, kid." He had to admit—Nzo was ridiculously cute like this.

The baby wiggled in his arms. "Me go pee-pee!" Nzo announced upon spotting the restroom.

"No." Hendrix tightened his grip, already sensing where this was going.

Nzo glared up at him, eyes burning with mischief. "Me poop ugly dress. Okie-okie!?" The baby's expression was no longer cute.

Hendrix narrowed his eyes. "Do it, and I'll smash your filthy diaper on your face."

Nzo bared his teeth and tried to bite Hendrix's hand. The two continued their childish bickering as they exited the airport, searching for a cab to take them to their hotel.

Just as Hendrix stepped outside, he froze. Something— Something familiar lingered in the air. A scent. A feeling.

"What-what!?" Nzo asked, suddenly alert.

Hendrix shook his head, brushing the feeling aside. "N-nothing." He hailed a cab, completely missing Naria walking just behind him. She moved in the opposite direction with Bufe and Rhailey, heading toward their waiting car.

Aboard the train, Lumen stretched lazily, feeling satisfied. Last night had been... fulfilling. The two men she had met? Well— She had a meal. They didn't.

She awoke in high spirits, but as she stepped into the next car, a new scent filled the air. And it made her salivate. Her stomach tightened in anticipation.

Seven compartments. Seven berhen. Pure, untouched teenage berhen. As young as thirteen. Lumen licked her lips. With effortless grace, she leapt into the other side of the train car, moving discreetly through the shadows.

"Hi, girls." The girls turned, startled, then smiled, unaware of the danger standing before them.

"Hi!" they greeted her cheerfully, so innocent, so trusting.

Lumen joined them as they leaned against the train's windows, watching the world blur past. "Where are you headed?" she asked.

"To Perlaz," one of them answered—a girl with thick, curly hair.

Lumen's smile widened. "Oh really? I'm from there," she replied sweetly. *More like imprisoned there*, she added silently, amused.

Another girl, the one who smelled the most delicious, looked up. Lumen's keen senses picked up on it instantly.

She's about to have her period. Her mouth watered. "Are you the one picking us up?" the girl asked innocently.

Lumen's lips parted, her hunger growing. "S-sure," she purred. *Picking your hearts apart? With pleasure.*

Then—

A voice interrupted. "Are you Reeva?"

Lumen turned, her expression instantly darkening. An older woman stood in one of the compartments, eyeing her expectantly.

Reeva.

Lumen clenched her jaw. Just then, the train reached the tarmac, and outside the window— She saw her. The young girl who sometimes brought her food in her prison. Reeva.

And now, Reeva was turning around— Facing her. Their eyes locked. And Lumen knew— She's walking straight into disaster.

<><><>

"Yes, how may I help you?" The woman at the counter greeted Vahitna with a polite smile.

From Cintru to Xego, Vahitna had traveled with no intention of attending the festival in the City of Ruinae. She had no time for distractions. After leaving the restroom, she headed straight for the ticket counter.

"Is there a way for me to buy a ticket to the boundary near Perlaz?" she asked, her voice steady but her mind racing. She had already decided—once she reached the edge of Xego, she would hike the rest of the way on foot until she reached the channaks' territory.

The teller tilted her head. "Depends. Are you visiting family there?"

Vahitna hesitated. "Y-yes," she answered quickly, the lie slipping out before she could think twice. In truth, she had once lived in a part of Perlaz. Back when she was still human. But did she still have living human relatives there? She doubted it.

"Alright, here are the ticket prices," the teller said, sliding a printed list across the counter.

Vahitna glanced at the prices, then smiled. Excitement thrummed through her veins. *Nzo needs to know what Kein is planning. They must avoid Hiro's public display.*

It was a trap.

A carefully laid snare, designed to lure out the bleeding sigbin—and deliver him straight into Kein's hands. Despite the suffering she had endured as Kein's toy, there was one advantage to it— She had access to information that no one else did. And now, that knowledge might be the key to stopping Kein.

<><>

The City of Ruinae was unlike anything Naria had ever seen. It was her first time traveling thousands of miles away from Perlaz, and despite her lingering doubts about why she had come in the first place—she couldn't deny the thrill of it.

Everything was marvelous. Bufe, honored as Kein's guest of honor, was treated like royalty.

From the moment they stepped off the plane in Xego, through the airport, to their hotel, every accommodation was luxurious. The technology here was far beyond anything Naria had ever known. She had never felt more small—more ignorant—than she did now, standing amidst the dazzling spectacle of the Avlam Festival, where humans and sigbin partied together beneath neon lights.

Music filled the air, and the streets were lined with an endless spread of food—free food—offered to festival goers. Skyscrapers stretched toward the sky, towering over elegant hotels and gleaming modern structures.

It was overwhelming. Beautiful, yes—but also suffocating. Bufe, however, was unimpressed. He hadn't come for the sights –his blind afterall. He hadn't come for the celebration. He had come to destroy this deceitful illusion—this grand facade that both humans and sigbin had blindly accepted.

Naria leaned against the terrace railing of their suite, gazing at the city. One building, in particular, caught her attention. "What's that?" she asked, eyes locked on the tallest, brightest skyscraper dominating the skyline.

"The famous Hajji Tower," Rhailey answered.

32

Lumen Naria

Unlike Naria, Rhailey had been to the City of Ruinae before—though never during the Avlam Festival. Sometimes, he assisted Reeva with the transportation of the berhen, and once, curiosity had drawn him to the city. Still, he found himself in awe of the tower.

It was more than a building—it was a fortress. "No one enters that facility without clearance," Rhailey murmured, almost to himself.

Bufe let out a weary sigh. "Rest for now. I'll see you all tomorrow." Though he couldn't see, he still turned and made his way toward his adjoining room. Rhailey followed closely behind, ready to assist him.

Just before disappearing inside, Bufe stopped and murmured quietly to Rhailey— "Stay close to Naria. Watch her carefully. This place is not safe for her."

Rhailey nodded. "What about dinner?"

"Just order in," Bufe said dismissively.

Then, turning back to Naria, he called out— "Naria."

She turned from the terrace. "Yes?"

Bufe's blind eyes seemed to pierce through her. His voice was firm. "Do not part with the vessel. No matter what."

Naria swallowed, gripping the strap of her backpack tighter. "I won't," she promised. But deep down—she wondered if she even had a choice.

<><><>

Lumen remembered the City of Ruinae—the place where she had grown up. Back then, it had been lively. And even now, the festival pulsed with energy, lights, and music.

The night was young. And she was starving. She had barely escaped when she encountered the group of berhen. As the train approached the tarmac, she spotted Reeva through the glass window, waiting.

Then—Reeva turned.

At that moment, a channak nearly caught her, but Lumen reacted fast. She bolted, leaping into the next car, hiding until Reeva and the berhen were gone. She had watched from the shadows as Reeva led them away.

And then, with the Koine codes she had stolen from the two men she had dined with—them being her food—she made her way to the famous city.

Now, after sleeping all day in her hotel room, she woke up excited. Her plan was in motion. "Hiro, my love... I'm coming," Lumen whispered, trailing her fingers along her bare skin.

Her body tingled with anticipation. Her fingers traced lower, teasing. She closed her eyes, imagining him—the way he used to touch her, the way he used to move and rock her world in bed.

Her breath hitched. But her fantasies weren't enough. They could never be enough. Still, she continued visualizing him sliding, curling, pushing against her—bringing her to the edge.

"Ohhh..." She moaned softly, her body growing slick with need.

Her breathing became deeper, her hands clutching the sheets as she imagined Hiro touching her again –taking her, filling her completely.

But it wasn't him. Not yet. Soon, though. Very soon. And when she finally saw him again— She would make sure he would never leave her side ever again.

<><><>

"Me Nzo see Hiro. Okie-okie? Where!?" Nzo asked, clinging to Hendrix's hand as they navigated the heart of the city.

The streets were packed. Crowds loitered along the avenues, buzzing with excitement. Neon lights flickered, and laughter echoed in the night. The sheer congestion of the festival made it nearly impossible for security cameras to track individuals—exactly what Hendrix had hoped for.

Nzo, however, looked ridiculous. Dressed in a frilly pink dress, his wrist adorned with matching balloons, he was the perfect picture of an innocent little girl—far from the troublemaker he truly was.

"It's to be announced. We have to wait," Hendrix muttered, keeping a firm grip on the disguised child's hand as they blended in, pretending to be nothing more than wandering tourists.

Nzo sighed dramatically. "Me Nzo drink. Okie-okie?!" After so long staying relatively sober, he couldn't wait to drown his sorrow with a bottle of the strongest alcohol available.

Hendrix shot him a glare. "No. And what kind of idiot drinks at a bar with a baby girl?" For a moment, he considered smacking Nzo upside the head for even suggesting it.

Nzo shrugged. "Me no baby, and me drink want- okie-okie?!"

Hendrix eyed the baby sigbin closely, having an idea why he's so grumpy. "You see Vahitna?"

"No, she left-left Nzo, okie-okie?!" Nzo shook his head, disappointment clear in his voice. "Me try see-see. Okie-okie?!" Then, without warning, he stretched his arms up, expectantly. "Up-up. Drix...up-up!?"

Hendrix sighed but scooped him up anyway, placing him on his broad shoulder.

◇◇◇

Earlier, after arriving in the city, the two had split up. Rather than risk staying in any of their old hideouts, they had booked a hotel under fake names.

Hendrix went out to gather intel on Hiro's upcoming public display while Nzo made a trip to Vahitna's old home. The visit had been disheartening.

"Oh, she's no longer living here," Vahitna's neighbor, eyeing the channak curiously, had informed Nzo's pretend mom that Hendrix hired for him.

"Move where-where!?" Nzo tried to keep his voice steady, blinking hard to keep the tears at bay.

"I don't know," the neighbor had replied, handing him a piece of candy.

Nzo had taken it, barely looking. Now, back in the festival crowd, the candy still sat in his palm. Out of sadness, he almost put it in his mouth—almost. But he knew better. Sugar was a one-way ticket to trouble for him.

Still sulking, he clung to Hendrix's sleeve. "Me phone. Vahitna. gadget, okie-okie!?"

Hendrix tensed. "No! We cannot risk any digital footprints. Not now, more than ever!"

They were still flagged. They could still be tracked. And as much as Hendrix desperately wanted to get his hands on a gaming console—he couldn't.

Nzo pouted. His tiny face scrunched up in frustration, and Hendrix recognized the signs— the channak was about to throw a tantrum. Hendrix groaned. He knew what this was really about. Vahitna's milk. He's dying for it.

Hendrix exhaled in defeat. "Fine, I'll buy you a drink," he muttered, knowing it was the only way to avoid a scene.

Nzo instantly brightened. "Sucker!"

Hendrix rolled his eyes. Tonight was going to be long.

<><><>

As Hendrix, carrying baby Nzo on his broad shoulder, moved through the crowded market, Naria caught a glimpse of his face through a tabletop telescope available at her room— And her heart nearly stopped.

Enjoying the view of the crowded night market from her room, a familiar face appeared in her line of sight. Bearded or clean-shaven, she would never forget it. It was him. Her breath hitched. A wave of emotions crashed over her, her pulse hammering wildly in her chest.

Don't come out of your room. Bufe's warning echoed in her mind. But she was already closing the door behind her, ignoring every ounce of reason. *I have to see him again!*

Without another thought, she hurried down the elevator— leaving the vessel sitting untouched on her nightstand.

<><><>

As Naria weaved through the crowded streets, another pair of eyes found her.

She was heading to her meeting when something stopped her. A scent. Pure. Unspoiled. A berhen. Her head snapped up, scanning the sea of people. Then— She saw her. A girl moving quickly, lost in the chaos of the festival. So innocent. So unaware.

Her mouth watered. The hunt was on. With predatory ease, she slipped through the crowd, following her prey.

Naria drifted through the sea of people, yet she saw none of them. Her mind was locked onto a single face—the one she was desperate to find again And then—

BUMP!

Naria collided into someone, nearly losing her balance. A pair of strong hands caught her before she could hit the ground. She gasped. "Oh!" Wide-eyed, she turned to see a beautiful woman holding her steady.

Lumen.

Their eyes met. And Lumen smiled. A slow, hungry smile. "Oh my goodness! I'm so sorry—I wasn't paying attention... I'm just so lost," Lumen said, her voice trembling with just the right amount of desperation.

Naria shook her head. "I-it's okay. I'm kinda lost too." She glanced around. The streets were too crowded. The festival's energy was overwhelming. Finding Hendrix like this... was like searching for a needle in a haystack.

Lumen tilted her head, studying her. "Where are you from?"

"Perlaz." "Perlaz?" They both laughed—Lumen with amusement, Naria with nervous relief. Lumen had guessed as much. Naria's wide-eyed innocence was obvious.

Perfect.

"Would you like to have dinner with me?" Lumen asked, lowering her voice just enough to sound vulnerable. "I don't like being alone in this big, unfamiliar city."

Naria hesitated, her eyes darting back toward the crowd. Her heart ached. Hendrix was gone. She had no idea where to look. And Lumen... Lumen looked scared. Naria knew that feeling all too well. "S-sure," she said hesitantly. "My hotel is just around—"

"I know a better place." Before she could finish, Lumen grabbed her hand— And led her away from the crowd.

<><><>

Kein stood in his penthouse atop Hajji Tower, the highest point in the City of Ruinae. The skyline stretched endlessly before him, bathed in dazzling lights, a testament to the thriving empire that Mr. Hajji had built.

He held the fruit in his hand, absentmindedly running his fingers over its smooth surface. But his thoughts drifted.

Bufe.

The hukluvan who despised him more than anyone—yet had suddenly chosen to visit. Kein smirked, his curiosity piqued. *What do you want, old man?*

A subtle shift in the fruit's color caught his attention. Lifting it closer, he inhaled deeply. A slow, knowing smile curved on his lips. "Soon, Father... soon," Kein murmured, pressing a reverent kiss against the fruit's surface.

A knock at the door. "Your guest is here, my lord," Caiphaiz announced as he stepped inside. Kein turned, his sweet smile masking the darkness behind his eyes. Time to see what the old man wanted.

<><><>

Lumen stood naked in the dark alley, her body slick with oil as she smeared it over herself, her hands moving with ritualistic precision. The full moon hung high above, casting an eerie glow over the city. She smiled. She didn't have to wait long for dinner.

The streets of Ruinae pulsed with life, but Lumen led Naria further and further away from the noise—down winding paths and narrowing alleys, where the city's neon brilliance faded into shadow.

She still knew her way around. This place was perfect. Dark enough to be avoided by tourists. Close enough to the festival for its music and revelry to drown out the screams.

Naria hesitated. "Ahm… are we lost aga—" A sudden, blinding pain struck the back of her head. Everything spun.

Then—blackness.

Lumen watched her crumple to the ground, utterly still. Normally, she loved playing with her food—letting it struggle, savoring its fear. But not tonight.

She had other plans.

A low, guttural moan escaped Lumen's lips as her body ripped apart. Her spine cracked. Her skin split. Her wings—black and leathery—erupted from her back, spreading wide into the night air. The pain was delicious.

Her teeth elongated into jagged fangs. Claws extended from her fingertips. Thick, dark fur swallowed her once-human body. She turned to the shattered reflection in the broken window of an abandoned building.

Magnificent. A human bat. Nasty. Deadly. Starving. Lumen hovered above her unconscious prey, her glowing red eyes locked onto Naria's chest. Her heart. Her berhen heart. Lumen's mouth foam with stinky, slimy, greenish oil. Just as she was about to strike—

"AZHUANG!" A voice tore through the alley.

Lumen snarled in frustration. She whipped her head around to see someone stepping between her and her meal.

Vahitna.

The woman stood her ground, shielding Naria behind her. Lumen growled. No drama! With one swift, vicious movement, she tore Vahitna's baby from her womb.

Vahitna's scream split the night air. Too loud. People would hear. Lumen didn't care. She devoured the infant in seconds, feeling the surge of power rush through her.

With a cruel smirk, she reattached herself to her lower body, tossed the baby's severed head toward Vahitna's trembling, healing form— And disappeared into the dark. "Your baby sucks!" Lumen called mockingly before vanishing.

Naria stirred. Her head throbbed. As her vision cleared, she realized she was surrounded by people—festival-goers drawn by the screams.

She noticed a woman lying on the ground, clutching her stomach, her face twisted in pain. Pregnant. Naria's instincts kicked in. She pushed through the crowd, kneeling beside the woman. "A-are you okay?"

The woman—Vahitna—slowly sat up, her breath ragged but her body healing before Naria's eyes. "I—I'm fine. Just fainted," she said quickly, brushing herself off.

Naria's pulse spiked. She knew. The shape of her philtrum—that distinct mark only sigbin had— She was one of them.

A pregnant hellspawn.

"You were attacked by an azhuang," Vahitna whispered.

Naria stiffened, the memory of Dimas flashing in her mind. "O-oh..." Her stomach churned.

She had no idea what an azhuang even was. But she did know—the flying demon she encountered back home that also attacked her.

Ugh! Why am I always the target? Naria helped Vahitna to her feet. Something was terribly wrong. "I was with a woman—she's from Perlaz—" Naria started, scanning the dispersing crowd.

Vahitna's face twisted. "That woman attacked you—" Then, she paused. "Wait. You're from Perlaz?" There was something in her tone. Something eager.

Naria hesitated, suddenly wary. "Y-yes...?"

Vahitna studied her for a moment, then sighed. "This place isn't safe for you. Let's get you back to your hotel." She accepted the coat Naria offered, wrapping it around her torn dress and bare belly. Without a word, she quietly followed the berhen leading the way. Vahitna wasn't tempted by berhen blood. But the scent of Naria—pure, sweet, intoxicating—lingered in the air. Still, Vahitna had bigger concerns.

She had just come from the airport. Her frustration still boiled inside her. "I'm sorry, ma'am, but you're wanted in Perlaz for several crimes..." The human ticket agent's voice had been shaky. "Something about... babies."

Vahitna had stood there, her rage barely contained as she listened.

"It says here you're only cleared for travel between Cintru and parts of Xego—not this far out." The agent's fingers twitched, shifting nervously. She was scared.

Vahitna had seen the wariness in her eyes. She didn't argue. She had retreated. And now— She needed to talk to Nzo.

Just moments ago, she had stepped out of the cab, frustrated beyond words— And then— She smelled it. A scent she hadn't encountered in so long—

Oil.

The kind her husband used to vomit when he transformed. Her heart pounded. Impossible. But her senses never lied. And then—she saw her. A shadow in the dark. A monstrous, bat-like creature—Deadly.

Just like James.

She barely had time to react before the azhuang struck. The attack had been brutal. Expected. But she had blocked it—just in time to save the berhen lying unconscious at her feet.

Now, as she guided the girl back, she clenched her fists. Another of her babies was gone. But she had kept the berhen alive.

For now.

<><><>

"Where have you been?" Rhailey's voice was sharp with worry as he rushed toward Naria the moment she stepped into the hotel lobby. He had been circling the area for what felt like hours, debating whether to report her disappearance to Bufe. Just as he was about to search one last time, she walked in.

His heart nearly gave out.

Naria hesitated, guilt creeping over her. "Sorry, I just..." She knew she had worried him. She just didn't know how to explain why she had left without telling him. Before she could finish, another voice chimed in—

"Hi, I'm Vahitna. Your friend here was almost att—"

"She's asking about Perlaz!" Naria cut in quickly, not wanting to alarm Rhailey any further. He already looked like he was about to faint from relief.

Vahitna blinked at the interruption but went along with it. "Ah, yes!" she said, recovering quickly. Then, turning to Rhailey, she asked, "Do you happen to know a channak named Nzo?" Her tone was eager.

Rhailey frowned, studying the heavily pregnant woman standing before him. He knew most of the channaks in Perlaz. But Nzo? The name didn't ring a bell. "No, sorry," he said carefully, still assessing her.

"Oh." The disappointment in Vahitna's voice was impossible to miss. But she wasn't giving up just yet. "H-how about R-rina? Or Veera?" she tried again.

Rhailey's brow furrowed—then realization flickered across his face. "You mean... Reeva?"

Vahitna's eyes lit up. "YES!" she nearly shouted, excitement surging through her.

<><><>

"Kein."
"Bufe."
The two men locked eyes.

That morning, Bufe had been picked up by a sleek black car Kein had sent for him. He had made sure Naria and Rhailey were safe at the hotel before coming here.

Now, he stood face-to-face with the one he despised most.

Kein studied him for a moment before offering a smirk. "Long time..." His words trailed off, uncertain.
Bufe's expression remained unreadable. "It is... very long."

The air in the conference room was thick with cold silence and unspoken history. Kein, impatient, leaned back in his chair, drumming his fingers against the armrest. "A surprise visit."
He was irritated—at first, because the Hukluvan had rescheduled their original evening meeting. But in the end, he was glad they had. Now, he was in the middle of something far more entertaining, only to have his time wasted on an old, blind man. *Why the hell do I have to put up with this old trash anyway?*
Bufe remained unfazed. "It is."

Kein sighed, rubbing his temples. "What can I do for you, then?"
Bufe didn't hesitate. "A private viewing of the sleeping sigbin."
Kein's interest piqued. Bufe wasn't one for small talk either, especially not with the creature he loathed most in this world.
Still, Kein raised an eyebrow. "M-May I ask why?"
Bufe's lips curled slightly, his voice steady. "Because I know how to wake him up."

<><><>

Nzo was desperate. Hendrix, instead of taking him to a bar, had dragged him to a store selling fresh breast milk. He hadn't protested.

Alcohol didn't interest him anymore. He had been sober for decades, thanks to Reeva, who had deprived him of it throughout his stay in Perlaz. He just craved it a while back because he was disappointed.

Now, sucking his thumb anxiously, Nzo declared, "Must see Vahitna. Now! Okie-okie?!"

Hendrix sighed, handing him a napkin. "Okay, just be careful." He had his own mission—getting tickets for Hiro's viewing or at least finding out where and when his friend would be displayed.

As soon as Nzo was a few blocks away from their hotel, he spotted a sigbin on the street and quickly borrowed a phone using his baby charming way. He had no time to waste. He knew what was coming. Knew that Lumen would be with Hiro—and they needed to act fast.

Desperate, he called someone he never thought he would reach out to again. The line clicked.

"Hello?" It was Mr. Hajji.

<><><>

With everything now set in motion, the destinies of five unlikely heroes would soon collide—leading them straight into the most dangerous quest of their lives.

–and the others?

Lumen carefully selected the most beautiful dress she had ever seen, preparing for her reunion with Hiro. After decades in a prison cave, she deserved to feel beautiful again.

Caiphaiz remained in the dark about Kein's true intentions.

Mr. Hajji, though surprised, was pleased to hear from Nzo—he had long wanted to question him about his son.

Hiro lay in peaceful slumber, his beautiful glass casket displayed in the very place where his journey began.

Rhailey, frustrated and angry, protested against Bufe's orders—only to be met with another smack on the head from his great-great-grandfather.

Reeva, stunned by Vahitna's revelations, prepares to return to Xego, her mind racing with uncertainty. "What is going on?!" She nervously typed out a request to Mr. Hajji, seeking approval for an unscheduled re-entry. She needed answers. And she needed them now.

<><><>

Naria fidgeted, shifting the vessel in her arms as it grew heavier and heavier with each passing second. Or maybe— It was just her nerves.

The elevator ascended higher and higher, pressing her deeper into the unknown. The Hajji Tower was a fortress, an endless maze of corridors, elevators, and interconnected buildings. She had lost track of how many they had passed through.

Her throat felt dry. She wished she could reach into her backpack, pull out her goblet, and pour herself a drink from the vessel. But she didn't dare. Not here. Not now.

Ding.

The elevator doors slid open. Naria's breath hitched. Before her lay a vast open arena, its sheer size overwhelming. Towering stadium seats stretched endlessly in every direction—large enough to hold hundreds of thousands of spectators.

Yet tonight, it stood eerily empty. A coliseum without its gladiators.

Naria shivered. It was awe-inspiring —But also deeply unsettling.

33

Azhuangs Unite

At the center of the arena, a figure awaited them.

"Bufe." The voice was smooth, calculated. It belonged to Caiphaiz. Kein's loyal servant.

Bufe's face darkened. "Caiphaiz." His tone was ice. He despised the priest just as much as he despised Kein. No pleasantries were exchanged. Without another word, they were ushered to the heart of the arena— Where the sleeping sigbin lay.

"Kein will be here soon," Caiphaiz informed them.

Bufe barely acknowledged him. His attention was elsewhere. His hands traced the glass casket, searching for a weakness—an opening, a flaw. He longed to cut him open, to touch his blood.

But the sleeping mystery, as Naria had described, remained locked in his slumber—his body preserved in the pristine, unyielding glass.

If only Bufe could smash it. If only the shards could pierce the sigbin's skin, spilling his blood into the open. Bufe's fingers twitched.

Then—

"You brought a guest." Caiphaiz's sharp eyes turned to Naria. *Not a sigbin, he's not into her uniqueness though.*

"Yes," Bufe answered without looking up. "She's the doctor I told Kein about."

Naria swallowed hard. She felt Caiphaiz's gaze scan her—assessing her, measuring her.

Then, another voice entered the fray. "Hi, I'm Mr. Hajji." Naria turned as a man extended his hand—not toward Bufe, but toward her. "Hiro's father."

Bufe didn't react. He couldn't see him anyway.

Tentatively, Naria shook Mr. Hajji's hand.

His grip was firm, but there was a trembling edge to it. "C-can you really cure my son?" Focused on Hiro, Mr Hajji was unfazed by Naria's scent.

Kein had already briefed him—had told him about a human doctor capable of waking Hiro from his eternal sleep.

Naria tightened her grip on the vessel. Her heart pounded. "I-I'll try," she whispered. And as she stood in the shadow of the glass casket, she couldn't shake the feeling— That she had just stepped into something far greater than herself.

◇◇◇

"How exactly did we get invited to this private viewing again?" For what felt like the nth time, Hendrix shot the question at Nzo as they rode the elevator toward the arena.

Nzo fidgeted. "We no-no invite. Me hear, okie-okie?!" he muttered, struggling to lie—though he had done so the first time Hendrix asked.

After calling Mr. Hajji, Nzo hurried back to their hotel and told Hendrix about a private viewing of the sleeping sigbin.

***

Hendrix had been skeptical from the start. "So, how exactly are we supposed to see him if we're not invited?" He had asked when Nzo first told him about it a day before last.

Nzo's response had been simple—"We go arena, okie-okie!?"

"Oh... arena... wait, Hajji Tower's arena? My arena?" The realization hit Hendrix like a brick. The last place he wanted to be.

The arena. Him. Hiro. Again. After decades.

He felt a lump in his throat. He couldn't wrap his head around it. Of all places—why there? Why the arena?

Nzo tugged on his sleeve impatiently. "Yes. You ask arena. Ask friend, okie-okie?!"

—and asking friend, Hendrix did.

Joreel's face lit up when Hendrix showed up at his door. "Whoa! Haruki?!" No hesitation. No suspicion. Just pure excitement in opening his door to a friend.

Joreel had always been a good kid. And Hendrix was counting on that.

Without asking too many questions, Joreel agreed for Hendrix to visit the arena.

***

Now, after stepping out of the elevator, Joreel led them to the back door of their office, offering a quiet entry.

As Hendrix stepped inside with Nzo on his shoulder, Joreel turned to him with excited curiosity.

"Are you running a secret simulation for Nzo's RPG Version 2?"

Hendrix stiffened for a second. *Darn.* Joreel must not know too much. He needed plausible deniability—for his own sake."Y-yeah," Hendrix lied smoothly.

"Finally!" Joreel grinned. "Can I watch?"

Hendrix kept his face neutral while accepting the access code Joreel handed him.

"We'll record it. You can check it out later," he said quickly, shifting gears. "Besides, don't you have that big party at the City Square? You don't want to miss it, right?"

Joreel hesitated—then nodded, grinning. "Right... okay. Enjoy!" He walked Hendrix to the door, waving goodbye.

The second Hendrix had the code, he and Nzo immediately made their way to the connecting bridge to Hajji Tower. They had made it past security unnoticed.

Now, inside the watch tower where Sandy and his team used to direct his fight simulations, Hendrix turned to Nzo. "Alright. What's our plan?"

Nzo let out a long sigh, staring at the floor. He had no idea. Finally, he mumbled, "Wait Lumen... then home."

Simple. Too simple.

They both knew it wouldn't be that easy. Hendrix exhaled heavily, rubbing the back of his neck. Yeah. This was going to be a mess.

<><><>

Naria stood in silence, watching Hiro sleep inside his glass casket. The stillness of his form, the unnatural peace in his expression—everything about it unsettled her. She wished she had brought her medical kit to examine him properly.

Can I really cure you? The doubt gnawed at her. She had confided in Rhailey, but the brigada general had been too busy complaining and pouting about being left behind. Bufe had commanded him to stay in the car, insisting that the meeting was no place for humans.

Naria sighed. Not that he would've been any help anyway. She turned her attention back to Hiro and hesitantly placed her hands on the casket's cover, attempting to open it— But it wouldn't budge.

"Hello, Bufe." The voice was smooth, laced with amusement.

Naria turned sharply—

Kein had entered through the nearest passageway, Vahitna, in his arms.

Naria's breath caught. "Y-you!" she whispered, stunned.

"Small world, right?" Vahitna smiled, though there was something guarded in her expression.

Kein tilted his head, eyes flicking between them. "You two know each other?" His gaze lingered on Naria, his senses immediately picking up on her scent. He was not interested at the moment, though. *He has other plaything and plans in mind.*

"We met at the city district the other night. By accident," Vahitna answered smoothly—though the truth was, she had mostly spoken to Rhailey that night.

"Oh, right! You're the pregnant sigbin Reeva talked about!" Rhailey suddenly perked up, excitedly recalling an old story from his childhood. "You helped her rescue the berhen a long time ago!"

Vahitna chuckled. "Yup! That's me." She was relieved that Reeva had spoken well of her. Without hesitation, Rhailey pulled out his device and contacted Reeva, allowing the two to catch up.

"Reeva, don't let them come here!" Vahitna's voice was urgent, her expression dark. She told Reeva everything she knew—about Kein, Hiro's viewing, and the danger waiting for them all.

There was a long pause.

Then, Reeva's voice came through the line, tight with worry. "It's too late. They're already there."

Vahitna cursed under her breath. With no other choice, she pleaded with Mr. Hajji to convince Kein to allow her entry into the private viewing.

<><><>

Kein flashed Naria a charming smile. "So, doctor, do your magic, please."

Bufe, however, wasted no time with pleasantries. "Open the casket," he commanded.

Without hesitation, Mr. Hajji placed his palm on the glass. The casket disappeared like a hologram, revealing Hiro lying motionless on the long table beneath.

Bufe took a step forward—

But Caiphaiz blocked his path.

The tension was palpable. Ignoring the confrontation, Naria moved closer to Hiro, her heart pounding. She gently tilted his head back, carefully opening his mouth. With steady hands, she slowly poured water from the vessel into his lips, drop by drop.

Then they waited. And waited. Nothing happened.

Naria bit her lip, checking Hiro's pulse— Stable. His body showed no signs of distress. He was simply... sleeping.

Then—

She noticed something. A single tear slipped from the corner of Hiro's closed eye. Naria leaned in, her breath hitching. *Tears? Is he dreaming?*

"Do you want to give him a berhen's kiss?" The voice was soft, sultry.

Everyone turned— And saw Lumen.

She walked toward them with effortless grace, her movements fluid, a goddess draped in crimson. The dress hugged every curve, making her glow like a temptress bathed in blood and moonlight. She was breathtakingly beautiful. And utterly dangerous.

"You!" "YOU!" Both Vahitna and Naria gasped in unison, their shock mirrored in each other's eyes.

But Lumen? She simply smiled sweetly, as if amused by their reactions. Then, without hesitation, she walked straight up to Kein— Slid her arms around his neck— And kissed him.

Long. Slow. Deep.

When she finally pulled away, Kein smirked, eyes dark with intrigue. "Hello, beautiful."

Lumen beamed.

◇◇◇

Back in her dark cave of a prison, Lumen thought she was dreaming. She could hear Hiro's voice—soft, distant, calling to her. How long had she been trapped in this dark, suffocating cave?

She didn't know.

All she knew was hunger. And pain. But not for food—for Hiro. She needed him more than she needed the filthy, rotting animals her prison guards tossed her way. She had begged her grandfather to let her die.

Just let me die. She had provoked him, done things she knew would anger him, hoping he would snap, lose his patience, and finally end her misery.

But her grandfather was just as twisted, just as cruel, and just as patient as she was stubborn. And so, she remained in the dark, her body aching—her mind slipping further into madness.

Until— A voice.

A voice she had never heard before. A voice that sent a shiver down her spine. "W-where are you?"

Lumen's breath caught. She froze. "W-who are you?" she whispered into the shadows. She was alone in the cave. Wasn't she?

"I can smell you," the voice said. It was Dimas.

"Help!" Lumen screamed, thrashing against the cave walls. "I'm in the cave! Please, let me out!" But no one could hear her. No one could.

This place wasn't meant to be found by just anyone.

Dimas followed the scent, the same scent that had drawn him through the dense, dark forest—a scent that felt familiar yet impossible.

A scent like his own.

But all he could see was wilderness, an unwelcoming channak-infested territory he knew he would never be allowed to enter.

And yet—somehow—

He could hear her. He could feel her voice through the lingering stench of her vomit, scattered across the forest floor. Washed away through an underground stream whenever the channaks cleaned Lumen's stinky prison cave. That's when they started to talk— And piece together the puzzle. The names they both knew.

The bleeding sigbin. And Hiro.

"Where is he?" Lumen's voice was desperate, her fingers digging into the dirt, her lips brushing against the filth she had been forced to live in.
"In Cintru. With my maker," Dimas answered, his mind drifting to Sofia—his Sofia. Meeting Lumen like this gave him hope.

Perhaps—

There was a way for them both (Sofia and Lumen) to escape their cages.
"Help me see him," Lumen begged. Again. And again.
But Dimas had his own price. "Tell me about the bleeding sigbin first," he bargained.

And so— She did. She spoke of Hendrix, of Hiro, of the trap that could be set for Kein to capture the bleeding sigbin.
And Dimas gave her something in return— A way out. "Dig a tunnel." Lumen's hands trembled, her fingers curling into the damp earth.

"I will meet you halfway," Dimas instructed. "Lead me using your vomit."

And with that, their escape had begun. But first— Dimas had a message to deliver.

<><><>

Upon connecting with Lumen, Dimas entered Cintru like a man walking into the lion's den. Every instinct screamed at him to run. But he didn't. Instead, he stood tall in front of Kein's underlings.

When they brought him before Kein, he met the god's gaze without flinching. Caiphaiz, standing at his master's side, fought to contain his shock.

Kein's expression was calm, but his eyes burned with silent rage. "How did a human like you survive getting here?" Kein's voice was low, dangerous -- sensing what kind of monster Dimas was.

Dimas didn't waver. "Because I have something you want."
Kein leaned forward, intrigued. "And what would that be?"
"Give me Sofia," Dimas demanded.

Even Caiphaiz flinched at the audacity. The priest had never liked Dimas—he hated him even more now.
"And in return?" Kein's voice dripped with amusement.
"I'll give you the bleeding sigbin."

Silence. Then—

Kein laughed. Not a mocking laugh. Not an angry laugh. But a laugh of pure interest. "Really? And how exactly do you plan to do that?"

Dimas held his gaze. "The sleeping sigbin and the bleeding one." He let the words sink in before continuing— "They are connected."

For the first time, Kein looked intrigued. And for a moment, allowed Dimas to speak to Sofia. It was a mockery of kindness, but Dimas took it anyway.

"My love!?" Sofia's voice was raw, desperate, filled with fear and disbelief. She screamed his name from the abyss where she had been imprisoned.

Dimas clutched the bars, heart pounding. "Don't worry, my love. I'll get you out soon."

Sofia shook her head, her tears falling freely. "He will kill you!" Her voice was filled with fear—not for herself. For him.

Dimas turned, looking at Kein over his shoulder. His expression was unreadable. But his meaning was clear. "He won't," Dimas whispered.

And for the first time— Sofia believed him.

After Dimas left, Kein sat in his office, fingers absently tracing the fruit in his hand.

Caiphaiz stood nearby, waiting. His maker's silence unsettled him.

Finally, Kein exhaled, his lips curling into a smirk. "Destroy the azhuang."

Caiphaiz straightened, prepared to carry out the order—

But then—

The fruit shifted color. Kein stilled. And then— A voice. A hiss in the darkness. "Find the bleeding sigbin at any cost," the serpent whispered.

Kein's eyes narrowed. His grip on the fruit tightened.

"Yes, my lord?" Caiphaiz prompted, awaiting confirmation. A beat of silence.

Then—

Kein smirked. "Don't touch the azhuang."
Caiphaiz hesitated. "But—"
"Let him be. For now."
Caiphaiz clenched his jaw, but in the end, he obeyed. "Yes, my lord." And just like that

— The game had changed.

<><><>

With aching limbs and bloodied hands, Lumen crawled through the final stretch of the tunnel she had painstakingly dug.

And then— Freedom.

She emerged into the night, the cold air hitting her skin like a forgotten lover's touch. For the first time in years, she was out. She waited. Just as she and Dimas had planned. But he never came.

She searched the darkened streets of Perlaz, her pulse racing. *Where was he?* They were supposed to meet here. But the longer she waited, the more restless she became. She couldn't stay exposed like this.

He is late. Something happened. Or worse— He's not coming. A flicker of doubt twisted in her gut, but she swallowed it down. She needed to move. And she needed to do it fast.

Lumen roamed the streets, aimless at first, trying to figure out her next move. She had no allies, no clear escape route. But she knew she had to get away from her grandfather before he realized she was gone.

Then—

A screen flickered to life above her. The city square was ablaze with neon lights, and a massive holographic projection lit up the sky. Her breath hitched. It was him.

Hiro.

Displayed for the entire world to see. Lumen's heartbeat roared in her ears. She barely registered the booming voice of the announcer, the extravagant visuals of the Festival of Avlam being held in the City of Ruinae.

All she saw was Hiro's sleeping form, encased in glass, surrounded by the city's brightest lights. For a moment, she forgot about Dimas. Forgot about their plan. Forgot about everything— Except him.

Her love. Her obsession. She didn't need to wait anymore. She didn't need Dimas. With new determination, Lumen turned away from the dark alleys of Perlaz. Her destination was clear.

The City of Ruinae.

She was coming for Hiro. And nothing—not Dimas' absence, not her grandfather, not even fate itself— Would stop her.

◇◇◇

"My Lord, your visitor is here." Caiphaiz's voice echoed through the lavish penthouse atop Hajji Tower.

Kein sat in his grand chair, gazing out at the neon-lit cityscape. At Caiphaiz's words, his lips curled into a smile. Excitement flickered in his eyes. Since his meeting with Bufe had been canceled, an unexpected—yet long-awaited—visitor arrived. Admittedly, curiosity got the better of him; he had been anticipating this moment for some time. To personally meet the mastermind behind his plan. Slowly, he turned—

And there she was. Lumen. She stepped forward with graceful confidence, her dark eyes gleaming with an unnatural hunger.

Then, she bowed. "My name is Lumen, my Lord."

Kein had never cared for the azhuang. He loathed their stink, their animalistic hunger, their vulgarity. Though he had lost all contact, the only one he had ever encountered was Dimas—and that one had proven useful.

It had been Dimas who had brought Lumen's name to him. "She says it's the only way to lure the bleeding sigbin out of hiding," Dimas had told him, his voice laced with conviction.

Kein smiled then, intrigued. The idea was brilliant. "Tell Lumen I will see her soon." He had been eager to meet her. And now, here she was— Standing before him.

A beautiful azhuang.

Unlike the disgusting creatures of her kind, Lumen had something special. She was elegant, her skin flushed with stolen life. Kein had lost interest in his pregnant toy and was looking for a new entertainment.

A semi-immortal hellspawn with blood. He couldn't help but wonder— *What would she taste like?* Kein strode toward Lumen, his curiosity deepening. "I have been waiting for you," he murmured. Before she could react, he pulled her into a tight embrace.

Lumen stiffened. His grip was firm, his body solid. He smelled of power, lust, and danger. And she— She smelled of oiled flesh, damp earth, and hunger. Ah... so she failed to feed before coming here.

Kein inhaled, his lips ghosting over her temple. "You're soft. Warm. Strange, but not unpleasant."

Lumen suppressed the urge to wince. She had just reattached herself after a botched hunt. She had been so close to devouring a berhen— Only for a pregnant sigbin to interfere. Now, she reeked of the struggle.

The scent of her own oil and vomit clung to her. She needed to wash it off. "May I clean myself first, my Lord?" Lumen asked smoothly, lowering her gaze. "I have just returned from an errand and..." She trailed off gracefully, letting him fill in the blanks.

Kein tilted his head, amused by her restraint. "Of course." He gestured toward the luxurious bathroom, lined with black marble and gold fixtures.

Lumen scrubbed herself clean, ridding her skin of the stench of failure. As she toweled herself dry, she froze. Something shifted in the air.

A scent.

A familiar, intoxicating scent. Her stomach clenched. A low, involuntary growl rumbled from her throat. She was hungry. Desperately hungry. Naked, pulse racing, she stepped out of the bathroom—
And found him. Kein. Waiting. Smirking. Bleeding. The rich, crimson trail ran down his body, pooling just above his navel— Dripping lower.

Her pupils dilated. Her breath hitched. Kein's voice was silk and sin. "Dinner?" He extended his hand mockingly, offering his bleeding flesh. Lumen dropped to her knees before him. Her lips parted, her breath hot against his skin.

Then—

She wrapped her mouth around him, sucking at the source of his wound. The moment his blood hit her tongue, she moaned. The intoxication was instant. Kein laughed, his fingers tangling in her wet hair. He had never tasted so sweet a sin. And neither had she.

34

The Arena

Kein played with his new toy all night. Lumen was like a human—but so much more. Her body was warm, soft, and breakable, yet unlike the others, she could take it. She could bleed and heal. She could scream and survive.

Kein suddenly regretted exterminating her kind all those years ago. Had he known they could be this much fun, he might have kept a few. He had his way with her, over and over, watching as she tore apart and stitched herself back together, every piece of her pliant beneath his hands. Flesh bruised. Bones cracked. Skin torn.

And yet—

Not a single complaint. Only moans, whimpers of pleasure and pain, a delirium that sent him spiraling deeper into madness. He loved breaking her. And she let him.

But then— She transformed.

Kein watched, fascinated, as her body split apart. Her lower half stood firm, as though it had a mind of its own, while her upper half hovered above him, still very much alive.

Kein's breath quickened. Slowly, he knelt before her severed lower half, tracing his fingers along her thigh. Above him, Lumen's detached torso arched— And moaned. Even separated, she could still feel him.

Kein grinned, his eyes gleaming with twisted delight. "Glorious," he whispered, his hands exploring her detached flesh, reveling in the unnatural perfection of her form.

Lumen growled, her voice raw with pleasure. Kein poured a single drop of his blood into her boiling intestines— And watched her legs convulse. The muscles twisted and locked, her body trembling as if gripped by rapture.

Her scream split the air, a cry of pure, agonizing euphoria, as she hovered above him, her torso writhing, desperate, starving.

Then—

She fell. Her legs moved on their own, stepping forward just in time to catch her crashing form.

Kein laughed, utterly enthralled. "What a magnificent creature," he mused, watching as Lumen's body reassembled itself, her form shifting— Becoming beautiful again. A new plaything, ready to be ruined once more.

Kein grabbed her, flipping her onto her stomach, his fingers digging into her flesh as he took her violently, his pace merciless, brutal, relentless. She split apart beneath him, her body almost torn in two, and still—

She moaned for more. "Ohhh," Lumen gasped, delirious, as Kein's hips crashed into her.

He drove deeper, harder, reveling in the way she trembled beneath him, in the way she broke and reformed, in the way she never stopped taking him.

Then—

As she shattered beneath him, her body convulsing in release— Kein slashed her throat open. A gush of hot, sweet blood spilled over him. His lips curled into a wicked grin as he drank her dry, the taste of immortality flooding his senses.

And in that moment— As her body stilled beneath him, her blood coating his tongue— Kein had never felt more alive. That's when he relented, allowing Lumen to take part in the meeting held within the arena.

<><><>

Chaos unfolds in the arena as Lumen clung to Kein's side, a satisfied smirk playing on her lips. "This is perfect. I have my lover with me, and now you've brought me food, my Lord." Her eyes glowed with hunger, flickering between Kein and Naria.

Kein chuckled, enjoying the thrill of the moment. "Well, if your plan works, I've already given you a gift." He gestured toward the sleeping sigbin, once again sealed within the glass coffin. Uncaring whether Hiro woke or not, for he was nothing more than bait in Kein's grand scheme.

The bleeding one would soon come for him. And as an added bonus— A delicious berhen.

"It will work, my Lord," Lumen assured him, stepping away. "But first, may I have her heart?" She turned toward Naria, her grin widening.

Naria stepped back, her instincts screaming at her to run. But as she turned— She collided with Hiro's casket. The vessel in her hands slipped— And shattered against the impenetrable glass.

"No!" Naria gasped, her hands trembling.

Bufe's head snapped up. Even though he couldn't see, he felt something shift in the air. "What's happening?!" his voice boomed.

Vahitna, standing near Kein, immediately moved to protect Naria. And then— A sudden gust of wind. A blur of motion.

From above, Hendrix descended, carrying Nzo in his arms. Nzo's eyes were wide, torn between shock and exhilaration from their flight. For the first time, Hendrix truly took in the scene below— And his breath hitched. Among the chaos, among the familiar and not so familiar sigbin— There she was.

Naria.

Focused on Lumen's arrival and the still form of his sleeping brother, Hendrix—watching from Joreel's booth above—paid no attention to the woman carefully pouring water from the vessel into Hiro's mouth. It wasn't until too late that realization hit him like a thunderclap—
Naria was here.
His pulse roared in his ears

– until.

"Grandpa!" Lumen's voice cut through the air, raw and filled with fury. She locked eyes with Hendrix— And for the first time in years, she saw the man who had once been her savior.
Vahitna darted forward, reaching for Nzo. "Nzo!"
"Mom!" Nzo almost forgot his true mission as he acted like that of a human baby, hungry for his mother's love.

Kein watched it all, utterly enthralled. He lifted the fruit in his hand, whispering softly— "He is here, Father. The bleeding one is here." The fruit glowed, its color shifting, becoming more radiant. Everything was falling into place.

"H-Hendrix!" The sound of his name left Naria's lips, her voice barely above a breath.

Hendrix took a step forward — And the moment their eyes met, his heart nearly stopped. "N-Naria!"

But before he could reach her— Lumen lunged. Her claws extended, her face twisted in a gleeful snarl. She was going to rip Naria's heart from her chest.

Hendrix snapped into action, grabbing Naria and launching into the air, just in time to avoid Lumen's killing blow.

Kein clapped his hands, utterly delighted by the unfolding spectacle.

Vahitna and Nzo, wrapped in a tight embrace, exchanged a meaningful glance. "Now!"

In one swift motion, Nzo fired a water gun directly at Mr. Hajji. The man staggered, then collapsed.

Caiphaiz reacted instantly, ready to strike— But Bufe was faster. The old man landed a solid punch straight into Caiphaiz's ribs, sending him stumbling backward. "I may be blind," Bufe growled, "but I am still capable."

The priest regained his footing, his expression darkening. He had never cared much for fighting— But he had no choice now.

Hendrix landed near Vahitna, his arms still wrapped around Naria. "Please, keep her safe," he pleaded.

Vahitna nodded, gently taking Naria from his arms. Then— The wind shifted.

Hendrix's body tensed. Too late.

"AHHH!" A powerful force struck Vahitna, lifting her off the ground. She was flung across the arena, crashing into the dirt with a sickening thud.

Naria screamed— But before she could react, Lumen's claws wrapped around her throat.

"LUMEN!" Hendrix turned, his voice desperate.

Naria struggled in Lumen's grip, her legs kicking uselessly, her breaths coming in short gasps. Lumen's half-body hovered above them, her grin filled with dark amusement. She had her prize.

And Hendrix—

Hendrix looked destroyed. "Please... Lumen... don't."

Lumen's smirk faltered. For a moment, she saw not the enemy— But the man she had once adored. The man who had saved her when she was nothing but a pitiful human girl.

She looked at Naria again – then at Hendrix. At the pain in his eyes.

"Please, Lumen. Not... not her." Hendrix took a cautious step forward, his hands raised in surrender. "I'll give you whatever you want," he whispered. "Just let her go."

Lumen's eyes darkened. Then—

Her laughter echoed through the arena. It wasn't the sweet laughter of the girl he once knew. It was ugly. Twisted. Corrupted. "You! You actually care for this girl?" She gasped—then laughed harder. "Oh no! Oh no, you love this girl!" Her grip on Naria tightened.

Hendrix took a shaky breath, but he didn't deny it. Lumen's eyes gleamed with wicked realization. She had loved him once—deeply, truly—but her love was never returned. "Then I'll make you suffer." She leaned in, her voice dripping with venom. "The way you made me suffer."

She tightened her grip, watching Hendrix crumble. "Now, I will make you feel the pain you gave me when you put Hiro to sleep, bleeding sigbin!"

Bufe staggered, the azhuang's words hitting him like a blade. His mind reeled. *So...it wasn't the sleeping sigbin?! The bleeding sigbin was... a young man named Hendrix.*

<><><>

Nzo watched, his small hands shaking. He had to make a choice. A choice he should have made long ago.
"ILLUMINATA!" His voice rang out.
Lumen turned just in time to see him pouring something into her severed lower body. Then— She screamed. A burning sensation coursed through her, her body twisting in agony. She thrashed, releasing Naria to save herself.

Hendrix lunged, catching Naria just in time as she collapsed to the ground, gasping for breath. "Naria!" He touched her face, checking for injuries.
"Hendrix..." Naria's voice was weak, but her arms wrapped around him tightly. She clung to him, trembling. For a moment, they forgot everything else. Then— A dark presence loomed over them.

Kein.

Hendrix felt a vice-like grip drag him away from Naria. Kein's breath was warm against his ear. "I'm afraid we haven't been properly introduced yet." And with that—

The real battle began.

<><><>

Vahitna rushed to Naria's side, steadying her as Hendrix was dragged away by Kein.

On the ground, Bufe and Caiphaiz were locked in a brutal struggle, rolling across the dirt in a battle of sheer will and skill.

Above them, Lumen hovered furiously, her body twisting and contorting in rage as she circled Nzo.

The toddler stood his ground, aiming and firing his water gun each time she got too close. Hendrix's blood burned Lumen's flesh, making her snarl and writhe in pain— But it wasn't enough to destroy her. It only slowed her down, infuriating her further.

And Nzo was now her prime target.

Hendrix clawed at Kein's powerful grip, his lungs burning as he fought to breathe. Through the chaos, he spotted Vahitna protecting Naria—

Good. He locked eyes with the self-proclaimed god and twisted his body, using raw strength to break free from Kein's chokehold. A swift knee to the chest sent Kein stumbling back—but only for a second.

Kein grinned, blocking every attack with incredible ease, despite using only one hand. His other hand? Still clutching his precious fruit.

Then—

A flash of unnatural speed. Kein seized Hendrix's throat, his long, razor-sharp nails slicing deep— A gush of blood sprayed through the air. Hendrix's vision blurred. *Go for it,* Hendrix thought darkly. *Let's end this.*

Kein licked the scarlet fluid from his fingers— And the moment Hendrix's blood touched his tongue— A violent shudder ran through his body. A rush of ecstasy, power, and revelation flooded him— "Ahhh..." Kein moaned, his entire body shaking from the high.

Then—

His eyes snapped open. Wide. Bright. Horrified. Kein staggered back, staring at Hendrix as if seeing him for the first time.

Then—

Laughter. Slow at first, then louder. Unhinged. "You... you are the missing soul!" Kein's entire being thrummed with energy, his fruit pulsing in his grip. "The one that will complete the serpent's transition into his true form—" His grin widened, teeth bared in animalistic delight. "—And turn me back into who I once was!"

Hendrix stared, confused. His blood does nothing to Kein.

Kein's eyes glowed as he stepped closer, his voice trembling with glee. "You're the reason we've been trapped in this forsaken existence! The key to everything!" His laughter erupted again, manic and unrestrained.
Before Hendrix could process it, Kein lunged— And sank his fangs into his neck.

Agony ripped through Hendrix's body. Not just pain— Something worse.
It felt like Kein was draining more than just his blood. He was pulling something deeper, something primal. Something Hendrix couldn't fight off. Hendrix thrashed, struggling with every ounce of strength

— But

Kein held him like a vice, consuming him bit by bit. Hendrix's body burned, his thoughts spiraling into darkness. His inked marks—the ones buried under his shirt—lit up in a fiery glow, flickering wildly.

With a final, desperate push, Hendrix wrenched away, feeling his flesh tear apart as blood poured from his throat. Kein staggered back, his lips and chin coated in crimson, his eyes wild with hunger.

Hendrix snapped. His fist flew up, colliding with Kein's throat in a devastating power punch. A shockwave rippled through the air. Both of them reeled back. Hendrix gasped—his own force was crushing his throat too.

Kein howled with laughter.

Hendrix twisted Kein's arm, attempting to snap the bone— But instead, his own bones shattered. A searing pain shot through him, making his vision blur with white-hot agony.

He fell to the ground, helpless—

And Kein was on him in an instant, sinking his teeth back into his neck. Hendrix screamed, smashing his fist into the dirt—

The earth trembled beneath them, erupting into a cyclone of debris that hurled them into the air. The winds roared, forming a hurricane of dust and dirt, swirling around Kein and Hendrix.

Blinded by the storm, Kein finally let go, staggering back with gritted teeth. But even as the earth howled, he dragged Hendrix with him— Twirling together in the chaos. Laughing. Enjoying the dance of destruction.

Hendrix had had enough. His frustration boiled over, his patience gone. He thought of heavy rain, and the skies answered. The clouds split apart, unleashing a torrential downpour. The dirt morphed into thick, sinking mud, drowning them both in the storm's wrath.

Kein remains unshaken, his grip unwavering. With a twisted smile, he lunged again—his claws raking across Hendrix's skin, tearing away the last remnants of his clothing. Naked. Drenched. Bleeding.

Hendrix was losing.

And Kein knew it. His laughter echoed through the storm. Hendrix's mind swam, his body too weak to move.

But then—

A spark. A memory. A surge of power. With everything he had left, Hendrix lifted his arm, his fingers trembling. A streak of fire shot into the sky— And the heavens answered in fury. A blinding bolt of lightning crashed down—

Striking Kein in the back with thunderous force. "AARRGHHH!" Kein's body convulsed, his flesh scorching, smoking. His grip finally broke.

Hendrix gasped for air, his own body spasming from the shared pain of the lightning's wrath. And in the heart of the storm, amid screams of agony and power—

Their battle raged on.

The hurricane of mud and lightning churned violently in the air, with Hendrix and Kein locked in a brutal struggle, their bodies convulsing from the relentless electric shocks. Their backs arched, their muscles spasming, but neither would let go.

Then—

"Hendriiiixxx!" The desperate scream cut through the storm. Hendrix's blurry vision snapped downward— And what he saw shattered him.

Below, on the bloodstained ground, Nzo lay screaming, Lumen's half-body straddling the child, her clawed fingers digging into his tiny frame. Nzo's young and fragile baby body was being torn apart

Vahitna, distracted while shielding Naria, gasped as she saw Lumen drive her talons into Nzo. Without hesitation, she bolted forward. "No!"

A fury Hendrix had never known before surged through him. His eyes locked with Nzo's— And in that brief moment, Nzo's gaze pleaded for what needed to be done. "Do it, Drixxxx okie-okie?!" Nzo's voice wasn't screaming in pain— It was something deeper. It was a desperate, unwavering plea.

Hendrix acted instantly, redirecting the lightning bolt coursing through Kein's back straight toward Lumen. At the same time, he summoned fire to his palm— A searing sphere of white-hot flames— And hurled it straight at her wings.

Lumen screamed as the electric charge surged through her, her wings igniting, turning to blackened embers. She convulsed, twisting violently, her screams shaking the air.

Then—

Hendrix's moment of victory shattered. Kein, unaffected by the storm, grinned viciously and lunged again— This time, his hand drove deep into Hendrix's ribcage. A sharp, unbearable pain tore through him.

Hendrix gasped, but it wasn't just the pain of being impaled— It was what Kein was reaching for. The spot on his ribs that always glowed in Naria's presence

— The light inside him.

Kein's eyes widened in awe as he tore open Hendrix's already tattered shirt, revealing his beautifully inked marks and skin aglow with light. His fingers traced the deep radiating mark, as if an old wound that had never quite faded.

Then he smiled. "There you are," Kein whispered, fascinated. He drove his hand deeper, trying to extract whatever power was buried inside Hendrix. "You're more than just blood, aren't you?" Kein chuckled. "I wonder how it will feel to devour you completely."

Hendrix shook violently, his body losing more than blood— He was losing his life.

Lumen, on the other hand, struggled to fly, her charred wings disintegrating, but before she could reach her severed body— Vahitna appeared behind her. Without hesitation, she grabbed Lumen's burning wings

— And ripped them off.

Lumen's agonized shriek pierced the night. She plummeted to the ground, her body bouncing in a deathlike stillness.

Ignoring Lumen, Vahitna sprinted to Nzo, her heart shattering at the sight of his wounds.

She tore open her blouse, cradled Nzo against her chest, and pressed her milk to his bloodied lips. "Here, baby... drink." Tears streamed down her face as Nzo, crying like a human infant, latched onto her— And began to heal.

"Bufe!" Naria rushed to the blind hukluvan, who had overpowered Caiphaiz in combat. Bufe's fists were bloody, and Caiphaiz's face was a torn mess, blood pooling beneath him. Some of that blood had splashed into Bufe's mouth—

And that's when it happened. A sensation unlike anything he had ever felt before. Bufe froze, his entire body shuddering as his tongue flicked over the warm taste.

Then—

A slow, wicked grin spread across his face. He leaned over Caiphaiz's motionless body— And licked the rest of the blood from his skin. A deep guttural laugh spilled from Bufe's lips. "I... I can see!"

Naria's stomach dropped. "Bufe!" She lunged, grabbing onto him

— But Bufe shoved her aside, his hands grasping for more blood. "No! I want more!"

Naria, without hesitation, slapped him. Twice. Bufe staggered, blinking in shock. "Remember your mission!" Naria shouted, shaking him hard. "Remember your purpose! We have to destroy Kein! Remember Yswh!"

Bufe's crazed expression wavered. For the first time, he seemed to return to himself. He looked down at Caiphaiz, who was stirring awake, already healing. A flicker of shame and rage crossed Bufe's face— Then he punched Caiphaiz again. And again. And again.

Vahitna, still holding Nzo, looked up at the sky. She saw Hendrix struggling against Kein, his body weak, trembling, dying. As she had feared. "Nzo, we have to help him."

Nzo, now fully healed, nodded. "Okie-okie!?"

Vahitna leaned in, **whispering something in the toodler's ear.**

Then—

She twisted her body, using every ounce of her strength, and launched Nzo toward the storm above.

"HENDRIIIIXXX!" Naria's scream broke through the howling storm, cutting through Hendrix's haze of pain. Her desperate cry yanked him back from the edge of unconsciousness.
Hendrix's head lulled forward, disoriented

— And then—
Something fast was flying toward him.

Nzo.

Launched like a cannonball, his small but powerful body spinning midair. Vahitna had aimed perfectly. Nzo collided into them, hitting Kein's hand. The fruit slipped from Kein's grip. Tumbling. Rolling. Until it landed at Naria's feet. She snatched the fruit up just as

— Kein screamed.

His hand burned, his power faltering. And finally

— He let Hendrix go.

Hendrix plummeted, crashing onto the ground, semi-conscious, covered in blood.
"HENDRIX!" Naria ran to him, kneeling at his side, clutching his broken body.

35

Cannonball

"Go! Go! Go! We have to leave!" Vahitna's voice rang out, thick with urgency.

Recalling how fiercely Kein guarded his precious fruit, she didn't hesitate. In one swift motion, she hurled a sharpened thorn—crafted from Lumen's wings—through Nzo and straight into Kein's wounded hand.

The thorn tore through his flesh, forcing him to release the fruit.

Kein let out a furious howl, his hand writhing as it struggled to regenerate. Seizing the moment, Vahitna rallied the others and drove them toward the nearest exit.

"CAIPHAIZ!!!" Kein's furious roar echoed across the arena.
The priest was still struggling to regenerate, his body slowly mending itself from the brutal beating he had taken. Not a fighter by nature, Caiphaiz had been no match for Bufe—the hukluvan had done a number on him.

He staggered, his steps unsteady, but at the sound of Kein's furious command, he forced himself to move, heeding the call despite the pain coursing through his body.

<><><>

In a flash, Caiphaiz and Kein charged toward them, their movements fast and deadly, closing the distance in seconds.

Without hesitation, Vahitna snatched the fruit from Naria's grasp— And with the precision of an athlete, she hurled it in the opposite direction.

As expected—

Kein's pursuit shifted instantly. His eyes widened in panic, his focus no longer on them but on the airborne fruit spiraling away.

"CAIPHAIZ!" Kein bellowed. "DON'T LET FATHER HIT THE GROUND!" The desperation in his voice was palpable.

Vahitna smirked, watching as the two heaven's rejects scrambled in a frantic race to catch it. She had always been good at sports, particularly throwing precision shots— A talent from her human days that was now proving useful in survival.

She didn't wait to see where it landed. Instead, she turned and ran with the others, knowing they had just bought themselves a precious window to escape. *Good luck finding that fruit today, Kein. For now*

— They were free.

<><><>

Something was wrong. Lumen could feel it—her body was failing, her strength fading fast. She struggled to pull herself together, crawling inch by inch across the arena floor, her severed halves barely reattaching.

She had only one place left to go. To him.

Hiro.

He was still lying in his glass casket, untouched, unaware—trapped in a sleep that felt eternal. The arena was silent, the chaos having moved elsewhere. But above them, the first rays of sunlight began creeping in— A countdown to her end.

Lumen summoned every last ounce of strength to drag herself toward him. Her trembling fingers reached the smooth surface of his casket, and with a weak press of her palm, the cover dissolved away, just as Kein had once shown her.

Slowly, painfully, she crawled inside, pressing her frail, broken body against Hiro's still chest. She had only seen him once since Kein allowed her access—

Once.

It hadn't been enough. She had wanted more time with him—awake or not. And now, she would never get it. Lumen cupped Hiro's face, her fingers brushing his cold skin. "Hiro, my love..."

She pressed her lips to his, tasting something sweet— The water Naria had poured into his mouth. A trace of hope. Lumen smiled faintly and kissed him deeper, savoring it. "I love you." Her voice shook. Tears spilled down her face, landing on Hiro's cheeks.

She kissed him again and again, her lips trailing over his face, desperate to memorize every part of him before it was too late. "Wake up," she whispered urgently. "Please wake up. I can't say goodbye to you like this... I'm dying, Hiro. Please—wake up for me!" Her sobs wracked her fragile body, her face buried in his neck, her arms clutching him tightly. She cradled his still form, weeping—

And Hiro heard everything. *Lumen!* Her name echoed in his mind, but his body wouldn't move. Hiro was trapped. The last thing he remembered was Hendrix's face, then darkness.

How long had he been in this void? He had no sense of time. But now— There was something different. A taste—sweet and fresh, something awakening his awareness.

Then—

Her voice. Her touch. Her pain. He could feel her sorrow, hear her cries, and it ripped him apart. *Ahhh, Lumen... You are the love of my life.* He tried -- tried so hard to move, to wrap his arms around her, to pull her close

— But nothing.

Only the burning ache of helplessness. He screamed inside his mind

— Desperate. Powerless. Trapped.

"Goodbye, my love..." Lumen's voice trembled, her words barely above a whisper. Her breath hitched— Then slowed.

Her body stilled.

And Hiro's heart shattered. *No!* Tears streamed down his face, slipping down the sides of his motionless expression. He couldn't move. He couldn't speak. But he could cry.

The sun crept higher, its golden light spilling over the arena. Lumen's skin began to sizzle. A searing pain tore through her body—but she didn't scream. She only clung to Hiro tighter, refusing to move even as the fire consumed her. Because being with him in her final moments was worth everything.

Hiro's soul howled. *No! No! NO!* Something inside him fought, raged, begged— But he couldn't stop it. Couldn't save her. His body remained still, but inside, he was dying with her.

Outside, the sleeping sigbin remained motionless. His face is peaceful. Unaware. But inside that body, Hiro was screaming. *LUMEEEEEN!* And as the sun rose fully, as her body crumbled into ashes against him

— Hiro's heart shattered completely.

<><><>

Reeva managed to smuggle Bufe and the others onto the plane without incident. With no berhen aboard aside from Naria, they all had room to breathe, collapsing into their seats, bodies aching from exhaustion.

"We need to take off before Mr. Hajji flags this flight. I couldn't secure his approval in time," Reeva muttered as they boarded, the plane taxiing down Mr. Hajji's private runway.

"Him no worry-worry, okie-okie?!" Nzo's voice was quiet but certain, his mouth still latched onto Vahitna's nipple, sucking absentmindedly. "He sleep-sleep, okie-okie, stupid?!"

Reeva glanced at him, her eyes narrowing. She was about to smack the kid until Vahitna shot her a warning glare. "Don't."

Reeva hesitated, then let out a frustrated sigh. "He's still mourning," Vahitna murmured, gently stroking Nzo's chubby cheek. Then, for the first time since Xego—Nzo cried. Vahitna cradled him closer, letting him grieve for Lumen in silence.

Reeva sighed again, this time in defeat. She, too, was grieving. Even though she had known, from the very beginning, that Lumen was a lost cause.

Rhailey, sitting nearby, watched Bufe warily. The old hukluvan was still lying down, his eyes glassy and unfocused, his face split in a wild, euphoric grin. "What's wrong with him?" Rhailey asked, frowning.

Bufe chuckled to himself, twisting an oxygen mask between his fingers like it was some precious treasure. "I can see..." he murmured dreamily. "This is nice... Look at it... the sun... I'm holding the sun in my hand..."

Rhailey raised an eyebrow. "Is he high?"

Vahitna barely spared Bufe a glance. "He'll be fine. The effects will wear off soon." She knew exactly what he was feeling—the intoxicating high of immortal blood.

"Where's Naria?" Rhailey asked, scanning the cabin.

"Treating Hendrix," Reeva replied, finally sinking into the seat beside Rhailey. She stole a quick glance at him, her expression neutral, but inside, her thoughts betrayed her. *If only I were human...* It was a thought she had too often whenever she was around him. But to Rhailey, she would always be his annoying little sister— And that thought alone made her want to groan in frustration. *Ugh.*

Rhailey scowled. "What for? You guys can heal yourselves, right?" His irritation was clear, jealous of Naria and Hendrix's closeness, but no one answered.

Vahitna and Reeva exchanged a knowing glance. Even Nzo, usually quick with a snarky remark, simply continued to nurse in silence.

Because they all knew the truth— This wasn't about healing wounds. It was about something much deeper.

◇◇◇

In the first-class cabin near the cockpit, Naria sat beside Hendrix, her hands working tirelessly to stop his bleeding. His neck and throat wounds were slowly healing, but the gaping wound on his rib refused to close, blood leaking endlessly through the soaked cloth.

Hendrix lay still, one arm draped over his eyes, his chest rising and falling in slow, steady breaths—but Naria knew he wasn't asleep. She reached for him again, lifting the bloodied bandage, replacing it with a fresh cloth, her fingers grazing the bruises along his torso.

Hendrix felt every touch. A comfort. A pain. *Stop. Go away. Your scent is... No. Stay. Stay here with me.* Hendrix remained silent, his body fighting itself. He needed strength, needed control—needed to stop himself from losing to the hunger she unknowingly awakened inside him.

You love her... Lumen's words echoed in Naria's mind, lingering, taunting. *Do you love me? Because I... I love you too.* Naria wanted to say it—the words burned inside her— But instead, she let her touch speak for her.

Her hand rose to his cheek, fingertips tracing the roughness of his jaw, lingering for a moment before softly caressing his face. "Tell me what you're feeling... Are you going to be alright?" She didn't expect an answer.

But she needed to hear his voice. Tears welled in her eyes. *Please don't leave me. Please.* Overcome with emotion, she stood up, ready to leave before her sobs could break her completely.

Then—

A strong but gentle grip caught her wrist. And in the next second— She was pulled down beside him, his arms enveloping her.

A rush of joy flooded Naria's heart, her tears soaking into his skin as she buried her face against his chest. His warmth. His scent. His heartbeat—steady, strong, alive. She held onto him, not caring about anything else, only that he was here with her.

Hendrix fought to steady his breathing as the concentration of her scent overwhelmed him. The beast inside him stirred violently. *No. Not now. Not her.* He gritted his teeth, forcing himself to hold back, to tame the hunger, to be the man she needed him to be. His grip on her tightened slightly, just enough to remind himself that she was fragile—that this wasn't a dream.

Naria lifted her head, her teary eyes searching his face. Finally— He removed his arm from his eyes, allowing her to see him fully. No beard. No mustache.

Just him.

And at that moment, words weren't needed. Their hearts knew everything. Her fingers touched his face again, tracing the contours she had longed to see without the barrier of disguise.

Hendrix lifted a hand, wiping away her tears with his thumb. Then— He was on top of her, holding himself up, looking deep into her eyes. *This is impossible. We can't be like this.* Hendrix knew this— But why did it feel so natural? So easy?

Naria's heart pounded uncontrollably, her mind spinning. *I loved Gabby... But this... this is different.* Her lips parted, ready to speak—

And that's when Hendrix kissed her. Soft. But deep. Passionate. Like he had been waiting for this moment forever. Naria's blood burned, heat spreading through her, her body trembling as the warmth of Hendrix's lips devoured her.

She could feel it— The way her ears burned, the way her skin tingled, the way her heart raced out of control. She had never kissed anyone before. But Hendrix's tongue guided hers, and she followed, melting into him.

Then—

He moaned softly against her lips. And it was the most beautiful sound she had ever heard. *Do I make you happy? I want to make you happy.*

She pressed closer, their tongues intertwining, their breaths mingling. For the first time, Hendrix didn't resist. She had opened her lips, and he had fallen into her completely.

Oh, softness... These lips— The ones he had dreamed of touching, craving, tasting— How could he ever resist them now? He had no excuse anymore. He had hoped—pathetically—that they would one day share a drink from the same cup, that he could place his lips where hers had been—

But this? This was so much more. And if it meant dying, then let him die like this— Drowning in her taste.

Then—

A sharp, searing pain tore through his rib. "Ahh!" Hendrix jerked back, the wound on his rib ripping wide open again.

Naria immediately sat up, eyes wide with concern, her hands frantically checking his side.

And then—
The light returned.
A blinding glow burst forth from his wound
— And

--in the next breath, the deep, gaping tear Kein had left behind vanished. No scar. No trace of injury. Just smooth, unblemished skin. Hendrix stared in disbelief. He had healed. But not on his own. Because of her.

"Oh...thank God!" Naria's voice broke as she threw herself into Hendrix's arms, sobbing into his chest.

Hendrix held her tightly, his own eyes stinging with emotion. Her love had saved him. And now, he never wanted to let her go.

<><><>

It took time and effort before the channaks and hukluvans managed to gather all the human leaders of Perlaz. But when they did— The course of history shifted. The meeting ended, and with it, the continent braced itself for war. They all understood—this wasn't just another battle.

This was a fight for survival.

The entire boundary surrounding Perlaz was placed under red alert. Miles before the border, intricate obstacle courses, snares, and deadly traps were set—stretching into the deserted territories of Xego, Zapad, and even Cintru.

The enemy could come from anywhere— And Perlaz would be ready. All human military reserves were activated. Soldiers were armed not only with traditional weapons but also with water guns infused with Hendrix's blood—a powerful new tool that could incapacitate both human and sigbin foes alike.

Every vulnerable citizen—most importantly, the berhen—were evacuated to the center of Perlaz, with the majority placed under heavy protection in Vincot. This was their final line of defense.

Bufe, standing before a continent-wide broadcast, addressed his people, his voice strong and unwavering. "My ancestors have already given you the playbook. We have prepared for this not just for years, but for centuries—thousands of years, even. The channaks and hukluvans have always known the truth— Kein was never our savior. And he never will be."

The weight of his words hung heavy in the air.

"He placed us here for his harvest. And now— The harvest season has come. But we will not stand by and let him take us. With Adonai on our side, we are not without hope!"

Rhailey, standing beside his grandfather, addressed the human forces of Perlaz. "Our enemies have technology far beyond ours. But our forefathers saw this coming. That is why— We remain dark. Zapad and Xego may have state-of-the-art, 40th-century technology, but we still communicate in the way of the 21st century. They cannot hack what they do not understand. They underestimate us, thinking us primitive— But this is our greatest weapon. We will use their blindness against them."

The soldiers listened intently, their determination hardening into steel. They were being briefed on Hendrix's powerful blood— A secret weapon that would turn the tide of battle against the sigbin army. And with every passing second—

Perlaz was readying itself for war.

<><><>

At the inner part of Perlaz, "Be careful." Grace's voice trembled, her eyes shimmering with unshed tears as she waved at her husband and father—both staying behind in Zalem to fight for their people.

Beside her, Sariah held baby Yzra tightly, pressing a long, lingering hug to Eze's chest. The weight of goodbye settled over them like a heavy fog.

Eze gently cupped Sariah's face, his expression torn between love and duty. "How about Naria?" he asked, his voice low but firm.
Sariah took a steady breath. "She will follow soon."
Eze nodded, though the worry never left his eyes. "She better be." He knew his wife's strength, knew she was capable—but this war was different. This war was for their very survival.

And while his heart ached to stay, he was ready to give his life for this cause. Because every able man had been called to fight— And they would stand as one.

<><><>

At the border, Bufe stood motionless, his mind drifting. A new vision had begun to take shape— And the future it revealed was one he dared not ignore.
Rhailey stepped cautiously into the dark cave, his heart pounding harder than he cared to admit. Even after everything they had been through, something about being alone with Bufe still unnerved him.
This unease had started as soon as they landed in Perlaz—the same strange heaviness in his chest that had driven him to crash through the arena gates at Hajji Tower, desperate to save Bufe and the others who ran toward him for their lives.
Some called it instinct. But this? This was something more. Something stronger. Something that terrified Rhailey

—especially now.

Bufe was no longer high when they arrived at the border, the effects of Caiphaiz's blood finally wearing off. His sight was gone again. The hukluvan was once more trapped in darkness.

Rhailey guided him to his bed, his grip steady but hesitant. "Careful, Grandpa," he murmured.

Bufe groaned as he settled onto the mattress, his voice harsh and worn-out. "Why is my whole body aching?"

Rhailey smirked. "Because you fought like a martial arts ninja in Xego, Grandpa." He bit his tongue to keep from adding— *And you acted like a darn fool on the plane, too.*

But just as Bufe began to relax—

It happened. A sudden grip—tight, unrelenting. Before Rhailey could react, Bufe's hands locked around his arms.

Then—

A forceful push. A blur of movement, weight, strength. Rhailey slammed onto the ground, the hukluvan on top of him, his sightless eyes clouded in a deep trance.

"Grandpa, stop!" Rhailey struggled, his muscles tensing against the unnatural strength of Bufe's grip. He tried to fight back, but the moment Bufe's palm pressed against his forehead—

His world vanished. Everything went white. How long they remained trapped inside the vision, Rhailey didn't know. Hours? Days? It didn't matter.

When they finally came back to reality, both of them were gasping for breath, hearts racing with terror. They had seen everything.

Kein's plans.

His legions of hellspawns from Zapad—vicious, bloodthirsty creatures who had hated humans for centuries. Goran -- Ehud's son -- the human smugglers, and his men were among them. They had all sworn their loyalty to Kein, worshipping him as their god.

And Kein?

He had one demand."I need the bleeding sigbin."

Rhailey watched the vision of Kein, standing before his army, his fingers tightening around the fruit he had nearly lost in his first encounter with Angelo Markado. His eyes burned with hunger, obsession, madness.

"I don't care if you slaughter every human and paralyze every channak and hukluvan in the process—just bring me the bleeding one! The missing soul!" Kein raised the fruit to his nose, inhaling deeply, his lips curving into a cruel smile.

Then—

A shadow moved. The serpent slithered out of the fruit, coiling itself around Kein's body like an old, familiar lover.

Rhailey's blood ran cold.

Kein's voice was soft at first, almost reverent— "It won't happen again, Father." The serpent hissed, pressing against Kein's skin—its dark, ancient energy merging with his being.

Kein's smile widened.

"This time, he will be ours—the missing soul that will complete your transition... the key to restoring you to your walking form... the way you were before you were cursed in the garden..." The air shook with power. "We will use him as a bargain with Adonai. He will give us what we want."

Then—

The serpent entered Kein's body. Merged with him. Became one with him. And the pain was unlike anything the world had ever seen.

Kein screamed.

A sound that shattered the air, ripped through existence itself— And every sigbin in Perlaz felt it. They transformed violently, their bodies writhing in agony as Kein's new power restructured them from within.

It was excruciating. It was unstoppable. And Rhailey, still trapped in the vision, could only watch in horror.

Because the war had already begun.

<><><>

Rhailey's warning came just in time. Because he had seen the vision ahead, the hukluvans and channaks were prepared for the agony that followed. The pain of their forced transformation, the way their bodies contorted and writhed under Kein's power—it was still unbearable, but at least they were not caught off guard.

And when the prophesied suffering arrived, there was no denying it anymore. Bufe and Rhailey had proven their vision true.

"Grandpa... do you know when the attack will happen?" Rhailey's voice was tight with urgency, but Bufe remained silent, his expression troubled. For days, the hukluvan had been desperately seeking another vision, but the answers remained elusive.

The date didn't matter. What mattered was— *How do we defeat Kein?* And as soon as the visions had passed through Rhailey's eyes, they gathered, each bringing their pieces of the puzzle to the table.

Bufe's vision about Naria. Hendrix's connection to the sleeping sigbin. Reeva's link to the kidnapping of the berhen and Mr. Hajji's involvement. Nzo and his granddaughter, who became azhuang. And Vahitna's knowledge of Kein's obsession with the bleeding one, and his mysterious fruit.

They knew the answer was here—hidden among these clues. But one thing still didn't make sense.

Bufe's brow furrowed deeply. Hendrix was the key. That much was clear. But what about Naria? Without the vessel, now shattered and discarded in some Xego garbage heap, how could she possibly fit into this prophecy?

Then—

A voice cut through the silence.

36

The Canaan Wedding

"They love each other." Everyone turned to Vahitna and Nzo, who had been watching what everyone else had refused to acknowledge. The truth was right in front of them.

The way Hendrix looked at Naria. The way Naria gravitated toward him, unable to stay away. No one spoke about it, but everyone saw it.

Because the impossibility of their love was a painful truth too heavy to bear. Saying it out loud wouldn't change anything. It would only hurt more.

"Grandpa?" Rhailey placed a cautious hand on Bufe's shoulder— And that's when it happened again. A sudden, violent pull— Then darkness.

Another vision.

And when Rhailey finally emerged from the trance, his face was pale, his entire body trembling. Then, to everyone's shock— He broke down. "No..." His voice was barely a whisper. Then louder. "NO! NO! Grandpa, NO!" Rhailey was sobbing uncontrollably, shaking his head in desperate denial.

Bufe placed a hand on his great-great grandson's shoulder. The old sigbin's expression grave, his heart heavy with sorrow. "It's the only way."

A moment of silence passed, the weight of those words settling over them like a storm cloud.

Then—

"Call everyone." Bufe's voice was steady, but his eyes were filled with an unspoken pain. "Everyone... except Hendrix." Because some truths

— Were too cruel to tell.

◇◇◇

The room fell into a heavy silence as Bufe finished narrating Rhailey's vision.

Then—

All eyes turned to Naria. Rhailey couldn't speak. He couldn't accept it. Ever since Bufe brought Naria into their lives, Rhailey had loved her—quietly, painfully. And though it tore him apart knowing her heart belonged to Hendrix, he had learned to live with it.

But this? This was too much. She wasn't just giving Hendrix her heart— She was giving it to him literally. Rhailey felt his chest tighten, his hands clenched into fists.

Beside him, Reeva gently held his hand. She said nothing—she didn't have to. Reeva had always supported Naria and Hendrix, despite knowing how impossible their love was. Because she wished it for herself, too. If only she wasn't frozen in this state. If only she could grow into the woman she was meant to be

— Maybe then, Rhailey would see her, too.

"That's the only way Hendrix can defeat Kein." Bufe's words sealed Naria's fate.

Reeva, still gripping Rhailey's hand, nodded grimly. "It makes sense," she murmured. "All of us carry Kein's demonic blood in some way. A house divided cannot stand. Hendrix must purge his monster side... Only then can he destroy the most evil of all."

"N-Naria..." Vahitna's voice shook.

Even Nzo, usually so indifferent, slid off Vahitna's lap and wrapped his tiny arms around Naria. She reminded him of Lumen in so many ways— But she wasn't Lumen.

And maybe that was why...

Hendrix loved her more. The truth was there for everyone to see. He may have had a soft spot for Lumen— But Naria? She was the one who truly held Angelo Markado's heart.

"There has to be another way!" Rhailey's rage boiled over. His fist slammed against the table, shaking everything in the room.

They had a plan. They had set everything in motion in Perlaz. They didn't need to do this!

"I'll do it." Naria's voice was calm, yet unshaken. She smiled nervously, but there was no doubt in her eyes.

"Naria!" Rhailey's voice broke, his disbelief shattering into grief.

But she didn't waver. "I have my family in Perlaz." She took a deep breath, as if preparing herself for the final step forward. "If there's a way for me to stop this war—if my death can save my home—then I will do it."

Rhailey shook his head, his heart pounding in his chest.

But Naria's gaze turned to Bufe, her expression earnest, unwavering. "Bufe, you always say this isn't our true home. That we will be with Yswh one day— That we will be with our families again in paradise." Her voice wasn't filled with fear—

It was filled with faith.

"You saw me in a vision before I was even born." She let out a nervous laugh, though her sincerity never wavered. "Maybe... maybe this is why I'm here." She turned to the others, her smile soft, yet resolute. "Maybe this is my purpose."

The room was silent. No one could speak. No one could deny that she was right.

Even Rhailey. Though every part of him wanted to scream, to shake her, to stop her— Deep down, he knew. She was choosing to fulfill her destiny.

And there was nothing he could do to stop it.

"Tonight." Naria took a deep breath –her decision firm and irrevocable. "So... I'll do it. I'll do it tonight." The words hung in the air like a death sentence.

And then—

"No!" Rhailey's cry of protest tore through the cave. And suddenly— Everyone was shouting. The cave erupted into chaos, voices clashing in heated debate.

Then—

A single voice cut through the noise. "Guys... Hendrix is coming." The room fell silent. Everyone froze. Standing at the entrance— Rebel's expression was grim.

And outside the cave— Hendrix was on his way.

"O-oh... why are you all here?" Hendrix stopped in his tracks, his eyes narrowing with suspicion. He had only come looking for Reeva to discuss the obstacle courses he was designing with the channaks—
But now, he found himself standing in the middle of something else entirely. A room full of tense, guilty faces. Something was wrong.

Then, from across the cave—

"Naria no want go Vincot. She want stay en fight. Okie-okie?!" Nzo's small, innocent voice cut through the silence.
"Kid!" Naria's sharp cry followed, a mix of anger and desperation. She knew exactly what Nzo was doing. And she was playing along.
"Naria!" Hendrix's growl was low and dangerous. His jaw clenched, his fists tightened.

They had already discussed this. She had agreed. She had promised. And now— She was going back on her word?
"N-naria gathered us here without you so we can convince you to let her stay." Vahitna's voice was calm—too calm. But the words hit Hendrix like a punch to the gut.
He whipped his head toward Naria, his eyes burning with betrayal. "You know I would never!" His voice was sharp, filled with a quiet fury. "We talked about this, Naria. If I have to drag you to Vincot myself—" He took a step toward her, his resolve unshakable. "I will."

Then—

"Do it." Bufe's voice rang through the cave like a command from the heavens.

All eyes snapped to him.

"Bufe! No!" Naria shot up from her seat, panic flashing across her face.

But it was too late. Hendrix was already moving.

"No! No!" Naria's screams echoed through the cave as Hendrix caught her mid-run. She thrashed in his grip, but Hendrix didn't falter. In one smooth motion, he threw her over his shoulder— And flew out of the cave.

Inside the cave, the silence that followed was unbearable.

Then—

Bufe's shoulders trembled. And to everyone's shock — He cried. And as if on cue

— So did everyone else.

****<><><>***

"Put me down! Put me down!" Naria's screams filled the air, her fists pounding against Hendrix's back as he carried her through the sky.

But then—

A sudden shift. Hendrix moved her from his shoulder, cradling her in his arms instead.

Naria froze. Her protests died on her lips.

Because now—

She was looking directly into his eyes. The eyes she had learned to love. The eyes that saw through her soul. *Please, Yswh... don't let him see the truth in mine.*

"You know I will not risk putting you in danger." Hendrix's voice was firm, filled with undeniable resolve. "I won't be able to fight if I know you're anywhere near harm."

Naria's chest tightened. She knew. She knew he would protect her at any cost.

But—

"I don't want to leave you." Her voice broke, the weight of her words hitting them both like a storm.

Hendrix's anger softened. Because when she said those words— He felt it. The love in her voice, the fear of losing him, the ache of separation that neither of them could control.

"I will come for you, Naria." His voice was gentle, steady, unshakable. "I promise."

Naria's fingers gripped his shirt tightly, her eyes searching his face. "Promise me..." She took a deep breath. "That no matter where I am... you will come find me." *Even if I have to wait a lifetime.*

Hendrix nodded, his gaze locked with hers.

Then—

He brushed his lips against hers. A kiss so soft, so fleeting— Because he knew— If he let himself go, he would want more.

And Naria...

She was already risking too much just by being in his arms.

Then—

A heavy downpour crashed from the sky, soaking them within seconds. As if on cue, heaven was crying too.
"Did you do this?" Naria sighed in frustration, her lips parted—ready to kiss him back.
But now? She knew now that Hendrix had a deep connection with water (among other elements)—not just the gentle flow of rivers, but the uncontrollable force of the storm itself. He didn't just move with the rain—he commanded it. Even the thunder seemed to answer him, roaring in response to his unspoken will.

The moment was stolen by the rain. Hendrix chuckled, his arms tightening around her. "No." His invisible wings shifted, carrying them toward a secluded place to wait out the storm.
"The treehouse!" Naria's eyes widened with excitement as they landed inside the cozy shelter. The very place they met each other for the first time. "Oh! I dreamt about this place!" She spun around, taking in every detail—the sturdy wooden beams, the scent of fresh rain against old timber, and the soft rustling of leaves outside.

Hendrix watched her with quiet amusement, his heart warming at her joy. Still drenched, Hendrix grabbed a thick blanket and wrapped it around Naria's shoulders. She shivered slightly, hugging the warmth against her skin.

Then, without hesitation— She turned around and removed her wet clothes.

Hendrix froze. He didn't look, but the sound of fabric rustling, the slight intake of her breath, and the sudden presence of her scent in the enclosed space—

It rattled him. When he dared glance up again—

She was wearing one of his old, torn t-shirts, its hem falling loosely above her knees. She wrapped the blanket around herself, her damp hair cascading down her back as she settled near the small fireplace.

Hendrix swallowed hard. He stepped outside just long enough to rip off his own soaked shirt, letting the cold air cool the fire burning inside him. By the time he returned, Naria was drying her hair with a small towel, her fingers gently twisting the strands, then releasing them again.

It was such a simple movement, but something about it— The way her delicate fingers combed through the damp strands— Sent an uncontrollable shiver down his spine.

He needed a distraction. "Are you hungry?" Without waiting for her reply, Hendrix reached outside the small window, plucked a ripe fruit from the tree, and handed it to her.

Naria's eyes sparkled in delight. "Wow!" She took a big bite, realizing for the first time how hungry she actually was.

Hendrix sat beside her, his shoulder brushing against hers as they both gazed at the fire. He grabbed a few wet branches, but with a simple rub of his hands, the wood ignited, crackling softly in the hearth.

Naria watched in fascination. She had seen him do so many things—things no ordinary sigbin should be able to do. "Do you ever wonder how you can do all that –make fire, fly high, move the ground around, command the heavens to make it rain, and God knows what else?" Her voice was soft, filled with genuine curiosity.

Hendrix only shrugged, his gaze fixed on the flames. "As long as I can use it to save you," he said, voice deep with sincerity, "it doesn't really matter."

Then, without hesitation—

He turned to her and kissed her forehead.

Naria stilled, feeling the warmth of his lips linger against her skin. A soft blush crept up her cheeks. "Hmmm." Without thinking, she leaned against him, resting her head on his shoulder.

Hendrix let out a slow breath, tilting his head slightly to rest against hers. Outside, the storm raged on. But inside the treehouse—

There was only warmth.

Hendrix tightened his arm around Naria, ensuring the blanket kept her warm. The rain pounded relentlessly against the treehouse, showing no signs of stopping. Hendrix knew he could make it stop—at least enough to fly her safely to Vincot and be back before anyone noticed.

But...

A few hours here wouldn't hurt. He didn't know when Kein and his army would strike, but one thing was certain— He would miss this. Miss being alone with Naria. Miss the quiet moments before war swallowed them whole.

Naria sat in deep thought, her fingers lightly tracing the fabric of the blanket. The treehouse—this was the perfect place for her plan. But now, she felt her stomach twist with nerves.

She had learned the traditions in Vincot—how every berhen had to attend a class on seducing their future husbands. She had barely paid attention back then, dismissing it as something she wouldn't need for a long time. Even with Gabby – her dearly departed husband — such intimacy never crossed their mind.

Now?

She regretted it. Her eyes drifted to Hendrix, who sat beside her, lost in his own thought.

Then—

He turned. And their eyes met. Her brain short-circuited. "What?" Hendrix's voice was low, curious, his golden eyes burning with intensity.

Naria wanted to say it. *I want to kiss you, but I don't know how to start.* Instead, she said— "I have an idea." She quickly stood up, rummaging through her wet backpack. Hendrix watched her, intrigued. "I'm thirsty." Naria pulled out her goblet, holding it up to the open window.

The rainwater filled the cup, glistening in the firelight. She took a sip, then turned to Hendrix, offering it to him.

"You're sharing your goblet with me?" Hendrix hesitated, recalling how particular she was with germs.

A soft laugh escaped Naria as she blushed, recalling the kiss they had already shared. Compared to that, drinking from the same goblet seemed nothing at all. *In fact, I want to share even more with you,* she almost whispered—but chose instead to say it with a smile.

Hendrix took the goblet, lifting it to his lips. He drank.

Then—

He froze. A strange look flickered across his face.

"What? What's wrong?" Naria asked, suddenly worried.

Hendrix licked his lips, staring at the goblet in confusion. "This is... this is rainwater?" He drank again, his brows furrowing.

"It is. I just tasted it," Naria said, reaching for the goblet. She took another sip— Then, her eyes widened.

The water... It tasted exactly like the water from the vessel. No— It tasted even more powerful. Naria's tongue flicked out, licking her lips just as Hendrix had.

"No way." Naria rushed to the window, quickly forming two makeshift cups from large leaves. She filled them with rainwater and handed one to Hendrix.

"Here, try this."

Hendrix took a sip. Then— He shrugged. "It's just water."

Naria frowned, filling the goblet again and drinking from it. As soon as the liquid touched her lips, her eyes went wide.

Hendrix noticed her expression and immediately snatched the goblet from her hands.

He drank—

And then, their eyes met. Shocked. Disbelieving. "It's wine..." "Alcohol..."

The rain outside poured harder, as if sealing the strange magic between them.

They inspected the goblet, turning it over in their hands, examining every worn-out detail. It was ordinary. Old. A cup so common that anyone could buy it from a regular market. Even Grace had one—she had even bought one for Hendrix once. Which he lost in three days.

She remembered scolding him endlessly about it, laughing now at the memory. Yet here they were— Drinking from it over and over again, trying to understand why this simple cup had the power to turn water into wine.

<><><>

Naria had no idea about the true history of the broken vessel she left behind at Xego. It was ancient. A relic from a time long before the sigbin demons walked the earth. It was the exact same vessel used at a wedding in Canaan, a town long lost to history.

The story went—

The celebration was not yet over, but the wine had run dry. And so, Yswh, in his first miracle, had turned water into wine inside that very vessel.

The newlyweds shared a single cup, into which the vessel's contents were being poured. And with that single act, their bond was sealed forever. A marriage beyond the physical— A spiritual, unbreakable connection.

The same had happened before, with Marie and Aaron— Drinking from a single cup being filled with water from the ancient vessel had made their love deepen, their connection stronger than before.

Now— Without realizing it—

Naria and Hendrix had done the same. With each shared sip from the cup once filled by the vessel's water, a quiet bond began to form between them. A marriage of souls beyond the boundaries of any ritual. With their lips having shared the goblet, their fate was sealed—they were now bound as husband and wife.

Soon thereafter, they were laughing, drunk, and lost in their own world— On what was, without them knowing, their wedding night. Along with the sweetness of wine shared with her husband, Naria received a blessing from above to put her plan in motion.

"Nzo did that to you? But he's so cute!" Naria was laughing so hard, shaking as she passed the goblet back to Hendrix, who filled it with rainwater again.
"He is evil." Hendrix took a long gulp. "Cute, but still... evil." His jaw ached from laughing as he told her about the first time he met Nzo. They talked for hours— About parents they lost. About childhood friendships— Naria with Gabby, Hendrix with Hiro.

As the night deepened—

The rain finally stopped. And their wine was gone. They lay on the wooden floor of the treehouse, side by side, drunk and breathless from laughter.

Then—Silence.

Naria turned onto her side, her heart pounding. It's time. For Hendrix to be separated from Kein's evil DNA, she knew what had to happen. Nzo had told her— In Xego, sigbin consumed the hearts of athenas during the act of intimacy.

But the athenas in Xego... They came back to life.
In her case, though— being a berhen human and all...
She knew. She would not.

Naria let out a soft sigh, accepting her fate. Then— She moved closer to Hendrix, her body trembling.

He was too drunk to resist.

Her fingers brushed against his chest, feeling the steady rise and fall of his breath. She looked at his lips—still tinted with wine.

And whispered

— "Hendrix..."

◇◇◇

Following that night, the first obstacle course surrounding Perlaz had been breached. Monstrous evil sigbin from Zapad and Xego landed in waves—choppers, planes, and military carriers flooding the borders. They marched in droves, eyes burning with hatred and hunger, their single goal clear—wipe out all resistance and make a few meals out of them.

Maharlika, Blake, and even Rebel laughed in glee, watching the city sigbin struggle in the traps they had meticulously set. Some of the invaders fell instantly, tangled in snare lines, impaled by sharpened stakes, or crushed under collapsing ground was filled with water diluted by Hendrix's blood. Others retreated, unwilling to continue through the maze of death that Hendrix had designed for them. For the channaks, it felt like a game. Hendrix had taught them well, treating the battlefield like a simulation in an RPG—each level increasing in difficulty. But unlike a game, the consequences here were real—a single mistake could mean mass slaughter.

The second alarm blared through the continent, shaking the ground beneath them.

The night deepened, darkness swallowing the land, but still, the hukluvans and channaks held their ground. Despite their confidence, Bufe and Reeva knew the truth—

They were battling creatures that never slept—unless Hendrix's blood touched them. Pain meant nothing to them. They didn't tire. And they couldn't die. Not ever.

This war was only beginning—and the real battle had yet to come.

"We have to trust Naria," Bufe whispered, eyes closed in prayer. "Yswh will guide us. He must."

37

The Blessed Vessel

Then—

A hurricane-like wind tore through the battlefield. A deafening sound, like a war drum echoing from the sky, rattled their bones.

Vahitna gasped. Her grip tightened around Nzo, pulling him close as her heart pounded in terror. Then she saw them. Thousands. Tens of thousands of Azhuang—their black wings stretching across the sky, blotting out the moon.

"Oh no..." "We're doomed..." "Sound the alarm for the humans—NOW!" Rhailey roared, as the brigada scrambled into formation at the heart of Perlaz.

Then—

An skyraptor helicopter descended, its engines roaring as it landed on the very spot where Kein had made his first deal with the channaks and hukluvans a thousand years ago.

Bufe and Reeva remembered that day. They remembered their deal with the devil—a deal made to save humanity and form Perlaz.

Now, Kein had returned to finish what he had started. Above him, his army of Azhuang hovered, waiting for his command.

And Kein— He laughed. A booming, thunderous laugh that sent a chill down everyone's spine.

Caiphaiz stood at his side, looking up at the sky, his expression twisted. The creatures above them—those dark, hungry monsters— They were his creation.

He had given his blood to turn humans into this. And Kein had known all along. How did he know? Caiphaiz wondered, but he dared not question his god. Kein knew everything.

"They will zero in on the berhen." Rhailey swallowed hard, knowing what that meant. The berhen—the purest hearts among them— They were walking beacons for the Azhuang.

"Bufe!" Kein waved mockingly from across the battlefield.

"Kein!" Bufe growled, his fists clenched in pure hatred.

"Happy to see me?" Kein smirked.

"Happy to see you die."

Kein chuckled. "Ah, old man. I'm afraid that's not going to happen." His grin widened as he stepped closer. "You see, I am cursed to live forever. And those who try to change that…" He sighed dramatically, eyes gleaming with malice. "…always end up dead."

Bufe smirked, unfazed. "Then let's see if I'll be the first to succeed."

Kein's thunderous laughter shook the ground, sending an eerie chill through the warriors of Perlaz.

Then—

A massive gust of wind tore through the battlefield again. A burning light shot down from the sky— Like a meteor crashing down between Kein and Bufe.

The ground trembled as dust and smoke rose into the air. Nzo's eyes widened in awe.

Then—

He laughed.
A genuine, giddy baby giggle, filled with joy and excitement.
Vahitna gasped. "What is it?!" She wasn't the only one.
All channak children—those seven and younger— Were reacting the same way. Their laughter filled the battlefield.
And when the smoke cleared

— There he stood.

Hendrix - Haruki - Angelo Markado stood tall, blood-soaked and bare-chested, his pants torn from battle. And on his skin— The inked marks of his power burned in the dark.

Fire and water glowed on both his shoulders.
The earth's strength wrapped around his legs.
A spear-like mark shimmered over his rib.
A massive, wing-shaped mark ignited across his back.
They were not just inked markings. They pulsed with light.

Reeva and the others gasped in awe.
Bufe felt it. Even without sight, he knew— Something had changed.
"Naria did it," Rhailey whispered, tears burning his eyes.

The channaks saw something more. Hendrix was not alone. He wasn't even flying on his own. Above him, a brilliant figure of light hovered— Holding onto the glowing wings etched onto Hendrix's back.

It was Azrael.

And the angel spoke inside Hendrix's mind. *"Remember what I told you. My breath is now inked inside you. You bear the marks of an angel. You are ANGELO MARKADO. I can only act upon your will. Solidify your purpose— And I will follow your command."*

Hendrix's eyes burned with resolve. He clenched his fists, his heart pounding with purpose.

"What is your will, Angelo Markado?" Azrael asked.

Hendrix took a deep breath. His entire soul ached—

For Naria.

For the promise he had made to her. For everything they had fought for. "To fulfill my promise to Naria." His voice was shaken with emotion

— But unbreakable in determination. "I will end this war. Now."

◇◇◇

Naria initiated the kiss—not because it was part of her plan, but because she wanted him. She had never wanted him more than she did now. Maybe it was the wine. Maybe it was something deeper, something she couldn't explain.

But every fiber of her being ached to be one with Hendrix, even if it meant losing herself completely. Even if it meant dying in his arms.

"N-Naria," Hendrix moaned against her lips, torn between his desire and the monster clawing inside him. He should stop. He should resist. But he couldn't. Not anymore.

"Don't think," she whispered, her voice trembling. "No thinking tonight... just love me. Make love to me, Hendrix." She was breathless, desperate, and something in her voice shattered the last of his restraint.

Hendrix growled—low and primal—before seizing her, crashing their lips together with a hunger that mirrored her own.

Naria moaned, feeling him pull the blanket from her body with urgency, his rough hands tearing the old shirt she had thrown on.

His hands shook as he explored her. The warmth of her skin against his calloused palms sent shivers up his spine. He traced the delicate curve of her waist, his touch hesitant yet reverent, before finally cupping the softness of her chest. "Beautiful," Hendrix breathed, his eyes dark with awe.

He had been with Beth, but Naria was nothing like he had ever known. She was alive in a way that set his blood on fire. He could hear her pulse, could feel the heat rising from her, could sense the way her heart pounded against his touch. Her blood sang to him, the rhythm intoxicating,

maddening—

And then she touched him. Her fingers trailed over his bare skin, brushing against the glowing marks etched into his body. "You're more beautiful..." she murmured.

Hendrix let out a shuddered breath as she ran her lips down his chest, her kisses slow and deliberate. Soft. Teasing. Deadly.

Naria was killing him, and he was willing to die. "Ah—" Hendrix's breath caught as she kissed lower, sending electric shocks of pleasure through his body.

But he wasn't about to let her win this war. With a swift motion, Hendrix pinned her beneath him, capturing her wrists and raising them above her head.

She gasped, eyes wide— Then smiled. There was no need for him to subdue her. She was his, and he was hers.

But then—

He did something with his lips and tongue that sent her over the edge. The sensation was unbearable. Her body arched off the floor, her breath coming out in ragged gasps.

She struggled, wanting to touch him, to reciprocate, but Hendrix was too strong. All she could do was moan his name, her legs trembling beneath him. "Ohhh—" she gasped, her hands tangling in his hair as he kissed lower, and lower still.

Her skin was burning, her body aching, her mind spiraling into oblivion. "No... yes... don't... please... yes..." she whimpered, helpless against the storm he was unleashing inside her. She felt like she was dying— And if this was death, then she welcomed it.

And then—

She shattered. A choked cry escaped her lips as pleasure ripped through her, leaving her breathless, trembling, undone.

Hendrix was still not finished.

But Naria had other plans. With whatever strength she had left, she pushed him onto his back, straddling him with a look in her eyes that made his breath hitch.

She was no longer the girl he had to protect. She was no longer afraid. She was a warrior. A warrior who knew exactly what she wanted. And right now— That was him.

Hendrix tried to move, to take control once more— But Naria placed a firm hand on his chest, holding him down. Her eyes blazed with hunger, her lips swollen and parted as she hovered over him, her breathing uneven.

Hendrix swallowed hard, his heart pounding. He had no choice but to surrender. To her. To the only woman he had ever truly loved.

Now, it was her turn to make Hendrix moan.

He still couldn't believe it—that he could have her like this. Everything about this moment told him he was exactly where he was meant to be. As if the universe had conspired to bring them together. He tried to be gentle, to hold back, fearing that she was too delicate, too fragile.

But she wasn't. She endured everything. And that shattered him. It blew his mind—this woman, his woman, accepting all of him, loving all of him. Hendrix couldn't get enough—couldn't stop kissing her, couldn't stop touching her, couldn't stop worshiping every inch of her precious body.

He was drunk, but not from the wine. This was something deeper. Something far more intoxicating. Something far more dangerous.

"Ahhh—" Hendrix bit his lip, trying to stifle his cry, his body shaking beneath her touch. He wanted to grab her, pull her closer, devour her whole— But he knew that if he did, he might hurt her. So instead, he gripped the blanket beneath them, his fingers clenching, threatening to tear it apart.

No. No. No. Hendrix wanted to scream—to protest. Because she was touching the part of him he loathed most. The beast within him was unusually silent. Hendrix had expected that familiar, gleefully wicked voice to snarl, *"She's mine."* But there was nothing. No sound. No claim.

Hendrix's breath hitched as he looked down—expecting to see his shame staring back at him. But it was gone. *No! Yes. How?!*

Naria was driving him to madness, and he didn't want to escape. He never wanted to escape. Delirious, lost in her, Hendrix snapped—grabbing her, crushing his lips to hers, kissing her with a hunger that could never be sated.

No more holding back. Their passion was no longer gentle, no longer hesitant— It was raw. Desperate. Hendrix was no longer controlling how hard he pressed into her, how fiercely he kissed her, how much he needed her.

And Naria— She laughed.

A dark, wicked laugh that made his entire body burn. She kissed the back of his ears, her lips tormenting him, her breath setting him on fire. Hendrix growled, struggling beneath her touch, losing himself.

She was driving him insane. So he fought back. Tickling her—from head to toe, gripping her thighs, making her squirm beneath him. She kicked at him, breathless with laughter, trying to escape—

But he chased her down. And when she finally collapsed into his arms, breathless, he melted into her warmth. Her body wrapped around him, soft and strong and perfect, as if she was made for him. Hendrix felt his blood boil, the heat of her searing through him. His heart pounded violently, his soul shaking as he realized—

He would never let her go.

Naria loved how every mark on Hendrix's body lit up whenever she kissed him, especially the one on his rib—the one shaped like a weapon, sharp and pointed like a spear.

"Ahhh—!" The initial shock sent a jolt through her body, and she instinctively gripped Hendrix's arms, her nails digging into his skin.

"S-sorry, I'm hurting you—" Hendrix jerked back, panicked, afraid he had lost control.

But Naria stopped him. Her hands caught his, fingers tightening around his wrist. "No." Her voice was soft, breathless. "Just... give me a minute to process... every... ohhh—"

And then, she kissed him, deeper than before, as if giving him permission to continue. Hendrix's heart pounded violently inside his chest.

She was ready. She was more than ready.

And it was driving him insane. He hesitated—because he knew what lurked inside him, what wanted to take over. His monster. It was silently waiting. Watching. Hungry. *If I take her... will I hurt her?*
No, you won't. She'll be fine. An unfamiliar voice echoed in his mind, distant yet distinct, and it startled him.
But then Naria moaned. "Yes... please... I want... more..." She was begging between kisses, grabbing at him, pulling him closer.

And Hendrix gave in. His resolve shattered. He claimed her. She opened herself to him, and Hendrix lost himself completely, needing her just as much as she needed him.
Like a storm meeting the sea, he crashed into her—over and over again, taking her in every possible way he could. She was his. And he was hers.
Their moans filled the treehouse, their bodies moving in perfect sync, rocking against the ancient walls, almost bringing the structure to ruin. When they finally slowed, breathless and dazed, they lay on their sides, gazing at each other adoringly.
"Ohhh..." Naria moaned, her legs still wrapped tightly around his waist.

Hendrix smirked, watching her delirious expression—her eyes fluttering shut, her lips swollen from his kisses, her face flushed with warmth.

She was beautiful. And he was utterly ruined. But Hendrix wasn't done. He kissed her deeply, then—without warning—he stood up, lifting her with him, her legs still wrapped around his hips.

"Ah!" Naria laughed, gasping as he playfully tickled her, carrying her around the treehouse.

Hendrix reached for the goblet, still filled with trickles of rainwater, and drank. The wine was sweet—intoxicating. He poured some onto Naria's waiting lips, watching as she sighed with satisfaction. Then he tilted the goblet, letting more trickle down her chin—catching the drops with his lips, kissing the wine off her skin.

They shared the sweetest wine, first from the goblet, then from each other's mouths. Naria giggled, feeling light-headed, feeling free, feeling more alive than ever before.

But Hendrix—

He was focused. He laid her down again, eyes burning, body on fire. He moved, and with one final thrust, Naria's entire world shattered.

"AHHH—" Her scream tore through the night, and Hendrix screamed with her, his body trembling, unraveling, surrendering.

But then—

Something dark awakened. Something is wrong. Somewhere deep inside him, the monster laughed. *Mine.* And with one final release, Hendrix unknowingly fed it—

The blood of Kein. The essence of Velial. The thing that had always been hungry—for a berhen's heart. And now—

It was inside Naria's womb.

<><><>

Outside, the treehouse erupted in a blinding, radiant light.

Naria saw everything—the way Hendrix's marks were permanently inked into his skin, how the wing-like glow on his back intensified, and then—out of that light—two hands emerged, holding onto him.

A presence descended from the sky.

Finally.

Azrael smiled from the clouds above, his ethereal form waiting for this exact moment. He entered the treehouse, his glowing fingers grasping the wings of light sprouting from Hendrix's back—the same wings formed by the angel's very breath.

And then— It was over.

Hendrix turned to Naria, panting, exhausted, thirsty, but somehow... free.

Naria felt it immediately. The moment the monster left Hendrix and entered her. A silent, eerie knowing settled in her chest. She was the vessel after all—not the holder of water, but the one destined to trap Hendrix's monster.

She reached out, her fingers tracing the sharp tip of the spear-like mark on his rib. Its warm light pulsed beneath her touch, and she swore she could feel it piercing through her—not painfully though.

Hendrix watched her, pulling on his pants. They saw the torn remains of the t-shirt she had been wearing, the one Hendrix had ripped apart in the throes of their passion.

She smiled sadly, knowing she wouldn't be needing it anymore.

For the first time in his immortal existence, Hendrix felt peace. But there was something else—something off. He looked at Naria, still alive, still glowing, still herself. Whatever miracle this was, he didn't understand it
—but he wanted to.
If this was Yswh's doing
—the God his parents had always worshipped
—then maybe, just maybe, he would finally start believing.

Hendrix turned his gaze to the bright midday sun, realizing how late it had gotten. "You're hungry," he said, brushing his fingers gently over her cheek before kissing her lips.

Naria's eyes fluttered closed, savoring the warmth of him. It took every ounce of Hendrix's sanity to accept the idea that he needed to bring her to Vincot, for her safety. She's no longer a berhen though—maybe that could be an excuse for them not to go. He felt like dying being apart from her, even now. "I'll grab us some lunch," he murmured, about to pull away.

But she stopped him. Her small fingers curled around his wrist, holding him back. Then, she motioned for him to lie down beside her again. "Later," she whispered, pulling him close.

Hendrix frowned slightly, sensing something different in her tone. "Why so serious?" he teased, trying to lighten the mood as he sank back into her embrace. "What, are you gonna tell me I was lousy in bed?"

Naria laughed softly, though it was a little strained. "No," she whispered. "You were the best."

Hendrix smirked. "You mean the beast?"

Naria's heart skipped a beat. She forced a smile, hiding the truth burning inside her. "Yes." But what she couldn't say was— *And now, your beast is inside me.*

<><><>

Hendrix held Naria tightly, his arms wrapped around her like he could somehow keep her there—keep her safe. Neither of them wanted to part. Now, they lay on their sides, facing each other, tangled in warmth, their breaths syncing in the quiet of the treehouse.

"I have to leave you now, but..." Naria began, her voice soft but steady.

"Yeah... Vincot," Hendrix murmured, trying to keep his voice light, though his heart clenched at the thought of being separated from her. They'd be there before nightfall.

Darn this war!

But Naria was thinking of somewhere farther than Vincot. "...But promise me," she whispered, tears slipping down her face, soaking into his bare chest.

Hendrix frowned, feeling the tremor in her body. He tried to tilt her chin up, searching for her eyes. "Naria...?"

"You'll avenge me, okay?" she choked on a sob, gripping onto him tighter. "And make sure you protect humankind. Stop this war for me, Hendrix. Finish what I started." Her fingers clutched at his skin. "Finish Kein for good."

Hendrix's blood ran cold. "What—what the heck are you talking about?"

She was shaking. Her tears were too many. And now he could see it—the pain carved into her expression.

"Naria..." he said, a warning, a plea.

She pressed her forehead against his chest, inhaling deeply.

"I took the monster from you," she whispered.

Hendrix's heart nearly stopped. "What?"

"It's inside me now," Naria said. "Your marks are permanently inked on your skin. You're free from the curse of Kein. Now, you and Azrael can finally do what Yswh has destined for you to do."

Her voice held a knowing finality, and it terrified him.

"What? Who the heck is Azrael?!" Hendrix growled, panic gripping his throat. He looked around frantically, sensing something was horribly, terribly wrong.

Then Naria pointed behind him. "Him."
Hendrix followed her gaze
—but saw nothing.
No one.

Naria pulled his face back to hers, forcing him to focus on her. She was no longer crying. Instead, there was peace. Acceptance.

And it was the most terrifying thing Hendrix had ever seen.

"Take care of Hendrix, okay?" Naria whispered, but not to him. She was speaking to something he couldn't see.

Hendrix's pulse pounded. Who the heck was she talking to?!

"I'll wait for you." Naria murmured, seemingly in pain. "I...love you, Hendrix." Naria closed her eyes, tears flooded her cheeks.

No. No, no, no! Hendrix's heart slammed against his ribs, panic surging through his veins like fire. "I love you..." His voice shook, raw and desperate. "Naria, you hear me? I love you so much!"

He meant every word. Words he never had the courage to say to Beth. Words he never whispered to Lumen. Words that, for the first time in his entire existence, felt right.

But why—

why did it feel like she was saying goodbye? Why did it feel like he was losing her? A gnawing fear clawed at his gut, a silent scream rising in his chest. Something was wrong. And Hendrix

—Hendrix didn't understand why.

"I'll be in paradise... waiting for you... on the other side." Her words were mumbled, almost a difficult whisper.

Hendrix shook his head wildly. "N-Naria—stop! You're not—"

Then she screamed.

Her entire body arched violently, her mouth open in a silent cry of agony.

Hendrix watched in horror as her chest split open—ripped apart— And from within, a massive serpent burst forth. Naria jerked backward, convulsing.

The serpent coiled in the wreckage of her ribs, its slimy, pulsating body dripping with blood.

Hendrix couldn't move.
Couldn't breathe.
And in the serpent's mouth
— It held Naria's heart.

Still beating.
Still alive.

Hendrix's scream shook the heavens.

38

The Spear Of Fate

Get up, Angelo Markado. Azrael's command echoed in Hendrix's mind, unyielding, relentless.

No! The first siren blared in the distance, a piercing reminder that the war had begun. But Hendrix didn't move. He sat motionless in the corner of the treehouse, cradling Naria's lifeless body.

Hours passed. Outside, the sun dipped below the horizon, shadows creeping in. Darkness was coming.

Pull yourself together! They are coming. Azrael's voice boomed inside his head.

No! The hell with this war! Hendrix screams internally. **This isn't even my war!**

But the voice wouldn't let him be. The monster inside him was gone, but in its place

—a new one was rising.

You promised her. Azrael's words were a dagger to the heart.

Hendrix choked back a sob, unable to answer. Because Azrael was right. Tears blurred his vision as he held Naria closer.

"Why did you do this to her?" His voice shook, barely above a whisper.

It was her choice. Azrael's tone was steady. *She made it for you.*

No. "If she did it for me, she wouldn't have left me like this..." He felt abandoned. Alone. Like an orphan all over again.

Loud crashes rang outside. The air was thick with tension. He could feel his friends waiting for him. But he didn't care.

Not anymore.

You will be with her soon. Azrael's voice was softer this time. *She was right, Hendrix. But first, finish what she started.*

Hendrix's breath hitched. He pressed his lips gently against Naria's forehead, then her lips, tasting the salt of his own tears. He laid her down, tucking the blanket around her.

But her chest
— It was empty.

The last thing he remembered was her voice, telling him she loved him. And before he could even answer—her blood was everywhere. Drenching his skin.

And then he saw it.

A monstrous serpent slithered out of Naria's open chest, her still-beating heart clutched in its jaws.

Hendrix snapped.

With a furious roar, he grabbed the serpent by the head.

Hendrix... it's me, remember? The voice—that voice! The one that had whispered to him all his life. The one that had tormented him, fueled his nightmares. It spoke like an old friend.

The sight enraged him even more. With a roar, he lunged at the now monstrous serpent that had swallowed Naria's still-beating heart. And after what felt like an eternity of struggle, Hendrix—his pants torn and shredded by the serpent's razor-sharp scales—finally found an opening. As the beast coiled tighter around him, he wrenched his arms free. With a roar of pure wrath, he seized its massive head and twisted with all his strength until a sickening crack echoed through the air. Then he ripped it apart. His fists slammed into its writhing body, over and over. He stomped. He smashed. He tore. Until the serpent was nothing but shreds.

"AHHHHHHH!!!!" Hendrix screamed in agony. But the rage, the violence, didn't change anything. When the serpent was finally gone, Naria was still dead.

His breathing was ragged as he pulled another blanket over her, leaving only her face exposed. He leaned down, one last time, and kissed her lips. Then her forehead.

Finally, he looked at Azrael.

Make her death worth it, Angelo. Don't put her sacrifice to waste. Azrael's golden eyes burned with expectation. *Are you ready to face Kein?*

At the mention of the name, Hendrix's jaw clenched. A low growl rumbled from his chest. He nodded. Azrael reached forward, grabbing the light from Hendrix's wing-like mark.

And together, they soared toward Kein.

<><><>

"Tell your demons to back off! I'm here. I'm what you want." Hendrix's voice rang through the battlefield, unwavering. Unshaken. He stepped forward, putting distance between himself and the sigbin who stood behind him

—his family.

Kein's lips curled into a smirk. "Why would I care about what you want?" he scoffed.

CRACK!

Without hesitation, Hendrix raised his hand. A bolt of lightning ripped through the sky coming out of his inked body.
The azhuangs shrieked as the electric surge struck them, sending their charred bodies plummeting to the ground. One by one. The moonlight burst through the cleared sky, illuminating the battlefield.

For the first time that night, Kein's smirk faltered.

Azrael spoke in Hendrix's mind, his voice calm yet commanding. *Kein doesn't want to rule. He wants to trap human souls here. His vaccine was never to save—only to enslave for their undying eternity. Azhuangs were humans too, free their souls...you must! Free them from Kein's slavery.*

Hendrix clenched his fists. "Call them off. Now!" He ordered. "Or I'll make sure you have nothing left to harvest."
A low growl rumbled from Kein's throat. Annoyed. Furious. "Caiphaiz..." he snapped, "tell them to back off."

Caiphaiz, hiding from afar, bowed his head. "Yes, my lord." As he issued the command, the hellspawns slithered back into the darkness. Some even grateful when they witnessed how powerful Angelo Markado was.

Bufe and the others exhaled in relief.

But Kein wasn't finished. He tilted his head, eyes narrowing. "What about them?" He motioned toward the sigbin behind Hendrix.

Hendrix laughed. "Afraid of babies and senior citizens, are you?"

Kein's jaw tightened. The channaks and hukluvans stood firm. "No, they can stay." Kein sneered. "They should witness your death." The immortal inhaled deeply, puzzled to see Angelo Markado covered in blood, as if he had just walked away from another war. "But I can't smell your berhen," he mused. "She should be here... to watch you die. Then, I'll kill her myself." A flicker of something dark and dangerous passed through Kein's expression.

Hendrix snapped.

He launched himself forward, fists clenched, ready to tear Kein apart. Kein laughed. Mocking. Taunting. But just as Hendrix was about to reach him—

He froze in midair.

Azrael was holding him back. *Don't attack to kill.* Azrael's voice was sharp. Urgent. *Kein cannot die, remember? Adonai willed it that way. Every attack you land on him will only ricochet back onto you. Just like what happened at the arena. It will be pointless.*

Hendrix's rage burned. *Then what should I do!?*

Trust me. Azrael's voice softened. *Naria is the reason I'm here. Trusting me is trusting her.*

Hendrix gritted his teeth.

Kein stood below, watching him. Waiting.
Then—
he moved.

The immortal god jumped high, straight for Hendrix. Aiming for his neck. For his blood.
Pain exploded through Hendrix's body.
Kein's claws slashed deep into his throat. Blood gushed in all directions, drenching them both. Kein moaned in pleasure, reveling in the sensation.
Hendrix fought back. Struggled.
But Kein was too strong. They plummeted to the ground, crashing into the dirt.

The sigbin on both sides watched in horror. Bufe clenched his fists, feeling the tension in the air. Rhailey gritted his teeth. Reeva gasped.
Hendrix felt himself slipping.
The anger—
the hatred—
the hunger for Kein's death—

Azrael's voice shouted in his mind. *WAIT! Stop thinking about his death and WAIT!*
But Kein wasn't stopping. His fangs neared Hendrix's exposed throat. His tongue flicked out

—hungry.
Starving.

Around them...

The children watched in awe, their innocent eyes fixated on Azrael hovering behind Hendrix. To them, the celestial being was a magnificent spectacle—his radiant, feathery wings stretched wide, glowing like the morning sun.

Hendrix exhaled sharply, pushing Kein away with a powerful kick to the chest.

Kein stumbled back but only for a moment. His eyes gleamed with madness.

His hunger—
his obsession—
was consuming him.

He craved more. Hendrix prepared to strike, his body ready to launch into another attack, but Azrael's voice echoed in his mind -- *Wait*

Hendrix clenched his fists. *Again?!*

As expected, Kein came at him again. Each of his attacks targeted Hendrix's neck. Again and again. Hendrix dodged, blocked, defended. Blood continued to drip from his previous wounds, but he ignored the pain. Instead, he used everything at his disposal.

Water, fire, earth, wind. He redirected the elements to counter every blow, controlling the battlefield itself.

Kein's frustration boiled over. His lips curled in rage. His pride was wounded. The self-proclaimed god—

humiliated by a mere sigbin.

Azrael hovered, arms crossed behind Hendrix. *Stop playing with him, Angelo. Now you're just showing off.*

Then—

Kein changed the game. He stretched out his hand and touched the earth. Instantly—

the land withered.

The lush greenery shriveled into decay. The tall trees, once full of life, collapsed into dust.

Hendrix's stomach twisted as he watched the forest die around them.

Kein grinned. "I will curse this land," he declared. "No green will ever flourish here again. Your humans will starve."

Hendrix's heart pounded. He thought of his treehouse. The branches that sheltered him and Naria. The place where he held her for the last time. Anger burned inside him, but he swallowed it down. He had to stay focused.

Kein lunged. Fangs bared. Nails sharp.

Hendrix let him.

A trap.

Kein sank his teeth deep into Hendrix's flesh—tearing out a chunk and drinking greedily. He threw his head back, laughing in ecstasy.

The blood of the bleeding sigbin...

Now one in body with Kein, Velial finally tasted the Bleeding One—and its insatiable hunger consumed him. Then it happened. A low, guttural laugh rumbled from deep within Kein's chest.

Another.
Deeper.
Hungrier.

His mouth stretched unnaturally wide. And from his gaping jaws

— a massive serpent slithered forth—hissing, coiling, starved beyond reason. Velial, a fallen angel, craved what lay within Hendrix: the angelic essence inked into his blood, a gift from Azrael himself.

Azrael's voice thundered. "NOW! Hendrix...now!"
Hendrix wrenched free, blood pouring from his wound.

The serpent lunged for him— ready to drain Hendrix down.

Kein screamed— face split in half.
And then Hendrix ran. The serpent chased him, slithering its massive body out of Kein's mouth.

Further.
Further.
Halfway out.

Kein twitched. Shook violently. His body wasn't his own anymore.

It was Velial's.

Azrael's voice rang out again. "DO IT, ANGELO Markado! Do it, NOW!"

With his hand gripping the glowing spear, Hendrix touched the burning mark inked on his rib – the same mark made by a spear that poked and wounded THE ONE crucified at the cross -YSWH.

A searing light erupted, illuminating the battlefield.

In one swift motion, Hendrix pulled out

– seemingly from his rib
– the divine spear and
—without hesitation
—plunged it deep into the serpent's head.

The beast shrieked, thrashing violently. Its skull split open, cracked in two.

But Hendrix wasn't finished. With a mighty roar, he scooped the writhing serpent from Kein's gaping mouth, twisting its massive body like a pretzel, coiling it in on itself.

The channak children gasped in delight. To them, it was like watching a grand spectacle in the sky, a battle between gods and demons straight out of their bedtime stories.

What the others, older channaks and hukluvan, didn't realize though was that Hendrix wasn't fighting alone. Azrael mirrored his every movement.

Step by step.

The angel's celestial form shimmered behind Hendrix, guiding him like a shadow of pure light. Then, in one powerful throw, Hendrix hurled the broken serpent toward Azrael.

The divine warrior caught it effortlessly. Azrael twisted the wounded demon even further, compressing its massive body until it shrank to the size of his palm.

"Hello, brother," Azrael whispered. "Father is waiting for you." With a flick of his wrist, he stuffed the serpent into a small satchel. Despite its previous enormous size, the creature fit inside as if it had always belonged there.

Hendrix turned back to Kein and his grotesque form. The immortal looked disoriented, weak, and dazed

—still high on Hendrix's blood while trying to regenerate.

"You want more?" Hendrix smirked, cutting his arm open with the spear. Dark crimson poured out. Before Kein could react, Hendrix shoved his bleeding arm straight into the immortal's mouth, forcing him to drink. "Here. Enjoy!"

Kein gagged, his body convulsing. The divine essence in Hendrix's blood overwhelmed him.

The unstoppable god of the evil sigbin shuddered, his eyes rolling back as the powerful blood coursed through his veins. Without Velial inside him and without his DNA inside Hendrix, Angelo Markado's blessed blood was lethal.

Azrael gave Hendrix one last knowing look before glancing at the wide-eyed channak children, winking at them. Nzo giggled, unable to help himself.

"Goodbye, Angelo Markado. Until next time." With a final wave to Nzo and the others, Azrael disappeared into the sky.

Kein gasped, choking on the divine corruption now consuming him. He stumbled, his once-mighty form collapsing. For the first time in eternity... Kein felt exhausted. He tried to fight it, but the weight of Hendrix's blood crushed him.

"No..." The world around him spun. His vision darkened. And then—Kein closed his eyes. His body went limp. He collapsed into a deep, unshakable sleep.

Hendrix kicked Kein's body aside like a discarded rag. "You don't die. But who says you can't sleep?"

"Sleep—forever."
Then...

A piercing scream shattered the silence. "AHHHHHH!!!!!"

Hendrix spun around, heart pounding.

Vahitna was on the ground—in labor. Reeva remained calm despite knowing that she was also bleeding -- her very first as a young maiden. She knelt beside Vahitna, steady hands working quickly. Tears streamed down Vahitna's face. With one final push, a beautiful baby girl entered the world, her tiny cries echoing through the battlefield.

The moment was surreal.

Fireworks erupted over Perlaz. Cheers. Laughter. Shouts of joy. Across the land, humans embraced. The alarm of victory sounded, spreading the news:

The war was over.

Reeva gently placed the crying infant against Vahitna's chest. The exhausted mother clutched her newborn, tears of joy mixing with her sweat.

Beside her, Nzo wept. Reeva lifted him up, letting him see the newborn for the first time. "Look, Nzo. You have a sister."

Nzo reached out, touching the tiny baby's cheek. Then he broke down, sobbing.

Meanwhile, Bufe—watching the scene unfold without seeing anything

—did something unthinkable.

He grabbed Rhailey's knife and sliced his own palm open. The moment his skin split

—red liquid oozed from the wound.

For the first time in thousands of years...

Bufe bled. "I can die...I can finally die!" The hukluvan leader threw his head back and laughed.

Meanwhile...

Hendrix

—still dazed

—turned toward the spot where Kein's body had fallen.

But...

Kein was gone along with the rest of his minions.

39

The Jabezzite Warriors

After the initial shock of what had transpired in Xego and Zapad, the sigbin

—now fully human again
—struggled to adjust to their newfound mortality.

But as time passed, chaos gave way to quiet. The world began to rebuild. With new births, deaths, and growth shaping the future, those who embraced change thrived.

Yet, not everyone welcomed this transformation. Those who clung to their frozen, immortal existence found themselves lost in despair. Many retreated to the distant, abandoned lands near Cintru, choosing isolation over adaptation.

In Perlaz, however, life moved forward. People embraced the cycle of existence—welcoming new life, mourning their losses, and celebrating growth.

<><><>

Bufe, the legendary hukluvan leader, spent his final moments holding Vahitna's newborn daughter. As he gently caressed her tiny face, his aged, battle-worn heart swelled with peace. And that night—for the first time in thousands of years—he closed his eyes... and never opened them again.

His watch was over.

Rhailey, now the sole inheritor of Bufe's visions, still saw glimpses of the future. Most of what lay ahead looked promising for humankind. But there was one vision that left him feeling unsettled.

A vision of himself—standing beside a grown-up Reeva. He couldn't explain why, but when he saw her smiling in the village that day, something shifted.

It made him feel awkward in her presence—a sensation he had never experienced before.

<><><>

"Nzo!" Vahitna's voice carried through the open yard.

Her son—now taller and more mature-looking—was playing with a group of kids in their backyard. They had settled into one of the peaceful villages inside Perlaz, where laughter filled the air instead of war cries.

"What, Mom!?" Nzo groaned, momentarily pausing his game.

"Watch your baby sister for a while, will you?"

Nzo dramatically stomped his foot. "Oh crap! Fine!" With a huff, he said goodbye to his friends, dragging his feet back toward the house.

But before he could take another step—

"I'm here! I'll watch her. Go and play." Reeva, still radiant with joy, scooped up the baby with ease. Being a young maiden, she was days away from settling in Vincot yet her heart felt light. Rhailey had informed her of his intention to visit once she was settled, and the thought made her smile more than she expected.

"Thanks!" Nzo's mood instantly shifted. With a quick nod, he ran back to his playmates, his laughter blending into the sound of children's voices filling the yard.

And just like that—life went on.

<><><>

Looking over the vast land of Hebron, rich with natural resources and teeming with life, Hendrix sat on the roof of his treehouse

—exhausted.

There was still a long road ahead to rebuild this part of Perlaz

—the land he now called Hebron.

He had been invited to lead the nation and join the world-rebuilding summit in Xego, but he refused. No more wandering. No more running.

Hendrix already found his purpose and his place in this world.

Thirsty from all the dirty work, he jumped off the roof and entered the house by the window. His long hair covered his face, his bare chest was streaked with dirt, and his pants were ragged.

He was the embodiment of wildness and freedom.

PAK!

A shirt smacked him on the face. "Ouch! What the—?" Hendrix muttered.

"PUT YOUR SHIRT ON!" Naria stood at the terrace window, hands on her hips, eyes narrowed. She threw him a towel next. "And clean yourself up before stepping inside! You're getting dirt all over the floor I just cleaned!"

Hendrix grinned, amused by his beautiful, angry wife. "Why are you always mad? Are you on your period or something?"

Naria gasped, appalled. "I'm mad because you—ayyy!" Before she could finish, Hendrix grabbed her, spinning her into his arms.

Her indignant protests were muffled by his scruffy beard as he pressed his face against her neck. "Ugh! You stink! Get off me, Hendrix! I'm serious!"

Laughing, he carried her toward the floor, mud and all, rolling with her in playful combat. Hendrix knew exactly how to change her bad mood—with the right touch, the right kiss, and the right whisper in her ear.

And as always, Naria melted in her husband's arms. She tried to resist, but when his hands traced familiar paths down her body, her protests became soft moans.

He kissed her, deep and knowing. "I love you."

Naria sighed against his lips, torn between frustration and undeniable desire. "I hate you," she grumbled, then gasped as he made her forget her irritation altogether.

That night, their home was filled with laughter, passion, and love.

Hendrix stared at the night sky, thinking about everything he had lost... and everything he had gained.

Yswh was right.

Sometimes, when God asks for something, He doesn't take it away—He only borrows it. And when He gives it back, it is always greater.

After the final battle with Kein, Hendrix left the battlefield broken, believing Naria was gone forever. He returned to the treehouse only to honor her body before joining her in death.

But when he walked in—

"You're back for me! You kept your promise!" Naria was waiting at the door, alive, smiling, arms open.

Hendrix froze.

This isn't real. It can't be real. "W-what? How—?" His voice broke, trembling as he stepped closer.
Naria wrapped her arms around him, holding him tightly. "I don't know... maybe Yswh isn't done with me yet." She pointed to the sky, eyes full of faith.

Hendrix collapsed into her arms, sobbing—thanking God, thanking fate, thanking whatever miracle had given her back to him.

It was the spear-shaped mark on Hendrix's rib that saved Naria. As she lay dying, she reached out and touched the light of the spear. Its power pierced through her soul, anchoring her to Hendrix.

The serpent had devoured her heart, but it could never claim her soul. The jagged scar across her chest served as a brutal reminder of the war—but her bond to Hendrix was eternal. And now, deep within her womb, something far greater had been set into motion.

A new life.

A child.

The one who would carry the bloodline of the Jabezzite warriors—destined to lead the next great battle, two thousand years later.

His name would be Jabez, and from his bloodline, Caleb and Vera would rise to continue the legacy their ancestor had begun – (Read the Sequel, Blood & Gospel Saga: The Vampires' Night Market)

<><><>

In the Shadows. Far away, hidden from the world, Kein lay sleeping inside a glass casket.

Caiphaiz stood over him, placing a fruit in his maker's hands. "It's not the same, Father... but one day, it will serve its purpose."
The door opened behind him. Hiro and Sofia entered, bowing before him.
"Is the laboratory ready?" Caiphaiz's voice was calm, measured.
Hiro nodded.
"Yes." Sofia glanced at Hiro

—a silent exchange of understanding passing between them.

They would ensure the rise of a new generation of immortals, destined to shape the future.

<><><>

In the Garden of Adonai, the serpent slithered once more before the Throne of God.

It faced Abba, the Great I AM, the Triune—YHWH Himself.

It trembled. "Father..." The voice was a whisper, a hiss.
"Welcome back, My child." God's voice was filled with unfathomable love.
The serpent bowed low, awaiting its punishment.

Azrael silently exited, his task complete. Now, he sat upon the clouds, looking down upon the world.

Watching.

Waiting.

"Make use of my light, Hendrix –Angelo Markado... you deserve your happiness."

He smiled, knowing that the story was far from over.

-END-

Grab the sequel...

BLOOD & GOSPEL SAGA:
The Vampires' Night Market
Sangre De Imago Dei
Ang Diyos Ng Bampira

Angelo Markado serves as a prequel to the tale of Caleb—a vampire who once purchased a human slave for food at Kamara, the vampires' night market—unaware that Vera's blood carried the IMAGO DEI (the Image of God, embodying Faith, Hope, and above all, Love). To save Vera's soul, Caleb must complete the Sacred Book of Adonai, the only means to counter the deadly dance of Salome, who is determined to present Vera's head on a platter to Kein, the sleeping immortal god of the sigbin, azhuang, and vampires.

www.ingramcontent.com/pod-product-compliance
Lightning Source LLC
LaVergne TN
LVHW040034080526
838202LV00045B/3338